Winning at New Products
Second Edition
Accelerating the Process from Idea to Launch

Robert G. Cooper

▲▲

ADDISON-WESLEY PUBLISHING COMPANY

Reading, Massachusetts • Menlo Park, California • New York
Don Mills, Ontario • Wokingham, England • Amsterdam • Bonn
Sydney • Singapore • Tokyo • Madrid • San Juan
Seoul • Milan • Mexico City • Taipei

Library of Congress Cataloging-in-Publication Data

Cooper, Robert G. (Robert Gravlin), 1943-
  Winning at new products : accelerating the process from idea to
launch / Robert G. Cooper.
       p. cm.
  Includes bibliographical references and index.
  ISBN 0-201-56381-9
  1. New products.   I. Title.
HF5415.153.C65 1993
658.5'75—dc20   93-18734
                                                                        CIP

Text printed on recycled and acid-free paper

ISBN 0-201-56381-9

10 11 12 13 14-MA-0099989796
Tenth printing, November 1996

Winning at New Products
Second Edition

To the three ladies in my life: my wife Linda and my two daughters, Barbara and Heather.

Contents

Preface

This book is about product innovation—more specifically, about how to win in the new products game. In it, I outline a new product game plan or process for bringing new products to market successfully and quickly.

This is my second managerial book about product innovation. My first book, simply entitled *Winning at New Products*, was published in 1986. It was based largely on research work done from 1972 to 1985 into what made a new product a winner, and on some consulting projects that I had been involved in. Much to my surprise, the book had a profound impact on the way many companies approached product development. Major corporations in both Europe and North America adopted the prescriptions outlined in the book, and in particular focused on designing and implementing a new product process.

This current or second book shares a lot in common with the first book. We probe new product success factors and try to discover what makes a new product a winner. Then we translate these into an operational game plan for success. To a certain extent, then, this book represents an expansion of the first one. And for those of you who purchased the first edition and see certain similarities, I can only point out that there was much that was sound and useful in that book; and those people who had made use of that original book in their companies recommended that certain topics remain in this second book. They are still valuable lessons.

This book is more than just an "updating," however. There is much that is new in it. Indeed, it has been made necessary by all the progress we have made since 1986. The new product game plan was largely untested at the time the first book was written. Since then, we have "installed" it as a "stage-gate" system in a number of firms. And other firms have done so on their own. (My publisher informed me that one U.S. firm bought two thousand copies of the first book simply to get everyone that mattered on board the new approach.) One result of all this testing has been that the game plan has been modified and refined over the last six years: today it is simpler and more streamlined.

A second reason for writing this book is that, today, we have hard evidence that the game plan or stage-gate system really does work. We also have the experiences—both good and bad—of implementing the game plan in a number of firms. And here some of the lessons have been painful: that the implementation is far more difficult than the design of a process. And so a chapter is included that is devoted strictly to seemingly mundane, but in reality, absolutely crucial implementation issues.

Another reason for writing this second book is that we know a lot more about new product success factors than we did in 1986. Since the mid-1980s, our own research into product innovation practices has probed hundreds of firms and new product projects, seeking the keys to success. Many of the lessons for success included in this book are based on these more recent studies. And other researchers have undertaken similar studies into winning and losing at new products that the current book benefits from. We also have new practices—for example, Quality Function Deployment (introduced to the U.S. in 1986) and the use of lead users as idea sources—which are relatively recent concepts, and are included in this book.

Finally, there are some new issues that were not quite as prevalent in '86, yet are front-and-center in this book. The first is the issue of speed. In the early- to mid-1980s, we were mostly concerned about getting successful products to market. That seemed like the major challenge! Avoiding product failure was the goal. Now, the goal is twofold: success coupled with speed. The goal is to have winners, but to make sure they're speedy ones too! This quest for success and speed is topical; it's also dangerous, as many quick fixes and instant solutions have been proposed by various pundits and authors. To no one's surprise, some of these quick fixes have been poorly conceived and untested, and they do great disservice to companies. By contrast, the solutions proposed in this book's 1990s game plan are tested ones—based on hard evidence from research, as well as real live installations.

Another key issue of the 1990s is globalization, or the international new product effort. While this is not a major focus of the book, I do introduce some of our most recent findings on the international dimensions of product innovation and encourage readers to think in terms of a global new product process.

A number of people have helped me in the writing of this book. Professor Elko J. Kleinschmidt is both a friend and a colleague: together he and I conducted much of the research on new product success factors that is reported in this book. Robert Davis of the Procter & Gamble company provided valuable insights into product innovation over the years, and many of his thoughts appear in the book. He was also one of the drivers behind P&G's implementation of a stage-gate system. Similarly Richard Collette, manager of Polaroid's product delivery process, provided many thoughts on the implementation process.

Other business contacts have also been of great help, as they have adopted elements of my game plan and provided feedback. In alphabetical order, they are: Jens Arleth (private consultant in Denmark), Dr. Larry Gastwirt (formerly of Exxon Chemicals, now at the Stevens Institute), Dr. David Greenley and Dr. Steve Krzeminiski (both of Rohm and Haas), Erik Lahn Sorensen (Danish Technological Institute), Brian Lanahan (Corning), Dr. Mike Martin (Tremco),

Paul O'Connor (the Adept Group), Alec Petit (private consultant in the U.K.), Don Sandford (formerly ICI-U.K., now president of ICAST, an R&D venture firm), Paul Seubert (Du Pont), Bill Smith (Du Pont), and Carol Urich (Polaroid).

I would also like to thank Richard Collette of Polaroid and Robert Davis of Procter & Gamble for reviewing the manuscript and providing superb feedback. Finally, thanks to my two daughters, who besides giving up many hours of "their" computer to me, also provided physical help: Heather, who helped with the computer graphics for the artwork; and Barbara, who did some of the typing.

1

Winning Is Everything

In war, there is no second prize for the runner-up.
Omar Bradley, U.S. General

New Products Warfare

America is engaged in a new products war. The battlefields are the marketplaces around the world for everything from consumer electronics to new engineering resins, from potato chips to electronic chips.

The combatants are the many companies who vie for a better position, a better share, or new territory on each battlefield or marketplace. They include the large and well-known combatants—the IBMs, Du Ponts and 3Ms, as well as an increasing number of foreign players—BASF, Sony, NEC, and Siemens. More recent entrants have gained prominence in the last few decades because of new product victories: Apple with computers, Glaxo with pharmaceuticals, Northern Telecom with telecommunications equipment.

The weapons are the thousands of new products developed every year in the hope of successfully invading chosen marketplaces. Sadly, most new product attempts fail. Increasingly the quest is for weapon superiority—seeking product differentiation in order to secure a sustainable competitive advantage. Positioning plays a key role too, as combatants deploy their troops to secure an advantageous position on the battlefield. They use tactics such as frontal assaults, out–flankings, and even attempts to reposition the enemy.

The combatants have their shock troops that lead the way into battle—the sales teams, advertising people, and promotional experts. The cost of these shock troops is enormous (it costs Proctor & Gamble about $100 million to launch a new brand in the U.S.). But the battle is often decided by the unsung heros—the infantry—the many engineers and scientists in R&D labs and engineering departments around the world—less glamorous and less visible, but at the heart of almost every victory.

The combatants have their generals—the senior executives who plan and chart direction, and attempt to define a business and technology strategy for their firm. The generals speak in terms of strategic thrusts, strategic arenas, and the need for strategic alignment. Sadly, many generals haven't really grasped the art of new product or technology strategy very well. So, as is often the case with ill-defined strategy, the battle is won or lost tactically in the trenches by the shock troops and infantry.

In the last few decades, the new products war has become a global confrontation. We've seen the advent of the world product and global product mandates. There are no national borders any more—domestic markets have become the enemy's international market.

As with recent wars, there are new ingredients for success: three are advanced technology, superior intelligence, and rapid mobility. Technology makes weapon superiority possible, and those combatants who have wisely invested in technology reap the benefits. Intelligence—market information and competitive intelligence—enables the most effective deployment of weapons and resources and often means the difference between winning and losing. And mobility or speed enables lightning strikes designed to seize windows of opportunity or to catch an enemy off guard.

As in any war, there are winners and losers. The winners are those firms, such as Merck, 3M, and Hewlett-Packard, who have a enviable stream of new product successes year after year. There are losers as well: General Motors, who throughout the eighties, failed to launch new products that captured the consumer's interest (while Ford glowed victoriously with winners such as Sable and Taurus). Sometimes the defeat is so great that the combatant collapses and simply disappears. Such was the fate of Coleco, the once-giant computer games producer, who misfired badly with new products in the home computer market and failed to launch the new generation of computer games while others, such as the makers of Nintendo, did.

As we enter the twenty-first century, this new products war looms as the most important and critical war the companies of the world have ever fought. Winning in this war is everything: it is vital to success, prosperity, and even survival of these organizations. Losing the war, or failing to take an active part in it, spells disaster: the annals of business history are replete with examples of companies who simply disappeared because they failed to innovate, failed to keep their product portfolio current and competitive, and were surpassed by more innovative competitors.

Success and Speed

In winning at new products, as in warfare or war games, the goal is victory—a steady stream of profitable and successful new products. On this new product battlefield, the ability to mount lightening attacks—well-planned but swift strikes—is increasingly the key to success. *Speed is the new competitive weapon.* The ability to accelerate product marketing—ahead of competition and within the window of opportunity—is more than ever central to success. And so this book is about more than success—it's about how to get successful products to market, but in record time.

There are major payoffs to speeding products to market.

- *Speed yields competitive advantage.* The ability to respond to customers' needs and changing markets faster than competition, and to beat competitors to market with a new product often is the key to success. But too much haste may result in an ill-conceived product, which has no competitive advantage at all!
- *Speed yields higher profitability.* The revenue from the sale of the product is realized earlier (Remember: money has a time value, and deferred revenues are worth less than revenues acquired sooner); and the revenues over the life of the product are higher, given a fixed window of opportunity and hence limited product life.
- *Speed means fewer surprises.* The ability to move quickly to market means the product as originally conceived is more likely to meet market requirements. The short time frame reduces the odds that market conditions will dramatically change as development proceeds. Contrast this with a seven-year development effort incurred by some U.S. auto companies: here, market requirements, market conditions, and the competitive situation are likely to have changed considerably from beginning to end of the project.

So speed to market is a preoccupation throughout this book—*but not at the expense of managing the project properly.* I will never recommend cutting corners or executing in a sloppy fashion in order to save time—it just doesn't pay off. In short, speed is important, but it is only one component of our overarching goal of profitable new products.

Strategy and Tactics

Books about war or war games highlight both strategy and tactics. So does this book.

- *Strategy:* The art of determining strategic direction for product innovation is a question of identifying and selecting strategic arenas or battlefields. We will look at how to define the areas of strategic focus or strategic thrust, how to determine what markets, products, and technologies to invest in, and, in light of these decisions, what is the best entry strategy?
- *Tactics:* Without tactics, strategy is nothing but words: tactics are the tools by which strategy is implemented. This too is the major theme of the book. That is, having decided on the strategic arena or battlefield, what does one do to win the battle? How does one plan and mount a swift attack? The tactical questions result in a game plan consisting or a set of moves or maneuvers designed to move a new product project from the idea stage through to a successful launch—quickly and effectively.

Although strategy and tactics are military concepts, they are terms increasingly used in sports arenas. Indeed, a sports or game analogy is often the more appropriate one when developing new product strategy and tactics, so terms such as "game plan" and "new product game" are common in this book.

Logically, strategy precedes tactics. But in this book, I reverse the order of presentation: we first tackle the tactical issues—the challenges at the new product project level. And, towards the end of the book, we focus on the "big picture"—a product innovation strategy or direction for the firm. Why this sequence? First, most problems lie within the tactical or implementation arena—at the project level! And second, tactics or the game plan is more concrete, easier to visualize, and certainly more "actionable"—you can see improvements more quickly here.

New Products: The Key to Corporate Prosperity

New product development is one of the riskiest, yet most important, endeavors of the modern corporation. Certainly the risks are high: you and your colleagues have all seen large amounts of money spent on new product disasters in your own firm. But then, so too are the rewards.

Countless corporations owe their meteoric rise and current fortunes to new products. For example:

- JVC, hardly a household word several decades ago, pioneered the VHS format for home VCRs.
- Glaxo, once a mid-sized British pharmaceutical house, rose to number two in the world on the coattails of a single anti-ulcer drug.
- Apple Computer, a small upstart firm, succeeded against the giant IBM, when for decades, much larger firms—GE, RCA, AT&T, and Honeywell—had tried and failed. But Apple did it with a steady stream of new products, the Macintosh being the most memorable.

New products account for a staggering 40 percent of company sales, on average. (Here I define a product as "new" if it has been on the market by that firm for five years or less.) And the figure has been going up dramatically: 33 percent in the years between 1976 and 1981; 40 percent from 1981 to 1986;[1] and 42 percent between 1985 and 1990. By 1995 new products are expected to account for 52 percent of company sales.[2]

New products have a similar impact on corporate profits. In the period from 1976 to 1981, new products contributed 22 percent of corporate profits; this had grown to 33 percent for the next-five year period (1981–86); and by 1995, the figure will rise to 46 percent. That is, profits from new products will account for almost half of the bottom line of corporations![3]

To support these new product targets, companies expect to increase the *rate of new product introductions by 21 percent* over the next five years: from an average of 37.5 new products per firm over the last five years, to 45.3 in the next five years.[4]

Research and development expenditures are also impressive: in the U.S., R&D expenditures recently reported amounted to $138 billion annually, or about 2.9 percent of the Gross Domestic Product (GDP) (but much of this has been for military work—49 percent of this U.S. R&D spending is financed by government);[5] in Japan and Germany, R&D spending is also about 2.8 to 2.9 percent of GDP (but much less is military—private industry finances 71 percent of Japanese and 64 percent of German R&D spending).

Certain industries, noted for their growth and profitability in recent decades, spend heavily on R&D. For example, office products and services, including computers, business machines, and software, averages 7.9 percent of sales on R&D; and electrical and electronics products (which includes instruments and semiconductors) averages 5.5 percent of sales on R&D (see Table 1.1 for an industry breakdown).

Why is product innovation so central to corporate success? Why is the world speeding up so much when it comes to new products? One factor is the financial market, which seems to dominate corporate behavior so much these days. An annual *Fortune* survey rates top U.S. corporations on a number of criteria, including "value as a long term investment." Using data supplied by *Fortune*,

Table 1.1:   R&D Spending by U.S. Industry (1991)

INDUSTRY	R&D SPENDING ($ BILLIONS)	R&D AS PROPORTION OF SALES (%)	R&D AS PROPORTION OF PROFITS (%)
All industry	70.0	3.4	46.8
Aerospace	3.9	3.7	90.5
Automotive	10.7	3.7	>100
Chemicals	5.2	3.9	40.9
Consumer products	1.9	1.4	13.0
Containers and Packaging	0.1	0.9	24.3
Electrical/Electronics	7.0	5.5	84.8
Food	0.5	0.7	8.9
Fuel	2.7	0.7	9.3
Health care	8.5	8.7	47.9
Housing	0.5	1.8	29.7
Leisure time products	1.8	5.1	125.3
Manufacturing (general)[a]	3.2	2.9	44.7
Metals and Mining	0.4	1.1	17.2
Non-bank financial	0.1	0.7	8.5
Office equipment and services	15.9	7.9	89.7
Paper and Forest products	0.4	1.1	14.6
Service Industries	0.1	0.8	47.1
Telecommunications	3.2	3.6	30.4

[a]   Includes general manufacturing, machine tools, tools, machinery, textiles.

Source: "R&D statistics" Business Week, Special 1991 Issue (Oct. 25, 1991): 173–208.

I studied various predictors of investment value. The results were provocative. *The single strongest predictor of investment value is "degree of innovativeness of the company."* A typical industry relationship—how innovativeness affects investment value—is shown for the chemical industry in Figure 1.1. The conclusion is that product innovation is not only important to remain competitive in the firm's marketplace, it also seems to be important to financial markets—in determining the worth or value of the company as a long term investment—and hence to the cost of capital to the firm.[6]

A recent *Fortune* survey[7] lists the ten most admired major corporations in America. Merck is number one. Coincidentally, two of the top three most admired are also listed as the three most innovative corporations in America. Again Merck is number one!

Innovation Drivers

New products are clearly the key to corporate prosperity. They drive corporate revenues, market shares, bottom lines, and even share prices. But why is the innovation game speeding up so much, and why is so much more emphasis being placed on our product innovation track records? Here are four innovation drivers as identified by senior executives.[8]

Figure 1.1:   How Innovativness Affects Value as an Investment: Chemical Industry

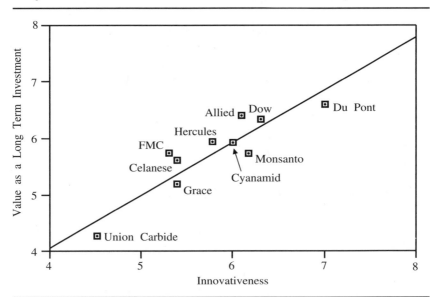

Source: *Fortune* and *Erdos & Morgan, Inc.*. "Stage-Gate Systems: A New Tool for Managing New Products." Reprinted from *Business Horizons*, May-June 1990. Copyright 1990 by the Foundation for the School of Business at Indiana University. Used with permission.

- *Technology advances:* The world's base of technology and know-how increases at an exponential rate, making possible solutions and products not even dreamed of a decade or so ago. What was science fiction yesterday—for example, hand-held computers or kitchen stove tops that operate by magnetic induction—is suddenly a technological reality today.
- *Changing customer needs:* Marketplaces are also in turmoil, with market needs and wants, and customer preferences changing regularly. The company that seemed omnipotent only a few years ago suddenly falls from favor with the consumer. Witness IBM's current problems, as corporate customers have shifted their desires dramatically away from mainframe computers (IBM's strength) and to much smaller computers in recent years. In other markets, customers have come to expect new product with significant improvements: we consumers have become like kids in a candy shop—we see what is possible, and we want it.
- *Shortening product life cycles:* One result of the increasing pace of technological change coupled with changing market demands has been shorter product life cycles. Our new product no longer has a life of 5 to 10 years, but within a few years, sometimes even months, it is superseded by a competitive entry, rendering our's obsolete, and necessitating a new product launch by us. The game has speeded up.
- *Increased world competition:* We now have access to foreign markets like never before, but at the same time, our domestic market has become someone else's international one. This globalization of markets has created significant opportunities for the product innovator: the world product targeted at global markets. It has also intensified competition in every domestic market. Both factors have sped up the pace of product innovation.

A quick review of all four drivers of product innovation reveals that none is likely to disappear in the next decade or two. Technology advances will continue to occur; so will changes in market needs and demands; world trade and globalization of markets marches on, spurred by the General Agreement on Tariffs and Trade (GATT) and the creation of free trade zones; and competition will drive life cycles to become even shorter. Product innovation will be even more critical to corporate prosperity in the years ahead than it has been in recent past.

Suggestion: If you haven't already done so, conduct a review of the strategic role—past, present, and future—of new products in your company. Key questions include:

1. What is your historical level of R&D spending as a percentage of sales? Has it been going up or down? How does it compare to your competitors' or industry level? Why is it higher or lower?

2. What proportion of your current sales comes from new products introduced by you in the last five years? What is the projection or objective for the future? What will your portfolio of products look like in five years?
3. Where will your sales growth come from? What proportion from new products? From new markets? From growth in existing markets? Or from increased market share?
4. Are the answers to the three questions above consistent with each other? Are you investing enough in R&D and new products to yield the results that you want?

In addressing the first question above, some managers ask, *"what is the appropriate level of R&D spending* for my firm?" There are no easy answers here. Remember that R&D spending is by no means the sole determinant of new product performance or even sales generated by new products. There are many factors that make a new product program a success. Indeed, using R&D spending as a measure of new product development activities may be misleading. R&D spending typically accounts for less than 40 percent of a firm's total expenditure for product innovation.[9]

More food for thought: In one of our studies on innovation strategies, R&D spending as a percentage of company sales was indeed found to be the strongest predictor of the new product sales (also expressed as a percentage of company sales). This comes as no surprise. *But the level of R&D spending explained only 16 percent of this revenue performance!* Many other factors also determined performance.[10] Finally, different strategies or means of introducing new products may not require similar levels of R&D spending. Such low–R&D approaches include acquiring technology from others, purchasing components and materials, or licensing products and technologies.

High Odds of Failure

New products are critical to long term success. They keep your current product portfolio competitive and healthy, and in many firms, provide you with long term and sustainable competitive advantage. The dilemma is that product innovation is a crap shoot: boasting a steady stream of successful new products is no small feat.

The hard realities are that the great majority of new products never make it to market. And those that do face a failure rate somewhere in the order of 25 to 45 percent. These figures vary, depending on what industry and on how one defines a "new product" and a "failure." Some sources cite the failure rate at launch to be as high as 90 percent. But these figures tend to be unsubstantiated, and are likely wildly overstated. According to Crawford, who has undertaken perhaps the most thorough review of these often-quoted figures, the true failure rate is about 35 percent.[11] Our own studies concur: in a review of the new product performances of 122 industrial product firms, the average success rate of fully developed products was 67 percent. But averages often fail to tell the whole story: this success rate varied from a low of zero percent to a high of 100 percent, depending on the firm![12]

Other studies point to the difficult times faced by new product managers. A Product Development and Management Association (PDMA) study reveals that new products have had a success rate of only 58 percent at launch over the last five years.[13] The Conference Board reports a median success rate of 66 percent for consumer products and 64 percent for industrial goods (defined as success in the marketplace after launch).[14] Booz, Allen & Hamilton cite a 65 percent success rate for new product launches.[15]

Regardless of whether the success rate is 55 or 65 percent, the odds of a misfire are still substantial. Worse, the figures cited above don't include the majority of new product projects that are killed along the way and long before launch, yet involved considerable expenditures of time and money.

The attrition curve of new products tells the whole story. One study revealed that for *every seven new product ideas, about 4 enter development, 1.5 are launched, and only 1 succeeds.*[16] A more recent investigation paints an even more dismal picture: For every 11 new product ideas, 3 enter the development phase, 1.3 are launched, and only 1 is a commercial success in the marketplace (see Figure 1.2).[17] The bad news continues. An estimated 46 percent of all the resources allocated to product development and commercialization by U.S. firms are spent on products that are cancelled or fail to yield an adequate financial return.[18] This is an astounding statistic when one considers the magnitude

Figure 1.2: The Attrition Rate of New Product Projects

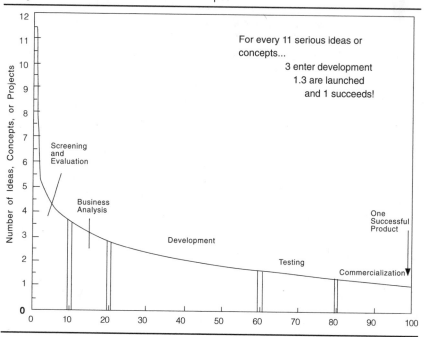

Source: A.L. Page, "PDMA New Product Development Survey: Performance and Best Practices" (Paper presented at PDMA Conference, Chicago, Nov. 13, 1991). Reprinted with permission from *New Product Management for the 1980's* (New York: Booz, Allen & Hamilton, 1982).

of human and financial resources devoted to new products. But a minority of firms (30 percent) did achieve an enviable 80 percent success rate: that is, 80 percent of the resources they spent on innovation went to new product winners. These few firms show that it is possible to outperform the average, and by a considerable margin.

Suggestion: How well is your company faring in the new product game? Do you even know? (Most companies cannot provide statistics on success, fail and kill rates, or on resources spent on winners versus losers.)

Keep score in the new product game. Key statistics to track include:

- success versus failure rates at launch.
- attrition rates: what percent of projects continue at each stage of the process?
- proportion of resources devoted to winners versus losers versus killed projects.

Beating the Odds

New products are much like a steeplechase horse race: relatively few new product projects succeed. About ten horses leave the starting gate and must clear various hurdles, hedges, or jumps along the way. And only one horse in ten crosses the finish line as the winner. The racetrack gambler tries to pick the one winning horse, but more often than not, places his or her bet on the wrong one.

New product management is even more risky than a horse race. True, the odds of picking a winner at the outset are somewhere in the order of ten to one. But the size of the bets is considerably greater—often in the millions of dollars. And unlike the gambler, the new product manager cannot leave the game—he or she must go on placing the bets, year after year, if the company is to succeed. New products is very much an addictive game: once into the game, it is difficult to quit!

Faced with these kinds of odds and risks, why would anyone want to play the new product game? Don't forget that there are some important differences between a horse race and new products. First, the payoff from a winning new product can be enormous—enough to more than cover all your losses. Second, and perhaps more subtle, the way the bets are placed is different. At a race track, *all bets must be placed before the race begins.* But in new products, *bets are placed as the race proceeds.* Imagine the horse race where bets could be placed after the horses clear each hedge or gate! Suddenly the odds are changed dramatically in favor of the shrewd gambler.

The new products race, then, is much more like a game of five card stud poker than a horse race. In five card stud, after each card is dealt, the players place their bets. Towards the end of each hand, the outcome—who will be the winner—becomes clearer; at the same time, the betting and the amounts at stake rise exponentially.

Many an amateur poker player has sat down with a professional, assuming that he had equal odds of winning. True, each player has the same odds of being dealt a winning hand: the cards are dealt randomly. But over the long term, the professional will always win—not because she gets better hands, but because of how she bets, knowing when to bet high, when to bet low, and when to fold and walk away. The trick is in the betting! The professional player counts cards and has criteria for betting.

Unfortunately, too many companies play the new products game like the amateur poker player. They start with an equal chance of winning. But because they don't count cards (that is, don't gather much information about the project, but operate on hunch and speculation instead) and lack solid betting criteria (that is, have poor or nonexistent decision rules for making Go/Kill decisions), they lose to the professional. And so the odds of losing—especially for the amateur player—are exceptionally high.

The point of these analogies is to show that new products is a much more complex game than a mere horse race: high risks, low odds of picking a winner, large amounts at stake, and an incremental betting process, with additional and increasing bets placed as the race proceeds. The second point is that effective betting is one key to winning. We all have the same odds of being dealt a good hand, but it's how we bet—the information we gather and the betting rules or criteria we use—that makes the difference between winning and losing.

What's New about a New Product?

Serious players keep score in the new product game. But in order to keep score, one must have a definition of what counts as a new product. One of the problems with some of the scores cited above is that they include different types of new products: for example, the attrition rates for truly innovative new products are much higher than for extensions and modifications of existing company products.

Defining Newness

How does one define a "new product," innovativeness, or "newness." There are many different types of new products. "Newness" can be defined in two senses:

- new to the company, in the sense that the firm has never made or sold this type of product before, but other firms might have.
- new to the market or "innovative": the product is the first of its kind on the market.

Categories of New Products

Viewed on a two-dimensional map as shown in Figure 1.3, six different types or classes of new products have been identified.[19]

1. *New-to-the-world products:* These new products are the first of their kind and create an entirely new market. This category represents only 10 percent

Figure 1.3:   Categories of New Products

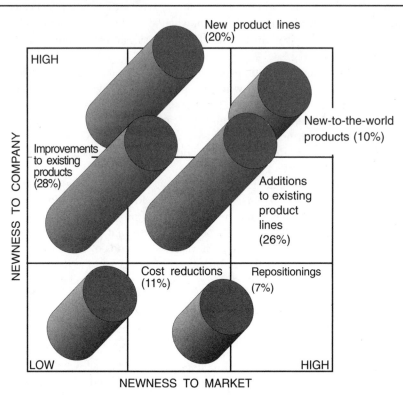

(Height of cylinder denotes number of introductions relative to total)

Reprinted with permission from *New Product Management for the 1980s* (New York: Booz, Allen & Hamilton, 1982).

of all new products, according to a Booz, Allen & Hamilton study. Well-known examples include the Sony Walkman, the first home compact disc player, and 3M's yellow Post-It Notes.

2. *New product lines:* These products, although not new to the marketplace, nonetheless are quite new to the particular firm. They allow a company to enter an established market for the first time. For example, IBM was not the first to launch an office version of a laser printer; Hewlett-Packard was, with its LaserJet. When IBM did introduce its version, it was clearly not an innovation, but it did represent a new product line for IBM, with all the investment that entailed. About 20 percent of all new products fit into this category.

3. *Additions to existing product lines:* These are new items to the firm, but fit within an existing product line the firm makes. They may also represent a fairly new product to the marketplace. An example would be Hewlett-Packard's introduction of its LaserJet II-P, a smaller and considerably less expensive version of its laser printers that is suitable for home computers. The printer is a new item within the LaserJet line, and its small size and low cost

made it somewhat novel or "new to the market." Such new items are one of the largest categories of new product—about 26 percent of all new product launches.

4. *Improvements and revisions to existing products:* These "not-so-new" products are essentially replacements of existing products in a firm's product line. They offer improved performance or greater perceived value over the "old" product. These "new and improved" products also make up 26 percent of new product launches. For example, Tremco, a B.F. Goodrich division, manufactures industrial sealants and caulking—a relatively mature business. A significant percentage of R&D efforts goes into product "tweaks"— that is, changes to existing sealant products that respond to a changing customer requirement or a competitive threat.

5. *Repositionings:* These are essentially new applications for existing products, and often involve retargeting an old product to a new market segment or for a different application. For years, aspirin (or ASA, as it is known in some countries) was the standard headache and fever reliever. Superseded by newer, safer compounds, ASA was in trouble. But new medical evidence suggested that aspirin had other benefits. Now aspirin is positioned, not as a headache pill, but as a blood clot, stroke, and heart attack preventer. Repositionings account for about 7 percent of all new products.

6. *Cost reductions:* These are the least "new" of all new product categories. They are new products designed to replace existing products in the line, but yield similar benefits and performance at lower cost. From a marketing standpoint, they are not new products; but from a design and production viewpoint, they could represent significant change to the firm. They represent 11 percent of all new product launches.

Most firms feature a *mixed portfolio* of new products. The two most popular categories, additions to the line and product improvements or revisions, are common to almost all firms, according to Booz, Allen & Hamilton. By contrast, the "step-out" products—new-to-the-world and new-to-the-firm product lines— constitute only 30 percent of all new product launches, but represent 60 percent of the products viewed as "most successful."

Sadly, many firms stay clear of these two more innovative categories: 50 percent of firms introduce no new-to-the-world products, and another 25 percent develop no new product lines. This aversion to "step-out" and higher risk products varies somewhat by industry, with higher technology industries launching proportionately more products that are innovative.

More recent data from industrial product firms in moderate-to-high technology businesses is shown in Table 1.2 and compared to industry at large. Note the importance of the two most innovative product categories to the moderate-to-high technology industries: a total of 58 percent of new products launched, compared to 30 percent in all industry.[20]

Suggestion: Review the new products that your firm or division has introduced in the last five years. Make a complete list. Then categorize them according to the six types in Figure 1.3. Questions to consider include:

Table 1.2:   Innovativeness of New Product Launches

PRODUCT CATEGORY	PERCENTAGE OF LAUNCHES	
	MODERATE-TO-HIGH TECHNOLOGY INDUSTRY	ALL INDUSTRY
New-to-the-world products	20%	10%
New product lines	38%	20%
Additions to existing product lines	20%	26%
Improvements/revisions to existing products	20%	26%
Cost reductions	2%	11%
Repositionings	1%	7%

Reprinted with permission from *New Product Management for the 1980s* (New York: Booz, Allen & Hamilton 1982). Reprinted with permission of the publisher from "The Impact of Product Innovativeness on Performance," by Robert G. Cooper and Elko J. Kleinschmidt. Thomas P. Hustad, Editor. *Journal of Product Innovation Management* 8: 240–251. Copyright 1991 by Elsevier Science Publishing Co., Inc.

1. What is the split of projects by type (percent breakdown)? Does it differ much from the all-industry averages shown in Table 1.2? Why?
2. What is the breakdown by product type in Figure 1.3 in terms of total resources spent . . . that is, to which types of products has the money and effort been devoted?
3. What is the breakdown by sales and profits . . . that is, which types of products are generating the revenues and profits? What is the success rate by type?
4. Is your current breakdown or split the desirable one? What should be the split of new products by type in Figure 1.3?

Performance and Innovativeness

One of the problems with reading too much into the new product success and performance data cited above or found in your own firm is that *performance depends to a large extent on the types of products and projects undertaken.* As you reviewed your own new product performance by innovativeness type, were the innovative ones more successful, or was it better to avoid breaking new ground? Two conflicting schools of thought might have emerged. The first is that innovative new products are more successful: they provide more opportunities for sustainable competitive advantage, and often open up more significant market opportunities. Remember that one conclusion of the Booz, Allen innovativeness study cited above is that the most innovative categories—new-to-the-world and new product lines—represented only 30 percent of the launches, but 60 percent of the most successful products!

The other school of thought is the "play it safe" school. The product innovator, because he or she is first into a market, often makes many mistakes. The number two entrant can learn from these mistakes, and succeed where the would-be pioneer failed.

So what types of new products, in terms of innovativeness, are the most successful? Our own research has pursued this theme of innovativeness and its impact on success rates.[21] To simplify things, consider just three classes of new products in terms of innovativeness:

- *Highly innovative products*, namely new-to-the-world products and innovative new product lines to the company (these represent 30 percent of the cases we studied).
- *Moderately innovative products*, consisting of new lines to the firm, with products that are not as innovative (that is, not new to the market); and new items in existing product lines for the firm (47 percent of cases).
- *Low innovativeness products*, consisting of all others: modifications to existing products; redesigned products to achieve cost reductions; and repositionings (23 percent of cases).

The impact of product innovativeness on new product success is not nearly as straightforward as expected: failure rates do not necessarily steadily increase (or steadily decrease) with increasing innovativeness! Figure 1.4 shows the results: a U–shaped relationship between product innovativeness and two key measures of performance—success rate and return on investment (ROI). Here, success rates and the mean ROI for each of the three innovation categories are shown as vertical bars.

The results are clear: Innovative products do well; so do noninnovative ones. *The problem lies within the huge middle category*—moderately innovative products—whose performance lags far behind the other two groups.

Figure 1.4:   Impact of Innovativeness on Profits

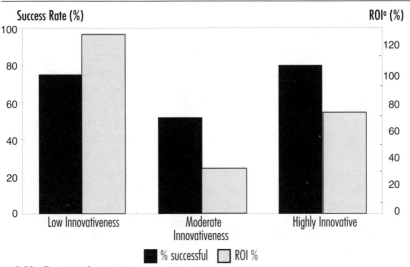

aROI = Return on Investment

The success rate (the percentage of products meeting the firms' financial criteria) is greatest for highly innovative products: 78 percent are successful. Success rates are almost as high for low innovativeness products as well (68 percent). But the success rate drops to 51 percent for the middle group—the moderate innovativeness products.

A similar U-shaped pattern is also evident for ROI: this time, highest for low innovativeness products (124 percent), followed by highly innovative products (75 percent), but dropping to a mean ROI of 31 percent for moderately innovative products.*

New product performance can be viewed in other ways as well: for example, market share, meeting sales and profit objectives, and opening new windows of opportunities for the firm. These alternative gauges of performance also show similar and striking U-shaped relationships with innovativeness. This curved pattern is clearly true across the board, and not just for one or a few measures of performance.

The message is this: First, *success rates and new product performance do depend on the product type or newness of the product.* So when you keep score, be sure to develop different innovativeness categories of new products. Second, the fact that highly innovative products do so well is a provocative finding: it helps to dispel certain myths about what types of projects are more successful, and may cause some management to rethink their "short pass" strategy.

Don't simply make the assumption that highly innovative products are too risky for your company, and that they have a negative performance. They don't: on average, they do very well! Perhaps it's time to have a hard look again at tackling more innovative projects.

An Introduction to the Game

In this chapter, we have seen that winning at new products plays a critical role in determining company fortunes. We have also witnessed some of the risks in product innovation: that new products is like a horse race with high odds of failure and significant rates of attrition. The key is on how you place your bets! Keeping score is an important facet of the game, so I laid out a scheme to help categorize new products in order that the scores would be more comparable. And finally, we looked at some par values or norms for these scores for different types of new products—from the truly innovative to the not-so-new—and witnessed the debunking of some old myths.

In the next chapter, we begin to take a hard look at the evidence. Our research into new product practices over the last 20 years has been widely published and has yielded perhaps the most thorough database on new product winners and losers—over 1,000 launches in about 350 companies in both Europe and North America. And from observing these many successes and failures, we learn the

---

* Just in case you get too enamoured with these high ROI figures, remember that these highly positiv returns must also cover the costs of the many new product projects that were killed prior to launch, a well as the misfires after launch.

keys to winning at new products: these investigations provide the basis for the book.

We begin our voyage in Chapter 2, with a look at the reasons why new products fail, and what goes wrong with product innovation. This is perhaps a negative way to start, but it's the right place too: here the hope is that we can learn from our past mistakes—that we are not doomed to repeat the same mistakes year after year.

Following that, Chapter 3 looks to new product successes and pinpoints what separates the winners from the losers. Here we see that there are clear patterns to success, and indeed, that new product success is both predictable and controllable. Chapter 4 integrates what we have learned into 15 key lessons for new product success—lessons that we build into our game plan for winning.

Chapters 5 through 9 deal with tactics or process: the development and implementation of a game plan or process for driving new products to market successfully and quickly. The game plan for new product success is introduced in Chapter 5, where the key lessons are translated into an operational blueprint for action. Chapter 6 lowers the microscope on the up-front stages of the game plan and provides a more detailed look at key early stages or "plays." Chapter 7 deals with picking the winners: it focuses on the gates or decision points in the game plan, where we look at ways to improve your "betting practices"—improving your odds of picking the right projects.

Chapters 8 and 9 follow the play as we move through development and towards the goal line: development, testing, and market launch.

Chapter 10 looks at implementation issues—what results were achieved within firms that have implemented new product processes or game plans—and how to handle the difficult job of implementation.

The final chapter deals with strategy: we stand back and look at how the game plan fits into the larger picture. This is the master strategy for new products: in which arenas should we play the game, and how should we enter each?

So read on! Become part of the new product game and observe the unfolding of the game plan—how to move down the field from idea to launch and be a winner at new products.

NEW PRODUCTS — PROBLEMS AND PITFALLS

2

Those that cannot remember the past are condemned to repeat it.
George Santayana, American philosopher.

We have forty million reasons for failure but not a single excuse.
Rudyard Kipling, *The Lesson.*

Skeletons in Our Closets

Most new product projects fail! An estimated 46 percent of the resources that firms spend on the conception, development, and launch of new products are spent on products that either fail commercially in the marketplace, or never make it to market.[1] And for every four projects that enter development, only one becomes a commercial success. Even at launch—after all the tests are complete and plans of action scrutinized—one project in three fails commercially.[2] Why the high failure rates?

A good place to begin our understanding of the keys to success is with an analysis of our past failures. This might sound like a negative beginning point, but consider this: One of the inherent weaknesses in books and articles that provide solutions and prescriptions to managers is that they tend to be based on practices identified from observing successful companies. The original *In Search of Excellence* and subsequent books by these and other authors follow this pattern.[3] But the approach is flawed—which may explain why many of those so-called excellent companies weren't doing so well several years later. Consider a fictitious illustration:

> Imagine that you and I embark on an investigation of Japanese companies to study their "secrets to success." We arrange interviews with senior managers in a dozen highly successful Japanese firms. Our approach is to observe what practices these companies share or have in common. When we identify these, we'll then conclude that these are the keys to success.

Sounds like a reasonable approach? Let's continue:

> On our first morning visit to a Japanese firm, we note that employees are vigorously doing callisthenics and singing the company song. We take note of this. Same thing at companies number 2 and 3—a lot of singing and exercising—and so on through the dozen firms.

> On our return home, we conclude that the practice that these successful Japanese firms had in common was singing the company song and doing callisthenics every morning. Since this was the common factor, it must be the secret to success. And we publish a best selling book!

Nonsense, you say, and you're right! The weakness of this type of investigation is that we only looked at one side of the coin—only at successful companies. Had we looked at an equal number of unsuccessful companies, we might have discovered that their employees also sang the company song and did callisthenics each morning. So what have we proven? Only that the Japanese like to sing and do exercises in the morning—but this likely has nothing to do with success.

The point is we have to look at both sides of the coin—at both successful case studies and unsuccessful ones too—in order to uncover what makes a winner. If we only look at winners, we may end up with some very naive conclusions, as we did with the invented example above.

Analyzing Failure

Let's begin with new product failures. Often a post mortem on new product failures will identify causes of failure, which can then lead to prescriptions for what to avoid. In this way, management can then take corrective action to avoid these pitfalls in the future.

Reasons for New Product Failure

The Conference Board has undertaken perhaps the most comprehensive analysis of new product failures over the last few decades.[4] Their management surveys have identified a number of failure reasons. Here's what they found in the most recent study:

1. *Poor Marketing Research:* Insufficient or faulty marketing research is what managers cite most frequently as the number one cause of new product failure: "A lack of thoroughness in identifying real needs in the marketplace, or in spotting early signs of competitors girding up to take the offensive, are often the findings of a new product post-mortem."

    The Conference Board report continues: Managers confessed to a serious misreading of customer needs, too little field testing or overly optimistic forecasts of market need and acceptance. Management often fell into the trap described by an executive in one industrial firm: "Simply stated, we decided what our marketplace wanted in this new product without really asking that market what its priorities were."

Another common mistake is to assume that because a product may be adequate in the eyes of the designers or R&D department, the customers will see it the same way. As one manager interviewed in the study put it: "The very important lesson we learned was to determine the requirements of the marketplace through market surveys, and then to interpret that need to our engineers for product development."

2. *Technical Problems:* The second most common cause of new product failure is technical problems in design and production. Difficulties in trying to convert from laboratory or pilot-plant scale to full-scale production are common, while manufacturing glitches and product quality problems frequently arise. In many cases, it is a failure to conduct the earlier phases more thoroughly—technical research, design, engineering—before moving to the commercialization phase. Other times, the technical problems stem from a lack of understanding of the customer's requirements—for example, trying to develop the "perfect product"—one that is simply overengineered (and too costly) compared to what the customer wanted.

3. *Bad Timing:* The penalties of moving too slowly, or too fast, stem not only from technical problems, but also from flawed planning, organization, or control. Numerous new product failures result from not moving quickly enough, given a limited window of opportunity. In some cases, there is a shift in customer preferences during the development cycle; in others, the competitor moves more quickly with a new product, and seizes the market opportunity.

The need to move quickly to market has created yet another set of timing problems: rushing a product through the process, and cutting corners to do so. Shortcuts are taken with the best intentions, but too often result in disaster. Key steps and stages are often skipped (or handled too quickly), such as market studies, prototype testing and field trials, with inevitable results: serious quality problems; the need for product redesign once into production; and marketing and sales weaknesses. There are ways to reduce the cycle time—we'll look at some in successive chapters—but doing things in a rush and cutting corners are clearly not the answers.

In another study by the Conference Board into why new products fail, a similar set of reasons was identified, but this time were quantified (See Figure 2.1).[5] Inadequate market analysis again emerged as the number one culprit, followed by product problems or defects. Often product problems were directly related to a failure to understand customer needs or do adequate field testing of the product. Insufficient marketing effort was the third cause: here management was guilty of "assuming that the product would sell itself" and simply failed to back the product's launch with sufficient marketing, selling, and promotional resources.

Figure 2.1:   Causes of New Product Failure

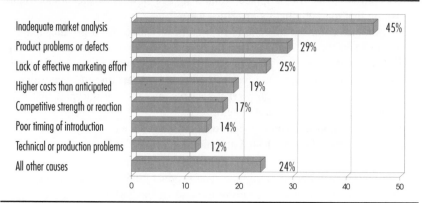

Adapted from D. S. Hopkins and E. L. Bailey, "New Product Pressures," *Conference Board Record* 8 (1971): 16-24.

Product development tends to be dominated by technology and technical issues; yet a review of the first five reasons for product failure in Figure 2.1 reveals that the principal deficiencies are not technological at all; rather, four out of five are directly or indirectly related to marketing deficiencies and problems!

Prescriptions

Some of the prescriptions gleaned from the Conference Board studies are obvious, but apparently not to everyone:

1. *More and better marketing research, market analysis and sales forecasting.* Note that traditional market research, such as large sample surveys, may not be appropriate for every project, however. But customer input and market information are, which has lead many firms to develop novel ways to include market information and the customer as an integral facet of their new product process. More on these approaches when we get into the details of the "new product game plan" in Chapter 6.

2. *Other suggestions.* These include more careful product positioning, more effective concept testing prior to the development phase, better test marketing, sharper evaluation of new product projects (including early screening), and better planning and execution of sales and promotional efforts.

3. *Specific recommendations* go further:

   - Make sure senior company executives are kept informed about the progress of each new product project, but aim to limit their personal involvement to no more than is appropriate or necessary.
   - Support a new product with ample selling effort and promotional resources in order to enable it to achieve its goals.
   - Be wary of proposed new products that stray too far from the company's area of technical and marketing expertise. This is especially true when trying to market a new product via a sales force accustomed to a different selling task—selling a different product category, or to a different type of customer.

- Don't discount competitive responses: the launch of a rival "me too" product, price cuts, or heavy promotion of existing entries.
- Educating customers about the use and value of a new product can be a much longer and harder process than anticipated, especially if the "customer's customer" must be reached.
- Get the positioning right—price, features, and quality—and not above or below customer expectations.
- Make a repeat check on expected costs, margins, revenues, and profitability whenever the original product specifications are significantly modified during the course of its development.

The Cooper Studies: Why New Products Fail

My own extensive investigations of new product winners and losers initially focused on 114 case histories in 114 industrial product firms.[6] Here our major focus was on *process*—what really happened during the course of the project. We asked each project leader to relate the story of his or her project from beginning to end—from idea through to market launch. A flow of activities, including initial screening, preliminary technical assessment, product development, prototype testing, and so on, was identified. Next, we lowered the microscope on each activity to determine quality of execution: whether a given activity had been done at all; in hindsight, should it have been done; and how well it was executed. The results are provocative (see Figure 2.2). Certain activities, considered crucial to success, are noticeable for their absence, and where done, are woefully inadequate.

Figure 2.2:   Deficiencies in the New Product Process

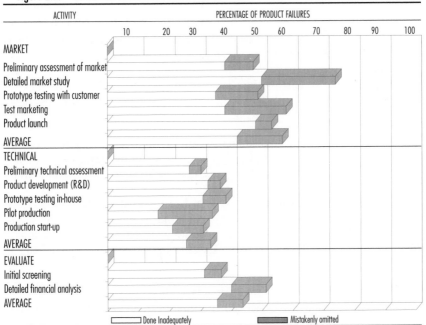

Reprinted with permission of the publisher from "Why Industrial New Products Fail" by Robert G. Cooper. James D. Hlaveck, Editor. *Industrial Marketing Management* 4: 315–26. Copyright 1975 by Elsevier Science Publishing Co., Inc.

Deficiencies in the New Product Process

The detailed market study is the most deficient activity in the entire new product process. *In 22 percent of the projects, no detailed market study was done at all,* but in hindsight, was considered a critical error of omission. In another 46 percent of projects, it was rated as "poorly done." That is, after adjustment for the few cases where a market study was inappropriate, in 74 percent of projects the detailed market study was scored as "deficient"—either poorly done or not done at all.

Other highly deficient activities (in rank order) include: test marketing or trial sell (omitted or poorly done in 58 percent of the projects); product launch (deficient in 54 percent of the cases); detailed financial/business analysis (omitted or poorly done in 52 percent of projects). Even the customer field trials and the preliminary market assessment were each rated deficient in about half the cases.

By contrast, the technologically oriented activities—preliminary technical assessment, product development, in–house product tests, pilot production, and production start–up—while not perfect, received much better ratings.

Rethinking Your Game Plan

Imagine that you are a coach of a North American football team. You've identified 12 key plays that make up a march to a touchdown. Think of the 12 activities in Figure 2.2 as these plays. You review the last 114 touchdown attempts by your team and sadly discover two things:

- On Play #1, the team fumbled the ball 48 percent of the time; Play #2 was worse—a fumble or missed pass 74 percent of the time; on Play #3, they dropped the ball 49 percent of the time; and so on. Very discouraging statistics indeed.
- Closer scrutiny reveals that the fumbles and missed passes mostly happen on one side of the field—there's a consistent pattern as to where the deficiencies lie.

As a coach, you would be distraught—how do we ever score a touchdown! Yet these are the statistics in a play-by-play analysis of the new product game. And if your company is typical, these statistics are likely not far from the truth for you!

One more point: these play-by-play statistics reported for the new product game are taken from a very biased sample of projects. Every one of these products was expected to be a winner; every one went to market; and all 114 failed! What we have here is the profile of a loser. If losing is your objective, then here are the rules.

- Don't do a detailed market study, or at best, do a fairly superficial one.
- Forget the test market or trial sell (no time or money), and make a feeble attempt at a launch.
- At all costs, avoid doing a detailed financial and business analysis.

Follow these and a few more patterns from Figure 2.2, and I can almost guarantee that you'll have a steady stream of failures. If your play-by-play statistics look like those in Figure 2.2, perhaps it's time to rethink your game plan!

A typical first reaction is that these results simply couldn't be valid for my company. We're not that bad! The point is that you don't know unless you've measured them. Subsequent to this study, I undertook private investigations using the same methodology in many firms, including well-regarded firms such as Du Pont, Procter & Gamble, and Emerson Electric. In retrospective analyses of these firm's new product failures, the results were provocative and alarming. Indeed, they were very similar to those reported above. At the beginning of one of these studies, one executive boasted that "we do everything well, all the time, every project. After all, we wrote the book on new products." When the study's results were finally available—and the results revealed many deficiencies in the way projects were carried out—his view had changed dramatically: "I guess we do many things well, in a lot of projects, much of the time—but we suffer from a lack of consistency." Consistent quality of execution was missing.

Suggestion: Undertake a post-mortem or autopsy of past new product projects in your firm. These should include both winners and losers, as well as aborted or killed projects, which were well into or past development. Undertake a strengths-and-weaknesses analysis on each, focusing on what was done well and what poorly. Go through each project from idea to launch—a play-by-play analysis, and search for good practices as well as areas that need improvement. A skeleton of the questionnaire that I ask project team members to complete when conducting such an audit is given in Appendix A.

Marketing: The Culprit

One recurring theme in the Conference Board, my own, and other studies is that many marketing activities are seriously deficient, and in particular, the lack of good market information hurt many new product projects. This is not a new theme—it was first pointed out in the 1960s—but it's a persistent one.

One facet of the problem is this: in the early stages of a new product project, we make many assumptions in order to justify the project. We make technological assumptions: we assume that the product is technically feasible; we map out a probable route to the technical solution; manufacturability at a certain cost is assumed; and so on.

There are also marketing assumptions: we make estimates of market size, growth, and need; we expect that the product's features or performance really are superior to competing products, and that "the world will beat a path to our door"; and we make competitive assumptions—for example, that the competitive response will be minimal.

Based on these assumptions, the project is given a Go decision. And then what happens? Considerable effort is devoted to verifying and validating the technological assumptions: a team of technical people undertake lab or engineering work, lab tests of prototypes, and trial or pilot product runs. But where is Marketing? Sadly, remarkably little marketing work gets done until the project is nearing completion.

A decided imbalance exists between technology and marketing in how firms allocate resources in an "average" new product project. In a study of industrial new product projects, *78 percent of the total effort (person-days) goes to technological and/or production activities,* while only 16 percent is devoted to marketing activities, and much of that goes to the launch![7] If launch is not counted, then marketing's share of effort drops to less than 10 percent of the project. This picture of where the time, money, and effort are spent provides strong evidence, that in spite of declarations of being "market oriented," marketing activities receive relatively little attention and are badly under-resourced in the new product process of many firms.

This evidence is strong: in most projects, precious little effort (in terms of people and time) is devoted to confirming the marketing assumptions until the product is actually in the launch phase. And only then *do* we learn the truth: the market isn't quite as large as expected; the product's features are a little off what the customer values; competitors *do* respond. Some of the original marketing assumptions or expectations are invariably wrong, and we failed to check them out. But by then it's too late—the damage is done.

Very often, this failure to undertake the needed marketing activities and the inability to obtain good market information stems simply from inappropriate resource allocation—the 78/16 split we saw above. The resources aren't in place! In our new product failure study, further questioning revealed that the most damaging resource deficiency was a lack of marketing research skills, capabilities, and people.[8] Other areas where resources were missing, and which contributed to these product failures, include a lack of general management skills and a lack of selling resources or skills. A lack of engineering, R&D, and production resources were rated much further down the list in terms of contributors to the failure.

Categorizing Failure

A convenient categorization scheme for new product failures was constructed from our failure case histories—a scheme which you might find helpful in undertaking new product post-mortems.[9]

Types of Failures: Six Scenarios

• *The better mousetrap that nobody wanted.* This is the most common type of failure (28 percent of cases) and typically describes a technology driven product. The product is conceived and developed internally with little attention paid to the real needs and wants of the marketplace. Carried away by the belief that they have a have a better mousetrap and that the world will beat a path to their door, managers push ahead with the project without checking their assumptions about the market and the customer's needs. Only after launch do they discover that no real need for the product, as designed, exists.

An expensive example was the introduction of IBM's first home computer, the PC Jr., in the 1980s. While it had many technological niceties, such as a cordless keyboard and totally new internal architecture, it didn't meet the fundamental needs of the adult target user. For example, the keyboard wasn't the traditional IBM-style keyboard, but more like a child's keyboard; the keys had a rocking motion, rather than up-and-down, and it quickly became known as the "Chiclets" keyboard—it felt like one was typing on Chiclets! The new architecture meant that the computer was not expandable via adding new boards—a feature that IBM users had come to expect. And so on. The PC Jr. was dead wrong for the market, and this misfire cost IBM $100 million.

- *The "me too" product meets a competitive brick wall.* This type of failure (representing 24 percent of cases) is the opposite extreme of the type described above. The project is often initiated when a successful competitive product is observed. The cry goes out: "We have to have one too!" The strategy is to develop a product remarkably similar to competitors' in the mistaken belief that simply being in the market will bring a "fair share" of sales. Once the product hits the market, sales fall below expectations. Management suddenly discovers that their offering is identical in features and price to that of an entrenched competitor. The customer has no reason to switch. Management learns that there is no such thing as automatically gaining "our fair share of the market": it must be earned. Merely "being there" is not enough: the product must be there and be better!

Vicks' attempt to penetrate the daytime allergy and cold remedy market with its Headway brand is an example. In spite of a massive launch effort, the product fell far short of sales expectations. It was essentially a "me too" product, almost identical in terms of chemistry, performance, and positioning to a leading and entrenched brand, Dristan. By contrast, new products introduced subsequently by other firms into this same competitive market in a variety of countries *offered new chemistry and distinctive consumer benefits,* namely the fact that their ingredients did not cause drowsiness. And these brands have been great successes.

These two types of failure scenarios—the better mousetrap nobody wanted, and the "me too" product meeting a competitive brick wall—together account for more than half of all new product failures. There are other less common scenarios, however.

- *Competitive one-upmanship.* Competitors may deliberately set out to upset or destroy a new product success (13 percent of cases). For example, a competitor may cut prices just prior to your launch; or it may initiate promotions, deals, or a sales push, again just prior to your own launch. Various tactics may be used to destroy your test market or trial sell; such as, disrupting your store or trade show display, price cutting, or heavy promotions. Finally, competitive product announcements may appear, which are designed to take the wind out of your sails. Often the competitive product is nonexistent or years away from the market; but the announcement is timed to hurt your new product's launch.

• **The technical dog.** The product simply doesn't work or falls short of performance requirements (15 percent of cases). A memorable example is the Adam home computer, which was rushed to the market just before Christmas. Unfortunately, there were technical bugs in the product, and reports soon began to appear in the media about the computer's shortcomings. The Adam was a well-designed home computer and gave good value for money. But because it was plagued by technical problems (which were subsequently solved), the product's reputation was badly tarnished, and eventually Coleco had to remove it from the market.

• **Price crunch.** The new product's price is too high (13 percent of cases). In some instances, competitors dropped their own prices when confronted with a new product on the market. More often, however, the pricing is a consequence of misreading the market: the product is overengineered, and too much is built into the product. As one manager put it, "The market wanted a Volkswagen, and we gave them a Mercedes."

• **Plain and simple ignorance.** Just about everything that can go wrong does go wrong (7 percent of cases). The product is wrong for the customer; competitors introduce similar products; the selling effort is inadequate and incorrectly targeted; or the product runs afoul of government regulations. The disaster results from a complete misreading of the external environment—customers, competitors, and government.

What Really Happens in the New Product Process

Can new product development really be this badly flawed? In a nutshell, yes! In countless firms, horror stories abound about mistakes made during new product ventures. These specific problems, pitfalls, and misfires were pinpointed in a more recent and extensive new product study we undertook.[10] Here we looked in detail at what happened in 203 actual new product projects in 123 industrial product companies. There were 123 commercial successes and 80 failures—a 61-percent success rate, which is fairly typical. Managers were asked to relate the story of each project—a "blow by blow" description of what happened from idea to launch. In particular, we focused on 13 key activities or plays that are often found as part of a new product project. (These activities are listed and defined in Table 2.1).

Table 2.1:   Thirteen Key Activities in the New Product Process

Initial screening	The first decision to go ahead with the project; the initial commitment of resources (people and money).
Preliminary market assesment	The initial market study: a "quick and dirty" assessment of the marketplace, possible market acceptance, and competitive situation; largely nonscientific and relying principally on in-house sources.
Preliminary technical assessment	An initial technical appraisal, addressing questions such as "can the product be developed? how? can it be manufactured? etc."; based largely on discussions, in-house sources, and some literature work.
Detailed market study	Marketing research: detailed market studies such as user needs-and-wants studies, concept tests, positioning studies and competitive analyses; involves considerable field work and interviews with customers.
Predevelopment business and financial analysis	The decision to go to a full development program; involves, for example, a financial analysis, risk assessment, and a qualitative business assessment, looking at market attractiveness, competitive advantage, etc.
Product development	The actual development of the physical product.
In-house product tests	Testing the product in-house under controlled or laboratory conditions; alpha tests.
Customer product tests	Testing the product with the customer; field trials, beta tests, or preference tests: giving the product to customers and letting them try it under live field conditions.
Trial sell	A trial sell or test market of the product: an attempt to sell the product to a limited number of customers or in a limited geographic area.
Trial production	A limited, trial, or batch production run, designed to prove production facilities.
Precommercialization business analysis	The decision to commercialize: a final business and financial analysis prior to launch.
Production start-up	Start-up of full-scale or commercial production.
Market launch	The full market launch of the product: the implementation of the marketing plan.

Holes and Omissions

Our study showed that what the literature prescribes and what most firms do are miles apart when it comes to the new product process! This was one provocative finding of the study. The literature features numerous process models or game plans that describe *how firms should develop new products*. Reality is much different! Reviews of what actually happened in the 203 projects revealed that many commonly recommended stages, activities, and practices are omitted altogether from the process. Figure 2.3 shows the frequency results; that is, in what proportion of the 203 projects a given stage or activity was carried out. Some highlights from our findings:

Figure 2.3:   Frequency of Activities in the New Product Projects

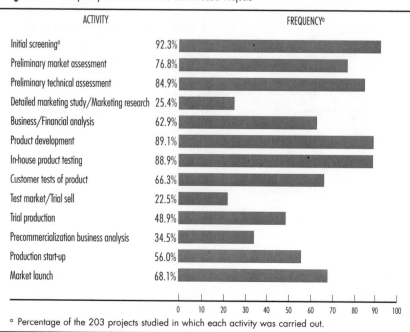

ACTIVITY	FREQUENCY[a]
Initial screening[a]	92.3%
Preliminary market assessment	76.8%
Preliminary technical assessment	84.9%
Detailed marketing study/Marketing research	25.4%
Business/Financial analysis	62.9%
Product development	89.1%
In-house product testing	88.9%
Customer tests of product	66.3%
Test market/Trial sell	22.5%
Trial production	48.9%
Precommercialization business analysis	34.5%
Production start-up	56.0%
Market launch	68.1%

[a] Percentage of the 203 projects studied in which each activity was carried out.

Reprinted with permission of the publisher from "An Investigation into the New Product Process: Steps, Deficiencies, and Impact" by Robert G. Cooper and Elko J. Kleinschmidt. Thomas P. Hustad, Editor. *The Journal of Product Innovation Management* 3: 71–85. Copyright 1988 by Elsevier Science Publishing Co., Inc.

- *Many key activities are simply left out altogether:* Commonly prescribed activities such as a market research study, a trial sell, and a detailed business and financial analysis were each undertaken in *less than half the projects studied.*
- The *weakest activities* (those most often omitted) were two of the market-related tasks, namely test market or trial sell and a detailed market study or marketing research. Three quarters of project leaders chose *not to do a detailed market study* in their project, in spite of the fact that a lack of market information remains the number one cause of product failure! A test market or trial sell was undertaken in even fewer projects: only 23 percent of projects featured such a market test of the product.
- *Other overlooked activities*—undertaken in less than half of the projects studied—were precommercialization business analysis and trial production.

The picture is bleak—a process full of holes and serious errors of omission. When one stands back and looks at the new product process, very few projects—only 1.9 percent—featured all 13 activities. Indeed, in the majority of the projects studied, less than 9 of the 13 possible activities were carried out—a very limited and truncated process. Further, in almost one-third of the projects, 7 activities or less were undertaken; that is, approximately half the new product process was left out! Could it be that what ails product innovation is that we're simply taking too many shortcuts—that we're leaving too many things out along the way?

Lame Excuses for No Action

No doubt there are good and valid reasons why certain commonly recommended actions may be omitted. Not every project needs a test market or trial sell, for example. But the frequency of omission of too many activities was substantial, certainly more than one might have expected from the occasional skipping over a step in the process. Moreover, often the excuses for omission were fairly lame. Some examples, along with our rebuttals:

> *Excuse #1 (from marketing):* "We had a limited window of opportunity, so we had to move fast. And that meant cutting out a few steps . . . things we might normally do if we had the time."
>
> *My reply:* This is probably the most popular of all lame excuses. More often than not, it results in disaster. Cutting corners, doing things in a rushed fashion, and leaving out important steps means, at best, having to cycle back to do them again; and, at worst, a significant product failure, the result of poor quality of execution.
>
> *Excuse #2 (from the R&D team):* "We didn't do a user study (market study) because we didn't have the budget. Besides there was nobody to do it . . . the marketing folks were too busy doing other things."
>
> *My reply:* "Maybe, but can you afford not to do it? Can you afford to assume that you really do understand customer needs and wants? And what will it cost you if you're wrong? Finally, if marketing won't help, maybe it's so important that you should do the customer contact work yourself!" Note that Procter & Gamble's R&D operation has had its own market research department for over 30 years!
>
> *Excuse #3 (from a project team):* "We don't usually do a detailed financial analysis prior to development. The numbers really aren't too reliable."
>
> *My reply:* "True. But maybe you should focus on getting better estimates of expected revenues, costs, etc.. And even if the analysis is not very reliable, at least some insight is gained into the financial viability of the project. The analysis acts as a 'sanity check'!"
>
> *Excuse #4 (from the product manager):* "We did alpha tests (in-house product tests) but no beta tests (field trials). We didn't want competitors to find out about the new product, which they might have if we had tested in the field."
>
> *My reply:* "Confidentiality is always a concern. But so is the fact that the product really does perform under live field conditions and in a way acceptable to the customer. Moreover, there are ways to preserve confidentiality in a field trial via tighter test controls, the selection of trusted customer partners, and a signed agreement with the customer."

Figure 2.4:   Quality of Execution of Activities in New Product Projects

Mean Scores (0–10) Proficiency		Activity		Need for Improvement Mean Scores (0–10)
	5.27	Initial screening	5.48	
	5.47	Preliminary market assessment	5.37	
	6.69	Preliminary technical assessment	4.60	
	5.74	Detailed market study	5.83	
	6.49	Business/Financial analysis	4.27	
	6.55	Product development	4.47	
	6.96	In-house product testing	3.87	
	6.69	Customer tests of product	3.99	
	6.86	Test market/ trial sell	4.59	
	6.79	Trial production	3.66	
	6.26	Precommercialization business analysis	3.95	
	6.31	Production start-up	4.37	
	6.36	Market launch	4.44	

10   9   8   7   6   5   　　　　　 3   4   5   6   7   8   9   10

Stronger　　　Weaker　　　　　Lower Need　　Higher Need

Reprinted with permission of the publisher from "An Investigation into the New Product Process: Steps, Deficiencies, and Impact" by Robert G. Cooper and Elko J. Kleinschmidt. Thomas P. Hustad, Editor. *The Journal of Product Innovation Management* 3: 71–85. Copyright 1988 by Elsevier Science Publishing Co., Inc.

What about Quality?

Errors of omission—simply leaving out too many tasks—were prevalent in our study of new product practices. But what about quality of execution? An activity may be carried out, but is it done well? Is there quality of execution, or is the activity undertaken in a rushed or sloppy fashion? We developed a "quality of execution" index for each of the 13 activities listed in Table 2.1. Figure 2.4 shows the average quality index (based on a scale of 0 to 10) for each activity. Some conclusions:

- *No activities are rated as top quality.* On average, there are no 10s, no 9s, not even any 8s or 7s. Even the best-rated activity, in-house product tests, scores just below 7 out of 10 on average—hardly a strong showing! What we witness is anything but a quality process: there is much room for improvement in the typical firm's new product process.
- *The worst-rated activities are typically the "up-front" actions.*The greatest weaknesses occurred in activities towards the beginning of the process (which coincidentally often are marketing activities). Particularly weakly handled activities include the initial screening, the preliminary market assessment, and the detailed market study.

Managers were also queried about whether each activity needed improvement or not; the mean responses are shown on the left side in Figure 2.4 (again on a 0–10 scale, where 10 means "great need for improvement"). Activities singled out for improvement by managers were, not surprisingly, the same three "up-front" activities cited as poorly done (and listed above).

A Blow-by-Blow Description

Let's now conduct a step-by-step review of the new product process based on the 13 activities outlined in Table 2.1, with a particular view to uncovering what goes wrong.[11]

Initial screening

Initial screening, although said to be undertaken in over 90 percent of the projects, was rated as the weakest activity overall, scoring lowest on the proficiency scale, and also cited as an activity greatly in need of improvement. Consider some of the ways that firms undertook screening:

- Sixty percent percent of firms indicated that screening was a group decision—a multidisciplinary group of decision makers from R&D, Marketing, etc. But no formal criteria were used to make the decision; this first commitment to the project boiled down to an informal discussion.
- In 24 percent of the projects, a single individual made the initial Go/Kill decision, again using no formal criteria. The assumption here is that one person in the company knows everything about technology, markets, production, and strategy— and more, that this person is so proficient at decision making that criteria are not needed!
- In only 12 percent of the projects did initial screening come even close to what it should have been: a multidisciplinary decision making group (in order to provide different inputs to the decision) armed with Go/Kill criteria upon which to base the decision.

Given the current practices above, it is little wonder that initial screening was singled out as one activity where improvement was sorely needed. Forty percent of managers sought better inputs at this decision point (e.g., from Marketing); another 23 percent wanted more consistent and formal procedures (e.g., decision criteria or Go/Kill screening rules).

Preliminary market assessment

Preliminary market assessment—the first but quick attempt to determine market potential and expected market penetration—was also rated as a weak activity. It was omitted altogether in almost one-quarter of projects: that is, the project charged ahead without even a cursory look at the marketplace; and when done, was rated a weak 5.47 out of 10 on the quality index.

What did a preliminary market assessment entail? *In less than half the cases was direct contact with customers made!* Other actions included discussions with the sales force, a review of competitors' products, a library search, and an "internal discussion among colleagues."

Preliminary market assessment was another activity singled out for improvement. A sharper, more focused definition of the market, more customer contacts, and the devotion of more time and effort were the suggestions most frequently made.

Preliminary technical assessment

Preliminary technical assessment—the first technical appraisal of the new product project—was rated more positively: it was undertaken in the great majority of projects (85 percent), and was rated as proficiently executed.

Detailed Market Study

The detailed market study was among the weakest of the 13 activities studied in the new product process. It was omitted in three-quarters of the projects! And when undertaken, it was rated as "poorly handled" on average—a quality index of only 5.7 out of 10.

The types of market investigations undertaken include (in descending order of mention):

- a study of competitive products and prices (26%)
- a study of what customers needed or wanted in the new product, to generate product specifications (19%)
- a study to determine market size (19%)

We have serious concerns that managers understand what is meant by the term "detailed market study" when the most frequently mentioned action is simply a study of competitive products and prices! By contrast, studies of customers to determine their needs (a user needs-and-wants study) and concept tests (a study of customer reactions to the proposed new product to gauge expected acceptance) were noticeably rare.

Suggestions for improvement were varied, but included better focus (better definition of the market or segment to be investigated); greater effort (more customer contacts and interviews, more depth); better definition of the product and technology before a customer survey is undertaken; and sharper market research objectives.

Pre-Development Business and Financial Analysis

Many firms (63 percent) conducted a business or financial analysis of the project prior to moving into full-scale development. Generally, this analysis was rated as moderately proficiently handled, and there was not a strong call for improvements here. Suggestions included: more multi-departmental inputs; more market information and inputs from customers; more time and effort spent on the business analysis; and more formal, consistent procedures.

Product Development

The product development phase—the actual design and development of the product—was perceived by managers as a well-executed activity, on average. There were some requests for improvement, however:

- a more formally laid out process, with better coordination among people and departments.
- more depth and detail regarding technical issues, problems, and questions during development.
- more resources, more and better experienced people, and better facilities.
- and more time and effort devoted to this phase.

In-house Product Testing

Following the development phase, the product was typically subjected to a set of in-house tests (89 percent of projects). This stage was rated as the strongest one, on average. Requested improvements included more time and effort to be spent on testing, and a more detailed, rigorous, and formal testing procedure.

Customer product testing

Customer tests of the product was a fairly well rated activity and one that was undertaken in the majority of projects studied (66 percent of cases). Most often, the customer test involved giving a sample or prototype of the product to the customer at no charge and letting the customer try the product (78 percent of cases). In a minority of cases (14 percent), there was a rigorously designed customer test, complete with written testing procedures. In a few cases (7 percent), the customer was brought to the company's premises for an on-site user test of the product.

Requested improvements included a more thorough testing program (more tests undertaken and at more test sites) and better control over the customer tests.

Trial Sell

The test market was undertaken the least frequently of all 13 activities in the process. Less than one-quarter of projects featured an attempt to gauge market acceptance based on a limited sell (for example, in one geographic area; or to a limited set of customers) prior to full commercialization. When undertaken, the activity was rated as proficiently executed, but improvements recommended included sharper definition of test market customers, and more objective and better measures of test market results.

Trial Production

Trial production was carried out in less than half the projects, but when undertaken, was rated positively. Trial production focused on either a test of the production system itselffor example, that the production equipment ran properly (54 percent of projects); or a test of the integrity of the product that the production system yieldedfor example, to see that the resulting product's specs were right (42 percent of projects). There were few improvements deemed necessary here.

Precommercialization Business Analysis

Managers were queried about whether or not a detailed business analysis was undertaken after product development, but before the full launch. Only a minority of projects (35 percent) featured such an analysis even though most experts recommend a full pre-launch business review.

Typically, if carried out, this prelaunch business analysis was executed in a quality fashion. Typical methods included a detailed financial analysis; a detailed market information review (sales forecasting, marketing costs); or a detailed cost review. Suggestions on how to make this final Go/Kill decision more effective included a total "start from scratch" review; revision and update of all data; and better market information, including input from a market acceptance or test market study.

Production Start-up

In the majority of cases, production start-up was a relatively straightforward activity, and tended to be rated proficiently. It involved either no changes to the existing production facilities (13 percent of cases) or few changes (35 percent).

Market Launch

The market launch stage was rated moderately positively on average. Surprisingly, in over 30 percent of the projects, *the launch stage was not recognized as a formal, distinct, or identifiable stage* or activity. Improvements thought needed were:

- more resources and efforts to be allocated to the advertising and promotion effort for the new product.
- a clearer definition of marketing objectives.
- better in-house communication among the sales, advertising, service, and production departments at launch.
- better training and preparation of the sales force.

Quality Is Missing

Many of the new product projects we studied above ran into serious trouble: they took too long; they fell below sales and profit targets; and in some cases, they performed so badly that they were eventually removed from the market. Why did they encounter so many difficulties?

What we witnessed throughout this extensive study of 203 projects was the *lack of a quality process*. Too many key activities were omitted; for other activities, it seems that the team just went through the motions; in still others, corners were cut or important tasks were overly rushed. In many cases, management or the project leader and team knew what had to be done, but simply failed to do it (or did it poorly). As one manager said: "we all know how to dance; but once on the dance floor, we don't dance so well." *Quality of execution is the missing ingredient* in the great majority of new product projects.

Suggestion: In undertaking your post-mortem or "retrospective analysis" of past new product projects, pay special attention to the various activities, actions, and tasks in the process (see Appendix A for the skeleton of an audit questionnaire). Measure quality of execution, and identify "good practices" and deficient actions throughout. If your company is typical, you'll be shocked at how many deficiencies there are. After the audit is complete, try to pinpoint where and why quality of execution is lacking, and what must be built into a new product game plan to ensure quality of execution.

Where the Resources Are Spent

One of the recurring themes throughout this study of 203 projects was the call for more time, money, and effort to be spent on various activities and actions. Managers constantly indicated that they had done a rushed or sloppy job on too many critical activities, and that there was a need for more time, care, and effort. These comments beg the question: just how are the resources allocated? Where is the time and effort spent in projects?

Where the resources are spent has rarely been the topic of detailed investigations. Mansfield and Rapoport provided some rough splits of innovation costs across major stages in the new product process[12]. They conclude that about 39 percent of the total costs of a new product project went to the R&D phase. Similarly Booz, Allen & Hamilton provide the breakdown of total company expenditures by major stage in the innovation process, and also the proportion spent on successes versus failures[13]. The approximate breakdown is shown in Figure 2.5.

The Booz, Allen results are provocative. (Note that Figure 2.5 shows a breakdown of total company spending, not a per-project analysis: there are far more projects at the beginning stages than at the end). This chart reveals that for every $1 million a firm spends on product innovation, roughly $150,000 is spent on exploration and screening—on exploratory research, idea generation, and on

Figure 2.5: Effectiveness of New Product Expenditures

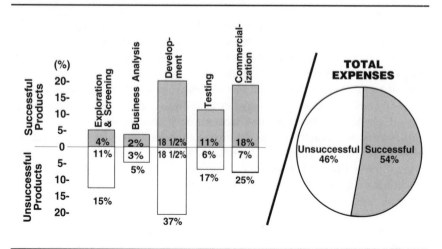

Reprinted with permission from New Product Management for the 1980s (New York: Booz, Allen & Hamilton 1982).

initial attempts to qualify the idea. Most of this goes to losers. This is no surprise: we must shovel a lot of earth to find a few diamonds! Remember the attrition curve in Figure 1.2 in the last chapter.

Next comes business analysis, where the concept is defined and the project justified. Here's where the detailed market, technical and manufacturing studies are done in order to build a business case and to weed out the bad projects. Relatively little is spent here: only 5 percent of the total.

Development takes the biggest piece of the pie, representing 37 percent of total spending or $370,000 of our $1 million. But here, *half the resources still go to unsuccessful projects.* One might have hoped that by the time development began, the "bad" projects would have been largely culled out. Not so. For even at this very expensive stage, and after all the up-front screening and business analysis work has been done, half the resources are still misspent! This apparent misallocation of resources raises serious questions about the goodness of steps that precede the development phase: for example, just how good a business analysis is being done? And is a 5 percent allocation really enough for the business analysis stage?

Testing follows and takes about 17 percent of the total. This includes field trials, trial production runs, and test markets designed to validate the product and project. The final stage is commercialization, which entails production start-up and market launch, and accounts for about 25 percent of the total, or $250,000 of our $1 million total spend. At this last stage, note that the majority of resources is devoted to successful projects—finally! By this final stage, many of the poor projects have been culled out, and the majority of resources are at last going to the good ones. But this is a bit late in the game to be figuring out which are the good projects—most of the money has already been spent!

These studies provide rough benchmarks that are useful for you to compare your company's spending patterns. They also raise serious questions and doubts—that spending or resource allocation is not as it should be; and that something is very wrong with the product innovation process. For example, why do half of development expenditures go to unsuccessful ventures? And why is it so late in the process before we finally figure out the correct priorities? And are we spending enough on business analysis—this homework phase is critical, but its 5 percent allocation appears pitiful.

By observing these spending patterns, we gain valuable insights into problems in product innovation. But these and other studies on spending do not yield the level of detail needed to permit meaningful diagnosis of problems and pitfalls in the innovation process. For example, the steps or stages considered were rather broad, and there was no breakdown of spending by specific activity such as "the market research study." Second, results were reported only in terms of dollars. This is obviously one important measure, but as many new project leaders will attest, often the issue is more one of time and people, and not so much a lack of money.

Our study of over 200 actual new product projects (above) also dissected spending and resource allocation.[14] Figures 2.6 and 2.7 show the percentage breakdown (for dollars and person-days, respectively) spent on the 13 activities outlined in Table 2.1.

The typical new product project is characterized by a very concentrated expenditure pattern. Of the 13 activities, three account for more than three quarters of the dollar expenditures. Not surprisingly, these activities are (see Figure 2.6):

Figure 2.6: Expenditures on Each Activity in the New Product Process

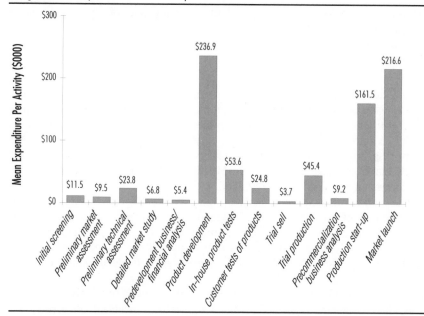

Reprinted with permission of the publisher from "Resource Allocation in the New Product Process" by Robert G. Cooper and Elko J. Kleinschmidt. James D. Hlavacek, Editor. *Industrial Marketing Management* 17(3): 249–62. Copyright 1988 by Elsevier Science Publishing Co., Inc.

Figure 2.7:   Person-Days Spent on Each Activity in the New Product Process

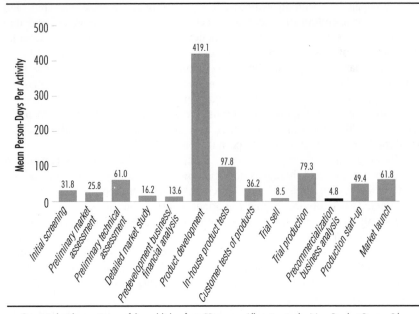

- *Product development*—the actual design and development of the product (29.3 percent of total dollars).
- *Market launch*—the formal launch of the product into the marketplace (26.8 percent).
- *Production start-up*—the acquisition of production equipment and production start-up (20.0 percent).

In contrast to these high expenditure areas, activities such as the pre-development business analysis and the detailed market study had few resources spent on them: less than 1 percent of total project costs for each! Indeed, of the 13 activities studied, a total of 6 add up to only 5 percent of total project costs. Not surprisingly, these 6 under-funded actions correspond quite closely to the "poorly executed activities" identified in Figure 2.4. Quality of execution and resources spent are clearly closely linked.

The market-oriented activities (with the exception of launch) are noticeable for their lack of expenditure. On average, only 1.2 percent of project costs were devoted to a preliminary market assessment; even less (0.8 percent) was spent on the detailed market study (partly a reflection of the fact that most project leaders did not do one at all!); only 3.1 percent was allocated to customer tests or field trials; and 0.5 percent spent on a test market or trial sell. These results provide strong evidence that the new product process is a relatively unbalanced one; that it remains largely dominated by technological activities; and that many critical marketing actions receive little attention and even fewer funds.

When person-days rather than dollars is used as the measure of resources spent, the picture remains almost the same. Figure 2.7 displays the results. Again, the product development function dominates, accounting for 46 percent of the person-days effort. Note that although the dollars spent on market launch and production start-up were high, the person-days spent here are considerably less: expenditures were not for people, but for out-of-pocket items such as equipment, plant, advertising and promotion. Other actions, such as in-house tests and trial production account for a relatively higher proportion of manpower.

In contrast, very little effort was devoted to activities such as the trial sell or test market (0.5 percent of the total person-days) or the detailed market study (1.8 percent of total).

When the dollars and people expenditures are collapsed into three categories, the picture becomes even clearer:

Type of Activity	Expenditures (% of total)	
	% Dollars	% Person-days
Technological and production	65%	78%
Marketing (including launch)	32%	16%
Evaluation (screening, project approvals, Go/Kill decisions)	3%	6%

Note that of the 32 percent of total dollars spent on marketing activities, 83 percent of that went to the launch.

If how people spend their time and money is any indication of the importance accorded different activities, *then clearly marketing activities remain a distant second in the new product process* for many firms. And most of the marketing effort boils down to one activity, namely market launch—sales force, advertising and promotion—with little going to earlier marketing actions, such as market assessments, detailed market studies and customer tests and trials. These results are frightening, especially when one recognizes that almost every study of new product failure has identified a lack of a market orientation and inadequate marketing inputs as the major culprit in new product failure!

Yet another way of looking at these resource allocation results is to *consider various major stages* of the new product process. For this analysis the process was subdivided into three major stages:

- *Predevelopment or "up-front" activities:* those actions from the idea stage up to (but not including) the product development phase—the "front end" of the process.
- *Development and testing:* the middle of the process, including product development, as well as in-house and customer tests of the product.
- *Commercialization:* the "back end" of the process, including market launch, production start-up, trial sell, and trial production.

Figure 2.8 shows the breakdown in expenditures for both dollars and person-days for the average project. What stands out in this exhibit is how much the typical new product project is loaded towards the middle and the back end. Only 7 percent of the dollars and 16 percent of effort (person-days) are expend-

Figure 2.8:   Resources Allocated to Each Major Stage in the New Product Process

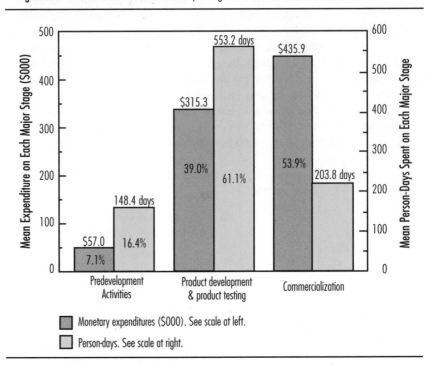

ed on the front end of the process. Some of this imbalance is inevitable, especially in projects where there is a major capital spend. But dollars aside, notice how little effort goes "up front"!

Yet it is the front end which houses so many critical and decisive activities central to new product success. The critical nature of these front end actions was highlighted in the Booz, Allen studies, which showed that successful U.S. firms devote more effort to the predevelopment activities, and that the Japanese spend even more here.[15] And it is in the up front activities where the seeds to so many new product disasters are sown—inadequate market analysis, poor screening and evaluation, and a failure to understand customers' needs.

The importance of getting the first few steps of the project right is obvious. But apparently the lesson hasn't been learned in the majority of firms: simply stated, *companies allocate very little effort and even fewer dollars to the front end or "homework" phases* of most new product projects! And the results are predictable.

Suggestion: Undertake a resource allocation appraisal for your new product efforts. Determine how many person-days and how much money is spent by people in various functions or departments on product innovation. Determine where and how it is spent. Get breakdowns by activity and by project. Then develop some of the charts you've seen in this chapter . . . the results will be provocative!

1. *Determine the total spending allocations* (dollars and person-days) by major stage, and what proportion is spent on winners versus losers at each stage (see Figure 2.5).
2. *Perform the breakdown on a per project basis.* That is, where do the resources go (by major stage and by specific activity) for the average project, and also for successes versus failures (see Figures 2.6, 2.7, and 2.8)?
3. Using the same data, *report the breakdown of resources per project by function* (in both person-days and dollars): R&D, Engineering, Marketing, Manufacturing, etc., to determine if you have a skewed distribution of effort, much like we saw in the results presented above.

Problems and Pitfalls

In this chapter, we've identified many of the problems and pitfalls that result in new product failures and a mediocre new product program. Let's review them.

1. *A lack of a market orientation:* Inadequate market analysis, a failure to understand customer needs and wants, and insufficient attention to the marketplace are consistently cited as major reasons for new product failure. Simply stated, firms tend to omit many of the critical marketing tasks, particularly those in the early phases of a project. Activities such as the detailed market study (to determine customer needs and wants and to assess likely market acceptance) and test markets or trial sells (to test the launch plan and determine market penetration) were most often omitted—in about three-quarters of projects. And activities such as preliminary market assessment and the detailed market study were plagued by poor quality of execution. Finally, marketing actions appear to receive a disproportionately small share of the total resources spent on projects: 32 percent of funding (most of which goes to the market launch); and only 16 percent of the effort (measured in person-days).
2. *Poor quality of execution:* The new product process is replete with deficiencies: errors of omission and errors of commission abound. Key actions, often considered central to success, are arbitrarily omitted: the typical new product process is very much a truncated one, with only a small minority of projects-less than 2 percent—considered to be complete. Certain pivotal activities are noticeable more for their absence than presence in the typical firm's process: activities such as the detailed market study, the test market, the precommercialization business analysis are undertaken in a minority of cases. When undertaken, the quality of execution is most often lacking. Quality of execution was rated as "mediocre" across a broad spectrum of actions, with some of the weakest areas being initial screening, detailed market study, precommercialization business analysis, production start-up, and market launch. *What we witness is the picture of a process that is very much in trouble.*

3. *Moving too quickly:* Many of these errors—the failure to do certain key tasks, or short-cutting others—are made in the interest of saving time. But these efforts are false economy: invariably, they come back to haunt the perpetrators. What little time may be gained by moving too quickly is usually lost several times over later in the project. When corners are cut, mistakes are made, the project moves off target, and activities have to be repeated; all at great time and money expense. Sometimes time-saving measures are fatal: a failure to undertake a needed market study or to cut short the field trials often leads to a product disaster.

4. *Not enough homework:* The three themes above—inadequate market analysis, poor quality of execution, and moving too quickly—all converge on the homework phase. For all the reasons above, the homework simply doesn't get done. The project moves from idea through a rather superficial "definitional and homework" phase right into a full-scale development. Management has adopted a cavalier or macho "ready, fire, then aim" approach when it comes to new products. The act of doing homework may be disliked, but it's got to be done! Sadly, the evidence is otherwise. The predevelopment activities receive a relatively small proportion of the total resources: 7 percent of the dollars and 16 percent of the effort. And these homework phases are the same ones which are plagued by errors of omission and commission. Yet these homework phases are central to success: it is here where the market and product are defined; where the obvious losers should be weeded out; and where the key decisions to commit significant resources are made.

5. *A lack of differentiation:* Too many new products are reactive efforts—a "me too" product that meets a competitive brick wall. The failure to do one's homework, a lack of willingness to seek customer input, and the desire to move quickly too often leads to a reactive, copy-cat product as the easy solution. Such products are one of the most popular ways of failing: There is no such thing as one's "fair share of the market." Advantage is essential to winning; and as we shall see in the next chapter, achieving product differentiation is critical to success.

6. *No focus, too many projects, and a lack of resources:* A lack of resources, particularly from certain departments in the company (e.g., Marketing) and for specific activities in a project (e.g., the up-front or predevelopment stages), plagues too many new product projects. This lack of time, money, and people is the root cause of many errors of omission and poor quality of execution, which in turn have such serious consequences for product performance. Why this lack of resources? In some firms, senior management has simply starved product innovation: it has grossly underestimated the resource requirements for an effective new product program. In most firms, however, it boils down to not enough focus and hence too many projects for the available resources; the result is that scarce resources are dissipated across many fronts, and that the truly deserving projects are underresourced.

From Losers to Winners

This chapter has begun our quest for the ideal new product game plan—a blue-print for new product success. We started with an understanding of our weaknesses: the problems, pitfalls, and deficiencies that beset new product projects. Six key weaknesses have been pinpointed. Correcting these weaknesses is the first step. But a word of caution: if we correct these deficiencies, does it stand to reason that success will be the result? If a football team fixes everything it does wrong, it doesn't necessarily win the game! The next chapter looks at winners: more specifically, we explore what makes a winner, and what separates winners from losers in the new product game.

What Separates the Winners from the Losers

The game is done! I've won, I've won.
Samuel Taylor Coleridge, *The Ancient Mariner.*

Winning isn't everything . . . it's the only thing.
Vince Lombardi, Green Bay Packers football coach.

A Critical Question

What makes a new product a success? And what can be done to improve the odds of winning at new products in my company? These questions have plagued senior executives for decades. But today more than ever, the answers are critical: the ability to develop and launch new products successfully and quickly is the key to business success as we move into the next century.

"Identify the top three factors in new product success!" a senior manager challenged the attendees at one of my seminars a few years ago. This seemingly innocent challenge proved much more difficult than first imagined. As we went around the room and listed each person's top three factors, it was clear that each of us had a very different view of the world. The problem was that each of us had a limited experience—participation in only four or five new product projects—and each of us was biased by the most recent one we had witnessed. The various success factors that managers in the room cited were typical, and fit into one of three types:

1. *Luck!* A minority of mangers attributed much of new product success to blind luck. And they cited countless examples, such as the hoola hoop, Post-It Notes, and Cabbage Patch Dolls, to prove their point: products whose success was likely due more to serendipity than to sound management practices.

   If you believe in the luck theory, the implications are simple: do a lot of projects, and the law of averages says that you're bound to get lucky on some! Operationally this means having a lot of people working on a large number of projects at any one time.

2. *Tailwind:* Factors outside the control of the project leader and team decide the success of the project—factors such as the nature of the marketplace, the competitive situation, and the existence of certain resources elsewhere in the firm that were available to the project team. The analogy here is that of an airplane pilot: the success of the flight—a smooth ride and arriving on time—depends more on factors outside the cockpit and over which the pilot and crew have no control (such as the weather, tailwind speed, and air traffic controllers) than on how that pilot flies the plane. The key to success, then, is not how you fly the plane, but which flight you pick!

If you believe in the tailwind theory, then the implications are straightforward: *Project selection is paramount.* Devote much energy to project selection, picking only those projects with the right tailwind factors.

3. *Actions:* The third theory argues that, while luck and tailwind do play a role, new product success hinges on the actions of the project team and leader: what they do, and how well they do it. Managers who voted for this theory pointed to countless projects in their firms that were floundering until a new project leader and team were put in place. This new team, through their actions—doing the right things and doing them well—turned the project around and transformed a would-be dog into a star. It's a common story we see repeated in many firms and new product projects. In short, the new product process and the players that execute it—the actions that occur from idea through to launch, and how well they are carried out—is central to success.

If you support the tactical actions theory, the implications are this: *Focus on your new product process and the team.* Make sure you have a process in place, build the process around proficient teams, and ensure that quality of execution is built into the process at every play.

Most of us would subscribe to all three theories: a little bit of luck, positive strategic tailwind, and sound actions or tactics. We can't do much about luck, but both tailwind and process (or actions) can be managed. So, an accurate understanding of precisely why new products succeed or fail—the success factors—is vital to improving new product performance for two reasons:[1]

- If the keys to success are indeed tailwind or strategic factors—*descriptors of the product, market, and technology, or their synergies*—then this knowledge can be built into project screening, selection, and prioritization decisions. The end result is that we become better at project selection—*at picking winners*; we make better use of scarce resources; and we become more focused.
- On the other hand, if what distinguishes winners from losers depends primarily on tactics—on the *players and the actions* they take and *practices they employ* from the idea stage through to launch—then our focus should be on improving the *new product process* itself.

The Keys to New Product Success

In the last chapter, we looked at why new products fail, and what goes wrong in product innovation. But identifying what makes a new product a winner is considerably more difficult than merely pinpointing reasons for failure. A number of experts have attempted to identify the factors in new product success. One of the earliest investigations, by Myers and Marquis, looked at 567 successful product innovations, and concluded that most are *market-pull* projects; only 21 percent are *technology push*.[2] Correct identification of an existing market need is the common ingredient among these success stories.

Internal sources of information are also critical to the innovation process, pointing to the need to foster interaction among departments involved in the new product process. External information obtained via nonstructured channels is also important. Myers and Marquis were among the first to recognize that a new product process—a "game plan"—exists: that some firms had in place a plan or process consisting of a logical flow of activities, from idea to launch. A simple five-step model was proposed as a result of studying these 567 successes.

The General Electric Laboratories provided another setting for an investigation of product success.[3] Roberts and Burke looked closely at six GE products and concluded that both technological and market variables decided their fates. These six successful products had several things in common:

- Market needs were recognized, and R&D was targeted at satisfying those needs.
- When a technological success did not meet a specific market need, the product was adapted to suit an identified need.
- Research managers communicated the possibility of a technological breakthrough clearly to other departments, which facilitated the identification of a market need.
- Communication existed between engineers and scientists and other involved (operating) departments.

Thus, in spite of the fact that the products were all moderate-to-high technology ones, emphasis was placed on market needs and market need identification.

In one of my early investigations of three significant high-technology new industrial products—a new milk packaging system by Du Pont of Canada, a new telephone handset by Northern Telecom, and a new turbojet engine by United Technologies—much was learned about what went into successful product development. The one common thread in these three developments was a *strong commitment and orientation to the marketplace.* In all three cases, there was extensive and careful analysis of the market; in fact, in two of the cases, 11 separate market studies were undertaken—from user needs-and-wants studies to concept tests, field trials, and test markets. These market studies, particularly those early in the project, dealt not only with the more obvious issues, such as market potential and size, but also with the nature of customer needs, the benefits they sought in a new product, and the design requirements that would achieve meaningful product differentiation.

The three cases dramatically demonstrated the importance of *marrying technological prowess to a strong market orientation,* and the need to undertake one's *homework before product development begins.* The result in all three cases was the development and launch of a new product that was not only technologically superior, but one that met customer needs and delivered unique benefits to end users far better than anything else on the market.

A second common facet of these three winning products was the *logical and stepwise flow of activities* as the projects moved from idea to launch. None of the firms at that time had a formal new product process in place; yet when we laid the flow charts that captured what happened in each of the three projects on top of one another, they were almost identical. It was almost as though the three firms, each in a different industry, had adopted the same game plan: similar steps and activities; similar sequencing and timing; and similar allocations of effort to each stage or step.

A final discovery was the extent of *interaction between people from different functional groups* within each firm. The project, from idea to launch, crisscrossed back and forth across the field between marketing, technical, and manufacturing groups and people. It was much like watching a rugby match. Although there was a product champion or project leader in each case, the effort was by no means a one-person or one-department show. A multidisciplinary approach, with strong interaction between players from different functions, was prevalent in all three cases.

Suggestion: We need to learn from history. Identify some recent new product successes in your company, and write up their stories: a chronology of events and actions from idea through to launch. Then, let a team analyze what happened, why the projects were successful, and what we can learn about what it takes to win. Build these case illustrations and lessons into your management training programs and into your company practices.

Success versus Failure

We can learn much from observing successful new products. Equally, there is much to be gained from doing post-mortems on failures. But as pointed out in the previous chapter, the fundamental flaw with both research directions is that they only look at one side of the coin: they report what successes have in common, or why products fail; but do not look at both types of projects—successes and failures—in the same study. Simply because a number of successes have one thing in common does not mean that this factor leads to success: perhaps failures also share the same characteristic! In order to uncover the keys to success, one must identify those *factors that separate winners from losers*—the discriminating variables—hence the need for a comparison of both types of projects in the same study.

The U.K. Experience

The first investigation to undertake such a comparison was the British investigation, Project SAPPHO. This classic study compared and contrasted 43 pairs of product innovations—successful products versus unsuccessful ones in the same industries—to identify factors that lead to success.[4] The most important discriminators between winners and losers were, in rank order:

- understanding of users' needs;
- attention to marketing and launch publicity;
- efficiency of development;
- effective use of outside technology and external scientific communication; and
- seniority and authority of responsible managers.

Note that the first two factors were market-related, and not the expected technological and technical prowess factors.

SAPPHO in Other Countries

A smaller study of the Hungarian electronics industry yielded comparable results.[5] In spite of the political, cultural, and economic differences between the two countries, a similar set of success factors was identified:

- market need satisfaction;
- effective internal communication;
- efficient development;
- a strong market orientation; and
- the role of key individuals.

The SAPPHO researchers also reported the results of a five-country study of innovation in the textile machinery industry. Here the focus was on firms rather than projects. High performance firms shared certain characteristics:

- they had superior marketing capabilities and frequent customer contact;
- they understood users' needs and were able to assess whether these needs could be filled economically; and
- they carefully matched specific sales strategies to market requirements.

Firms that employed qualified scientists and engineers were more able to produce successful breakthroughs, and more radical innovations stemmed from those firms with technically qualified chief executives.

Other Success/Failure Studies

Kulvik's study of successes and failures in Finland yielded similar results, but identified additional facilitators, namely various synergies: a good "company/ product fit," the utilization of technical know-how in the company, and familiarity with both the new product's markets and its technologies.[6] Another study on European and Japanese successes versus failures identified marketing proficiency, product advantage, early market need recognition, a high degree of customer contact, and top management initiation as the keys to success.[7]

Fifty-four significant facilitators for success were identified in Rubenstein's study of U.S. new products.[8] High on the list were the existence of a product champion, marketing factors (such as need recognition), superior data collection and analysis, planned approaches to venture management, and strong internal communications.

NewProd™ I

My original Project NewProd* in the late 1970s was an exploratory study into success versus failure, which sought to identify those characteristics that separated 102 new product successes from 93 failures in 102 industrial product firms.[9] Three important factors were uncovered that distinguished successes from failures:

1. A unique, superior product *in the eyes of the customer,* one with a real differential advantage in the marketplace.
2. A strong market orientation—building in solid market knowledge and sound market inputs, and undertaking the market research and marketing launch tasks well.
3. Technological synergy (both development and production technology) and competence in the technological tasks in the project.

Secondary factors that also had an impact on success included marketing and managerial synergy (a good fit between the needs of the project and the firm's marketing and managerial resources); positive value-in-use for the customer (the product saved the customer money over its lifetime); dynamic market situations (customer needs in a state of flux, and competitors launching many new products); large, high-need growth markets; a strong marketing communications, sales force, and launch effort; and finally weak competitors (whose customers were dissatisfied with them).

The Stanford Innovation Project

A more recent success/failure study, the Stanford Innovation Project looked at high-tech electronic firms and new products.[10]

In this comparison of success versus failures, winning products had the following factors in common: (1) the new product had a high performance-to-cost ratio (the result of an in-depth understanding of the customers and the marketplace); (2) a market launch was proficient, and backed by strong resources; (3) the product yielded a high contribution margin; (4) the R&D process was well

---

* NewProd is a registered tradename of the author. For more information see: R.G. Cooper, "Selecting Winning New Products: Using the NewProd System," *Journal of Product Innovation Management* 2 (1987): 34–44; and: R. G. Cooper, "The NewProd System: The Industry Experience," *Journal of Product Innovation Management* 9 (1992): 113–27. NewProd is available commercially in the U.S. from the Adept Group, Jacksonville, FL, for most industries, and from Temple, Barker and Sloan for the electronic and telecommunications industry; in the U.K. from Alec Petit New Product Consultancy, Rickmansworth, U.K.; and in Scandanavia from the Danish Technological Institute, Copenhagen, Denmark (marketed under the name DanProd).

planned and executed; (5) the create, make, and sell functions were well interfaced and coordinated; (6) the product was introduced into the market early—that is, ahead of competition; (7) there existed marketing and technological synergy; and, (8) top management support existed for the project, from development through to launch.

More recent studies by Stanford Project researchers on the U.S. electronics industry (86 successes and 86 failures) identified these main factors separating winners from losers:[11]

- Successes have a quality R&D effort, but based on strong interfaces with both manufacturing and the customer. Here, "interfaces with the customer" means a detailed understanding of the customer's problems, and a sound visualization of how the new product will solve the customer's problems.
- Winning products are technically superior, and feature strong product uniqueness.
- Successful products have a positive market environment: they are first in the market and enjoy a large and growing market.
- Winning products provide significant value to the customer.
- Successes build upon the firm's existing technological and organizational competencies (but strengths in the marketing and manufacturing departments did not contribute to success in this study of the electronics industry).

Booz, Allen & Hamilton

An investigation of new product practices in 700 firms by Booz, Allen & Hamilton in the 1980s identified a number of characteristics that contributed to higher new product success rates:[12]

- product fit with market needs;
- product fit with internal functional strengths;
- technological superiority of the product;
- top management support;
- use of a formal new product process;
- favorable competitive environment; and
- structure of the new product organization.

The study then went on to determine the existence of common characteristics in companies which were more successful with their new products. Here are some of the differences between successful and unsuccessful firms.

1. *Operating philosophy:* Successful companies are more committed to growth through new products developed internally. They are more likely to have had a formal new product process in place for a longer period of time. They are more likely to have a strategic plan that includes a certain portion of company growth from new products. They are also likely to prescreen new product ideas more thoroughly, considering almost 10 times fewer new product ideas per successful new product as unsuccessful companies.

2. *Organizational structure:* Successful companies are more likely to house the new product organization in R&D or engineering, and are more likely to allow the marketing and R&D functions to have greater influence on the new product process. They also keep the senior new product executive in place for a longer period of time.

3. *The experience effect:* Experience in introducing new products enables companies to improve new product performance. New product development costs conform to the experience curve: the more you do something, the more efficient you become at doing it. For the 13,000 new product introductions studied in these 700 firms over a five-year period, the experience effect yields a 71-percent cost curve: at each doubling of the number of new product introductions, the cost of each introduction declined by 29 percent. This experience advantage stems from the acquisition of a knowledge of the market and of the steps required to develop a new product.

4. *Management styles:* Successful companies appear not only to select a management style appropriate to immediate new product development needs, but also to revise and tailor that approach to changing new product opportunities. Three styles were identified:

   • an entrepreneurial approach, associated primarily with new-to-the-world products.

   • a collegial approach, associated with entering new businesses and adding new items to existing lines.

   • a managerial approach, most often associated with developing new products that are closely linked to existing businesses.

The study concludes with a list of "best practice prescriptions" for new product management:

• *Commitment:* Firms must make a long term commitment to new products. They must look inward for their future product opportunities, and be committed to internal product development as the major source of growth. They must be willing to mount well-defined new product efforts that are driven by corporate objectives and strategies. They must support these efforts with consistent commitments of the necessary funds, as well as management and technical skills.

• *Strategy:* At the core of a company specific approach to a sound new product program is a well-defined new product strategy. A new product strategy links the new product process to company objectives, and provides focus for idea/concept generation and guidelines for establishing appropriate screening criteria. The outcome of new product strategic planning is a set of strategic roles, used not to generate specific new product ideas, but to help identify markets for which new products will be developed.

• *Process:* The multistep new product process is an essential ingredient in successful new product development. And there is a new step in this process, namely strategy formulation. This revised new product process focuses the search for ideas, reduces the attrition rate of ideas, and contributes to a higher success rate. The net result of the improved process has been better expenditure allocations: companies have been able to increase the portion of total new product expenditures going to products that are ultimately successful.

The Hewlett-Packard Studies

Ten factors differentiated successful from the unsuccessful new product projects in an internal study undertaken at Hewlett-Packard using the Cooper NewProd methodology:[13]

1. *Understanding user needs:* The product's potential users and customers, and the product's contribution to the customer were totally understood by the project team.
2. *Strategic alignment:* There was alignment of the project with the strategy of the business unit, clear identification of the specific target segment, and a consistent charter in the development organization.
3. *Competitive analysis and product superiority:* The competitors' solutions for customer problems were well understood, and every effort was made to create a product plan that ensured that the new solution would be better than the competitors' at the time of market launch.
4. *Regulation compliance:* All regulatory issues in the product's arena were identified and addressed: patent infringement issues; industry standards and approval body regulations; environment, health, ergonomic, and globalization issues.
5. *Priority decision criteria list:* Priority decision criteria were defined before development began in order to make sound trade-off decisions during development. These decision criteria include the manufacturing cost target, the target time-to-market, key product features, the strategy for extending the technological platform, the reliability goals, and the design for manufacturability goals.
6. *Risk assessment:* The priority decision criteria list (above) also identified high-risk areas including piece-parts, processes, and marketing plans, so that they could be addressed early in the development phase.
7. *Product positioning:* The product was positioned correctly, based on an in-depth understanding of users' needs and purchase motivations, in order to provide higher value to the user than competitive products.
8. *Product channel and support:* Successful products had the right channel of distribution and support plan for the product.
9. *Project endorsement by upper management:* Upper management knew about the product development effort and provided support.
10. *Total organizational support:* Management provided adequate financial and human resources from all functions to complete the project as per plan.

One finding was that successful projects studied within Hewlett-Packard, with very few exceptions, had *no "holes" or deficiencies in the ten practices* listed above, whereas unsuccessful projects had numerous inadequacies in these ten areas.

Organizational Structure

Many of the studies above probed characteristics of the projects—the way the project was undertaken, and the nature of the project, product, and market. But what about organizational structure—the way the project is organized? The relative effectiveness of different *project management structures* for product development was assessed in a large empirical success/failure study by Larson and Gobeli.[14] The researchers identified five types of structure on a continuum from single-function segments to the multifunctional project team:

1. *Functional:* The project is divided into segments, which are assigned to relevant functional areas or groups. The project is coordinated by functional and upper levels of management.
2. *Functional matrix:* A project manager with limited authority is designated to coordinate the project across different functional areas. The functional managers retain responsibility and authority for their specific segments of the project.
3. *Balanced matrix:* A project manager is assigned to oversee the project and shares the responsibility and authority for completing the project with the functional managers: there is joint approval and direction.
4. *Project matrix;* A project manager is assigned to oversee the project and has primary responsibility and authority for the project. Functional managers assign personnel as needed and provide technical expertise.
5. *Project team:* A project manager is put in charge of a project team composed of a core group of personnel from several functional areas. The functional managers have no formal involvement. Project teams are also referred to as tiger teams or venture teams.

The results of the study indicate that there is no one best way to organize a new product project, but that some are better than others. The three multifunctional team approaches (structure types 3, 4, and 5 listed above) yield the best performance: project team, project matrix, and balanced matrix structures all have roughly the same high success rates. By contrast, the two functional approaches (structure types 1 and 2 above) fare much more poorly: success rates drop dramatically in the case of both functional matrix and functional organization. Projects using either of these two management structures lag behind the others in terms of schedule, cost, and technical performance.

Project teams (type 5) appear to be best suited to very complex projects, but are not as appropriate for less complex projects. By contrast, project matrix structures (type 4) work equally well for both complex and simple projects, and as well as project teams for complex projects. Functional structures (types 1 and 2) fared poorly for both complex and simple projects.

Finally, there is a decided preference among managers in the study for structures that provide *strong project leadership:* although the project manager may be able to rely on informal sources of influence to manage the project, the results of the study indicate that these need to be bolstered by formal designations of authority.

NewProd III

Is there *really a pattern* to new product success? And if so, what separates successful new product projects from unsuccessful ones? In spite of the many investigations, these and similar questions continue to plague senior managers charged with improving new product performance.

The answers were sought in our Project NewProd III, perhaps the most extensive new product success/failure study to date, where we studied more projects and more characteristics with greater depth than ever before.[15] NewProd III is a retrospective analysis of 203 actual new product projects in 125 industrial product firms. The products studied had all been launched into the market; some were successes, and others failures. By studying what the successes shared in common, and how they differed from failures, we uncovered the important success factors.

Ten Key Factors Underlying Success

There *is* a pattern to success: indeed, significant differences emerge between successful and unsuccessful projects when we look at the nature of the product and market, the level of synergy, and other strategic variables along with activities undertaken as part of the project. Here new product success was defined in a number of ways, including:

- a simple success/failure measure: whether the product's profits met or exceeded the company's financial or profitability criterion for success;
- the profitability level;
- the new product's market share after year 3;
- the degree to which the product met company profit and sales objectives.

New product success was most strongly decided by ten key factors. The impacts of these factors are described below; Figures 3.1 through 3.10 show the magnitude of the most important factors visually. In each figure, the 203 projects are divided into three categories: the top 20 percent, the middle 60 percent, and the bottom 20 percent of projects when rated on each factor. Then we looked at the success rates for each of the three categories: these are shown by the heights of the bars (the percentage of projects that met or exceeded the firms' profitability criteria). Other measures of performance are also illustrated, including market share (shown as a percent of the target market), and three other measures: rated profitability, and how well the product met both sales and profit objectives ranked at the bottom of each figure on zero-to-ten scales. A score of 10 is exceptionally positive.

Here, then, are the ten key factors (in descending order of importance):

1. A superior product that delivers unique benefits to the user.

Superior products that *deliver real and unique advantages to users* tend to be far more successful than "me too" products with few positive elements of differentiation (see Figure 3.1). When we contrasted high-advantage products (the top 20 percent) with those with the least degree of differentiation (the bottom 20 percent), we found that the superior products:

- had an exceptional success rate of 98.0 percent, versus only 18.4 percent for undifferentiated ones;
- had a market share of 53.5 percent, versus only 11.6 percent for "me too" new products;
- had a rated profitability of 8.4 out of 10 (versus only 2.6 out of 10 for undifferentiated products); and
- met company sales and profit objectives to a greater degree than did undifferentiated products.

What did these superior products with real customer benefits have in common? These winning products offered unique features not available on competitive products; they met customer needs better than competitive products; they had higher relative product quality; they solved a problem the customer had

Figure 3.1:   Impact of Product Superiority on Success

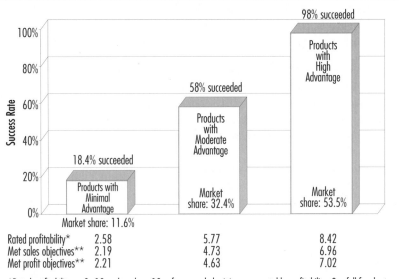

Rated profitability*	2.58	5.77	8.42
Met sales objectives**	2.19	4.73	6.96
Met profit objectives**	2.21	4.63	7.02

*Rated profitability on 0–10 scale, where 10 = far exceeded minimum acceptable profitability; 0 = fell far short

**Degree to which product met sales or profit objectives on 0–10 scale, where 10 = far exceeded objectives; 0 = fell far short

Robert G. Cooper and Elko J. Kleinschmidt, *New Products: The Key Factors in Success*. American Marketing Association, Chicago, 1990.

with a competitive product; they reduced the customer's total costs—high value in use; and they were innovative—the first of their kind on the market.

These six ingredients of a superior product provide a useful checklist of questions in assessing the odds of success of a proposed new product project. In short, the six items above logically become top-priority questions in a project screening checklist.

The central role of product superiority also provides prescriptions for the management of the new product process. The development of a new product with real advantages and customer benefits becomes paramount. Simply being "equal to the competition" or "having good product/market fit" is not enough; the goal must be superiority and advantage.

To maximize product advantage gained via unique benefits to customers:

- *Start with the customer:* Build in extensive market research and work closely with customers/users to identify customer needs, wants, and preferences, and to define what the customer sees as a "better product."
- *Apply creative translation:* Armed with this customer "wish list," use appropriate technical skills and creative problem-solving skills to translate customer needs into a technically viable solution.
- *Test and verify:* Undertake extensive customer tests—concept tests, customer tests during development, field trials with customers, and even a trial sell or test market—to ensure that the final product scores high with the customer.

2. A well-defined product prior to the development phase.

Successful products have *much sharper definition prior to development.* Projects that had these sharp definitions were 3.3 times as likely to be successful; had higher market shares (by 38 share points on average); were rated 7.6 out of 10 in terms of profitability (versus 3.1 out of 10 for poorly defined products); and did better at meeting company sales and profit objectives (see Figure 3.2).

What type of definition did these winners have? Before the project was allowed to proceed to development, winning products had a clear and agreed-upon definition of items such as the target market; customer needs, wants, and preferences; the product concept—what the product would be and do; and the product's specifications and requirements.

The role of sharp product definition prior to the commencement of a development program cannot be understated:

- Build in a definitional or protocol* step and checkpoint into your new product process.[16]
- This definitional step should occur before the door to development is opened—a "must have" before development can proceed.
- This definition must be based on solid evidence; it should force discipline into the preceding steps.

* A term which means in this context, an all party agreement to the definition of this product.

Figure 3.2:   Impact of Early Product Definition on Success

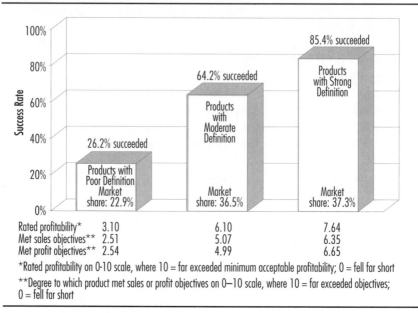

Rated profitability*   3.10   6.10   7.64
Met sales objectives** 2.51   5.07   6.35
Met profit objectives** 2.54   4.99   6.65

*Rated profitability on 0-10 scale, where 10 = far exceeded minimum acceptable profitability; 0 = fell far short
**Degree to which product met sales or profit objectives on 0–10 scale, where 10 = far exceeded objectives;
0 = fell far short

Robert G. Cooper and Elko J. Kleinschmidt, *New Products: The Key Factors in Success.* American Marketing Association, Chicago, 1990.

3. Quality of execution of technological activities.

Projects where the *technical activities* are carried out in a *quality fashion* are considerably more successful (see Figure 3.3). For example, they had 2.5 times the success rate; and a higher market share, by 21 share points. These successful products had particularly high ratings for quality of execution for actions such as: the preliminary technical assessment, product development, in-house product or prototype testing, trial or pilot production, and production start-up.

The implications are clear: quality of execution is critical. How well these technological tasks are undertaken is strongly tied to new product success. The challenge for management is to build quality of execution into the new product process by design rather than as an afterthought.

4. Technological synergy.

Successful projects feature a strong fit between the needs of the project and the firms's R&D or product development resources, its engineering skills and resources, and its production resources and skills (see Figure 3.4). Such products had 2.8 times the success rate, and were rated higher in terms of profitability and in meeting company sales and profit objectives.

The message here is attack from a position of technological strength. The ability to leverage in-house technological strengths and resources is a key success factor. These elements of technological synergy are critical screening criteria in the evaluation and prioritization of projects.

Figure 3.3: Impact of Quality of Execution of Technological Activities on Success

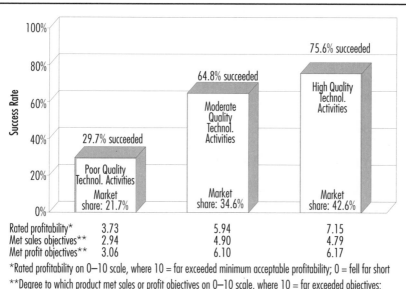

Rated profitability*	3.73	5.94	7.15
Met sales objectives**	2.94	4.90	4.79
Met profit objectives**	3.06	6.10	6.17

*Rated profitability on 0–10 scale, where 10 = far exceeded minimum acceptable profitability; 0 = fell far short

**Degree to which product met sales or profit objectives on 0–10 scale, where 10 = far exceeded objectives; 0 = fell far short

Robert G. Cooper and Elko J. Kleinschmidt, *New Products: The Key Factors in Success.* American Marketing Association, Chicago, 1990.

Figure 3.4: Impact of Technological Synergy on Success

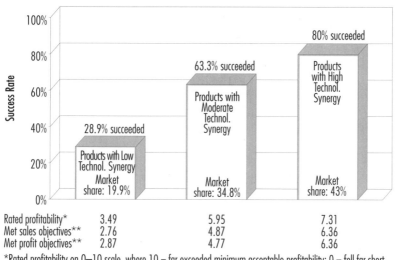

Rated profitability*	3.49	5.95	7.31
Met sales objectives**	2.76	4.87	6.36
Met profit objectives**	2.87	4.77	6.36

*Rated profitability on 0–10 scale, where 10 = far exceeded minimum acceptable profitability; 0 = fell far short

**Degree to which product met sales or profit objectives on 0–10 scale, where 10 = far exceeded objectives; 0 = fell far short

Robert G. Cooper and Elko J. Kleinschmidt, *New Products: The Key Factors in Success.* American Marketing Association, Chicago, 1990.

5. Quality of execution of predevelopment activities.

Products that feature a high quality of execution of activities that precede the development phase are more successful. Figure 3.5 shows that these products had:

- a success rate of 75.0 percent (versus only 31.3 percent for projects where the predevelopment activities were found lacking);
- a higher-rated profitability (7.2 out of 10 versus only 3.7 for projects where predevelopment activities were deficient); and
- a market share of 45.7 percent (versus 20.8 percent).

These predevelopment activities that were found to be so pivotal to new product success include: initial screening, preliminary market and technical assessment, detailed market study, and business or financial analysis.

These five key predevelopment activities must be built into the new product process as a matter of routine rather than by exception. In too many projects, we witnessed a new product idea that moved directly into development with very little in the way of homework to define the product and justify the project. These "up front" activities are also closely linked to the product definition (item 2 above): unless these predevelopment actions are carried out well, then product definition is likely to be weak, vague, or at best, based on hearsay evidence.

Figure 3.5:   Impact of Quality of Execution of Predevelopment Activities on Success

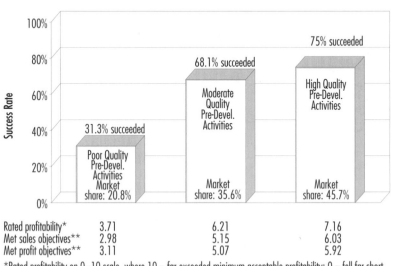

Rated profitability*	3.71	6.21	7.16
Met sales objectives**	2.98	5.15	6.03
Met profit objectives**	3.11	5.07	5.92

*Rated profitability on 0–10 scale, where 10 = far exceeded minimum acceptable profitability; 0 = fell far short

**Degree to which product met sales or profit objectives on 0–10 scale, where 10 = far exceeded objectives; 0 = fell far short

Robert G. Cooper and Elko J. Kleinschmidt, *New Products: The Key Factors in Success.* American Marketing Association, Chicago, 1990.

6. Marketing synergy.

Successful products feature a strong fit between the needs of the project and the firm's sales force and distribution system, its advertising resources and skills, its marketing research and intelligence resources, and its customer service capabilities. Where marketing synergy existed, the success rate was 2.3 times as great; the rated profitability was higher (a rating of 6.6 versus 3.7 out of 10); and market share was 14 share points higher than for products where marketing synergy was lacking (see Figure 3.6).

When selecting and prioritizing projects, remember the critical importance of marketing synergy. These four measures of marketing synergy (above) become logical criteria for screening and selecting projects.

7. Quality of execution of marketing activities.

Many companies were particularly deficient in the way they handled the marketing side of projects. Success was more often the result when the following activities were proficiently executed: preliminary market assessment; the detailed market study or marketing research; customer tests of the product prototype or sample; the trial sell or test market; and the market launch itself. When these activities were well executed, the success rate was 2.2 times as great, and market share rose 18.5 share points (see Figure 3.7).

A dedication to *building in* marketing activities is central to new product success. Too often these actions were not an integral facet of the project, and when

Figure 3.6: Impact of Marketing Synergy on Success

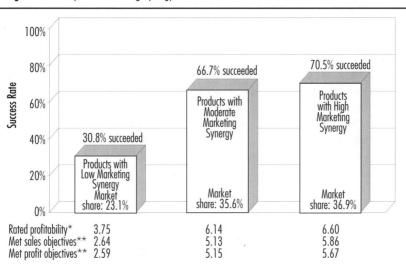

*Rated profitability on 0–10 scale, where 10 = far exceeded minimum acceptable profitability; 0 = fell far short

**Degree to which product met sales or profit objectives on 0–10 scale, where 10 = far exceeded objectives; 0 = fell far short

Robert G. Cooper and Elko J. Kleinschmidt, *New Products: The Key Factors in Success.* American Marketing Association, Chicago, 1990.

Figure 3.7:   Impact of Quality of Execution of Marketing Activities on Success

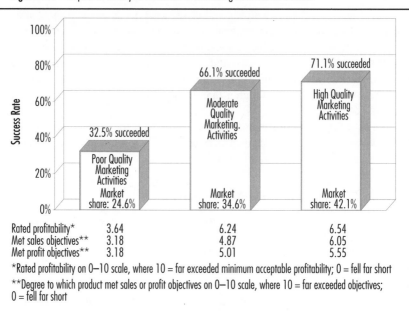

Rated profitability*	3.64	6.24	6.54
Met sales objectives**	3.18	4.87	6.05
Met profit objectives**	3.18	5.01	5.55

*Rated profitability on 0–10 scale, where 10 = far exceeded minimum acceptable profitability; 0 = fell far short

**Degree to which product met sales or profit objectives on 0–10 scale, where 10 = far exceeded objectives; 0 = fell far short

Robert G. Cooper and Elko J. Kleinschmidt, *New Products: The Key Factors in Success.* American Marketing Association, Chicago, 1990.

done, were often included as an afterthought or were poorly resourced. The message is that a strong market orientation coupled with quality of execution of these vital actions is essential.

8. Market attractiveness.

Products targeted at more attractive markets were more successful. They had 1.7 times as high a success rate, and also were rated much higher in terms of profitability and meeting sales and profits objectives. But market shares were only marginally higher in such attractive markets (see Figure 3.8).

In this study, attractive markets were defined as large ones with a high growth rate, and markets in which the customer had a high need for the product and considered the purchase to be an important one.

9. and 10. The competitive situation and top management support.

Factors that originally were thought to affect success, but were found to have a *lower impact than expected*, included top management support and the competitive situation (see Figures 3.9 and 3.10).

Products aimed at highly competitive markets were only marginally less successful than those targeted at less competitive markets. By "competitive markets," we mean markets with intense competition, considerable price competition, high-quality and strong competitive products, and competitorss whose sales force, channel system, and service was rated as strong. The message is

Figure 3.8: Impact of Market Attractiveness on Success

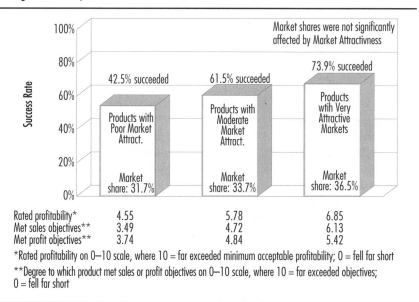

Rated profitability*	4.55	5.78	6.85
Met sales objectives**	3.49	4.72	6.13
Met profit objectives**	3.74	4.84	5.42

*Rated profitability on 0–10 scale, where 10 = far exceeded minimum acceptable profitability; 0 = fell far short

**Degree to which product met sales or profit objectives on 0–10 scale, where 10 = far exceeded objectives; 0 = fell far short

Robert G. Cooper and Elko J. Kleinschmidt, *New Products: The Key Factors in Success.* American Marketing Association, Chicago, 1990.

that *products succeeded in spite of the competitive situation*—because they were superior and well defined, were executed well, and had certain synergies with the firm.

Figure 3.9: Impact of Competitive Situation on Success

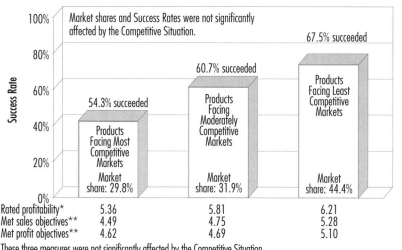

Rated profitability*	5.36	5.81	6.21
Met sales objectives**	4.49	4.75	5.28
Met profit objectives**	4.62	4.69	5.10

These three measures were not significantly affected by the Competitive Situation.

*Rated profitability on 0–10 scale, where 10 = far exceeded minimum acceptable profitability; 0 = fell far short

**Degree to which product met sales or profit objectives on 0–10 scale, where 10 = far exceeded objectives; 0 = fell far short

Robert G. Cooper and Elko J. Kleinschmidt, *New Products: The Key Factors in Success.* American Marketing Association, Chicago, 1990.

Top managers supported failures with almost the same frequency as successes. That is, top management support seemed to make little difference to the success rate and other measures of performance (see Figure 3.10). Those projects where top management was committed, was involved directly in the management of the project, and provided considerable guidance and direction for the project were only marginally more successful.

Process versus Environment

What emerges from a review of the key success factors is provocative. Of the hundreds of characteristics measured in NewProd III, only the ten factors outlined above had any consistent impact on success. But their impact was anything but equal: note that all ten factors above had been thought by one expert or another to be central to new product success. But NewProd III reveals that these ten factors are certainly not all equal, and that there are distinct patterns to the results.

At the beginning of this chapter, we looked at three theories:

1. New product success is luck.
2. New product success depends on strategic or tailwind factors—market attractiveness, synergies, competitive situation, etc.

Figure 3.10: Impact of Top Management Support on Success

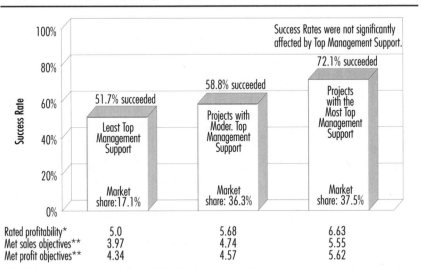

Rated profitability*	5.0	5.68	6.63
Met sales objectives**	3.97	4.74	5.55
Met profit objectives**	4.34	4.57	5.62

These three measures were not significantly affected by the Competitive Situation.

*Rated profitability on 0–10 scale, where 10 = far exceeded minimum acceptable profitability; 0 = fell far short

**Degree to which product met sales or profit objectives on 0–10 scale, where 10 = far exceeded objectives; 0 = fell far short

Robert G. Cooper and Elko J. Kleinschmidt, *New Products: The Key Factors in Success.* American Marketing Association, Chicago, 1990.

Table 3.1:   Breakdown of Success Factors: Process Vs. Environment

Importance to success (rank ordered)	Factors that portay the innovation process	Factors that describe the project setting (tailwind)
1	1. Product superiority	1. Product superiority
2	2. Early and sharp product definition	
3	3. Quality of technological activities	
4		4. Technological synergy
5	5. Quality of predevelopment activities	
6		6. Marketing synergy
7	7. Quality of marketing activities	
8		8. Marketing attractiveness
9		9. Top management support
10		10. Competitive situation

Robert G. Cooper and Elko J. Kleinschmidt, *New Products: The Key Factors in Success.* American Marketing Association, Chicago, 1990.

3. New product success is more tactical in nature—it depends on process: on the team, on their actions, and how well they execute.

Luck can be ruled out as a dominant success factor. While luck no doubt played a role in some projects, the ten factors listed above *explain almost all the performance differences* between projects. Tailwind factors and actions together decide new product success, not luck.

Which of these two is most important? Consider the breakdown in Table 3.1, where the ten success factors are split into two groups—actions and tailwind—in rank order of importance.

Overall, factors that describe the way the project was undertaken—process, tactics, and actions—are found nearer the top of the list. By contrast, strategic factors that tend to portray the setting—tailwind descriptors, such as synergies, market attractiveness, and competitive situation—are somewhat less important.

Note that Product Superiority is the number one success factor, and is linked to both process and tailwind: product superiority is the result of both a well-executed new product process, *and* tailwind factors such as synergies and competitive situation.

Quality of Execution

Our NewProd III study also looked at the quality of execution of the 13 key activities detailed in Chapter 2. Here we contrasted successes with failures, in order to uncover which activities are pivotal—where are the greatest quality differences between winners and losers? Figure 3.11 shows the results. The conclusions are provocative, and raise many concerns about the way we conduct new product projects.

The greatest differences lie in the *first few steps of the new product process*—the up-front or predevelopment steps. Simply stated, the first few plays of the game seem to decide the outcome!

Figure 3.11:   Quality of Execution: Success versus Failure

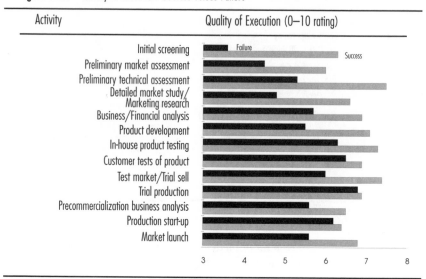

Reprinted with permission of the publisher from "An Investigation into the New Product Process: Steps, Deficiencies, and Impact," By Robert G. Cooper and Elko J. Kleinschmidt, Thomas P. Hustad, Editor. *The Journal of Product Innovation Management* 3: 71–85. Copyright 1988 by Elsevier Science Publishing Co., Inc.

The dilemma is this: These up-front actions are critical, and make all the difference between winning and losing. Yet we continue to "back end load" projects, throwing resources at projects at the middle and latter stages. Look how little time and energy we devote to these vital predevelopment steps—only seven percent of the dollars and 16 percent of the effort!

We saw in Chapter 2 that quality of execution was lacking in the new product process. But does it really make a difference? Does high quality of execution truly lead to success? NewProd III's results are convincing: *successful products feature better quality of execution across the board.* Regardless of the activity, the pattern is consistent (see Figure 3.12).

For some activities, true, the differences aren't great: for example, trial production was done almost as well for failures as for successes—it wasn't a big discriminator. For the majority of actions, however, the differences between winners and losers are striking. For example, successful project teams executed the following actions far better than their failure counterparts: initial screening, preliminary technical assessment, the detailed market study, product development, preliminary market assessment, business and financial analysis, market launch, and test market (or trial sell).

One key to success, then, is ensuring that *every step of the new product process is executed in a quality fashion:* quality consistency is key!

The allocation of resources within projects helps to explain why some steps and activities closely tied to success and failure were so poorly handled. Figure 3.12 provides an analysis of the number of person-days spent on a typical project, broken down across the various activities, for all 203 projects. (A similar breakdown for dollars spent was also determined but is not shown here.)[17] This figure is similar to Figure 2.8, except this time, expenditures are

Figure 3.12:   Person-Days for Successes versus Failures for Each Activity in the New Product Process

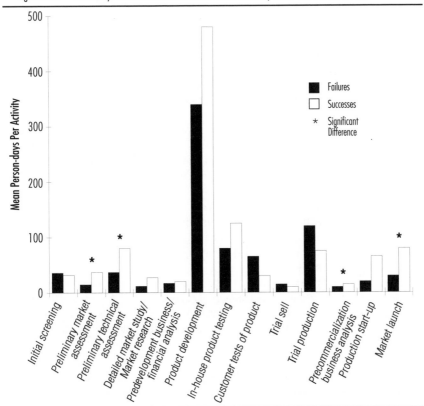

broken down for *successes versus failures:* again the black bars show the resources spent on failures; the white bars denote successes.

What stands out in an analysis of these spending patterns is how little is spent on product failures on some of the up-front or predevelopment activities. For example, for the typical failure, the detailed market study represented only 1 percent of the total project effort, yet deficiencies here remain the number one cause of new product failure. Successes fared somewhat better with more than 2 percent devoted to this pivotal market-oriented activity, but still the effort was small. Similar patterns emerge for other predevelopment activities.

Another conclusion is that successes generally had more time and money spent on them. This is particularly true in the early stages of the process: overall, successful products had about 75 percent more person-days devoted to the predevelopment activities than did failures.

The only steps where failures received more effort were in the activities immediately following development: customer tests, trial sell, and trial production. By this point in the process, troubles had already appeared in the project. People resources were allocated in a desperate attempt to "fix" the project, but the effort was in vain: the product failed. Had some of this energy been applied much earlier in the project, the evidence suggests that the results would have been more positive.

Consistency in Execution

The 13 activities studied represent a fairly ideal or "text book" view of how a new product project *should be undertaken.* Indeed, in many of the companies studied, senior management believed that this list of activities was "current practice" in the company.

The truth is that only a small minority of projects actually followed this text book ideal. We saw in Chapter 2 that in only 1.9 percent of projects were all 13 activities undertaken. That is, 98 percent of projects omitted one or more of these 13 steps. And half the projects had less than 9 activities done; that is, 4 or more potentially vital activities were left out in half the projects.

But does this matter? The answer is "Yes." The relationship between success rate and number of activities completed is strong: 75 percent of the variability in new product performance can be accounted for by how complete the new product process is (see Figure 3.13). Leaving out steps or activities drops the success rate dramatically!

One key to new product success, then, is consistency in action: simply *making sure that the key activities do indeed get done.* Sadly, current practice is far from ideal—far too many key actions simply omitted in too many projects. Correcting these errors of omission alone would go a long way to improving new product success rates.

Figure 3.13:   Impact of Completeness of the New Product Process on Success Rate

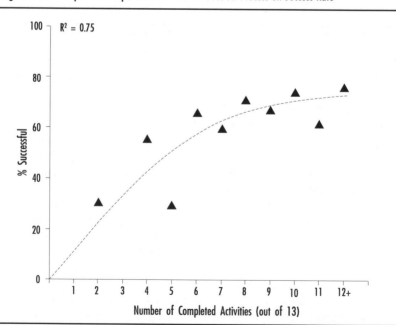

Robert G. Cooper and Elko J. Kleinschmidt, *New Products: The Key Factors in Success.* American Marketing Association, Chicago, 1990.

The Role of an International Orientation

The globalization of markets—1992 in Europe, and the North American Free Trade Agreement—has an obvious impact on product innovation. Concepts such as "world product mandates" and "global products" were often discussed during our interviews. A number of questions were therefore posed to determine the impact of an international orientation on new product success.[18]

Two dimensions of an international orientation were investigated—markets and products:

1. *Target market:* Was the principal target market for the new product a domestic one or international? And if international, was this for "nearest neighbor" countries (e.g., within North America for U.S. or Canadian companies) or for the world?
2. *Product design:* Was the product principally a domestic product, which was later modified to be sold abroad? Or was the product developed with international requirements in mind from the outset?

These two strategy dimensions together yield six possible orientations or scenarios, as shown in Figure 3.14.

New product success rates are profoundly affected by the particular orientation elected. For example, those project leaders who opted for a product with

Figure 3.14:   Impact of an International Orientation on New Product Success

	Product Type	
	International Design	Domsetic Design
Domestic	International product aimed at domestic markets Success rate: 61.5% (23.7% of cases)	Domestic product aimed at domestic markets Success rate: 43.1% (31.1% of cases)
Nearest Neighbor	International product aimed at nearest neighbor market Success rate: 78.1% (18.3% of cases)	Domestic product aimed at nearest neighbor market Success rate: 45.5% (6.7% of cases)
World	International product aimed at world market Success rate: 84.9%* (17.2% of cases)	Domestic product aimed at world market (3.0% of cases but too few to assess)

(Target Market is labeled along the left vertical axis of the table.)

* Success rates were significantly different for these various product/market orientations.

Robert G. Cooper and Elko J. Kleinschmidt, *New Products: The Key Factors in Success.* American Marketing Association, Chicago, 1990.

international design aimed at world markets achieved an enviable 85-percent success rate (see Figure 3.14). Unfortunately, only 17 percent of projects fit this scenario.

The most popular orientation, not surprisingly, was a domestic product strategy aimed at a domestic market. About one-third of all cases were classified in this scenario. Here, the success rate fell to a low of 43 percent.

Developing international products and electing world export markets also yields superior new product results when gauged on other measures of new product performance: for example, market share, profitability, and meeting company sales and profits objectives.

The message is this. On all performance measures, products that are designed to meet international requirements (versus only domestic) and that are targeted at world and nearest-neighbor export markets are the top performers, and by a considerable margin. As expected, such products do better in foreign markets; *they also do better at home!* And most important, they do better overall—profitability, and meeting sales and profits targets.

In marked contrast, products that are designed and developed to meet only domestic requirements and that are marketed at home and often to a nearby neighbor, fare much more poorly: a high failure rate, low profitability, low market shares, and low sales growth.

These results make a strong case for adopting an international focus in one's product design and development efforts. The results also point to defining the world, or at minimum, nearby export markets, as one's target market in product innovation.

NewProd in the Chemical Industry

The chemical industry in four countries provided the setting for our most recent success/failure study.[19] This NewProd investigation uncovered many of the same success factors as did previous studies. But there were some new insights gained as well:

- *Source of the idea:* Supplier-derived new product ideas, although representing only a handful of projects, had the highest success rate (86 percent). Next were customer derived ideas (77 percent success rate). The worst source of ideas was competitors—products developed in response to a competitive introduction—only 59 percent successful. (Note: the average success rate was 66 percent.)
- *Order of entry:* The strategies of "first in" versus "be a follower" are just about equal. Products that were first into the market had a marginally higher success rate: 71 percent. Success rates dropped off with later orders of entry: down to 57 percent for third into the market or later.
- *Product life cycle:* The stage of the product life cycle (PLC) of the new product's market has some impact on performance. Products aimed at markets or product categories in the introductory PLC stage yielded high failure rates: 58 percent. By contrast, new products in early growth phase categories fare well (81 percent successful), with a gradual falling off of success rates with successive stages (down to 58 percent successful for new products aimed at mature markets or categories).

- *Differential advantage:* As in virtually every new product study, competitive or differential advantage proved critical to success. Elements of product advantage were decisive: relative product quality, good value for money, superior to competing products in meeting customers' needs, and superior price/performance characteristics. By contrast, nonproduct elements of differential advantage—for example, brand name, company image, aggressive sales force or advertising effort—had relatively little impact on new product financial performance, except customer service.
- *Benefits delivered:* The exact nature of the benefit delivered did not decide success or failure. The two exceptions were:
  — lower price as a benefit strategy was not effective: the success rate dropped to 29 percent!
  — improved customer service level pays off! This was the principal benefit in a small minority of cases, but the success rate was an impressive 88 percent.
- *Organization:* Projects undertaken by multifunctional teams were far more successful than no teams or single-department teams. Success rates were also higher for projects where the team was *responsible and accountable* for the project from beginning to end (no hand-offs to another group partway through the project). And where the team leader was strong, empowered, and dedicated to that project, projects had a higher success rate.

Suggestion: Why not do what Hewlett-Packard tried? Undertake a NewProd study in your company. Take a sample of new product projects in your firm— known successes and failures. Then characterize each, using the descriptors, factors, and variables outlined in this chapter. Appendix A provides a skeleton questionnaire. Take a close look at what was done in each project (and how it was done), and at the way the project was organized—team and leader. Examine other aspects of each project—the marketplace, competitive situation, synergies, and product advantage. Then try to determine what your successes shared in common that distinguished them from the failures. Finally, make up a list of prescriptions—lessons that can be learned from your own winners and losers.

What Makes a Winner?

What emerges from a review of the many studies into new product success and failure is that *clear patterns exist.* New product success is not so much a matter of luck. Rather, it is fairly predictable, and in many cases, quite controllable.

Overall, factors that describe the way the project is organized and undertaken—*actions, process, and players*—dominate the list of reasons for success. By contrast, factors that portray the setting—*tailwind factors* that describe the nature of the marketplace, the competitive situation, the existence of certain resources and synergies in the firm—while having a bearing on success, are somewhat less important.

In the next chapter, we take these many findings and conclusions and fashion them into a concise set of 15 key lessons for successful product innovation.

Lessons for Success

I am the master of my fate;
I am the captain of my soul.
  W. E. Henley, *Invictus.*

Fifteen Key Lessons for Success

The challenge is to design a game plan for successful product innovation—a process by which new product projects can move from the idea stage through to a successful launch. Before charging into this game plan, reflect for a moment on what we have learned from the many investigations into new product performance. A number of underlying themes and recurring messages emerge as one examines the experiences of companies. Consider now the more evident lessons; reflect on how you can benefit from each lesson; and how you can translate each into an operational facet of your new product game plan (See Table 4.1 for summary of the key lessons).

1. The number one success factor is a unique superior product: a differentiated product that delivers unique benefits and superior value to the customer.

Product superiority—delivering unique benefits and product value to users—separates winners from losers more often than any other single factor. That product advantage, superiority, or differentiation is the key determinant of success is a recurring theme in many new product studies.

This result should come as no surprise to product innovators. Apparently it wasn't obvious to everyone, however: a number of studies point out that "tired products" and "me too" offerings are the rule rather than the exception in many firms' new product efforts. The NewProd investigations revealed that much time and energy is devoted to projects that yield "copycat," undifferentiated products; and 82 percent of such efforts fail!

Table 4.1:   Fifteen Key Lessons for New Product Success

1.   The number one success factor is a unique superior product: a differentiated product that delivers unique benefits and superior value to the customer.

2.   A strong market orientation—a market-driven and customer-focused new product process—is critical to success.

3.   Look to the world product: An international orientation in product design, development, and target marketing provides the edge in product innovation.

4.   More predevelopment work—the homework—must be done before product development gets under way.

5.   Sharp and early product definition is one of the key differences between winning and losing at new products.

6.   A well-conceived, properly executed launch is central to new product success. And a solid marketing plan is at the heart of the launch.

7.   The right organizational structure, design, and climate are key factors in success.

8.   Top management support doesn't guarantee success, but it sure helps. But many senior managers get it wrong.

9.   Synergy is vital to success—"step-out" projects tend to fail.

10.   Products aimed at attractive markets do better; market attractiveness is a key project-selection criterion.

11.   New product success is predictable; and the profile of a winner can be used to make sharper project-selection decisions to yield better focus.

12.   New product success is controllable: More emphasis is needed on completeness, consistency, and quality of execution.

13.   The resources must be in place.

14.   Speed is everything! But not at the expense of quality of execution.

15.   Companies that follow a multistage, disciplined new product game plan fare much better.

Consider how high your new product scores on each of the following ingredients of a unique, superior product:

- has unique features for the customer;
- meets customer needs better than competitors' products;
- has high relative product quality;
- solves customers' problems with competitive products;
- reduces customers' costs; and,
- is innovative or novel.

If it does, then your new product project has a good chance of success, and it should be prioritized accordingly. These ingredients are useful screening criteria for rating and ranking new product projects—a checklist. But if your project is like many and scores low on these product superiority items, then take care! Its odds of winning are poor.

The challenge the product developer faces is to ensure that the elements of product superiority are built into each and every new product. In short, the list of these six ingredients of product advantage above become personal objectives of the project leader and team, and must be molded into the game plan.

But how does one invent or build in product superiority? Note that superiority is derived from design, features, attributes, specifications, and even positioning.

The important point here is that "superiority" is defined from the customer's standpoint, not in the eyes of the R&D or design departments. More than unique features are required to make a product superior, however. Remember: features are those things that cost you, the supplier, money. By contrast, benefits are what customers pay money for! Often the two—features and benefits—are not the same. So, in defining "unique benefits," think of the product as a "bundle of benefits" for the user; and a benefit as something the customer views as having value to him or her.

The definition of "what is unique and superior" and "what is a benefit" is from the customer's perspective; it must be based on an in-depth understanding of customer needs, wants, problems, likes, and dislikes.

1. *Determine customer needs at the outset.* Start with a user needs-and-wants study—market research—to probe customer needs, wants, preferences, likes, and dislikes. Determine the customer's "hot buttons"—the order winning criteria, and what the customer is *really looking for* in a much-improved or superior product. Let the customer help design the product for you.

2. *Do a competitive product analysis.* There is no such thing as a perfect competitive product. If we can understand the competitor's product weaknesses, then we're halfway to beating him or her. Remember: the goal is product superiority, and that implies superiority over the current competitive offering. Take the competitor's product apart in your lab; and when you do the market research, be sure to ask your customers for their opinions about the strengths and weaknesses of the competitor's product.

3. *Test and verify all your assumptions about your winning product design.* Once the product concept and specs are defined (based on user inputs), test the concept with users—make sure they indicate a favorable response. Continue to involve the customer throughout the development process, even as the product takes shape: let the customer react to working models, rapid prototypes, and final prototypes as the development progresses. Build in field trials to test product acceptance, and even consider a test market or trial sell.

This disciplined approach to discovering product superiority is decidedly customer focused, which leads to Lesson #2, the need for a strong market orientation.

2. A strong market orientation—a market-driven and customer-focused new product process—is critical to success.

A thorough understanding of customers' needs and wants, the competitive situation, and the nature of the market is an essential component of new product success. This finding is supported in virtually every study of product success factors. Recurring themes include:
- need recognition;
- understanding user needs;

- market need satisfaction;
- constant customer contact;
- strong market knowledge and market research;
- quality of execution of marketing activities; and,
- more spending on the up-front marketing activities.

Conversely, a failure to adopt a strong market orientation in product innovation, an unwillingness to undertake the needed market assessments, and leaving the customer out of product development spells disaster. Poor market research; inadequate market analysis; weak market studies, test markets, and market launch; and inadequate resources devoted to marketing activities were common weaknesses found in virtually every study of why new products fail.

Sadly, a strong market orientation is missing in the majority of firms' new product projects. Marketing activities tend to be the weakest-rated activities of the entire new product process. And relatively few resources and little money are spent on the marketing actions—particularly those that occur in the early stages of the project.

To be successful, a market orientation must prevail throughout the entire new product project. It begins with *idea generation:* Companies must devote more resources to market-oriented–idea generation activities, such as focus groups with customers; market research to determine customer need areas; using the sales force to actively solicit ideas from customers; and developing relationships with lead users.

A market orientation also has a vital role in the *actual design of the product*—when the product's specs and requirements are being defined. Too often, market research, when done at all, is misused in the new product process. It tends to be done as an afterthought: after the product design has been decided and to verify that the proposed product indeed has market acceptance. If the results of the market study are negative, most often they are conveniently ignored and the project is pushed ahead regardless.

The mistake is clear: market research must be used as an *input to the design decisions*, and not solely as an after-the-fact check. Investigations to determine users' needs, wants, and preferences; and to identify competitive product strategies, strengths, and weaknesses provide insights which are invaluable guides to the design team *before* they charge into the design of the new product.

Even in the case of *technology-push* new products (where the product emanates from the lab or design department, perhaps the result of a technological breakthrough), there still should be considerable marketing input as the technology is shaped into a final product design. That is, following the technical discovery, but before full-fledged development gets under way, there is ample opportunity to research and interact with the customer to determine needs and wants, to shape the final product the way the customer wants it, and to gauge likely product acceptance.

Customer inputs shouldn't cease at the completion of the up-front market studies. Seeking customer inputs and testing concepts or designs with the customer is very much an interactive or "back and forth" process. During the actual development phase of the project, and after the market research is done, *constant and continuing customer contact* remains essential. Keep bringing the customer into the process to view facets of the product as the prototype or final product takes shape. Develop rapid prototypes, working models, or facsimiles of the product as early as possible to show to the customer in order to seek feedback regarding market acceptance and needed design changes. Don't wait until the very end of the development phase—the field trials—to unveil the product to the customer. There could be some very unpleasant surprises!

3. Look to the world product: An international orientation in product design, development, and target marketing provides the edge in product innovation.

Here the evidence is clear. International products targeted at world and nearest-neighbor export markets are the top performers, according to the NewProd studies described in Chapter 3. By contrast, products designed with only the domestic market in mind, and sold to domestic and nearest neighbor export markets fare more poorly. The magnitude of the differences between these international and exported new products versus domestic products is striking: differences of two- or three-to-one on the various performance gauges. And the fact that international new products aimed at foreign markets also do better in the home market—almost double the domestic market share versus domestic products—is a provocative finding.

The comfortable strategy of "design the product for domestic requirements, capture the home market, and then export a modified version of the product sometime in the future" is myopic. It leads to inferior results today; and with increasing globalization of markets, it will certainly lead to even poorer results in the years ahead. The threat is that our domestic market has become someone else's international market: to define the new product market as "domestic" and perhaps a few other "convenient countries" severely limits one's market opportunities. For maximum success in product innovation, the objective must be to design for the world and market to the world.

This international dimension is an often overlooked facet of new product game plans, or one which if included, is handled late in the process, or as a side issue. For example, 3M is often cited as a model for successful innovation. But even 3M's new product process deals with the international facet somewhat late in the process: for example, in one 3M division, the game plan calls for the International Group to commence product testing outside the US, but at a much later stage in the process than US field trials—almost as an afterthought.[1]

One implication of this need to adopt a global orientation is the design and implementation of a *global new product process*. This global requirement increases the complexity of product development considerably; it means that, more than ever, firms must adopt a systematic and consistent new product process or game plan. This global new product process is one that both domestic and international units utilize, and that integrates actions across country borders. This means forming international project teams: team members may re-side in different countries and different tasks may even be undertaken in different countries; global criteria for Go/Kill decisions replace the traditional domestic ones; and international customer contact is the rule: for example, market studies and field trials in a variety of countries are built into the game plan.

4. More predevelopment work—the homework—must be done before product development gets under way.

We all learned in fifth grade how distasteful homework was. Many of us haven't forgotten: we hate homework! But then, as now, homework is critical to winning. The NewProd and other studies reveal that the steps that precede the actual design and development of the product—screening, market studies, technical feasibility assessment, and building the business case—are key factors separating winners from losers. Errors and omissions in these vital activities can and often do spell disaster later in the project.

Studies of new product failures show that weaknesses in the up-front activities seriously compromise the projects. Inadequate market analysis and a lack of market research, moving directly from an idea into a full-fledged development effort, and a failure to spend time and money on the up-front steps are familiar themes in product failures. Most firms confess to serious weaknesses in the "up front" or predevelopment steps of their new product process. The evidence from the data on resources spent in the NewProd studies shows pitifully small amounts of time and money devoted to these critical steps: 7 percent of the dollars and 16 percent of the effort.

More homework prior to the initiation of product design and development has been consistently found to be a key factor in success. The quality of execution of the predevelopment steps—initial screening, preliminary market and technical studies, market research, and business analysis—is closely tied to the product's financial performance. And successful projects have over 1.75 times as many person-days spent on predevelopment steps as do failures. The emphasis that the Japanese devote to the planning stage of the new product process is described by Havelock and Elder:

> Japanese developers make a clear distinction between the "planning" and the "implementation" phases of a new technology initiative. . . . The objective of planning is complete understanding of the problem and the related technology before a "go" decision is made. It is reported to be an unrushed process which might look agonizingly drawn out to Western eyes.[2]

Finally a Booz, Allen & Hamilton study finds that Japanese firms and successful U.S. firms devote considerably more time to the homework stages before entering development than does the average U.S. firm.[3]

The predevelopment activities are important because they qualify and define the project. They answer key success questions such as:[4]

- Is the project an economically attractive one? Will the product sell at sufficient volumes and margins to justify investment in development and commercialization?

- Who exactly is the target customer? And how should the product be positioned?
- What exactly should the product be to make it a winner? What features, attributes, and performance characteristics should be built into it to yield a unique superior product?
- Can the product be developed and at the right cost? What is the likely technical solution?

"More homework means longer development times" is a frequently voiced complaint. This is a valid concern, but experience has shown that homework pays for itself in reduced development times and improved success rates:

- First, all the evidence points to a much higher likelihood of product failure if the homework is omitted. So the choice is between a slightly longer project or much increased odds of failure.
- Second, better project definition—the result of sound homework—actually *speeds up the development process.*[5] Many projects are poorly defined when they enter the development phase: vague targets and moving goalposts. This is usually the result of weak predevelopment activities: the target user is not well understood, user needs and wants are vaguely defined, and desired product features and performance requirements are clouded. With a poorly defined product and project, R&D or design people waste considerable time seeking definition, often recycling back several times as the project parameters change.
- Third, rarely does a product concept remain the same from beginning to end of the project. The original idea that triggered the project is seldom the same as the product that eventually goes to market. Given this inevitable product design evolution, the time to make the majority of these design improvements or changes is *not* as the product is moving out of development and into production. More homework up-front anticipates these changes and encourages them to occur earlier in the process rather than later, when they are more costly. The result is considerable savings in time and money at the back end of the project, and overall a more efficient new product process.

The message is that more time and resources must be devoted to the activities that precede the design and development of the product. These initial screening, analyses, and definitional stages are critical to success. Managers must resist the temptation to skip over the up-front stages of a project and move an ill-defined and poorly investigated project into the development phase.[6]

5. Sharp and early product definition is one of the key differences between winning and losing at new products.

How well the project is defined prior to entering the development phase is increasingly cited as a key success factor.[7] Crawford implores managers to include a "protocol step" just prior to the development phase, where the requirements of the product are clearly spelled out and agreed to by all parties involved in the project.[8] Getting the product definition right was also uncovered as the key to success in an internal study undertaken by Hewlett-Packard.[9] And the NewProd studies find that sharpness of product definition prior to development is the number-two factor in new product success, right after product advantage: Sharply defined products had over three times the success rates of less-defined products!

Some companies undertake excellent product and project definition before the door is opened to a full development program. This definition includes:

- specification of the target market: exactly who the intended users are.
- description of the product concept and the benefits to be delivered.
- delineation of the positioning strategy.
- and a list of the product's features, attributes, requirements, and specs (prioritized: "must have" and "would like to have").

This definition is developed with inputs and agreement from the functional areas involved: marketing, R&D, engineering, manufacturing, etc.; and a signed agreement between team members and senior management from these functions is obtained: this is the essential "buy in."

Projects that have sharp project definition prior to development are considerably more successful. Here's why:

- Building a definition step into the new product process forces more attention to the up-front or predevelopment activities. If the homework hasn't been done, then arriving at a sharp definition that all parties will buy into is next to impossible.
- The definition serves as a communication tool and guide. All-party agreement or "buy in" means that each functional area involved in the project has a clear and consistent definition of what the product and project are—and is committed to it.
- This definition also provides a clear set of objectives for the development phase of the project, and the development team members. With clear product objectives, development typically proceeds more efficiently and quickly: no moving goalposts and no fuzzy targets!

6. A well-conceived, properly executed launch is central to new product success. And a solid marketing plan is at the heart of the launch.

Whoever said "Build a better mousetrap and the world will beat a path to your door" was a poet, not a businessman. This old adage may never have been true, and it certainly hasn't been true for at least several decades. Not only must the product be superior, but its benefits must be communicated and marketed aggressively.

The best products in the world won't sell themselves! A strong marketing effort, a well-targeted selling approach, and effective after-sales service are central to the successful launch of the new product. But a well-integrated and properly targeted launch does not occur by accident; it is the result of a *fine-tuned marketing plan*, properly backed and resourced, and proficiently executed.

Marketing planning—moving from marketing objectives to strategy and marketing programs—is a complex process. Entire books have been devoted to the subject. But this complex marketing planning process must be woven into the ideal new product game plan. For example, the selection of a target market and the development of a positioning strategy, one of the core steps in developing a marketing plan, logically is part of the definitional or "protocol" step just before development begins (item 5 above). And answers to many key questions—how do customers buy? via what channels of distribution? what are their sources of information? what servicing do they require?—are central to developing the nuts-and-bolts of marketing programs. Answers to these questions must come from market research investigations that are built into the new product process or game plan.

I make three important points regarding new product launch and the marketing plan:

- The development of a marketing plan is an *integral part of the new product process*: it is as central to the new product process as is the development of the physical product. Thus the marketing planning process must be overlaid atop the new product game plan.
- The development of a marketing plan *must begin early* in the new product process. It should not be left as an afterthought to be undertaken as the product nears commercialization; or as one manager indicated, "when the product's rolling down the production line, that's when our sales and marketing people become involved." Critical facets of the marketing plan must already be in place before the product's design and development phase even begins. Some of these facets will be concrete, such as target market definition, positioning strategy, and product design requirements; others will be more tentative, such as the pricing strategy, or promotional approach.
- A marketing plan is only as good as the *market intelligence* upon which it is based. Market studies designed to yield information crucial to marketing planning must be built into the new product game plan.

7. The right organizational structure, design, and climate are key factors in success.

Design your organization for product innovation. Product innovation is not a one-department show! It is very much a multidisciplinary, multifunctional effort. Organizational design—how you organize for new products—is critical. Except for the simplest of products and projects—line extensions and product up-dates—product innovation must cut across traditional functional boundaries and barriers.

The evidence is compelling: Investigations into new product success consistently cite interfaces between R&D and marketing, coordination among key internal groups, multidisciplinary inputs to the new product project, and the role of teams and the team leader. Successful new product projects feature a balanced process consisting of critical activities that fall into many different functional areas within the firm: marketing and marketing research, engineering, R&D, production, purchasing, and finance, to name a few. Maidique and Zirger's study of new product launches in high-technology firms reveals that a critical distinguishing factor between success and failure is the "simultaneous involvement of the create, make, and market functions."[10] And our NewProd studies in the chemical industry show that projects undertaken by empowered multifunctional teams were more successful. Similarly, analyses of Japanese successes emphasize their attention to manufacturability from the start of development efforts, the location in one place of engineers, designers, and manufacturers, and the conception of management unconstrained by traditional American functionalism.[11]

How does one design a *process that integrates* these many activities and multifunctional inputs? And how does one ensure quality of execution of these varied tasks, which are spread throughout the organization? One answer is to develop a systematic approach to product innovation—a game plan—that cuts across functional boundaries and forces the active participation of people from different functions. Make every step or stage a multifunctional one. That is, the game plan builds in different tasks and provides checks and balances that require the input and involvement of these various functions.

For example: a project cannot proceed into a full-scale development effort until a detailed market assessment has been completed, and until a manufacturing appraisal is complete. Without the active participation of both manufacturing and marketing people, the project does not get released to development—it goes nowhere!

A second and equally important answer lies in *organizational design*. What type of organization structure will bring many players from different walks of life in the company together in an integrated effort? In short, how do we take a diverse group of players and turn them into a team?

It's clear that the traditional functional organizational structure does not suit many of the needs of product innovation. Indeed, functional and functional matrix approaches led to the lowest new product performance, according to one study we saw in Chapter 3. Companies must move to team approaches that cut across functional lines. The three approaches that appeared to work best were:[12]

- *Balanced matrix:* A project manager is assigned to oversee the project and shares the responsibility and authority for completing the project with the functional managers: there is joint approval and direction.
- *Project matrix:* A project manager is assigned to oversee the project and has primary responsibility and authority for the project. Functional managers assign personnel as needed and provide technical expertise.
- *Project team:* A project manager is put in charge of a project team composed of a core group of personnel from several functional areas. The functional managers have no formal involvement nor authority.

Peters, in *Thriving on Chaos*, argues strongly in favor of project teams: "the single most important reason for delays in development activities is the absence of multifunction (and outsider) representation on development projects from the start."[13] Peters continues: "The answer is to co-mingle members of all key functions, co-opt each function's traditional feudal authority, and use teams." Project teams appear to be best suited for large, complex projects, whereas a project matrix approach works best for both complex and simpler projects.

Regardless of which of the three structures above you elect, *strong project leadership*—a dedicated and empowered project leader—appears essential for timely, successful projects. The leader must have *formal authority* (this means co-opting authority from functional heads); and the leader and team must be empowered to make project decisions, and not be second-guessed, overruled, or "micro-managed"* by the functional heads or senior management.

To work well, team members should be located close to each other. "Physical proximity is one of the keys to good teamwork," is the conclusion of studies done in a number of firms. 3M reports that physical distances beyond 100 yards thwarts team interaction severely. Co-location is one solution—team members from different functions in the company are relocated in one area or department. A team office is another solution. Although many people may work on a project during its life, the *core team* should number no more than eight people, according to studies done at AT&T; the ideal number is five to seven; and core team members should be dedicated to the project 100 percent of their time!

The final organizational ingredient essential to making this multifunctional team work is *climate and culture.* The climate must reward and encourage creativity and innovation. For example, 3M provides cash awards to about 10 percent of its employees annually for doing innovative and creative things. Milliken has a hall of fame, whereby individuals and teams are publicly recognized for their contributions to innovative projects.

At the same time, the climate must avoid punishment for failure. The only way to ensure no failures is to take no chances. So if failures are punished, expect little in the way of risk-taking and entrepreneurial behavior.

Additionally, the resources must be available to enable people to do creative and innovative work. Some companies have a deliberate policy to make resources available to innovators. 3M provides its technical people with about one day per week to work on their own pet projects; and many a successful new product project has been initiated as a "boot-strapped" project—using spare time and spare money. Du Pont has implemented a fund to provide seed money to cover cash expenses for would-be "intrapreneurs" working on their own projects.

8. Top management support doesn't guarantee success, but it sure helps. But many senior managers get it wrong.

Top management support is a necessary ingredient for product innovation. But it must be the right kind of support. Many managers get it wrong!

---

* "Micro-manage" is a term used to describe the behavior of senior management: day-to-day meddling in the affairs of the project team.

The Stanford project and the Hewlett-Packard study both found top management support to be directly linked to new product success. But NewProd III found a different twist. Top managers supported failures with almost equal frequency as successes: those projects in which top management is committed, is involved directly in the management of the project, and provides considerable guidance and direction for the project are only marginally more successful.

Where top management support is critical, however, is in getting the product to market. When one considers killed projects versus launched products in the NewProd III study, here top management support is important.[14] Top management can muster the resources, cut through the red tape, and push the right buttons to get the project done.

The message is that top management's main role in product innovation is to *set the stage* for product innovation to occur, to be a "behind-the-scenes" facilitator, and not so much to be an actor, front-and-center.

This stage-setting role is vital: Management must make the long term commitment to internal product development as a source of growth; it must develop a vision, objectives, and strategy for product innovation that is driven by corporate objectives, and strategies.[15] It must make available the necessary resources and ensure that these resources aren't diverted to more immediate needs in times of shortage. It must commit to a disciplined game plan to drive products to market. And most important, senior management must empower project teams and support committed champions by acting as mentors, facilitators, "godfathers," or sponsors to project leaders and teams—acting as "executive champions," as Peters calls them.[16]

Senior management's role is *not to get involved* in projects on a day-to-day basis, nor to be constantly meddling and interfering in the project, nor to "micro-manage" projects. This meddling behavior is wrong for two reasons: it usurps the empowerment of the team (and hence defeats the empowered team concept); and frankly, senior management doesn't do such a great job at either picking winners or managing projects!

9. Synergy is vital to success—"step-out" projects tend to fail.

Synergy is the common thread that binds the new business to the old. When translated into product innovation, synergy is the ability to leverage existing and in-house strengths, resources, and capabilities to advantage in the new product project. "Step-out" projects take the firm into territory that lies beyond the experience and resource base of the company.

If at all possible, "attack from a position of strength" when it comes to new products. That is, leverage your in-house resources and skills, seeking synergies in product development programs. This has been the message from a number of studies into new product success and failure. The reasons for the impact of synergy are clear:

1. *Resources are available and at marginal cost.* In short, if the product can be developed using existing and in-house technical skills, this is much less ex-

pensive (and less risky) than seeking outside technology and skills. Similarly, if the product can sold to existing customers through an already-established sales force or channel system, then this, too, is less expensive, less risky, and less time-consuming than seeking new distribution channels or building a new sales force.

2. *Experience.* The more often one does something, the better one becomes at doing it. If new product projects are closely related (synergistic) to current businesses, chances are, there has been considerable experience with such projects in the past. The result is that it costs less (29 percent at each doubling of the number of new introductions, according to Booz, Allen & Hamilton),[17] and there will be fewer unpleasant surprises: uncertainty is less.

Two types of synergy are important to product innovation:

- *Technological synergy:* the project's ability to build on in-house–development technology, utilize inside engineering skills, and use existing manufacturing resources and skills.
- *Marketing synergy:* the project/company fit in terms of sales force, distribution channels, customer service resources, advertising and promotion, and market-intelligence skills and resources.

The impact of these two synergy dimensions operating together is shown in Figure 4.1, based on the NewProd study results. Note that highly "step-out" projects—which lack both marketing and technological synergy—those in the upper-right cell—suffer a failure rate of 77 percent. By contrast, more synergistic projects have much higher success rates. (Note that some cells in the figure had too few cases to draw meaningful conclusions.) Ironically, the best place to operate seems to be projects with medium-to-high technological synergy coupled with moderate marketing synergy—a 71- to 82-percent success rate! Indeed, those projects that featured extremely high synergy in both technology and marketing dimensions (lower-left cell) were few in number (8.6 percent of cases) and had about average success rates (53 percent successful), raising questions about staying "too close to home."*

In designing new product strategies and selecting which new products to develop, never underestimate the role of synergy. Arenas and projects that lack any synergy invariably cost the firm more to exploit. Further, unsynergistic projects usually take the firm into new and uncharted markets and technologies, often with unexpected pitfalls and barriers. There are simply too many unpleasant surprises in arenas that are new to the firm.

10. Projects aimed at attractive markets do better; market attractiveness is a key project-selection criterion.

Market attractiveness is an important strategic variable. Porter's "five forces" model considers various elements of market attractiveness as a determinant of industry profitability.[18] Similarly, various strategic planning models—for exam-

---

* These very close to home projects most often were incremental products, modifications and tweaks: highly synergistic, but providing little opportunity for product differentiation.

Figure 4.1:   The Impact of Synergies on New Product Success

		High	Medium	Low
Marketing Synergy	**Low**	No cases	40.9% successful (12.6% of cases)	22.7% successful (12.6% of cases)
	Medium	82.4% successful (9.7% of cases)	71.1% successful (47.4% of cases)	33.3% successful (8.6% of cases)
	High	53.3% successful (8.6% of cases)	No cases	Too few cases

High   Medium   Low

Technological Synergy

Robert G. Cooper and Elko J. Kleinschmidt, *New Products: The Key Factors in Success.* American Marketing Association, Chicago, 1990.

ple, portfolio models used to allocate resources among various existing business units—employ market attractiveness as a key dimension in the two-dimensional map or portfolio grid.[19]

In the case of new products, market attractiveness is also important, but perhaps *not as much* as one might have anticipated. Clearly, products targeted at more attractive markets are more successful; but market attractiveness is not at the top of the list of success factors in any study, nor is it a success factor at all in many studies. There are two dimensions of market attractiveness:

- *Market potential:* positive market environments, namely large and growing markets,[20] markets where a strong customer need exists for such products, and where the purchase is an important one for the customer.[21] Products aimed at such markets are more successful.

- *Competitive situation:* negative markets characterized by intense competition, competition on the basis of price, high quality, and strong competitive products; and competitors whose sales force, channel system, and support service are strongly rated. Products aimed at such negative markets are only marginally less successful, according to both NewProd and the Stanford project.[22]

The message is this: products succeed in spite of the external environment they face: They succeed because they are superior and well defined; are executed in a quality fashion and driven by a multifunctional team; and have certain synergies with the firm. While a positive external environment—having a large and growing market with weak competition—helps pave the way for a success, don't count on external conditions to make up for a multitude of internal sins and weaknesses. In short, if the product and project are weak, the external environment will not save the day! Nonetheless, because both elements of market attractiveness—market potential and competitive situation—do have moderate impact on the new product's fortunes, both should be considered as criteria for project selection and prioritization.

11. New product success is predictable; and the profile of a winner can be used to make sharper project-selection decisions to yield better focus.

Most new product projects are unfit for commercialization: they are simply "bad" ideas—a weak market, no fit with the company, or no competitive advantage. But new product resources are too valuable and too limited to allocate to the wrong projects. The desire to weed out bad projects, coupled with the need to focus limited resources on the best projects, means that tough Go/Kill and prioritization decisions must be made.

Sadly, in too many firms, project evaluations are either weak, deficient, or nonexistent. In the NewProd studies, many managers confessed to weak evaluation and prioritization decisions. For example, initial screening was one of the most poorly handled activities of the entire new product process. In 88 percent of the projects studied, screening was judged as deficient: the decision involved only one decision-maker, and/or there were no criteria used to screen projects.[23] Further, 37 percent of projects did not undergo a business or financial analysis prior to the development phase, and 65 percent did not include a precommercialization business analysis. In many cases, managers confessed that projects simply aren't killed once they're into development: "Projects get a life of their own," and become like "express trains, slowing down at the stations, but never with the intention of stopping until they reach their final destination, market launch."

Often the problem of poor project evaluation boils down to a lack of criteria against which to judge projects: what is a "good" project? The many studies into success and failure provide insights in what criteria to use. New product success is *fairly predictable:* Certain project characteristics consistently separate winners from losers, and in a strong way. These characteristics can and should be used as criteria for project selection and prioritization.

Three important characteristics that discriminate successful from unsuccessful projects include:

- *Product superiority:* (described in Lesson 1 above);
- *Synergy:* (described in Lesson 9 above); and

• *Market attractiveness:* (described in Lesson 10 above).

These three factors, and the list of items comprised by them, should be an integral part of firms' screening and project-evaluation decisions. Checklists of questions that capture product superiority, synergy, and market attractiveness can be used as criteria to make more effective Go/Kill decisions. (For example, a computer-based new product screening-and-diagnostic model, the NewProd Model, has been constructed from the NewProd results.[24] (More on this NewProd model in Chapter 7.)

12. New product success is controllable: More emphasis is needed on completeness, consistency, and quality of execution.

New product success is very much within the hands of the men and women leading and working on the project. Certain key activities—how well they are executed, and whether they are done at all—are strongly tied to success. These activities include undertaking preliminary market and technical assessments early in the project, carrying out a detailed market study or marketing research prior to product design, performing a detailed business and financial analysis, and executing the test market and market launch in a quality fashion.

These activities are all within control of the project leader and team. Conversely, omitting some or all of these activities (or poor quality of execution) is strongly linked to failure. In short, success is not so much a matter of technology, market, or product, but how well the project is undertaken.

Quality of execution of the project is the key to success. Note the major impact of factors that capture quality of execution of technological, marketing, and predevelopment activities in the NewProd studies. Similarly, the completeness of the process—what activities and how many activities are actually undertaken—is an important success determinant. Finally, the expenditures on different activities—of people-hours and dollars—for successes versus failures reveal the impact of resource commitment.

The message is this: *there is a quality crisis in product innovation.* No, not the usual product quality problems, but rather serious weakness in quality of execution. The best way to double the success rate of new products in your company is to strive for significant improvements in the way the innovation process unfolds. Management and project teams must develop a more disciplined approach to product innovation. The way to save time and money is *not* to cut corners, execute in a hurried and sloppy fashion, or cut out steps. This is false economy: it results in more time and effort spent later in the project; and results in a higher failure rate.

The solution that some firms have adopted is to treat product innovation as a process: they use a formal product-delivery process or game plan. And they *build into this process quality assurance approaches*: for example, they introduce check points in the process that focus on quality of execution, ensuring that every play in this game plan is executed in a quality fashion; and they design quality into their game plan by making mandatory certain key activities and actions that are often omitted, yet are central to success.

13. The resources must be in place.

Having a sound game plan does not guarantee success. There must be players on the field as well—not just part-time or Saturday afternoon players, but full-time dedicated resources. Too many projects simply suffer from a lack of time and money commitment. The results are predictable: much higher failure rates.

This lesson, at first glance, is a trivial one. Sadly, too many managers don't get the message. As the competitive situation has toughened, companies have responded with restructuring (down-sizing) and doing more with less. The result is that product innovation, rather than being treated as an investment, is viewed as a cost, which must be reduced. And so resources are limited or cut back.

This short-term focus takes its toll. Certain vital activities, such as market-oriented actions and predevelopment homework are highly underresourced, particularly in the case of product failures.[25]

A strong market orientation is missing in the typical new product project. And much of this deficiency is directly linked to a lack of marketing resources available for the project. Only 16 percent of the project's total dollar costs and 32 percent of the person-days go to marketing actions, and most of these at the back-end or launch phase of the project. The conclusion is that new product marketing activities are typically underfunded; and that a market orientation exists in name only, and not in terms of dollars and effort.

By contrast, successful projects have far more dollars and person-days committed to marketing activities than do failures. Overall successes have more than twice as much money spent on marketing activities (other than the launch) than do failures. Moreover, these trends are consistent across marketing activities: double-to-triple the spending on each marketing action for successes versus failures. The message to managers is this:

- Consider how much (or how little) you now devote to these new product marketing activities—preliminary market assessment, marketing research, customer tests, trial sell, and market launch.
- Next consider the fact that managers who take winning products to market spend considerably more on these activities than managers who are responsible for failures.

Armed with this evidence, now is the time to rededicate the company to more spending and resources for these critical marketing actions.

Another serious pitfall is that the homework doesn't get done. Again much of this deficiency can be directly attributed to a lack of resources: simply not enough money, people, and time to do the work. Only 7 percent of the dollars and 16 percent of the effort spent on new product projects go to these vital up-front actions.

Again the evidence is clear: Successful projects have considerably more spent on the front-end stages of the new product process. More than twice as much money and 1.75 times as many person-days are spent on the up-front activities for successes versus failures. Management must recognize the importance of the first few steps of the new product process, and realize that money spent here appears to have a major positive impact on product performance.

14. Speed is everything! But not at the expense of quality of execution.

Speed is the new competitive weapon. Speed yields competitive advantage; it means less likelihood that the market or competitive situation might change; and it means a quicker realization of profits. So the goal of reducing the development cycle time is admirable. But a word of caution here: *speed is only an interim objective . . .* a means to an end. The ultimate goal, of course, is profitability. But many of the practices naively employed in order to reduce time-to-market ultimately cost the company money—they achieve the interim objective—bringing the product quickly to market—but fail at the ultimate objective: profitability. An example is moving a product to market quickly by shortening the customer-test phase, only to incur product reliability problems after launch—resulting in lost customer confidence and substantial warranty and servicing costs!

Be careful in your quest for cycle-time reduction: too often the methods used to reduce development time yield precisely the opposite effect, and in many cases are very costly: they are at odds with sound management practice. Short-cuts are taken with the best intentions, but far too frequently result in disaster: serious errors of omission and commission, which not only add delays to the project, but often lead to higher incurred costs and even product failure.

Here are five *sensible* ways to reduce cycle time—ways that are totally consistent with sound management practice and are also derived from our lessons for success outlined above. In short, not only will *these five methods increase the odds of winning, but they also reduce the time-to-market!*

- *Do it right the first time:* Build in quality of execution at every stage of the project. The best way to save time is by avoiding having to recycle back and do it a second time. Quality of execution pays off not only in terms of better results, but also by reducing delays (see Lesson 12).
- *Homework and definition:* Doing the up-front homework and getting clear project definition, based on fact rather than hearsay and speculation, saves time downstream: less recycling back to get the facts or redefine the product requirements; and sharper targets to work towards (see Lesson 4).
- *Organize around a multifunctional team with empowerment:* Multifunctional teams are essential for timely development. "Rip apart a badly developed project and you will unfailingly find 75 percent of slippage attributable to: (1) 'siloing', or sending memos up and down vertical organizational 'silos' or 'stovepipes' for decisions; and (2) sequential problem solving," according to Peters.[26] Sadly, the typical project resembles a relay race, with each function or department carrying the baton for its portion of the race, and then handing off to the next runner or department (see Lesson 7).
- *Parallel processing:* The relay race, sequential, or series approach to product development is antiquated and inappropriate for the nineties. Given the time pressures of projects coupled with the need for a complete and quality process, a more appropriate scheme is a rugby game, or *parallel processing.* With parallel processing, activities are undertaken concurrently (rather than

sequentially)—thus more activities are undertaken in an elapsed period of time. The new product process must be multidisciplinary with each part of the team—marketing, R&D, manufacturing, engineering—working together and undertaking its parallel or concurrent activity. Note that the play is a lot more complex using a parallel play or rugby scheme (versus a series approach), hence the need for a disciplined game plan (see Lesson 15 below).

- *Prioritize and focus:* The best way to slow projects down is to dissipate your limited resources and people across too many projects. By concentrating resources on the truly meritorious projects, not only will the work be done better, it will be done faster. But focus means tough choices: it means killing other and perhaps worthwhile projects. And that requires good decision-making and the right criteria for making Go/Kill decisions (see Lesson 11).

15. Companies that follow a multistage, disciplined new product game plan fare much better.

Product innovation in most firms is a woefully inadequate process: it is a process plagued by errors of omission and commission; it lacks consistency and quality of execution; and it is a process very much in need of repair. These are the findings of study after study. They reveal that many firms' new product processes are deficient or nonexistent, and point to the need for a complete and a quality process. A game plan is the solution to which many firms have turned.[27]

Managing a new products program without a game plan in place is like putting a dozen players on a football field, with no huddles and no preplanned plays, and expecting them to score. It works once in a while, but over the long run, the better-disciplined competitor will win. A number of companies have indeed implemented formal new product processes or disciplined game plans.[28]

The term "game plan" means a conceptual and operational model for moving new product projects from idea through to launch. It is a blueprint or road map for managing the new product process to improve efficiency and effectiveness. The model outlines the key plays and huddles necessary to score a goal, hence the analogy with North American football or rugby, and the term "game plan."

Operationally, game plans break the new product process into a series of multifunctional stages or plays composed of multiple, parallel activities; each stage is preceded by a gate, decision point, or huddle. The stage and gate format leads to names such as "gating" or "stage-gate" or "toll-gate" systems.

The evidence in support of a new product game plan is strong. Booz, Allen & Hamilton found that companies that had implemented such game plans are more successful; and that those firms with the longest experience here were even more successful.[29] As one vice president put it, "The multistep new product process is an essential ingredient in successful new product development."

Later in this book, we'll look at what happened to a handful of firms that have implemented such game plans: the results have been dramatic—faster new product introductions, less recycling to redo steps, and a higher success rate of launched products.

If your firm does not have a new product game plan in place, its design and implementation should become a top-priority task. The next chapter outlines a skeleton of a typical game plan—a step-by-step procedure for turning a new product idea into a winning new product in the marketplace.

Towards a Game Plan

This chapter has given us fifteen key lessons for new product success. They are lessons based not on hearsay and wishful thinking, but on fact—on the many research studies that have probed new product success and failure. Now the challenge begins: to translate these lessons into operational reality. That's the role of the game plan. In the next chapter, we'll fashion these fifteen lessons into a road map, a blueprint, or a game plan that is designed to drive new product projects from idea through to launch—successfully and in a time-efficient manner.

The New Product Process—The Game Plan

A process is a methodology that is developed to replace the old ways and to guide corporate activity year after year. It is not a special guest. It is not temporary. It is not to be tolerated for a while and then abandoned.
  Thomas H. Berry, *Managing the Total Quality Transformation.*[1]

Stage-Gate Systems

A game plan for product innovation is one solution to what ails so many firms' new product programs.[2] Facing increased pressure to reduce the cycle time yet improve their new product success rates, companies are increasingly looking to new product game plans, or "stage-gate systems," to manage, direct, and control their product-innovation efforts. That is, they have developed a systematic process—a blueprint or road map—for moving a new product project through the various stages and steps from idea to launch. But most important, they have built into their road map the many lessons for new product success in order to heighten the effectiveness of their programs. Consider these examples:[3]

- With a rather dismal track record for new products and models throughout the eighties, General Motors is now trying to beat the Japanese at their own game: fast-paced innovation. GM has implemented its copyrighted Four Phase system for product design and introduction—a methodology that has already drastically cut the concept-to-launch time of a new car model. This Four Phase new product game plan—essentially a stage-and-gate system— looks remarkably like new product processes found at Japanese car makers.
- 3M has traditionally had an enviable new product track record. An innovative corporate culture and climate are often cited as 3M's secret to success. But for years 3M has also had in place various stage-gate systems for managing the innovation process. Thus creativity and discipline are blended to yield a successful new product program.
- Procter & Gamble, always noted for its forward-thinking management methods, has recently faced tougher times in its new product efforts. A se-

nior management task force tried to find out why. One fact uncovered was that back in 1964, the company had implemented a new product gating system at a time when most people hadn't dreamed of the concept. The system worked well for 15 years, but fell from favor in the late 1970s with the advent of a new generation of managers. Throughout the 1980s, new product performance in the company had been mediocre. One recommendation of the task force: "Let's get back to basics and redesign and reimplement the stage-gate process." The company has. In 1991, P&G relaunched a 1990s version of its game plan: a six-stage model or "product launch road map" for driving new products to market.

- Northern Telecom—a telecommunications equipment manufacturer, which has successfully penetrated the world market in the last few decades—implemented a stage-gate system for new products in the early 1980s. The model cost approximately $1 million to design and implement, but paid for itself on the first major project. The documented results are impressive: shorter times-to-launch, fewer mistakes, less recycling and rework in the process, and a more successful development effort.

- In the U.S., other firms have implemented new product game plans or stage-gate systems, including Polaroid, Corning, Exxon Chemicals, Hewlett-Packard, Ethyl Corporation, and various divisions at Du Pont, Emerson Electric, and B. F. Goodrich.

Game plans work! So, the challenge in this chapter is this: given the 15 lessons gleaned from new product success-and-failure experiences (last chapter), how can we translate these into an operational and effective new product game plan? For example, how does one build in quality of execution, or a strong market orientation, or better predevelopment homework? Let us begin the design of this game plan with a quick look at what this new product process must achieve.

Six Goals of a New Product Game Plan

Goal # 1: Quality of Execution

The argument that the proponents of total quality management make goes something like this: "The definition of quality is precise: it means meeting all the requirements all the time. It is based on the principle that all work is a process. It focuses on improving business processes to eliminate errors." The concept is perfectly logical and essentially simple. Most smart things are. And the same logic can be applied to new product development.

Product innovation is a process: it begins with an idea and culminates in a successful product launch. But processes aren't new to the business environment. There are many examples of well-run processes in business: for example, manufacturing processes, information processes, and so on.

A quality-of-execution crisis exists in the product innovation process, however. We saw in the last two chapters clear evidence that the activities of the new product process—the quality of execution and whether these activities are carried out at all—have a dramatic impact on product success or failure. Further, there are serious gaps—omissions of steps and poor quality of execution—in the new product process. These serious gaps are the rule rather than the exception. And they are strongly tied to product failures.

This quality-of-execution crisis in the product innovation process provides strong evidence in support of the need for a more *systematic and quality approach* to the way firms conceive, develop, and launch new products. The way to deal with the quality problem is to visualize product innovation as a process, and to apply *process management* and *quality management techniques* to this process. Note that any process in business can be managed, and managed with a view to quality. Get the details of your processes right, and the result will be a high-quality end product or output. Manufacturing processes, for example, have had much focus on quality these last few decades.

Quality of execution is the goal of the new product process. More specifically, the ideal game plan should:

1. *focus on completeness:* ensure that the key activities that are central to the success of a new product project are indeed carried out—no gaps, no omissions, a complete process.
2. *focus on quality:* ensure that the execution of these activities is proficient—that is, treat innovation as a process, emphasize DIRTFooT (doing it right the first time), and build in quality controls and checks.
3. *focus on the important:* devote attention and resources to the pivotal and particularly weak steps in the new product process, notably the up-front and market-oriented activities.

The new product process or stage-gate system is simply a *process management tool.* We build into this process quality of execution, in much the same way that quality programs have been successfully implemented on the factory floor.

Goal # 2: Sharper Focus, Better Prioritization

Most firms' new product efforts suffer from a lack of focus: too many projects, and not enough resources. This focus and resource problem stems from inadequate project evaluation: the failure to set priorities and make tough Go/Kill decisions, and failure to undertake these in a timely fashion. Most of the critical evaluation points—from initial screening through to precommercialization business analysis—are characterized by serious weaknesses: decisions not made, little or no real prioritization, poor information inputs, no criteria for decisions, and inconsistent or capricious decision-making.

The need is for sharper project evaluation. By building in tough Go/Kill decision points (or bail-out points), the poor projects are weeded out, scarce resources are directed towards the truly meritorious projects, and more focus is the result.

One solution is to build the new product process or game plan around a set of gates or Go/Kill decision points. These gates are the bail-out points where we ask, "Are we still in the game?" They are analogous to the *quality-control check points* on a manufacturing assembly line. They serve to check the quality, merit, and progress of the project. Like a production line, gates are preset at different points throughout the new product process.

Each gate has its own set of *metrics and criteria* for passing, much like a quality-control check in production. These criteria and questions deal with various facets of the project including:

1. Does the project continue to make economic and business sense? Does it continue to meet or exceed our business and return-on-investment criteria?
2. Have the essential steps been completed—those steps or activities necessary to pass through the gate? Is the quality of execution of these activities first rate?
3. Is the project on time and on budget? Have the milestones since the last gate been hit?
4. What steps and actions need to be undertaken in the next stage of the project? And what are the deliverables for the next gate?

These gates, like quality-control check points in manufacturing, serve to map and control the new product process. They signal a "Kill" decision in the event of a project whose economics become negative, where the barriers to completion become insurmountable, or where the project is far over budget or behind schedule. Gates prevent projects from moving ahead to the next stage until all critical activities have been completed and in a quality fashion. And gates chart the path forward: they determine what tasks and milestones lie ahead, and the budgets and time frames for these tasks.

Goal # 3: Fast-Paced Parallel Processing

New product managers face a dilemma. On the one hand, they are urged by senior management to compress the cycle time—to shorten the elapsed time from idea to launch. On the other hand, the manager is urged to improve the effectiveness of product development: cut down the failure rate—do it right! This desire to "do it right" suggests a more thorough, longer process.

Parallel processing is one solution to the need for a complete and quality process, yet one that meets the time pressures of today's fast-paced business world. Traditionally, new product projects have been managed via a *series approach*— one task strung out after another, in series. The analogy is that of a relay race, with each department running with the project for its 100 yards. Phrases such as "hand off," "passing the project on," "dropping the ball," and "throwing it over the wall" are common in this relay approach to new products.

In marked contrast to the relay or sequential approach, with parallel processing many activities are undertaken *concurrently* rather than in series. The appropriate analogy is that of a rugby football match rather than a relay race.[4] A team (not a single runner) appears on the field. A scrum or huddle ensues, after which the ball emerges. Players run down the field in parallel with much interaction, constantly passing the ball laterally. After 25 yards or so, the players converge for another scrum, huddle, or gate review, and another stage of activities takes place.

With parallel processing, the game is far more intense than a relay race and more work gets done in an elapsed time period: three or four activities are done simultaneously and by different members on the project team. Second, there is less chance of an activity or task being overlooked or handled poorly because of lack of time: the activity is done in parallel, not in series, and hence does not extend the total elapsed project time. Moreover the activities are designed to feed each other—the metaphor of the ball being passed back and forth across the field. And finally, the entire new product process becomes multifunctional and multidisciplinary: the whole team—marketing, R&D, engineering, manufacturing—is on the field together, participates actively in each play, and takes part in each gate review or scrum.

Goal # 4: A Multifunctional Team Approach

The new product process is multifunctional: it requires the inputs and active participation of players from many different functions in the organization. The multifunctional nature of innovation coupled with the desire for parallel processing means that a *team approach* is mandatory in order to win at the new product game: The game plan or stage-gate system demands the presence of a new product team.

Essential characteristics of this team are:

1. It is multifunctional, with active teams players from the various functions and departments whose contributions to the project are needed.
2. The team may be organized as a *project team* for more complex projects (where the project manager has complete charge, with no formal involvement or authority by functional managers), or as a *project matrix team* for normal projects (where the project manager is assigned to oversee the project and has primary responsibility and authority, while functional managers assign personnel as needed).[5]
3. The team captain or leader has formal authority (this means co-opting authority from the functional heads) and the leader and team are empowered by senior management.
4. The team structure is fluid, with new members joining the team (or leaving it) as work requirements demand. But *a core group of responsible, committed, and accountable team players should be present from beginning to end.*

Goal # 5: A Strong Market Orientation

A market orientation is the missing ingredient in too many new product projects. A lack of a market orientation and inadequate market assessment are

consistently cited as reasons for new product failure. Moreover, the market-related activities tend to be the weakest in the new product process, yet are
strongly linked to success. While many managers profess a market orientation,
the evidence—where the time and money are spent—proves otherwise.

   If high new product success rates are the goal, then a market orientation—
executing the key marketing activities in a quality fashion—must be built into
the new product process as a matter of routine rather than by exception. Marketing inputs must play a decisive role from beginning to end of the project.
The following actions are *integral and mandatory plays* in the new product
game plan (but they rarely are):

- *Preliminary market assessment:* an early, relatively inexpensive step designed to assess market attractiveness and to test market acceptance for the
  proposed new product.
- *Market research to determine user needs and wants:* in-depth surveys or
  face-to-face interviews with customers to determine customer needs, wants,
  preferences, likes, dislikes, buying criteria, etc., as an input to the design of
  the new product.
- *Competitive analysis:* an assessment of competitors—their products and
  product deficiencies, prices, costs, technologies, production capacities, and
  marketing strategies.
- *Concept testing:* a test of the proposed product to determine likely market
  acceptance. Note that the product is not yet developed, but a model or representation of the product is displayed to prospective users to gauge reaction
  and purchase intent.
- *Customer reaction during development:* continuing concept and product
  testing throughout the development phase, using rapid prototypes, models,
  and partially completed products to gauge customer reaction and seek feedback.
- *User tests:* field trials using the finished product (or prototype) with users to
  verify the performance of the product under customer conditions, and to
  confirm intent to purchase and market acceptance.
- *Test market or trial sell*: a mini-launch of the product in a limited geographic area or single sales territory. This is a test of all elements of the marketing
  mix, including the product itself.*
- *Market launch:* a proficient launch, based on a solid marketing plan, and
  backed by sufficient resources.

Goal # 6: Better Homework Up-front

New product success or failure is largely decided in the first few plays of the
game—in those crucial steps and tasks that precede the actual development of
the product. It is here that the product is defined, and that the case for develop-

---

* A test market or trial sell is both expensive and time consuming, yields information that can be
sometimes obtained via other methods, and hence is not always appropriate for every project.

ment is constructed. Ironically, most of the money and time is devoted to the middle and back-end stages of the process, and the up-front actions suffer from errors of omission, poor quality of execution, and underresourcing.

The ideal new product game plan ensures that these early stages are carried out before the project is allowed to proceed—before the project is allowed to become a full-fledged development. Activities essential to building the business case become mandatory plays before the project is given formal approval for development.

What are these essential up-front activities in a well-designed game plan? They include:

- *initial screening:* the initial decision to spend time and money on the project.
- *preliminary technical assessment:* an initial attempt to prove technical feasibility, assess manufacturing implications, and identify technical risks and issues.
- *preliminary marketing assessment:* highlighted above, this is the first-pass market study.
- *detailed technical assessment:* detailed technical work (not development) to prove technical feasibility and address technical risks.
- *manufacturing assessment:* technical work to determine manufacturing implications, capital expenditures, and probable manufacturing costs.
- *detailed market studies:* includes the user needs-and-wants study, competitive analysis, and concept tests outlined above.
- *financial analysis:* probes the expected financial consequences and risks of the project.
- *product definition and business case:* integrates the results of the technical, manufacturing, marketing, and financial analyses into a product definition (protocol), project justification, and project plan.
- *decision on business case:* a thorough project evaluation and decision to go to full development.

Suggestion: Take a close look at the new product process within your firm. Does the process ensure quality of execution? Is it built around a set of gates, or evaluation and decision points to get rid of bad projects and focus resources on the truly deserving ones? Does it emphasize parallel processing—a rugby match—or does it resemble a relay race? Does it use the project matrix or project team approach—an empowered, multifunctional team headed by a leader with authority? Or are you still largely functionally based? Does it emphasize a market orientation, and what proportion of project expenditures go to marketing actions? Do you devote enough resources to the up-front or homework phases of the process?

If some of the answers are no, then perhaps the time is ripe to rethink your new product process or game plan. Look to a stage-gate system or formal new product process to provide you with some needed solutions.

Managing Risk

The management of new products is the management of risk. So the game plan must also be designed to manage risk. Indeed, if you look closely, you see that most of the 15 lessons outlined in the last chapter dealt with ways of reducing risk. Total risk avoidance in new product development is impossible, unless a company decides to eschew all innovation—and face a slow death.

Most of us know what is meant by the phrase "a risky situation." From a new product manager's perspective, a high-risk situation is one in which much is at stake (for example, the project involves a lot of money or is strategically critical to the firm), and where the outcome is uncertain (for example, it is not certain that the product will be technically feasible or will do well in the marketplace). The components of risk are: amounts at stake and uncertainties (See Figure 5.1).

A Life-or-Death Gamble

Imagine for a moment that you are facing the gamble of your life. You've been invited to a millionaire's ranch for a weekend. Last night, you played poker and lost more money than you can afford—around $50,000. All of the other players are enormously wealthy cattle and oil barons. Tonight they've given you the opportunity to cash in. Each of the other ten players antes into the pot $1 million. That's $10 million in thousand-dollar bills—more money than you are ever likely to see again stacked in front of you.

Here is the gamble. One of the players takes out a six-shooter pistol, removes all the bullets, and in full view of everyone, places one live bullet in the gun.

Figure 5.1:   Components of Risk in a Decision Situation

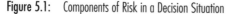

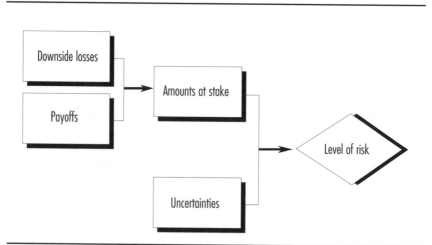

Adapted with permission from R. G. Cooper and R. A. More, "Modular Risk Management: An Applied Example," *R & D Management* 9 (Feb. 1979): 93–99.

He then spins the chamber. For $10 million, you are asked to point the gun at your head and pull the trigger. Will you take the gamble?

The situation exhibits the key elements of risk: a great deal at stake (the $10 million or your life) and a high degree of uncertainty—the bullet could be in any location.

Reducing the Stakes

This hypothetical gamble represents an unacceptable risk level. Yet this is precisely the way many managers play the new product game: huge amounts at stake coupled with high levels of uncertainty. How can the risk be reduced? One route is to *lessen the amounts at stake*. For example, use blank bullets and earmuffs to deaden the noise, and point the gun, not at your head, but at your foot. The potential downside loss, if the gun were to fire, is now merely humiliation in front of a group of friends.

But upside gains are inevitably tied to downside losses. So, instead of anting in $1 million, every player now puts in one dollar. Will you still take the gamble? Most would reply, "Who cares?" There is no longer enough at stake to make the gamble worthwhile or even interesting. The risk is now so low that the decision becomes trivial.

Some Gambling Rules

Rule number one in risk management is: if the uncertainties are high, keep the amounts at stake low. Rule number two is: as the uncertainties decrease, the amounts at stake can be increased. These two rules keep risk at a minimum.

There is another way in which risk can be managed in our hypothetical example. The pot remains at $10 million, a live bullet is used, and the gun must be aimed at your head. But this time, your opponent, in plain view, marks the exact location of the bullet on the chamber. He spins the chamber and asks you to reach into your pocket and give him $20,000 in return for a look at the gun to see where the live bullet has ended up. Then you decide whether or not you still wish to proceed with the gamble.

Most of us would consider this a "good gamble" (assuming we had the $20,000)—one with an acceptable risk level. A relatively small amount of cash buys a look at the gun and the location of the bullet. Having paid for the look and determined the bullet's location, you then make your second decision: are you still in the game?

The risk has been reduced by converting an "all-or-nothing" decision into a two-stage decision: two steps and two decision points. Your ability to purchase information was also instrumental in minimizing risk: information has reduced the uncertainty of the situation. Finally the ability to withdraw from the game—to bail out—also reduced risk.

Three more gambling rules designed to manage risk evolve from this second gambling situation. Rule number three is: incrementalize the decision process—break the all-or-nothing decision into a series of stages and decisions. Rule number four is: be prepared to pay for relevant information to reduce risk. And rule number five: provide for bail-out points—decision points that provide the opportunity to fold, walk away, or get out of the game.

Risks in New Product Management

These five rules of risk management apply directly to the new product game. Near the beginning of a project the amounts at stake usually are low, and the uncertainty of the outcome is very high. As the project progresses, the amounts at stake begin to increase (see Figure 5.2). If risk is to be managed successfully, the uncertainties of outcomes must be deliberately driven down as the stakes increase. Further, the stakes must not be allowed to increase unless the uncertainties do come down. Uncertainties and amounts at stake must be kept in balance.

Unfortunately, in many new product projects the amounts at stake increase as the project progresses while the uncertainties remain fairly high (see Figure 5.3). Additional spending fails to reduce the uncertainties! By the end of the project, as launch nears, management is no more sure about the commercial outcome of the venture than it was on day one of the project. The amounts at stake have increased, uncertainty remains high, and the risk level is unacceptably high.

Figure 5.2:   Relationship between Uncertainties and Amounts at Stake

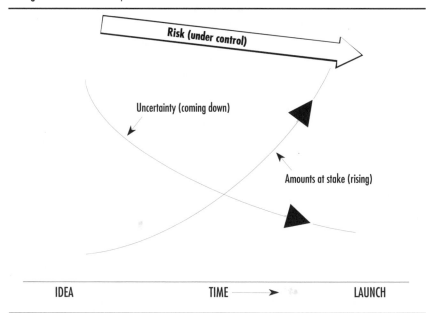

Adapted from R. G. Cooper and B. Little, "Reducing the Risk of Industrial New Product Development," *Canadian Marketer 7* (Fall 1974): 7–12.

Figure 5.3:   Risk Out of Control in the NewProduct Process

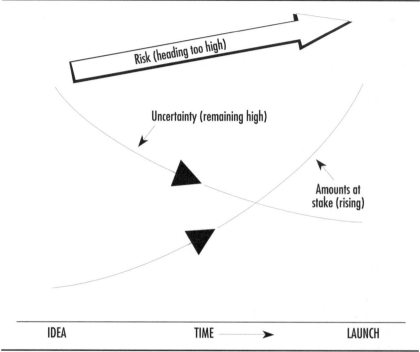

Adapted from R. G. Cooper and B. Little, "Reducing the Risk of Industrial New Product Development," *Canadian Marketer 7* (Fall 1974): 7–12.

For every thousand-dollar increase in the amounts at stake, the uncertainty curve in Figure 5.2 must be reduced by an equivalent amount. To do otherwise is to let risk get out of hand. In short, every expenditure in the new product process—every notch up on the amounts-at-stake curve in Figure 5.2—must bring a corresponding reduction in the uncertainty curve. The entire new product process, from idea to launch, can be viewed as an uncertainty-reduction process. Remember the five gambling rules:

1. When the uncertainties of the new product project are high (that is, when the prospects of success are fuzzy), keep the amounts at stake low. When you don't know where you're going, take small steps.
2. As the uncertainties decrease, let the amounts at stake increase. As you learn more about where you're going, take bigger and bigger steps.
3. Incrementalize the new product process into a series of steps or stages. Each step should be more costly than the one before.
4. View each stage as a means of reducing uncertainty. Remember that information is the key to uncertainty reduction. Each step in the process that creates an expenditure must reduce uncertainty by an equivalent amount. "Buy a series of looks" at the project's outcome.

5. Provide for timely evaluation, decision, and bail-out points. These decision points pull together all the new information from the previous stage and pose the questions, "are we still in the game? Should we proceed to the next stage, or kill the project now?"

Suggestion: The five decision rules outlined above apply to almost any high-risk situation. Does your company follow them in its day-to-day management practices? Review your firm's new product practices, perhaps using an actual case, and assess whether your management group is handling risk appropriately.

A Systematic Game Plan

We have made seven points so far in this chapter:

1. The new product process must be a *quality process*. There is a clear need for a systematic new product process or road map to guide and facilitate the new product project from idea to launch.

    This game plan or stage-gate system is one solution to correct the serious deficiencies and the quality-of-execution crisis that are common to many firms' new product efforts. These deficiencies and holes are glaring and pervasive, and sadly, they impact strongly and negatively on performance.

2. The process or game plan must be designed to *manage risk*; a multistage and gate framework is most appropriate.

    Build the five gambling rules into the process. The innovation process is broken into a series of stages, each stage more costly than the one before. Expenditures for early stages are kept low, but allowed to increase as uncertainty is reduced. Each stage is viewed as an information acquisition stage. And timely bail-out points (in the form of gates) are provided.

3. *Gates are central* to the new product game plan.

    These gates serve several functions: they act like quality-control check points and provide the quality-control mechanism in the process. Before a project is allowed to proceed to the next stage, essential tasks and deliverables must be complete. Gates also provide for bail-out points—Go/Kill decision points—to weed out bad projects and focus resources on the meritorious ones. And gates help chart the path forward, determining the tasks and deliverables for the next stage.

4. *Parallel processing* balances the need for a complete and quality process with the desire for a speedier process.

    The game plan is designed much like a rugby match (rather than a relay race). Activities and tasks are undertaken concurrently and in parallel rather than sequentially. The result is a faster, more intense process; there are fewer temptations to delete key activities due to lack of time; and a multifunctional process is the outcome.

5. The game plan requires a *multifunctional, empowered team* headed by a team leader with authority.

The multifunctional team approach is one critical ingredient, and is essential to the success of the stage-gate game plan. The team is multifunctional with active involvement and commitment by players from different functions in the firm; it must be empowered by senior management; and the leader is given formal authority over the resources (people) on the team.

6. The game plan is *market-driven* and *customer-focused.*

Customer inputs and constant customer focus throughout the process is paramount. Eight key marketing actions—from preliminary market assessment through to launch—have been identified and are a central feature of the game plan.

7. Up-front or *predevelopment homework* is crucial to success, and these activities must be built into the game plan in a consistent and systematic way.

The seeds of success and failure are sown in the first few steps of the new product process. Like the marketing actions, those steps that precede the development of the project are typically weak, yet make all the difference between winning and losing. Nine key up-front actions have been pinpointed—from initial screening up to the business case—and these too are built into the game plan.

The Structure of the Stage-Gate Game Plan

These seven key points, together with the fifteen lessons from the last chapter, have been fashioned into an effective new product game plan.

The stage-gate new product game plan is a conceptual and operational model for moving a new product project from idea to launch.[6] It is a blueprint for managing the new product process to improve effectiveness and efficiency. Stage-gate systems break the innovation process into a predetermined set of stages, each stage consisting of a set of prescribed, multifunctional, and parallel activities. The entrance to each stage is a gate: these gates control the process are serve as the quality control and Go/Kill check points. This stage-and-gate format leads to the name "stage-gate system."*

The game plan is based on the experiences, suggestions, and observations of a large number of managers and firms and on my own and others' research in the field. Indeed my observations of what happened in over 60 case histories laid the foundations for the game plan.[7] Since this stage-gate system first appeared in print, it has been implemented in whole or in part in dozens of firms in North America, including Exxon Chemicals, Procter & Gamble, Du Pont, Polaroid, US West, BF Goodrich, Corning Glass, The Royal Bank of Canada, and the Lawson Mardon Group, all of which have provided an excellent "laboratory setting" to further refine and improve the game plan. In Europe, firms such as ICI, Waven division of Shell, Courtalds and Lego have similarly provided case examples for stage-gate implementation.

* Although many other names are used besides stage-gate, including PDP (Product Delivery Process), NPP (New Product Process), Gating System, and Product Launch System.

Figure 5.4:   A Generic Stage-Gate New Product Process

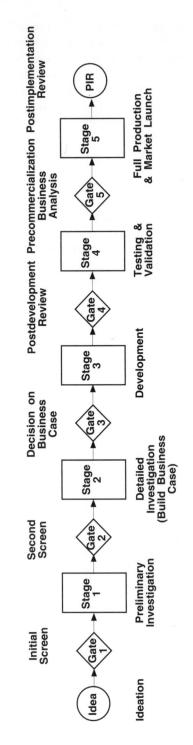

Reprinted from *Business Horizons*, May–June 1990. Copyright 1990 by the Foundation for the School of Business at Indiana University. Used with permission.

The Stages

The stage-gate system breaks the new product project into discrete and identifiable stages, typically four, five, or six in number. Each stage is designed to gather information needed to progress the project to the next gate or decision point. Each stage is multifunctional: There is no "R&D stage" or "marketing stage"! Each stage consists of a set of parallel activities undertaken by people from different functional areas within the firm. These activities are designed to gather information and drive uncertainties down. And each stage costs more than the preceding one: the game plan is an incremental commitment one.

The general flow of the typical or a "generic" stage-gate process is shown pictorially in Figure 5.4. Here the key stages are:

1. *Preliminary investigation*: a quick investigation and scoping of the project.
2. *Detailed investigation* (build the business case): a much more detailed investigation, leading to a *business case*, including project definition and justification, and a project plan.
3. *Development*: the actual design and development of the new product.
4. *Testing and validation*: tests or trials in the marketplace, lab, and plant to verify and validate the proposed new product, and its marketing and production.
5. *Full production and market launch*: commercialization—beginning of full production, marketing, and selling.

There are two additional stages not formally designated in the above scheme. One of these is *idea generation:* it's shown on the flow model, but isn't numbered as a stage per se. Idea generation is a critical activity, but one that occurs prior to beginning the new product process: ideas are the inputs or triggers of the new product process.

The other nondesignated stage is *strategy formulation*, also an essential activity. This strategy formulation stage is left out of the game plan model for now, not because it's unimportant, but because it is "macro" in nature—strategically oriented as opposed to process or tactics. Thus, strategy formulation is best superimposed over (or atop) the model; it is a prerequisite to the game plan, and is the topic of Chapter 11.

The Gates

Preceding each stage is a gate or a Go/Kill decision point. The gates are the scrums or huddles on the rugby football field. They are the points during the game where the team converges and where all new information is brought together. Gates serve as quality-control check points, as Go/Kill and prioritization decisions points, and as points where the path forward for the next play or stage of the process is decided.

Gates are predefined and specify a set of "deliverables," a list of criteria, both "must meet" (which are mandatory) and "should meet" (which capture desirable characteristics), and an output (for example, a decision and approved path forward). Gates are usually manned by senior managers from different functions, who own the resources required by the project leader and team.

An Overview of the Stage-Gate Process

Let's have a bird's eye look at the stage-gate model—an overview of what's involved at each stage and gate. In the next chapter, we'll lower the microscope on the up-front or predevelopment stages and gates. Chapter 7 then takes a close look at how to design and operate gates or decision points. And Chapter 8 focuses of the middle and back-end stages of the process. But for now, let's just have a quick run-through of the model, which you can follow stage-by-stage in Figure 5.4.[8]

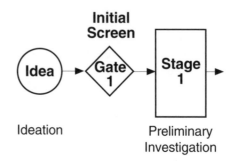

Idea

The process is initiated by an idea. Ideation activities include basic research, seed or unfunded projects, and a variety of customer-based and creativity techniques. More on ideation in Chapter 6.

Gate 1: Initial Screen

Initial screening is the first decision to commit resources to the project: the project is born at this point. If the decision is Go, the project moves into the preliminary investigation stage. Thus, Gate 1 signals a preliminary but tentative commitment to the project: a flickering green light.

Gate 1 is a "gentle screen" and amounts to subjecting the project to a handful of key "must meet" and "should meet" criteria. These criteria often deal with strategic alignment, project feasibility, magnitude of opportunity and market attractiveness, differential advantage, synergy with the firm's resources, and fit with company policies. Financial criteria are typically not part of this first screen. A checklist for the "must meet" criteria and a scoring model (weighted rating scales) for the "should meet" criteria can be used to help focus the discussion and rank projects in this early screen.

Consider the following illustration. Exxon Chemicals has implemented a new product process whose initial screen has a handful of key criteria: strategic fit, market attractiveness, technical feasibility, and supply route identified (within the company). The gatekeepers include both technical and business (marketing) people. These criteria are reviewed using a paper-and-pencil approach at the Gate 0 (or "Start Gate") meeting: this list of "must meet" criteria is scored (Yes/No), and the answers to all questions must be Yes; a single No kills the project.

Stage 1: Preliminary Investigation

This first and inexpensive stage has the objective of determining the project's technical and marketplace merits. Stage 1 is a quick scoping of the project, often done in less than one calendar month's elapsed time, and for 10–20 person-days' work effort.

A *preliminary market assessment* is one facet of Stage 1 and involves a variety of relatively inexpensive activities: a library search, contacts with key users, focus groups, and even a quick concept test with a handful of potential users. The purpose is to determine market size, market potential, and likely market acceptance.

Concurrently a *preliminary technical assessment* is carried out, involving a quick and preliminary in-house appraisal of the proposed product. The purpose is to assess development and manufacturing routes, technical and manufacturing feasibility, possible times and costs to execute, and possible technical, legal, and regulatory risks and roadblocks.

Stage 1 thus provides for the gathering of both market and technical information—at low costs and in a short time—to enable a cursory and first-pass financial analysis as input to Gate 2. Because of the limited effort, and depending on the size of the project, very often Stage 1 can be handled by a team of just several people—perhaps from marketing and from a technical group.

Consider this example of a preliminary technical and market assessment:

A firm had developed the technology for a plasma arc device with sufficient power to break down chemically inert molecules to their basic elements. One application they asked us to investigate was the development of a toxic waste destruction system. (Currently even toxic wastes, such as polychlorinated biphenyls (PCBs), are incinerated.) A preliminary technical appraisal had already been undertaken: it was largely a conceptual discussion among scientists to probe technical feasibility and costs. What remained was a first cut, quickie market assessment: to determine the market for PCB destruction.

We first contacted various government sources by telephone, namely environmental agencies. By midmorning, several reports listing toxic chemicals and quantities in various parts of the country were on their way to us. One government agency actually had a consultant's report that reviewed the many systems for disposing of toxic chemicals, and sent us a copy. Next, a library search: our reference librarian undertook a key word search through a number of journals and publications and produced a wealth of abstracts. We went through the list and chose the ones we wanted. Next, private contacts were pursued: who handles PCBs and should know about them? Manufacturers of transformers, of course. So environmental experts within GE and Westinghouse were contacted. One source had collected quite a file on the PCB problem, and with some encouragement, agreed to photocopy and send it to us. And so on through the week we continued . . . following our nose, almost like a detective or investigative journalist.

By the end of the week, we had a good understanding of the market: quantities and locations of toxic chemicals; current methods of disposal, their costs to use, and their strengths and weaknesses; a list of firms with toxic waste problems (potential customers); and even a first indication of the likelihood that users would opt for our new solution.

Gate 2: Second Screen

The project is subjected to a second and somewhat more rigorous screen at Gate 2. This gate is essentially a repeat of Gate 1: the project is reevaluated in the light of the new information obtained in Stage 1. If the decision is Go at this point, the project moves into a heavier spending stage.

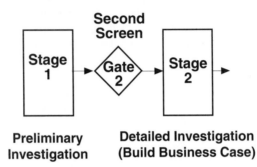

Preliminary
Investigation

Detailed Investigation
(Build Business Case)

At Gate 2, the project is again subjected to the original set of "must meet" and "should meet" criteria used at Gate 1. Here additional "should meet" criteria may be considered, dealing with sales force and customer reaction to the proposed product, potential legal, technical, and regulatory "killer variables"— all the result of new data gathered during Stage 1. Again, a checklist and scoring model facilitate this gate decision. The financial return is assessed at Gate 2, but only by a quick and simple financial calculation (for example, the payback period). Another example:

> Tremco Inc., a division of the chemical company, B. F. Goodrich, has implemented a stage-gate new product process model. At Gate 2, the Divisional Operations Group meets to make Go/Kill and prioritization decisions on projects ready to proceed to the next stage. Tremco employs a set of mandatory or "must meet" criteria similar to those at Gate 1: strategic fit, technical feasibility, consistent with company's policies, etc. Tremco also introduces a set of desirable project characteristics via a scoring model. The 14 characteristics capture the project's synergy, market attractiveness, competitive advantage, existence of the champion, and payback period. Each characteristic is rated by the "gatekeepers"; the ratings are added (in a weighted fashion—for example, elements of competitive advantage are weighted more heavily than elements of market attractiveness); and a total score of 50 out of 100 must be achieved for a Go decision.

Chapter 7 provides more detail on how to design a scoring model such as Tremco's.

Stage 2: Detailed Investigation (Build the Business Case)

The business case opens the door to product development. Stage 2 is where the business case is constructed: this stage is a detailed investigation stage, which clearly defines the product and verifies the attractiveness of the project prior to heavy spending. It is also the *critical homework stage*—the one found to be so often weakly handled.

The definition or *protocol for the winning new product* is a major facet of Stage 2. The elements of this definition include target market definition; delineation of the product concept; specification of a product positioning strategy and the product benefits to be delivered; and spelling out essential and desired product features, attributes, requirements, and specifications.

Stage 2 sees *market and market research studies* undertaken to determine the customer's needs, wants, and preferences—that is, to help define the "winning" new product.

> For example, Hewlett-Packard used extensive market research (including consumer choice modeling studies) to pinpoint desired features and attributes that customers desired in a hand-held calculator. What came out of the study was the desire to see results graphically, which lead to H-P's new graphics display calculator (where the graph or equation is shown visually on an LED display). The product has been a great winner for H-P.

Competitive analysis is also a part of this stage. Another market activity is concept testing: a representation of the proposed new product is presented to potential customers, their reactions are gauged, and the likely customer acceptance of the new product is determined.

> H-P also uses concept tests extensively to gauge market acceptance before initiating a development program. In developing a new line of portable computers, H-P put together a display of portable computers—competitive products and mock-ups of proposed H-P products. The target audience—sales reps—were invited in for a demonstration, and then asked to play with or "experience" the various units on display. They were then questioned (via a questionnaire) about products, concepts, and even features they liked and didn't like.

A detailed *technical appraisal* focuses on the "do-ability" of the project at Stage 2. That is, customer needs and "wish lists" are translated into a technically and economically feasible solution. This translation might even involve some preliminary design or laboratory work, but it should not be construed as a full-fledged development project. A manufacturing (or operations) appraisal is often a part of building the business case, where issues of manufacturability, costs to manufacture, and investment required are investigated. If appropriate, detailed legal, patent, and regulatory assessment work is undertaken in order to remove risks and to map out the required action.

Finally, a detailed *financial analysis* is conducted as part of the justification facet of the business case. This financial analysis typically involves a discounted cash flow approach, complete with sensitivity analysis to look at possible downside risks.

The result of Stage 2 is a *business case* for the project: the *product definition or protocol*—a key to success—is agreed to; and a thorough *project justification* and *detailed project plan* are developed.

Stage 2 involves considerably more effort than Stage 1, and requires the inputs from a variety of sources. Stage 2 is best handled by a team consisting of multifunctional members—the core group of the eventual project team.

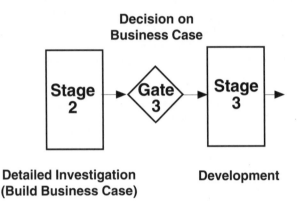

Gate 3: Decision on the Business Case

This is the final gate prior to the development stage, the last point at which the project can be killed before entering heavy spending. Once past Gate 3, financial commitments are substantial. In effect, Gate 3 means "go to a heavy spend." Gate 3 also yields a "sign off" of the protocol or product definition.

The qualitative side of this evaluation involves a review of each of the activities in Stage 2, and checking that the activities were undertaken, the quality of execution was sound, and the results were positive. Next, Gate 3 subjects the project once again to the set of "must meet" and "should meet" criteria used at Gate 2. Finally, because a heavy spending commitment is the result of a Go decision at Gate 3, the results of the financial analysis are an important part of this screen.

If the decision is Go, Gate 3 sees commitment to the product definition and agreement on the project plan that charts the path forward: the development plan and the preliminary operations and marketing plans are reviewed and approved at this gate. The full project team—an empowered, multifunctional team headed by a leader with authority—is designated.

Stage 3: Development

Stage 3 witnesses the implementation of the development plan and the physical development of the product. For lengthy projects, numerous milestones and periodic project reviews are built into the development plan. These are not gates per se: Go/Kill decisions are not made here; rather these milestone check points provide for project control and management. Some in-house or lab testing usually occurs in this stage as well. The "deliverable" at the end of Stage 3 is a lab-tested prototype of the product.

The emphasis in Stage 3 is on technical work. But marketing and manufacturing activities also proceed in parallel. For example, market-analysis and customer-feedback work continue concurrently with the technical development, with constant customer opinion sought on the product as it takes shape during development. These activities are back-and-forth or iterative, with each development result—for example, rapid prototype, working model, first prototype, etc.—taken to the customer for assessment and feedback. Meanwhile, detailed test plans, market launch plans, and production or operations plans, including production facilities requirements, are developed. An updated financial analysis is prepared, while regulatory, legal, and patent issues are resolved.

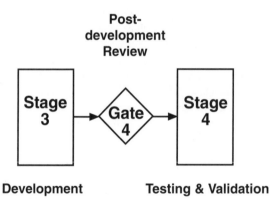

Gate 4: Postdevelopment Review

The postdevelopment review is a check on the progress and the continued attractiveness of the product and project. Development work is reviewed and checked, ensuring that the work has been completed in a quality fashion, and that the developed product is indeed consistent with the original definition specified at Gate 3.

This gate also revisits the economic question via a revised financial analysis based on new and more accurate data. The test or validation plans for the next stage are approved for immediate implementation, and the detailed marketing and operations plans are reviewed for probable future execution.

Stage 4: Testing and Validation

This stage tests and validates the entire viability of the project: the product itself, the production process, customer acceptance, and the economics of the project. A number activities are undertaken at Stage 4:

- *In-house product tests:* extended lab tests to check on product quality and product performance under controlled or lab conditions.
- *User or field trials of the product:* to verify that the product functions under actual use conditions, and also to gauge potential customers' reactions to the product—to establish purchase intent.
- *Trial, limited, or pilot production:* to test, debug, and prove the production process, and to determine more precise production costs and throughputs.
- *Pre-test market, test market, or trial sell:* to gauge customer reaction, measure the effectiveness of the launch plan, and determine expected market share and revenues.
- *Revised financial analysis:* to check on the continued economic viability of the project, based on new and more accurate revenue and cost data.

An illustration:

In the development of their new film recorder for PC graphics, the CI 3000 and 5000, Polaroid first undertook extensive alpha tests in their own lab to ensure that the product met all design specs. Next the product went to the field for field trials. Here potential customers were given the opportunity to use (and in some cases, abuse) the product in order to verify that the product did work under live field conditions and to establish purchase intent: "The field trial was very positive. . . . it did change some of the features and ergonomic factors. But it confirmed high demand in the marketplace and it was more a matter of fine tuning . . ."

Another illustration:

During the development of a new telephone handset, a major telephone manufacturer assembled 100 prototype units. Fifty of these were used for in-house reliability tests (lab tests). The other 50 were installed in customers' homes. The customer trials proved crucial to the product's eventual success, when a potentially disastrous flaw in the product's design was uncovered: in the wall-phone design, the receiver fell off the hook when a nearby door was slammed hard enough to jiggle the wall. The lab, of course, had solid concrete walls, and the problem went undetected until the customer test. A minor design modification overcame the problem before thousands of phones with faulty receivers found their way into households.

Ironically, the same company was not quite so lucky in a subsequent product development some years later. In the interest of saving some time, the field trials were cut short. And it wasn't until the product was commercialized that the design flaw was discovered: the fact that the phone's circuitry picked up local radio signals, something that was not found in the lab, but was unfortunately discovered in thousands of households following launch!

Gate 5: Precommercialization Business Analysis

This final gate opens the door to full commercialization—market launch and full production or operations start up. It is the final point at which the project can still be killed. This gate focuses on the quality of the activities at the Testing and Validation Stage and their results. Criteria for passing the gate focus largely on expected financial return and appropriateness of the launch and operations start-up plans. The operations and marketing plans are reviewed and approved for implementation in Stage 5.

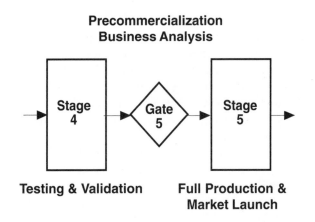

Precommercialization Business Analysis

Stage 5: Full Production and Market Launch

This final stage involves implementation of both the marketing launch plan and the production or operations plan. Given a well thought out plan of action and backed by appropriate resources, and of course, barring any unforeseen events, it should be clear sailing for the new product . . . another new product success!

Postimplementation Review

At some point following commercialization (often 6–18 months), the new product project must be terminated. The team is disbanded, and the product becomes a "regular product" in the firm's product line. This is also the point where the project and product's performance is reviewed. The latest data on revenues, costs, expenditures, profits, and timing are compared to projections to gauge performance. Finally a post-audit—a critical assessment of the project's strengths and weaknesses, what we can learn from this project, and how we can do the next one better—is carried out. This review marks the end of the project. Note that the project team and leader remain responsible for the success of the project through this postlaunch period, right up to the point of the postimplementation review.

What the Stage-Gate System Is Not!

With this overview of the new product game plan fresh in our minds, and before we get into its details in the next chapter, let's deal with some potential misconceptions right now. The stage-gate game plan is designed to *facilitate and speed products to market.* Here are some of the things the system *is not*:

1. Not a Functional, Phased Review System

Don't confuse this game plan of the nineties with the traditional "phased review" process of the 1960s. This phased review process, endorsed by NASA and others, broke the innovation process into stages, each stage reporting to a function or a department. Implemented with the best of intentions, the process managed to almost double the length of developments. Why? The process was designed like a relay race—activities in sequence rather than in parallel; there were hand-offs throughout the process, as one team or function passed the project on to the next department (and with hand-offs, there arise the inevitable fumbles!); and there was no commitment to the project from beginning to end by any one group or team—accountability was missing.

By contrast, the nineties game plan is built for speed. The stages are multifunctional: they are not dominated by a single functional area (for example, the notion of an "R&D stage" followed by a "manufacturing stage" and then a "marketing stage" is obsolete). The play is rapid, with activities occurring in parallel rather than in series, and with defined gates and criteria for efficient, timely decision making. And the game plan is executed from idea to postlaunch by a dedicated and empowered team of players drawn from the functional areas, and headed by a leader.

2. Not a Rigid System

The game plan or new product process outlined in Figure 5.4 is fairly typical. Most companies tailor the model to their own circumstances and build flexibility into their game plans. For example, not all projects pass through every stage or gate of the model:

- In some firms, management defines two or three categories of projects, based on project scope, investment, and risk level. These range from sales developments or product modifications (relatively simple, short–time frame and low-risk projects) through to major projects involving heavy expenditures and high risks. And appropriate routes are decided for each type of project, with lower risk projects typically omitting some stages and gates.

• In any one project, stages, gates, and activities can be omitted or bypassed. Similarly, activities can be moved from one stage to another—for example, moving an activity ahead one stage in the event of long lead times. The point is that the game plan is a guide or road map, and that deviations or detours are made consciously and deliberately, and with full awareness of the facts, consequences, and risks. Decisions to skip over, delete, or shift activities or gates are not ad hoc, arbitrary, and made for the wrong reasons; rather, they are decided thoughtfully, and agreed to by the team and gatekeepers at the preceding gate.

3. Not a Bureaucratic System

Properly implemented, the stage-gate system fosters all the attributes of a timely, successful development effort: a clearly visible road map with defined deliverables and objectives; a multifunctional team approach with empowerment; and defined decision points with spelled-out criteria. Sadly, some managers see any system as an opportunity to impose more paperwork, more meetings, and more red tape. Remember: the objective here is a systematic, streamlined process, not a bogged-down bureaucratic one!

Built-in Success Factors

The logic of a well-designed game plan, such as the stage-gate system in Figure 5.4, is appealing because it incorporates many of the factors and lessons vital to success and speed that I highlighted in the previous chapters. For example:

1. The process places much more emphasis on the homework or predevelopment activities. Stages 1 and 2—the preliminary investigation and the detailed investigation—are essential steps before the door to development is opened at Gate 3.
2. The process is multidisciplinary and multifunctional. It is built around an empowered, multifunctional team. Each stage consists of technical, marketing, production and even financial activities, necessitating the active involvement of people from all of these areas. The gates are multifunctional too: gates are manned by gatekeepers from different functions or departments in the firm—the managers that own the resources needed for the next stage.
3. Parallel processing speeds up the process. Activities in each stage are undertaken concurrently, rather than sequentially, with much interaction between players and actions within each stage.
4. A strong market orientation is a feature of the game plan. Marketing inputs begin in Stage 1, and remain an important facet of every stage from beginning to end of the process. Projects cannot pass the gates until the marketing actions have been completed in a quality way.
5. There is more focus. The game plan builds in decision points in the form of gates. These gates weed out poor projects early in the process and help focus scarce resources on the truly deserving projects. They also ensure quality of execution by requiring that project team members and the leader meet certain standards in terms of quality of actions.

6. A product-definition step is built into the process at Stage 2, the detailed investigation. It is here that the project and product are both defined and justified. This product definition is a key deliverable to Gate 3; without it, the project cannot proceed to Development.
7. There is a strong focus on quality of execution throughout. The stages and recommended activities within each stage lay out a road map for the project leader and team: there is less chance of critical errors of omission. The gates provide the critical quality-control checks in the process: unless the project meets certain quality standards, its fails to pass the gate.

Suggestion: As soon as you finish this chapter, take a hard look at your own new product process in your company. First, do you have a process? If yes, lay it out in front of you. Go through the seven success factors listed just above, and ask yourself: "Does my new product process build in each of these items?" If not, read on.

Towards a New Product Process

Many investigations, including our NewProd studies, have provided clues and insights into how to mount a successful product innovation program. This chapter has translated these insights and lessons into the skeleton of a carefully crafted new product process—a game plan that provides a road map and discipline, focuses on quality of execution, builds in the up-front homework, is strongly market-oriented, and is backed by appropriate resources.

The benefits of the stage-gate process are evident. The model puts discipline into a process that, in too many firms, is ad hoc and seriously deficient. The process is visible, relatively simple, and easy to understand and communicate: as one manager exclaimed, "At least we're all reading from the same page of the same book." The requirements are clear: for example, what is expected of a project team at each stage and gate is spelled out. The process provides a road map to facilitate the project, and it better defines the project leader's objectives and tasks: the deliverables for each gate become the objectives of the team and leader.

But the design and implementation of a stage-gate game plan is more complex than simply photocopying a flow model from Figure 5.4 of this book and displaying it on the office bulletin board. The next three chapters provide a much more detailed examination of the elements of this stage-gate model. We begin in Chapter 6 by focusing on the vital predevelopment stages: from idea through to the point of product development.

The Early Game—From Idea to Development

6

Ideas won't keep. Something must be done about them. When the idea is new, its custodians have fervor, live for it, and if need be, die for it.
Alfred North Whitehead, English philosopher and mathematician.

The First Few Plays of the Game

The game is won or lost in its first few plays. In Chapter 2, we saw that the seeds of disaster were often sown in the early phases of a new product project—poor homework, a lack of a customer orientation, and poor quality of execution (especially in the early stages). In Chapters 3 and 4, we witnessed that the keys to new product success often lie in the up-front or predevelopment activities. Sadly, these early stages receive little time, effort, and attention.

The steps where an idea, often crude and poorly explained, is miraculously transformed to a winning product concept and solid product definition—one ready for development—is the topic of Chapter 6. Here we focus on the critical up-front actions that precede the actual physical development of the product, yet are so crucial to the product's ultimate success. These steps are laid out in the form of a more detailed flow model—Figure 6.1—which takes us from the project's inception—the idea—through Stages 1 and 2 and up to Gate 3, the door to development.

Ideas Are the Trigger

The trigger for the process is a new product idea. An idea occurs when technological possibilities are matched with market needs and expected market demand. Ideas may be generated by the marketplace—a recognition of unsatisfied customer needs, direct requests from customers, or a competitive product. Such market-pull ideas represent the source for the majority of new product projects. But technology-push ideas—which are generated by research, from science or technology, or the result of a serendipitous discovery—also play an important role, particularly in radical innovations or breakthrough products.

Figure 6.1:   The Game Plan up to Gate 3

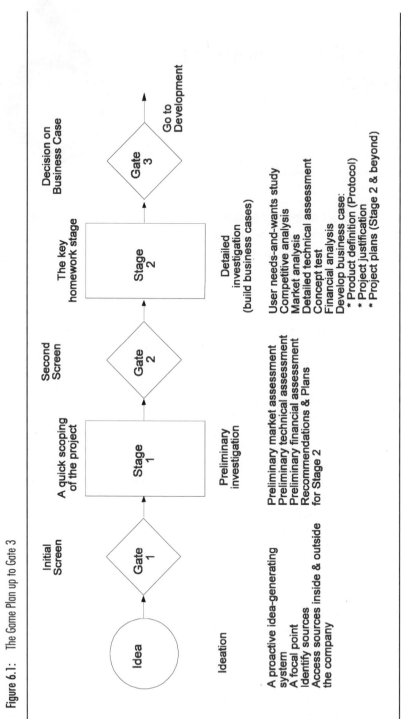

Figure 6.1   Reprinted from *Business Horizons*, May–June 1990. Copyright 1990 by the Foundation for the School of Business at Indiana University. Used with permission.

A good new product idea can make or break a project: ideas are the feedstock of the new product process. Since it is the product idea that initiates the whole process, there is a great need for new product ideas—both quality and quantity. The attrition rate of new product ideas and projects is large, and many firms are bankrupt of enough good new products ideas. An important facet of a successful new product program is the development of an idea generating system.

Suggestion: Review new product idea generation in your company. Where do new product ideas come from? Where should they be coming from? Are the ideas good ones? Do you have enough of them? How does your company actively solicit new product ideas? Do you have a new product idea generating system in your firm? If the answers to these questions make you uneasy, don't worry: this chapter suggests some concrete actions that can be taken to improve idea generation.

Eleven Ways to Get More and Better New Product Ideas

1. Establish a focal point.

Idea generation is everyone's job and no one's responsibility. There's no one in the company or business unit charged specifically with the responsibility of idea generation. And often when ideas do surface, there's no one to send it to for action.

The first step in setting up an idea generating system is to assign one person the responsibility of stimulating, generating, and receiving new product ideas—a focal point for ideas. This person identifies the sources of ideas both inside and outside the company, and then sets about establishing flow lines or mechanisms to generate or solicit ideas from these sources. The focal point also is the person that employees phone, fax, or write to about a new product idea.

Implicit in this role is action: the focal person moves the idea to the next step in the process; Gate 1 or the initial screen. The commitment here is that if an idea is submitted, then it gets a hearing and a decision. Further, the focal person is also responsible for providing feedback from Gate 1 to the idea submitter: a timely answer is essential in order to encourage further submissions.

2. Identify the sources of ideas.

Where do new product ideas come from in your company? And where should they be coming from? The second step is to make a list of possible sources of ideas. Table 6.1 provides a starting point. Note that while ideas from inside the company are the obvious place to begin, Von Hippel argues that the majority of good new product ideas in many industries are derived from the customer.[1]

Step 3 is to establish flow lines or mechanisms to solicit ideas (or stimulate idea generation) from each source. Let's spend a moment on each.

Table 6.1:   Primary Sources of R & D Ideas in 40 Companies

INTERNAL SOURCES	NUMBER OF COMPANIES
Research and engineering	33
Sales, marketing, and planning	30
Production	12
Other executives and board of directors	10
EXTERNAL SOURCES	
Customers and prospects	16
Contract research organizations and consultants	7
Technical publications	4
Competitors	4
Universities	3
Inventors	3
Unsolicited sources	3
Advertising agency	2
Suppliers	2
Government agencies	2

Adapted from B.V. Dean, *Evaluating, Selecting, and Controlling R & D Projects*, research study no. 89 (New York: American Management Association, 1968).

3. Use customers as a source.

Customers represent a huge and often untapped potential source of ideas. Here's how to tap these:

1. *Use group discussion with customers:* Try mounting several focus group discussions (professionally moderated) with groups of invited customers or potential users. The group discussion can focus on problems customers are having with your or competitive products. Alternately, a brainstorming session with customers can identify possible solutions or customer wishes for new products.

   One major electrical equipment manufacturer arranged a weekend for a management retreat to identify new product opportunities. Almost as an afterthought, half a dozen key industrial customers were invited. The customers enthusiastically accepted, and in fact proved to be the source of the most original and promising ideas.

2. *Set up customer panels:* A permanent panel of selected customers that meets on a regular basis is another good source of ideas. This approach has been used successfully in industries from sporting goods (panels of minor or little league coaches) to consumer packaged goods (panels of heads-of-households).

3. *Survey your customers:* Develop a research questionnaire, pick a representative sample of customers (or potential customers) and phone or visit them to identify your next new product winner. The most straightforward survey is fairly traditional: direct questioning to identify customer needs, wants,

and preferences; the order-winning criteria; customer likes and dislikes; and stated problems regarding current products. New product ideas often emerge. More difficult is to probe customer *latent needs and problems:* this usually means studying the customer to understand how he or she uses the product, what problems and difficulties he or she has, his or her real needs, and what a "better solution" might be.

4. *Work with lead users:* Von Hippel's work on the customer as a source of ideas and new products leads to a number of specific suggestions.[2] Von Hippel sees customers not only as a source of potential ideas, but sometimes as a source of partially completed new products. In many cases, the customer has actually experimented with your product, making improvements and modifications to suit his or her needs. Identify these lead users—they typically represent only a small proportion of your customer base—and work with them to find out if they've modified your product or what suggestions they have. Traditional market research targets the "average" user and asks "what are you looking for?" By contrast, lead-user research focuses on the leading edge customer and asks, "What have you done lately?"—a much more concrete question.

4. Competitors trigger ideas.

Competitors represent another valuable source of new product ideas. The objective is not to copy your competitors—copycat products have a much lower chance of success—but to gain ideas for new and improved products from competitors. Often the knowledge of a competitive product will stimulate your team in arriving at an even better product idea.

Routinely survey your competition. Periodically perform a complete review of competitive products, particularly new ones. Obtain a sample of your competitor's new product. Once obtained, undertake a thorough evaluation of the product from a technical standpoint. Arrange an internal brainstorming session aimed at improving on your competitor's product. Determine how well the product is doing in the marketplace from published data or from your sales force and customers. Finally, obtain copies of the advertising and literature for the product: knowing what the competitor is emphasizing or how it is positioning the product can yield new insights for your own new products.

5. Trade shows—an excellent source.

Trade shows present the perfect opportunity to uncover dozens of ideas at relatively little expense. Where else can you find all that's new in your field displayed for public consumption? And where else can you find customers ready to give their opinions on new products presented at the show?

Organize a trade show visitation program. Get a list of the relevant trade shows in your industry. Arrange to have at least one person visit each show, even if your firm is not displaying, for the sole purpose of getting new product ideas. This should not be a social event but a serious intelligence mission. Arm your intelligence officer with a sketch pad, a notebook, and a list of key exhibitors. His or her task is to visit each of the key exhibit booths and to itemize and describe new products on display. Sketches and brochures add detail to this description. At the end of the trip, your intelligence officer's task is make a formal presentation to the rest of the new products group: "here's what I found that was new at the show, and here are some product ideas that we might build on."

6. Trade publications provide ideas from around the world.

As most intelligence officers will attest, the majority of "intelligence information" is in the public domain—it's just a matter of gaining access to it in a regular and coordinated fashion.

Trade publications report new product introductions via advertisements and new product announcement sections. Like a trade show, these publications provide the stimulus for your group to conceive an even better idea. Don't ignore foreign publications: in certain countries, new products may be years or months ahead of yours, while foreign publications may feature unfamiliar competitors who offer products that you've never seen before. So hire an outside clipping service, domestically and abroad, to clip relevant ads, articles, and announcements in selected journals. Alternately, set up an internal clipping service, assigning different publications to each person in your group.

7. Patents—the universal clearing house.

The files in the U.S. patent office contain millions of American and foreign patents, and thousands more are added each year. To keep abreast of developments and to stimulate their new product ideas, some firms keep a close eye on the weekly *Official Gazette*, which provides a precise record of the recent patents issued.

8. Idea brokers—the idea middlemen.

The trade in ideas is big business. Over the last several decades an army of middlemen has sprung up—people in the idea trading, selling, and licensing business. The number of "go-between" firms precludes a complete listing here; many are local organizations or specific to one industry. How many of these idea brokers is your firm in regular contact with? If the answer is none or few, find out from a trade directory who the appropriate patent, license, and idea brokers are in your field, and make contact; get on their mailing lists and assign someone the task of regularly reviewing their offerings.

9. Suppliers—an untapped source.

Suppliers are often a good source of new product ideas and help. This is particularly so when the supplier is a large firm with well-funded R&D and customer applications or technical service facilities. Suppliers too are looking for new applications for their products, and often come up with ideas for their customers. Have your technical and marketing people regularly visit your supplier's lab and technical service facilities; and stay in close touch with your supplier's technical people. Chances are they're working on a development that could lead to your next new product winner.

10. Private inventors—an ignored source.

Yet another source of new product ideas, and sometimes fully developed new products, is the private inventor. For example, Black & Decker makes use of "do-it-yourselfers" who use their tools, and who often have new product ideas and inventions worthy of investigation. The problem with this source is the legal risk—how to handle the unsolicited idea in the context of the law relating to trade secrets and patents. Just in case you think it can't happen to you, consider the plight of General Electric. The case involves a private inventor (a university professor at MIT), who claims that he gave GE the idea for R&D work leading to a new structure for a synthetic industrial diamond. As if the legal problems weren't enough, GE is suddenly faced with bad publicity as the news show, *60 Minutes,* aired a segment on the dispute; and Tom Clancy, noted author of books such as *The Hunt for Red October,* has publicly gone to bat for the beleaguered professor.

The point is this: If your firm is working on the product and receives an unsolicited idea for the same product or invention, you may stand to be accused of stealing the idea. As a result, some firms simply refuse to deal with the private inventor. This is unfortunate, because the outcome is lost opportunities. Even a refusal can land you in legal difficulties. Crawford studied what happened when 35 unsolicited ideas were submitted to 166 companies.[3] The results were shocking: two-thirds of the ideas were handled in a legally dangerous way! Crawford recommends the following procedure:

1. Get the idea in writing (refuse oral submissions).
2. The receiver should forward the idea immediately to the firm's legal department. Don't read the idea!
3. The legal department gives the submission a number or identifier, and sends a form letter to the submitter, indicating the conditions under which the company considers unsolicited ideas, and that a waiver form must be signed. The waiver should stipulate that the submission is made free of obligation on the firm's part, that the firm may be working on a similar project, and that the firm may use all or part of the idea and pay what it feels is reasonable.
4. Only after the signed waiver is received should the submission be reopened and considered.

11. Universities—a brain trust in your back yard.

University professors and researchers are a source of ideas. Scholars working in science, engineering, or medicine can offer a wealth of information on developments in their fields. They may lack an appreciation of the commercial potential of their work or the ability to commercialize it, however. To exploit this source, consider establishing contact with key researchers in your field at various universities. Innovation centers or technology transfer centers have been set up at a number of schools to help professors commercialize their inventions. So survey the universities to locate these innovation centers and make contact with them.

Suggestion: A number of possible outside sources of new product ideas have been identified. Not all will be applicable to your firm, but some will. With your new idea "focal point" person in place, the task becomes one of identifying the appropriate sources. Next, determine how best to gain access to each source—how to establish a "flow line" between the source and your company's idea person. Start with the suggestions made above; once an attempt is made, you will probably discover other idea sources and more convenient ways of accessing them. Then you will be on your way to having an effective external idea-generating system in place.

Getting Ideas from Inside the Company

How many people are employed in your company? Several dozen, a hundred, five thousand, more? Is it not unrealistic to assume that each employee might have one new product idea during his or her career at the company? Employees are often an excellent source of new product ideas, but all too often they're not heard from. Why? Here are some frequently cited reasons:

- *Our employees aren't very creative*: Nonsense! Just about everyone has the potential for being creative. So what has your company done lately to encourage that latent creativity?
- *Our employees submit dumb ideas—ones that are way off base:* This may be partly true. But then, maybe your employees should be told what kind of ideas your looking for—what's on base versus off base. Not all ideas will be good ones, of course. But if you discourage all ideas simply because many are bad ones, you'll be missing out on a handful of potentially good ones.
- *Even if an employee did have a good idea, he or she wouldn't know what to do with it—where to send it for action:* This is a common problem. The designation of an idea person or focal point, together with some in-house publicity, will overcome this obstacle.
- *People who submit ideas get discouraged; they send in ideas but never get any feedback:* The best way to kill internal idea generation is to keep people in the dark. Not only does the focal person act as an idea receiver, but his or her job is also to get a response on the idea (i.e., take it to Gate 1 for an Initial Screen) and to provide timely feedback to the submitter.

In short, many of the potential barriers to internal idea generation can be easily removed. Given the number of employees in your firm and the potential for generating new product ideas, isn't it worth a little time and effort to encourage them to develop and submit their ideas?

Now let's look at several approaches to internal idea stimulation: suggestion schemes, group creativity sessions, and "scouting time."

Suggestion Schemes

Probably the least expensive way to solicit new product ideas is to implement a suggestion scheme. Most companies have cost-savings suggestion schemes. Posters are mounted on bulletin boards throughout the office and factory urging employees to submit their cost-saving ideas. Often employees share in some of the cost-savings dividends. But new product suggestion schemes are much rarer. Does management assume that employees are quite creative in generating cost-saving ideas, but real dullards when it comes to money-making ideas? Experiences in many firms prove this assumption quite wrong!

Try implementing a new product idea suggestion scheme for your employees. There are several possible formats:

- an ongoing suggestion scheme whereby employees fill out an idea suggestion form and drop it in a box or fax it to the idea person.
- a contest, perhaps an "Idea of the Month" contest, with prizes and awards made every month or two for the best ideas.
- a targeted effort, such as sending memos to targeted employee groups asking them for their new product ideas.

The following tips will help you set up an internal suggestion scheme:

1. *Publicize the scheme widely.* Make sure that every employee is aware of the program. Use posters, memos, the company magazine, sales conferences, and employee meetings to generate enthusiasm at all levels.
2. *Handle ideas promptly and provide timely feedback* to the submitter. You must have a process in place to handle this front end relatively quickly: perhaps a very quick and cursory prescreen to weed out the obvious misfits, and then a Gate 1 screen to review the more serious ideas. Your response to the submitter must make it clear that the idea was carefully considered, and, if rejected, on which criteria it failed to meet the mark. The need for clear and visible criteria at Gate 1 becomes paramount (see Chapter 7).
3. *Welcome all ideas.* Never belittle an idea (or submitter) and certainly, you shouldn't expect a high proportion to be winners. Even though the idea may appear to be inane, the person should be thanked anyway. Remember: you must shovel a lot of earth to find a few diamonds.
4. *Provide guidance and assistance.* Make it easy for the submitter. Develop a submission kit, including a guide booklet. In this guide, spell out what kinds of ideas you're looking for (for example, in which markets or product areas). List the criteria against which ideas will be judged, and provide an idea submission form—perhaps one page with topic headings—to aid the submitter. And spell out the prizes or awards!

5. *Offer incentives.* Different companies have different cultures, of course, and what is an acceptable reward or recognition in one firm may not be in another. Develop what you believe to be appropriate rewards or recognition for the individual or team submitting a good idea. And don't wait for years until the product is on the market to recognize the submitter. Make the rewards fairly rapidly after submission: for example, if the idea clears Gate 1 or Gate 2.
6. *Manage the suggestion scheme.* Management should set objectives: for example, a specified number of ideas per year. The ideas program should be an ongoing one (not a one-shot event), and it should be given periodic publicity boosts. Finally, the efficacy of the program should be annually reviewed.

Group Creativity Methods

Given the right environment, *most people can become quite creative.* This is the theory underlying group creativity techniques—methods designed to enable people, working in groups, to arrive at creative ideas or solutions. These methods include: brainstorming, synectics, reverse brainstorming, attribute listing, focus groups, and others. Rather than reviewing each method in detail, let's take a closer look at the most popular one (and one you can run yourself), namely brainstorming.

Creativity will flourish in a noncritical environment, even with a group of seemingly uncreative adults. Brainstorming creates the right environment: it is a group session in which all criticism or attempts to evaluate or judge ideas are banned.

The problem with most business meetings is that they tend to focus on the evaluative rather than the creative. Consider the two modes that occur in any meeting: *ideation* and *evaluation.* A meeting is convened to solve a problem. One person suggests an idea—that's *ideation* at work. Immediately the rest of the group comments on the suggestion—on its pros and cons—that's the *evaluation* mode. The difficulty is that in adult meetings, one mode—evaluation—tends to dominate. Indeed we adults are much more comfortable critiquing, judging, and evaluating than we are at suggesting new ideas. That's the stuff of children!

The notion behind brainstorming is that *we can only operate effectively in one mode at a time*—in this case, the ideation mode. All criticism, judgement, or critiquing is taboo in the meeting. The objective is ideas and lots of them.

Here are some tips in organizing a brainstorming session:

1. *Invite an eclectic group.* Try to avoid inviting the same old people. Rather, go to other departments, functions, divisions, and even countries in your company for your list of invitees. Seven to ten people work best. If possible, try to invite some outsiders—some distributors, customers, or an industry

expert (but be aware of the downside: proprietary information cannot be discussed, which may limit the effectiveness of the group).

2. *Run the session off-site.* Stay away from the office: you don't want people constantly interrupted or running for the phone. That's not good for creativity.
3. *Have a presession mailing.* Send some background information to participants ahead of time, so that their brain has already begun to churn the problem or issue. Make sure they understand the purpose of the session before arrival.
4. *Ensure that the "rules" of brainstorming all well understood by everyone:* that there is to be no judgement of any kind—negative words, facial expressions, or body language; and get each and every participant to agree to these rules. (Some groups use a penalty: ten dollars in a pot for every negative word; or the offender wears a dunce cap for being critical.)
5. *Have a moderator who runs the session.* This can be you. The moderator's role is to welcome all attendees, restate the objectives of the session, run a warm-up session (or some game to get people into the mood), act as a referee (ensuring that no one violates the "no criticisms" rule), and record the ideas on flip charts.

Many brainstorming sessions are poorly handled: the participants aren't clear on the purpose; the same old gang attends; there are constant interruptions, and the moderator isn't tough enough to enforce the "no criticisms" rule. Sadly, the results are predictable—few good ideas! But properly done, brainstorming can be a most effective way to generate dozens of solid ideas for new products.

Suggestion: Try running a brainstorming session at your company. You can be the moderator. Invite a multifunctional, eclectic group. Explain the rules of brainstorming, and follow the five points listed above. You'll be pleasantly surprised at the results of the session.

Scouting Time

A handful of progressive firms encourage select groups of employees to be creative by providing free time—"scouting time"—and some financial help for pet projects. For example, some divisions at 3M have a day-a-week rule for technical employees: R&D people are encouraged to work on their own "discovery" projects with the hope that some useful idea—for example, another Post-It Notes product—will result. Rohm and Haas provides about 10 percent of a technical person's time for scouting work to devote to pet projects. And money can usually be found "under the table" or from some other research account to cover out-of-pocket costs (for example, equipment needs). Du Pont has a seed money fund to support innovative, embryonic projects that have been rejected and have not received funding via normal sources. Not every employee takes part in these free time projects, of course; but the hope is that a handful of creative people will, and that innovative ideas will be the result.

Perhaps the only negative facet of these free time allocations is that they are usually restricted to technical people. Why shouldn't a creative marketing person have 10 percent of her time off to explore innovative market opportunities—ones that are "outside of the nine dots" of this year's strategic plan?

Using this scouting time, it is often possible to "progress" a project well down the pipe before asking for formal approval and funding. "Isn't this dangerous?" ask some people. Yes and no—it depends on how far down the road the project progresses. Some companies, which have implemented formal new product processes, are happy to see these scouting projects arrive as late as Gate 2 or even Gate 3 (that is, Stage 1 and 2 have been undertaken "outside the system" and using scouting time). I agree. My argument is that highly innovative, embryonic ideas are fragile things; and perhaps a select few should be handled in a special way. But the majority won't follow this route, nor should they. Otherwise we truly *would have* chaos!

The Idea Bank

Not all new product ideas get acted upon. For some the timing is wrong; others aren't sufficiently developed—they need a little more work; for still others, there simply aren't the resources available, or they don't mesh with the company's current priorities. One danger is that some potentially good ideas may be lost forever. Consider setting up an "idea bank"—a holding tank for inactive ideas. In this bank are ideas that need more work, ideas that have been rejected at Gate 1 (or simply haven't been moved ahead), or even ideas that no one has taken to Gate 1.

Some companies make this idea bank an open file: the inventory of ideas is publicly displayed on E-mail. The hope here is that some creative person in the company will add to an existing idea, or figure out a solution to a barrier, or perhaps even arrive at original ideas him- or herself as a result of reading the idea list.

Suggestion: I've identified a number of potential outside sources of ideas and have suggested ways to tap into them. Similarly internal techniques—from creativity sessions to contests—have been outlined. These are summarized in the 25 ways to increase the effectiveness of idea generation listed in Table 6.2. Pick the sources and approaches from the list that are most appropriate for your firm, and then design your own proactive idea generation system. If you do, you'll be blessed with a plethora of good ideas, ready for an initial screen and to move in to Stage 1 of the new product process.

On to Stage 1: Preliminary Investigation

Assume that we've done a good job of idea generation. We've got lots of good ideas. Now the task is to sift and sort through these ideas to see which ones are worthy of more time and money. That's the role of the Initial Screen, Gate 1. Designing these gates, screens, or decision points is no easy task, so I devote

Table 6.2:   Twenty-five Action Items for Generating New Product Ideas

1. Establish a *focal point*—a person to stimulate and handle ideas.

2. Identify possible sources of new product ideas, prioritize, and access these sources.

3. Use *focus groups* of customers.

4. Set up a *user panel* to discuss needs, wants, and problems that might lead to new product ideas.

5. Survey your customers.

6. Observe customers as they use (or misuse) your product.

7. Identify your lead users—the *innovative customers*.

8. Hire sales and technical people who can recognize potential new products. Train, encourage, and motivate them to do so.

9. Routinely survey your competition. Analyze their products, strategies, and business successes.

10. Organize a trade show visitation program.

11. Set up a clipping service for domestic and foreign trade publications. Look for new product announcements.

12. Examine the patent files and the *Official Gazette* regularly.

13. Get on the mailing list of relevant *idea brokers* and product license brokers in your industry.

14. Attend product licensing shows.

15. Visit your suppliers' labs and spend time with their technical people.

16. Set up a procedure for handling ideas submitted by private inventors in a legally sound way.

17. Visit key universities and researchers. Consider putting several university researchers on a retainer.

18. Set up a new product *idea suggestion scheme* in your company.

19. Run a new product *idea contest*.

20. Run some *group creativity sessions*. Use the methods suggested in this chapter.

21. Organize creativity sessions involving *sales and technical people in the same session*.

22. Invite lead or *highly innovative users to a creativity or brainstorming session*.

23. Provide *free time* or scouting time for employees to work on pet projects. Set up a *seed money fund* to support creative projects.

24. Set up an *idea bank*. Make it an open file so that everyone can see the ideas and add to them.

25. *Do something with the ideas*—don't just let them sit there! Get them evaluated (Gate 1) and provide feedback to the idea originator. And if the idea is sound, then progress it to the next stage.

Chapter 7 to this task. But for now, let's walk the idea through the first two stages of the new product process: let's let the idea pass Gate 1 and give it a green light for Stage 1, Preliminary Investigation.

The spirit of Stage 1 is to "spend a little money, gather some information, so that the project can be reevaluated at Gate 2 in the light of the better information." Therefore, this first stage is a quick and inexpensive assessment of the technical merits of the project and its market prospects. Preliminary market, technical, and financial assessments make up Stage 1.

Expenditures at this preliminary stage are quite small. Although Stage 1 is the first stage where resources are formally allocated to a new product project, note that Gate 1, the initial screen, was a fairly tentative commitment—a flickering green light. Indeed, some firms place a tight limit or ceiling on Stage 1 spending and time. In short, the output of a Go decision from Gate 1 can be expressed thus: "On the basis of the very limited information available, this idea or proposal has merit. Spend no more than $10,000 and 10 person-days, and report back in one month at Gate 2, armed with much better information for a more definitive review."

Preliminary Market Assessment

Preliminary market assessment involves a quick-and-dirty market study. The purpose is to determine if the proposed product has any commercial prospects:

— to assess market attractiveness and potential;
— to gauge possible product acceptance; and
— to size up the competitive situation.

The task is to find out as much as you can about market size, growth, segments, buyer interest, and competition by a specified deadline and for a very small budget.

Given the limited budget and the short time duration of the study, this type of market assessment is clearly not a professional and scientific piece of market research. Rather it's "grunt work": getting hold of available information in-house (for example, talking with the sales force, distributors, and technical service people); examining secondary sources (for example, reports and articles published by trade magazines, associations, government agencies, and research and consulting firms); contacting potential users (for example, via a phone blitz or focus groups); and canvassing outside sources (for example, an industry expert, magazine editor, or consultant). It's tough work, much like playing detective and following up on leads, but it's surprising how much information about a product's market prospects can be gleaned from several days of solid sleuthing.

Here are some sources of market information that can be accessed relatively inexpensively for Stage 1:

• *Your library:* Your reference librarian is worth his or her weight in gold in conducting a preliminary market assessment. Use a computer search with keywords to hunt through trade magazines, journals, etc., for articles on the market and competition for your new product. If your company doesn't have its own library, try a major public library or a library at the local university's business school.

• *Key customers:* Stage 1 is premature for a detailed, large sample size customer survey. But insights from a limited number of leading, key, or trusted customers can prove very useful at this early stage:

— Hold focus groups with a handful of customers, either consumers or industrial users. In spite of their limitations, focus groups remain a cost-effective way to gain insights into customer needs, wants, and preferences, and relatively quickly.

— Have direct, face-to-face discussions with a few customers. These need not be based on a detailed questionnaire, and can even be unstructured and exploratory. For industrial goods, try to pick trusted yet representative or leading users. Talk to several people within each firm. If budgets are tight and time is pressing, try telephone interviews.

- *Advertisements:* Get your hands on your competitors' advertisements and trade literature. Find out what they are saying about their products—features and performance characteristics, as well as how competitors are trying to position their products.
- *Your own people:* Interview your own sales force and service representatives. These people are your front line troops—the eyes and ears of the company. Often they can provide you with superb information on customer habits, likes, and dislikes and the order-winning criteria, on product preferences, and on the competitive situation and pricing practices.
- *Consulting and research firms:* Some consulting and research firms publish multiclient or standardized reports that provide an overview of an industry. While not specific to your new product perhaps, these reports or studies are a cost-effective way to gain information on market size, trends, competition, etc.
- *Financial houses:* Stock brokers can even be a help. Many keep up-to-date files or can provide an overview of companies listed on the stock market. Annual reports are a help, as is the 10K report that publicly listed firms must submit to the stock exchange.
- *Government agencies:* Governments collect a myriad of data. Finding it is the problem. But don't give up before you begin. Often a phone call to a state, provincial, or federal government office will identify the right department; and that department just happens to have the report or statistics that you were looking for.
- *Industry experts:* Hire an industry expert or guru for a day or two, and pick his or her brain. Although the per diem fee may be high, the knowledge gained may save you weeks of work.
- *Editors:* Editors of trade magazines are not the normal source of market information, but on occasion have proven very useful in tracking down reports, studies, and even informed individuals. A good editor usually has a good breadth of knowledge about what's going on in an industry
- *Trade associations:* Some industries have excellent trade associations that provide excellent market data. Contact these associations. And while on the telephone, be sure to talk to the association secretary or president to seek advice about where to go for the other information you're looking for.

Here's a real-life illustration of a market assessment for Stage 1. A small firm, Isofab Inc., makes insulation products. The firm wanted to develop a new product, a sound-absorbing brick. The idea came about as a result of some lab work on ceramic spongelike materials. The product would be used chiefly in highway sound barriers. Management had no idea of market size, pricing structure, or market acceptance for the proposed premium-priced product. Development costs were estimated at about $500,000—a sizable amount for this small firm.

The owner-manager contacted a nearby business school and acquired the services of a graduate student. The student's instructions were to phone every highway department in every state and province in the U.S. and Canada; to talk to the sound abatement engineer; and to ask ten minutes' worth of questions. The questions related to the number of miles of past and future installations of sound barriers, types of barriers used, cost per square or linear foot, problems with current products, and the engineer's reactions to the new product idea. The budget for the study was $5,000.

The phone blitz was finished in less than two weeks, the student was $1,500 richer, and the owner-manager saved himself a half-million-dollar disaster. It was discovered that the market was shrinking; current barrier products, although they only reflected rather than absorbed sound, were considered adequate (they met federal regulations); and the price per foot was of prime concern to governments. Clearly there was little opportunity for a premium-priced product with features that were not perceived as benefits by the customer.

This example shows that market studies are not the sole domain of the large firm. The costs can be kept down, and one person can gather considerable and valuable information from customers or experts in a week or two of hard work.

Preliminary Technical Assessment

The *preliminary technical assessment,* a second facet of Stage 1, subjects the proposed product to the firm's technical staff—R&D, engineering, and manufacturing engineering—for appraisal. The purpose is to establish preliminary rough technical and product performance objectives; undertake a very preliminary technical feasibility study; and pinpoint possible technical risks. Specific tasks might include discussions among in-house technical and manufacturing people (occasionally outside experts will be used); a preliminary literature search (for example, a titles search); a preliminary patent search; and acquisition and review of competitive literature. The key questions concern the technical viability of the product:

- Approximately what will the product requirements or specs be? (Note that the product definition may still be fairly vague and fluid at this early stage.)
- How would these requirements be achieved technically—is there a foreseeable technical solution?
- What are the odds that it's feasible? How, and at what cost and time?
- Can the product be manufactured? How, with what equipment, and at what cost?

- What about patent and regulatory issues? Note that regulatory, patent, and manufacturability issues are introduced and considered at this early stage!
- What are the key technical risks? And how might we handle each?

Preliminary Financial Assessment

Following preliminary technical and market assessment comes the preliminary or first-pass *business and financial assessment.* At this early stage, estimates of expected sales, costs, and investment required are likely to be highly speculative and largely conjecture. Nonetheless it makes sense to undertake a cursory financial analysis here, more as a "sanity check"—to ensure you're not spending $10 million on a one-million-dollar opportunity.

This financial analysis amounts to little more than a payback calculation based on ballpark estimates: what's the investment required in the venture; what's the probable annual income; and how many years before we see our money back?

Table 6.3 offers a summary of Stage 1. At the end of this Preliminary Investigation stage, a recommendation for the project is developed, along with proposed plans of action for Stage 2. The project now moves to Gate 2, where is it again subjected to scrutiny. But this time, the decision is to move to a much more *extensive and expensive* stage, namely the detailed investigation.

On to Stage 2: Detailed Investigation (Build the Business Case)

The detailed investigation, where we build the business case, is the last of the upfront stages before serious product development work begins. It is perhaps the most difficult and certainly the most expensive of the predevelopment stages; moreover this is the *critical homework stage*—the one that makes or breaks the project—and coincidentally the stage that we found was so often weakly handled. Stage 2 actions are summarized in Table 6.4.

What is a business case? The *business case* is the *key deliverable* to Gate 3, the decision point that opens the door to a full-fledged development project. The business case has three main components:

Table 6.3:   Summary of Stage 1 Actions: Preliminary Investigation

Preliminary market assessment	Quick scoping of market prospects for product; *not* detailed market studies or marketing research; detective work only, relying on readily available sources.
Preliminary technical assessment	Conceptual assessment of technical feasibility, probable technical solution, manufacturability, patent and legal, and possible technical risks.
Preliminary financial assessment	A sanity check: an extremely rudimentary and quick check of financial prospects; the possible payback period.
Recommendation and plans for Stage 2	A Go/Kill recommendation or proposal is developed for Stage 2, along with Stage 2 action plans.

Table 6.4:   Summary of Stage 2 Actions: Detailed Investigation (Build the Business Case)

User needs-and-wants study	Detailed market study or marketing research; face-to-face interviews, in depth; based on formal design and questionnaire; determines what is value and what is a benefit; seeks to define a winning product concept from customer's perspective; probes customers' needs, wants, preferences, choice criteria, likes, dislikes and trade-offs regarding product requirements; also product use and economics; seeks competitive product ratings.
Competitive analysis	Detailed competitive analysis; relies on varied sources; determines who the competitors are, product strong points and deficiencies, competitor strengths and weaknesses; strategies and performance.
Market analysis	Pulls together all market information from the two studies above, plus all the secondary sources noted in Stage 1; looks at market quantification, segmentation, buyer behavior, and competitive situation.
Detailed technical assessment	Translates these market inputs into a technically feasible product design or concept; may involve some lab or physical work; maps out the technical solution and technical route; highlights technical risks and solutions; looks at patent, legal, regulatory and safety issues; considers manufacturability, capital requirements, and costs; may use tools such as Quality Function Deployment (QFD).
Concept test	The final test prior to full commitment to develop product; tests the proposed product concept with the customer; market research involving face-to-face interviews; gauges interest, liking, preference, and purchase intent; may capture price sensitivity.
Financial analysis	Detailed financial analysis to justify the project; includes cash flow methods such as payback and discounted cash flow (net present value) along with sensitivity analysis.
Develop plans of action	Development of recommendation for project (Go/Kill) and a detailed development plan for Stage 3; also tentative test plans for Stage 4 and tentative marketing and manufacturing plans for Stage 5. A launch date is specified.

- definition,
- justification, and
- project plan.

Consider each component:

1. *Definition:* This answers the "what and for whom?" questions. Here the *product is defined*—that is, the "protocol" or all-party agreement spells out who the product will be targeted at, and exactly what the product will be: its benefits, features, and design requirements. Remember the importance of having sharp product definition prior to the development work beginning! This definition was discovered to be one of the key factors in success: it provides a target for development and forces discipline into Stage 2. Otherwise, the development team faces a vague product definition, one which is often a moving target.

   Inherent in this definition is the need to put "meat" on the product idea— to move from the fairly preliminary and sketchy product definition (the one we had in Stage 1) to a *sharp, clear, and complete definition* by the end of Stage 2. Also implicit in this definition is the need to build in the ingredients of product superiority: this is the opportunity to shape the product's requirements, features, and specs into a set that delivers unique and real benefits to customers.

The protocol or product definition includes:

- definition of the target market: exactly who the intended users are (be precise here!).
- description of the product concept and the benefits to be delivered.
- delineation of the positioning strategy.
- and a list of the product's features, attributes, requirements, and specs (prioritized: "must have" and "would like to have").

2. *Justification:* This second component of the business case answers the "why?" question. That is, why should your company invest in this project? This question boils down to a review of business, financial, profitability, and risk considerations. Because financial data are likely to be in error, note that this justification should also be based on nonfinancial criteria and considerations as well: qualitative issues such as competitive advantage, synergies, and market attractiveness.

3. *Project plan:* This final component of the business case answers the questions "how and by whom?" It lays out the plan of action from development through to launch, usually in the form of a time line or perhaps critical path plan. Resources required—money, people, and equipment—are also spelled out. And a launch date is specified in the business case, complete with preliminary marketing launch and manufacturing plans. Given the uncertainties of future events, however, most often these plans through to launch are very tentative. The recommendation is that the plan for the next stage (Stage 3, development) be defined in some detail—activities, events, milestones, time line, and resources required; and that plans for subsequent stages be sketches or "throw-away plans."

So what makes up this pivotal Stage 2? Figure 6.2 maps out the key actions. Building the business case involves, first of all, thorough market studies: a user "needs and wants" study to define what must be built into the product; a competitive analysis; and a concept test of the product to gauge market acceptance. Technical work, largely conceptual, translates the market "wish list" into a technically feasible concept. A business case is developed for the project: the product definition or protocol is agreed to; and a thorough project justification and detailed project plan are developed.

Let's look at each of these Stage 2 actions in more detail.

User Needs-and-Wants Study

A user needs-and-wants study is the detailed market study that is so often omitted, with disastrous consequences. Its purpose is to probe the customer in order

Figure 6.2: Stage 2: Detailed Investigation and Building the Business Case

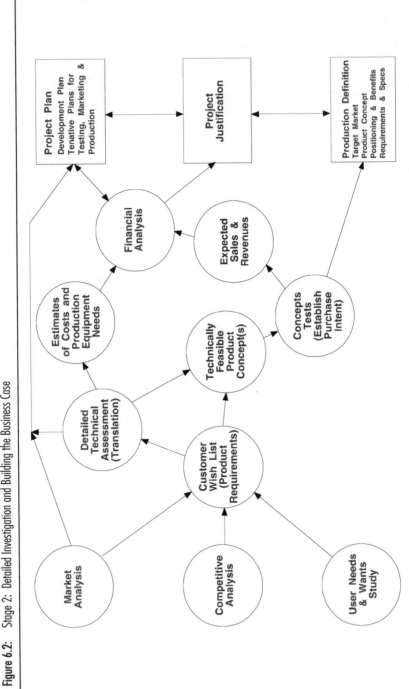

Figure 6.3:  The Means-End Link that Determines Product Value

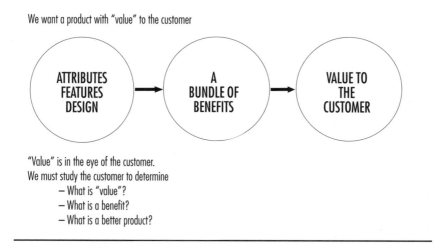

We want a product with "value" to the customer

ATTRIBUTES FEATURES DESIGN → A BUNDLE OF BENEFITS → VALUE TO THE CUSTOMER

"Value" is in the eye of the customer.
We must study the customer to determine
   — What is "value"?
   — What is a benefit?
   — What is a better product?

to put meat on the idea—to take a rather skimpy idea and develop a complete description of the product: benefits, features, performance characteristics, and design requirements. The problem is that *most of us already have a fixed idea of what the customer is looking for,* so we conveniently skip over this critical market study. We usually get it wrong!

A superior product—one that delivers *unique benefits to customers*—is the number one success factor. Never forget this fact! But how do you define this unique and superior product? This user needs-and-wants study provides the big opportunity: it enables you to fashion your sketchy product idea into a concrete and winning new product concept.

The objective here is to deliver a product with real value to the customer (Figure 6.3). Product value is in turn derived from the benefits built into and surrounding the product. And these in turn come from the product's design—its features, attributes, and performance characteristics and even its positioning.

The point is that you must understand the means-ends chain between value, benefits, and product features and performance (shown in Figure 6.3). So you must listen to the voice of the customer in order to get the product design right! That's why this user needs-and-wants study is so critical.

Specific research questions to address in this study include:

- What is value to the customer? What does he or she really value and by how much?
- What is a benefit? That is, what specific product deliverables would the customer see as being of benefit—enough to pay more for?
- What features, attributes, and performance characteristics translate into benefits and value for the customer?

Only by understanding the interrelationships between physical characteristics (i.e., product features) and customer perceptions (i.e., a customer-perceived benefit) are you in a position to sit down and design the winning new product.

The user needs-and-wants study identifies these relationships and answers the key research questions above about value and benefits. You can start with qualitative research—for example, focus groups of customers—to gain some insights into product value and desired benefits. But a focus group is a start only, and certainly not a substitute for a broader-based study. Face-to-face interviews and quantitative market research are usually required in order to gain the depth of understanding needed to proceed with product design.

The specific information objectives of this user needs-and-wants study often include:

- to determine customer needs, wants, and preferences in a new product;
- to identify the order-winning criteria, and their relative importance;
- to pinpoint areas of likes and satisfaction with current (competitive) products and also areas of dislikes, dissatisfaction, and problems with these products;
- to study how the customer uses the products—his or her use system—and what problems he or she faces in its use; and
- to understand the customer's economics of use—the total cycle costs to the customer.

Here are ten specific questions that frequently are addressed in customer interviews as part of a user needs-and-wants study:

1. How is the potential customer now solving his or her problem? For example, what current product is he or she using, and why this particular make or brand?
2. If the customer had a choice, which product or brand would he or she buy now? Why this one? Which one or ones would he or she not buy? And why not?

   These types of questions are important in that they are methods of inferring what the customer is looking for, and what he or she wishes to avoid. Here we're trying to uncover what the customer sees as having value and what his or her "hot button" is!
3. What are the customer's choice criteria—the criteria that the customer uses to make a purchase decision? And what is the relative importance or weight of each criterion in the decision?
4. How do current (competitive) products rate on each of the choice criteria? Which competitor scores highest on each criterion? Who's the lowest? And why does the customer say this—what is it about their products that causes the customer to rate them so high or low on each criterion?

   These fairly traditional questions on choice criteria and competitive ratings are important for several reasons. First, an understanding of how the customer makes his or her choice and what criteria are used is a critical input into product design: at minimum our new product must address and score high on the important criteria. Second, understanding how competitors' products score identifies areas of potential opportunity—for example, a competitive product weakness—that can be exploited via an improved design. A knowledge of the reasons that underlie these competitive ratings also provides valuable insights to the product designer regarding what to build into your new product and what to avoid. Finally, different patterns of responses among customers may suggest the existence of two or more market segments, and point to a market niche that had been missed by competitors, and can be successfully targeted by you.

5. What does the customer specifically like about competitive products? And what does he or she dislike?

6. What problems is the customer having using competitive products?

Often competitive products do have many positive design aspects, which can be borrowed and built into your new product. There's nothing wrong with copying the good facets of a competitor's product, providing one goes well beyond a mere copy. For example, in developing its successful luxury automobile, the Lexus, Toyota took a hard look at luxury cars around the world, and in particular European ones. And Toyota borrowed the best ideas from these, so that many of the design concepts in the Lexus are simply copied. A knowledge of what the positive facets of competitive products are is obviously a valuable input to the designer. Similarly identification of dislikes and problems that customers see with competitive products opens up opportunities for significant design improvement. Remember: the objective is to design a *superior product*—that means superior to the leading competitive products. So an understanding of where the competitor fails—where its Achilles heel is—is half the battle!

7. What specifically is the customer looking for in a new product? What features, attributes, and performance? Which of these are "must haves" and which are only "desirable but not essential?"

8. What trade-offs is the customer prepared to make (for example, trade-offs among various possible performance deliverables, or product features, or features versus price)?

An understanding of the customer's stated requirements—both musts and shoulds—is obviously a critical design input. But note that this customer-stated wish list is usually fairly sterile, and not enough upon which to build a winning new product design. A knowledge of customer trade-offs reveals the relative preference among various product features and attributes, and indicates relative value or importance of difference design features to the customer.

9. How does the customer use (and abuse) the product? What is the customer's "use system" in which the product must operate? And how does it fit into (or interact) with other components of the system?

10. What are the customer's economics? And how does our potential product affect his or her economics in use?

These last two questions are both critical and difficult. The first looks beyond the product itself: it probes the role the product plays in the total system. And it applies to products from prepared food entrées (the kitchen and household are the system) through to telecommunications components. The economics or "value in use" is fundamental to understanding how you can deliver a product that yields better economic value—for example, by saving the customer money over the total life of the product or in some other facet of his system.

Consider the following example:

A consumer goods firm, which markets a wide variety of cleaning products, wishes to enter the window cleaner market with a new product. The product idea was born in the marketing group, largely because of the magnitude of the market, the dominance of a single competitor's brand, and the gap in the firm's product portfolio. But the idea for the new product is fuzzy—there are no winning concepts on the table. In fact, the project almost fails a preliminary evaluation, simply because there is no competitive product advantage. The idea is sterile!

A user needs-and-wants study is commissioned. Qualitative research, undertaken via consumer focus groups, provides some insights to the project team about what is important to buyers and what is wrong with competitive products. The search for product advantage is underway. Next, observation is used, whereby users are videotaped as they use the competitors' products to clean windows. Personal interviews are conducted with consumers to determine their needs and wants, likes, dislikes, and problems.

These market studies reveal competitor weaknesses and also things consumers are looking for in their "ideal window cleaner." For example, the competitors' products:

- go on too wet—why not a drier spray?
- tend to streak—surely there's a better way here—perhaps a different surfactant?
- aren't tough enough—don't get that baked-on grime off exterior windows.
- can't be used for anything except cleaning windows—why can't they be multipurpose?
- are ergonomically deficient—you need three hands to hold the spray bottle, hold the roll of towels, and wipe the window!
- don't solve the *real* problem, which is "we hate cleaning windows!" Why not a dirt repellant for windows—the equivalent of Scotch-Guard for windows?

Given this information, what new product concept would you develop? The chemists and marketers met to discuss the results of these studies and to develop technically feasible concepts. Because participants were armed with the market information, there was some direction to the discussion: everyone was looking for solutions to real problems. The key benefits that the team elected—ones thought to deliver real value to the customer—were "streak free" and "multipurpose."

Postscript: In late 1991, Procter & Gamble introduced *Cinch*, a new window cleaner, which yields streak-free performance and is multipurpose. In test markets to date, results are very positive.

A positioning study can also be an integral part of this user needs-and-wants investigation. In a positioning study, we attempt to determine the key dimensions by which customers perceive and differentiate among competitive products or brands. For example, in pharmaceutical products, often these key dimensions are "side effects" and "efficacy." Positioning studies also attempt to identify the positions of the competitors' products in the buyer's mind—how he or she views various offerings, for example, in terms of the key dimensions. Finally positioning studies try to pinpoint possible new and desirable positions—niches or holes in the marketplace that are not occupied by a competitive product, yet have appeal to the customer.

In designing this critical user needs-and-wants market study, here are some tips and hints:

1. Think carefully about your *information objectives.* Remember that information only has a value to the extent it improves a decision. So outline the key design decisions you must make. And then identify the information that you need to make these design decisions. Put these information objectives in writing. And only then are you ready to begin crafting the questions you wish to address to customers.

2. Use a *structured questionnaire* for interviews. You may think that you're good at interviewing—at directing the conversation and remembering answers. But if you plan on interviewing more than one or two customers, you'd better develop a questionnaire. Why?

   • *Completeness:* to ensure that you cover all the questions you want answers to.

   • *Consistency:* to ensure that each respondent is questioned in the same way, with the same wording.

   • *Recording:* to provide a consistent method of recording the response.

3. Are you seeking the *right information?* Do a "preposterior" analysis—that is, before charging out to do interviews, imagine that the study is done— that you have the answers to the questions. Given these answers, can you make the design decisions? If there are any doubts, now is the time to rethink and revise your questionnaire—not after the interviews are finished!

4. Make sure the interviewees are *representative*—not just a handful of people or customers selected strictly for convenience. Get a list of prospective users in your target market, and select randomly from the list (or partition the list into subgroups or strata—for example, small, medium, and large users—and randomly select from each subgroup).

In the case of *industrial clients,* never rely on one or two interviews per client firm. Remember: One person does not speak for his or her company! There are many influencers in the purchasing company, and focusing on one or two people in the mistaken belief that they represent the company can lead to very erroneous information.

5. Get your *technical people involved* in the interviews too. Market information is too important to be left solely to the marketer. This is especially true for technology-based products, and where customers are technically sophisticated. The marketer may be best for setting up the interviews, designing the questionnaire, and handling the general questions; but the technical person has much more depth of knowledge about what is technically possible and what is not, and can engage the customer in a much more probing and profound conversation, which can lead to identification of desired product features and performance that the marketer would have missed.

6. Study the *customer's system or use environment.* Don't just stop at asking questions about what product features or performance he or she wants. Investigate the use system and how the product fits into the whole system. And try to gain an understanding of how the system works, so that you can better appreciate the needs for and demands placed on your product.

When Xerox introduced its color copier, it made the mistake of doing market research on the product only. A fine job was done on determining what product attributes and levels of performance were desired in the ideal product. What Xerox missed entirely was the nature of the office system into which this color copier had to fit. What they failed to detect was that the office system was a black-and-white one—not color: there were few color originals to copy. This was discovered after launch, at which time Xerox found itself facing the difficult task of changing the office system: it had to encourage the use of color originals, for example, via color kits.

Suggestion: Does your company do a solid job in terms of a user needs-and-wants study? Do you go to your customers, and via face-to-face meetings, try to understand their needs, wants, likes, dislikes, and preferences before development begins—in short, everything you'll need to know to sit down and design a truly superior product? Or are you like most firms: you arrive at a concept internally; you then use market research strictly to test product concept; but you don't really listen to the voice of the customer to help you develop and refine the concept.

In your next significant new product project, why not build in a user needs-and-wants study before development begins. Let the results of this study help shape your product design or product specs, translating an otherwise mundane idea into a real winner!

Competitive Analysis

A second key to building a superior new product is competitive analysis. There are several purposes to such an analysis. The first is to understand the competitor's product and its strengths and weaknesses. If your objective is to deliver product superiority, then the standard for comparison—the competitor's product—must be totally understood. Second, a knowledge of how the competitor plays the game—how it competes—can provide valuable insights into the keys to success and failure in this business. Finally, an appreciation of competitive strategy and how the competitor's product fits into its portfolio may be clues about expected competitive response to your product launch: for example, will it invoke a defense?

Here are some of the key questions to address in a competitive analysis:

1. Who are the key players—the direct competitors—whose product yours will replace (or take business away from)?
2. What are their products' features, attributes, and performance characteristics? What are their products' strong points and deficiencies?

   It's important to understand just who the "enemy" is and the exact nature of the product that yours must overtake. Understanding its strong points gives clues as to what to build into your product; its weaknesses reveal areas to exploit in a superior design.
3. What other strengths and weaknesses does each competitor have—for example, sales force, customer service, technical support, advertising, and promotion? For what is each competitor held in high regard? And where are its weak points?

   You must compete not only on the basis of product but also on non-product elements. While product advantage is clearly desirable, sometimes the main points of competitive advantage will be found in other elements of the marketing mix.
4. How does each competitor play the game? For example, on what types of customers (or segments) does each competitor focus? And what is the basis for competition? That is, how does each competitor get business—by pricing low? via product advantage? by having a larger or highly skilled sales force? or via a heavier promotional effort?
5. How well are the competitors doing? What are their market shares, and what has been the trend for each of their shares? And why is each doing so well (or poorly)—what's the secret to its success (or demise)?

   Here the focus is on what it takes to win. We witness different players with different strategies and approaches, and observe their results. From this comes valuable lessons about what succeeds and what fails in this marketplace.
6. (If possible) What are the competitors' cost pictures? Their production volumes and capacities? And their profitability—both contribution and net? And how important a product is this one to their operations and to their total profitability?

   These often-confidential data give insights into the strategic importance of the competitors' products to this business, their ability to respond (for example, how far they could cut price), and their likelihood of mounting an aggressive defense against your new product.

Unlike customer-oriented market research, there are no tried-and-proven methods for competitive analysis. It's more like playing detective and tracking down a variety of leads. Some suggestions:

- Get your hands on all possible *competitive literature* and competitive *advertising.* This is virtually all in the public domain: your own sales force should be able to help with trade literature, and clipping (or securing) advertisements displayed in print (or electronically) is straightforward.
- Do a keyword search through various *trade publications,* looking for information on competitors: announcements, new product introductions, plant expansions, or financial results.
- Try to acquire your *competitors' products.* If they are openly for sale and not too expensive, this is no problem. A friendly customer may also help out here as well—giving you access to a competitive product. And if the product is intangible—a new service product—utilize "mystery shopping" by posing as a customer and experiencing your competitors' service product first hand.
- Visit *trade shows.* Where else can you find under one roof the best and the newest that your competitors have to offer? It's all there—open for public viewing.
- Talk to your own *sales and service people.* They spend much time in the field and have the opportunity to see competitive products, practices, and prices. They also attend conferences and trade shows, and often have friends in other firms. In many cases, they are a storehouse of valuable competitive information.
- While doing your *user needs-and-wants study,* be sure to build in questions that seek opinion from your target customers about competitors: ratings and insights on competitive products, their sales force, service, and pricing.
- Talk to *suppliers* about your competitors. From suppliers you might be able to learn about the installed competitor capacity (what equipment and capacity it has), and current production volume (based on materials purchased). Some indication of the competitor's production operation and operations costs might also be gleaned from listening to suppliers.
- Use *financial sources* to learn about your competitors. For example, obtain a copy of their annual report. Ask your stock broker for his or her investment firm's written appraisal of the competitor. To be publicly traded, many stock exchanges require considerable information on the operations of a company (much of which would be considered confidential)—ask your investment house to secure this information from the stock exchange—for example, the 10K report. And undertake a keyword search through the many financial papers and magazines hunting for your competitors' names—*Fortune, Business Week,* the *Wall Street Journal,* etc.

- Hire a *consulting firm* that is expert on competitive intelligence. Often such firms have detailed intelligence files as well as considerable experience in employing some of the methods listed above.

Market Analysis

These two market studies discussed above—the user needs-and-wants study combined with the competitive analysis—are crucial to designing a superior product. But more information about the market is required in Stage 2. The numerous secondary and other sources of market information highlighted in the preliminary investigation section (Stage 1) can be reaccessed, but this time, much more thoroughly for Stage 2. The goal here is to develop a detailed portrait of the marketplace—a market analysis—which includes:

- market size, growth, and trends.
- market segments: their size, growth, and trends.
- buyer behavior: the who, what, when, where, and how of the purchase situation.
- the competitive situation.

When we develop a detailed marketing plan, this market analysis becomes even more essential. We revisit market analysis in Chapter 9, where we'll take a closer look at developing the marketing plan.

Detailed Technical Investigation

The user needs-and-wants study coupled with the competitive analysis should yield a set of guidelines—a wish list—of what should be built into your new product to truly delight the customer and to up-stage the competitor. Properly designed and executed, your market research should reveal what the "winning product" is from the customer's perspective as well as the product requirements that will yield product superiority over the competition.

This customer wish list must now be translated into something that is technically and economically feasible. This is where market needs and wants and technical possibilities must be married, in order to arrive at a proposed product design. In short, technical people must find a means of satisfying expressed customer needs and preferences. This is a creative process: it may be enhanced by creative problem solving techniques, but to a large extent, successful translation depends on the technological prowess and brainpower of your technical people. But a clear definition of what is required to meet customer needs and yield competitive advantage will certainly sharpen and focus this creative process.

The questions that are addressed in this detailed technical investigation include:

1. What is the probable technical solution that will yield a product to meet marketplace requirements?

2. What is involved in arriving at this technical solution? Is invention required? Or is this simply a matter of applying fairly well known technology?
3. What are the technical risks and potential roadblocks? And how might these be dealt with? Can alternate technical solutions be pursued in parallel?
4. What are the key steps involved in arriving at a prototype product? How long will each step take and how much will each cost? What are the personnel requirements?
5. What legal or patent, regulatory, and safety issues might arise? And how would we deal with each?
6. How might the product be manufactured or produced? In our plant or operations facilities? Or would new facilities, equipment, and production personnel be required? What would the production volume be? At what capital cost?
7. What is the cost per unit of producing the product?

The end result is a solid idea of what the product will be from a technical standpoint, what the probable technical solution and technical route are, and a reasonably high confidence that this solution and route are technically feasible. While some technical work—for example, lab work, experimental work, or modeling—may occur here, limit this technical work in Stage 2. Be careful that work that is more appropriate to Stage 3 doesn't move forward into this business case stage. The depth of technical work here in Stage 2 was put nicely by Rohm and Haas's Biocides business unit in their new product process:

> If lab work is conducted in Stage 2, the purpose is *not* to produce a prototype or final product; rather the spirit is to spend a limited amount of time to see if one can arrive at something remotely close to the desired product, enough to provide confidence that with more effort, it could be done.

Quality Function Deployment

Quality function deployment (QFD) is one technique adopted by a number of firms that helps to *translate customer needs and wants into a technique concept or design*. Thus QFD has particular applicability to Stage 2. It was developed in 1972 in Japan, and brought to the U.S. by Ford and Xerox in 1986.[4] The claim is that in some applications, QFD has reduced design time by 40 percent and design costs by 60 percent while maintaining and enhancing design quality.[5] Others claim that QFD's greatest success occurs when the model is used conceptually, but not in its detailed form as it is usually described.

QFD uses the model of four "houses" to integrate the informational needs of market, engineering, R&D, and management. The House of Quality (HOQ) is the first house, shown in Figure 6.4. This represents the translation between the marketing input (customer needs, wants, and perceptions) and R&D factors (design attributes and specs) via a relationship matrix. Griffin and Hauser stress

Figure 6.4: The House of Quality in Quality Function Development

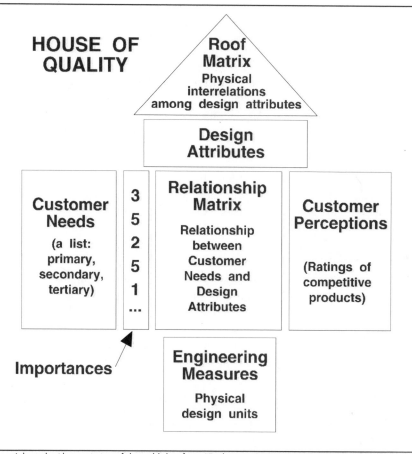

Adapted with permission of the publisher from "Evaluating QFD's Use in Firms as a Process for Developing Products," by A. Griffin. Thomas P. Hustad, ed., *The Journal of Product Innovation Management*, 9 (3): 17–82. Copyright 1992 by Elsevier Science Publishing Co.

that "the HOQ (as well as QFD) is an integrative process in which marketing and R&D participate as equal partners in all aspects of the communications process. . . . Much of the benefit of the HOQ comes from the mutual understanding of the problem and of one another that comes as marketing and R&D work together for a joint solution."[6] In developing this first house, the HOQ, we must listen to *both* voices—the customer's and the engineer's.

The voice of the customer. The results of the user needs-and-wants study provide critical inputs to QFD and the first house:

1. *Identifying customer needs:* Customer needs are first identified. A customer need is a description of a benefit the customer may want fulfilled by the

product. The user needs-and-wants study outlined above provides this needs-and-wants list.

2. *Structuring the needs:* To make the lengthy list of needs manageable (often there are 100–400 items), they are structured into a hierarchy of primary, secondary, and tertiary needs. The primary needs are strategic ones—the top five to ten needs that set the strategic direction for the new product. The secondary needs are tactical, essentially elaborations of the primary needs; there may be 20 to 30 of these. And tertiary needs simply provide the details.

3. *Importances of the needs:* These are indicated on the HOQ diagram (Figure 6.4) and come from the user needs-and-wants study.

4. *Customer perceptions:* These describe how the customer rates competitive products in terms of their abilities to meet customer needs. Again these come from the user needs-and-wants study (for example, see questions 4, 5, and 6 in that section).

The voice of the engineer. Specific input from R & D includes:

1. *Design attributes:* Customer needs are translated into measurable design requirements. These are measured in physical units that become targets for R&D work. But they are not solutions. These are listed at the top of Figure 6.4.
2. *Engineering measures:* These engineering measures (bottom of Figure 6.4) measure competitive products on the same physical units specified by the design attributes.
3. *Relationship matrix:* The project team then judges which design attributes in Figure 6.4 influence which customer needs. These influences or impacts are shown in each cell or element in the relationship matrix (center of Figure 6.4). Only the stronger relationships are highlighted, and most of the matrix may be blank. Experiments can be used to measure these impacts, but majority of impacts are based on team member judgments.
4. *Roof matrix:* The roof matrix shows the interrelationships among the design attributes. For example, adding more of one attribute may take away from another.

Once the HOQ is complete, the project team can use the relationships to establish design targets—that is, specific performance values of the design attributes that the product will deliver. "To make these decisions the team considers the cost and difficulty of achieving these targets, the influence of these targets on other design attributes, the influence of these targets on fulfilling customer needs (relative to competition), and any other relevant input of which the team is aware."[7]

Other Houses. The first house of QFD links customer needs to design attributes, and thus arrives at a technically feasible design concept or product definition. There are three other houses (not illustrated):

- *The second house of QFD:* These design attributes from the first house are next linked to solutions. Here, design attributes are placed on the left side of the house, and solutions are placed at the top of the house. When this second house is linked to the HOQ, these solutions are based on customer needs. This second house is thus a useful tool either at Stage 2 or even at Stage 3, development, in the new product process.
- *The third house:* Design solutions from the third house are linked to process operations (marketing, R&D, manufacturing, and delivery are coordinated). This time, design solutions are placed on the left, and process operations are located at the top of the house.
- *The fourth house:* This links process operations to production requirements to complete the cycle.

QFD has gained many proponents: "QFD works because it provides procedures and processes to enhance communication between, and structure decision making across, marketing and R&D and because it provides a translation mechanism from the language of the customer to the language of the engineer. It overcomes many of the barriers to communication. . . . The enhanced communication leads to reduced cycle time."[8] But others see it as too complex and cumbersome, and use it more as a conceptual tool.

Concept Test

Will the new product be a winner? Before pushing ahead into Stage 3 with product development, you must be certain that the product will meet customer needs and wants better than competitive products and will achieve your sales targets. Remember that your product is the new entry into the market, and it has to give the customer a reason to switch.

A problem faced by many firms is one of interpretation and translation. A thorough market study is undertaken that identifies customer needs and wants. The project team then translates these into a tentative product design—a set of product specs, perhaps using QFD. But something goes wrong in the translation. The final product isn't quite what the customer wants, or it lacks that special something that differentiates it from what the customer is already buying: it just doesn't quite delight the customer or push the customer's "hot button."

In order that this needs-identification-and-translation process works well, two assumptions must be true:

1. The customer understands his or her needs, and is able to verbalize these to you during the user needs-and-wants study.
2. You interpret these needs correctly and do a good job in translating these needs into the final product specs.

Both assumptions are rather doubtful. Even the most knowledgeable customer may not totally understand his or her needs, or these may not be accurately conveyed during the face-to-face discussions. Even if needs are understood, there may be errors in translation: the needs and wants are misinterpreted, resulting in the wrong set of product specs. The concept test is the final test prior to the development stage that validates that the product concept (and hence, the proposed product) is indeed a winner: it checks that customer needs were correctly understood, interpreted, and translated, and makes final course adjustments in the product design before it is too late.

Prospecting versus testing. It makes sense to build in a concept test as part of Stage 2 and before proceeding to product development (see Figure 6.2). There is a fundamental difference between this concept test market study and the user needs-and-wants study outlined above. The user needs-and-wants study is a *prospecting one*: no product or product concept was available to show the customer, but hints, clues, and insights were obtained from the customer about what should be built into a winning product design.

Once the technical investigation has yielded a technically feasible concept, then a full proposition concept can be shown to the customer—a model, a set of drawings, a story board, a spec sheet, or a dummy brochure—and his or her response gauged: "Given what you've told us, this is what we've come up with in terms of a proposed product; now, what do you think of it? Would you buy it?"

The concept test is not a prospecting study, but rather a *test or validation* that the proposed product concept is indeed a winner—intent to purchase is established. Note that at this early stage you still don't have a developed product. The purpose of this concept test is to see if you're heading in the right direction. By this time you should have, at minimum, a written description of the product and its benefits, features, performance characteristics, and likely price. In addition, you may have something concrete to show the customer—line drawings, artists renderings, a model, a slide show, or a crude working model of one or more versions of the product.

Designing the Concept Test

The design of a concept test is similar to that of the user needs-and-wants study. At minimum, you might use several focus groups of customers to gauge reactions to the proposed product. Although such focus groups give useful feedback on the product, remember that the limited sample size, the fact that group members are often not representative of the entire market (for example, a self-selected group), and the nature of the group dynamics (for example, one powerful person can sway the group) mean that the group's vote on the product may not be a true reflection of your target market. So a broader and more representative sample of customers should be contacted via a survey: mail, telephone, fax, or personal interview, or some combination of these.

Concept tests differ from user needs-and-wants studies in two major ways: first, in a concept test you have something to show the customer to solicit feedback; and second, you are seeking very different types of information than in a user needs-and-wants study.

Presenting the new product proposition. For the most reliable results, try a *full-proposition concept test*. That is, go beyond a simple written description—the traditional 100-word paragraph portraying the product concept. In order to respond intelligently, the customer must fully understand the product as it will be. The better you are able to convey what the final product will be and do, the more accurate gauge of purchase intent you will get. So get as close to the "final product" as you can in your concept presentation:

- Use written descriptions in conjunction with visuals: artists' renderings of the product, line drawings, dummy spec sheets, dummy brochures, or perhaps even a slide show showing the product concept and the product in simulated use.
- For consumer goods, pictures or drawings showing the product and its packaging can be displayed. Better yet, use a story board slide show presentation with a sound track.
- Use models (for example, crude working models) or rapid prototypes to show to the customer. Often a crude prototype or sample can be put together quickly and inexpensively as part of the detailed technical investigation in Stage 2.
- If the risk and amounts at stake are great enough, try a full proposition presentation using a video show or perhaps an interactive presentation on laserdisk.

For example, GM used an interactive, laser-disk–driven presentation on its electric car project, to bring the customer into the future via a simulated shopping trip. The cost of a video or interactive presentation is significant; but it is still much less than the cost of developing the product.

What information to seek. A concept test seeks customer reaction to the product in an attempt to assess market acceptance and expected sales revenues. Information objectives typically include the following:

- a measure of the customer's interest in the proposed product and a determination of why interest level is high or low
- a measure of the customer's liking for the product concept, and what facets he or she likes most, and what he or she likes least
- a comparative measure—a measure of the customer's preference for the concept relative to competitive brands or products the customer now uses, and the reasons for these preferences
- an indication of what the customer might expect to pay for the product

Figure 6.5:   Typical Questions in a Concept Test

Face-to-face interview:

(The respondent is asked to look over the proposed concept or concepts . . . a written description, or a sketch or drawing, etc.)

1a.   First, what's your reaction to the proposed product? You can answer using this 0-to-10 scale, where 0 means very negative and 10 means very positive. (Show him/her the scale.)

Very negative   0   1   2   3   4   5   6   7   8   9   10   Very positive

1b.   Why so positive (or negative)? _____

2a.   How interested are you in the concept? (Show response category scale.)

| _____ | _____ | _____ | _____ | _____ |
| not interested at all | not too interested | somewhat interested | quite interested | very interested |

2b.   Why did you answer the way you did? _____

3a.   To what extent do you like the proposed product? Please answer on this 0- to-10 scale, where 10 means "like very much" and 0 means "don't like it at all."

Don't like it   0   1   2   3   4   5   6   7   8   9   10   Like it very
at all   much

3b.   Why did you like/not like it? _____

4a.   What is the likelihood that you would buy this product at a price of $XX?

| _____ | _____ | _____ | _____ | _____ |
| definitely not | probably not | maybe | probably yes | definitely yes |

4b.   Why or why not? _____

5a.   What do you see as the product's main strengths? _____

5b.   Its main weaknesses? _____

5c.   Would you like to see anything changed? What are your suggestions? _____

- an indication of the customer's purchase intent at a specified price
- information useful in finalizing the position strategy

Figure 6.5 shows a typical questionnaire format. Note that there is a combination of closed-ended questions (to which the customer selects an answer, for example on a 1–5 or 0–10 scale), and open-ended questions (which result in a verbal answer or discussion). The closed-ended questions provide concrete, numeric data that can be aggregated and analyzed across many customers. But numbers alone tend to be sterile, hence open-ended responses are also sought to lend richness and greater understanding.

Be sure to use a structured questionnaire to ensure that all relevant questions and issues are covered, and that answers are recorded in a consistent way. Even when conducting personal interviews, it is good practice to follow a standardized questionnaire or interview guide, perhaps even showing the customer the written questions via a desk-top flip chart. Seek quantitative answers where possible: let the customer indicate his or her response on the various scaled measures, using a pointer and a scale, for example, to express his or her opinion.

It is also good practice to design a standard format for a concept test and to use that format consistently from product to product. In this way you will develop a history of data and establish benchmarks for comparison. For example, when 30 percent of those surveyed check off the "definitely would buy" box, what does this mean—is this a good result or poor one, and what market share might this score translate into?

> Hewlett-Packard investigated the development of a new computer pointing device to replace a mouse, namely fixed mounted cylinders that are twirled with the operator's thumbs. The product had not yet been developed, but customer reaction was sought via a full-proposition concept test. Customers were shown a film, which demonstrated a mock-up and simulation of the product, while a simulation on a computer screen was used to vividly portray how the new device would work. Note that although H-P did not actually have a prototype or product to test with the customer, this concept test came very close to it—well before development had begun!

Using the Results of a Concept Test

Use the results of a concept test with caution. They merely provide an indication of likely product acceptance—there are no guarantees. Nor should the results be used blindly. For most new products, particularly concepts in categories familiar to the customer, concept tests are likely to *overstate the market acceptance.* For example, a result of "30 percent of respondents definitely would buy" is not likely to translate into a market share of 30 percent for several reasons. First, respondents tend to have a positive response bias. There are many reasons for this: the so-called Hawthorn effect, whereby people under observation tend to respond more positively or enthusiastically than those not being studied; the desire to give socially acceptable or pleasing answers to the interviewer; and the fact that it's easy to say yes when there's no money or commitment involved. Second, although a respondent might say that he'll buy your product, in the case of a frequently repurchased product, he may continue to buy the competitor's as well: split purchases. If he buys both equally, the "30 percent definitely would buy" actually translates into a 15-percent market share. Third, not all potential buyers in your defined target market will be exposed or exposed sufficiently to your new product. Your advertising, promotion, and sales force may reach less than half of the total target market. The "intent to purchase" figure must be cut down by a factor that reflects your market exposure (or audience reach) on launch.

There are other problems as well that render the concept test results suspect. A common problem is obtaining feedback from the wrong respondents: this is particularly troublesome in industrial buying settings, where the one person interviewed may not speak for the entire company. Another problem is overselling the product concept—either promising things that the final product won't or cannot deliver, or using too much hype in the presentation of the concept (this is a test, not a sales pitch!).

For more innovative products, however, that represent new or unfamiliar product categories to the customer, the concept test results may actually *understate the product's acceptance.* Unfamiliar concepts tend to elicit a negative response initially, and it may be only after the customer has had a chance to use the product for a while (or see others using it) does he or she begin to appreciate the product's benefits. In short, there is a learning process here that occurs over time—one that cannot be measured in the short time frame of a snapshot concept test. For example, the initial consumer reaction to the introduction of automatic teller machines by banks was very negative—it was an alien, somewhat scary concept. It was only after we used these machines for several years that we saw their advantages, and our comfort level increased. A purchase-intent concept test today would yield very different results to one done in the early seventies (which would have predicted a very low market acceptance).

Here are some tips and hints in undertaking a concept test to gauge expected market acceptance:

1. *Be realistic* in preparing the concept presentation. The concept presentation should reflect the real-world environment that will exist when you launch your product. Control your zeal, highlighting benefits and performance characteristics that will be realistically included in the final product, and which you will be able to communicate to the customer at launch.

   The importance of being realistic is obvious. But countless examples exist where lack of realism was the culprit. A well-known firm in the female personal products business investigated the viability of a new woman's body lotion. A concept test was undertaken, where the concept description showed a unique product with a number of benefits. Based on the high-scoring concept test, the company moved the product into development and finally test market. The commercials for the test market were skillfully prepared, but in a 30-second time slot, only one of the key benefits could be stressed. The test market was a failure.

   The company assumed there was something wrong with the advertising or marketing support, so it took a second shot. The elements of the marketing mix were revised and the advertising stressed a different benefit.

   Again the product failed. The reason was clear: there was no way to convey all the features and benefits that had been displayed in the concept test in a live launch situation—a 30-second commercial, with lower viewer attention levels and less time to tell the story, made the task impossible.

   The key lesson to be learned here is this: don't develop or test a concept presentation that can't be replicated in the real world!

2. *Don't oversell.* Remember—this is a test to gauge customer reaction to the product concept; it is not a test of your selling ability; nor is it a preselling

exercise. Overselling what the product can do and the use of too powerful a presentation can lead to inflated and misleading results.

One telephone company had developed the concept for a new office data retrieval system, using telephone and cathode ray tube (CRT) technology. A concept test on target users was undertaken. A slick and professional video presentation was developed, showing a simulation of the product in action in an office—complete with a powerful sound track and music, and a dramatization showing happy, satisfied users. Potential customers were brought into a small theatre, shown the half-hour video, and then asked to respond to typical concept test questions.

The results were extremely positive, and the company proceeded into development and launch of the INET 2000 product. But market launch results were very disappointing. The lesson learned here is that customers were responding not so much to the concept, but to a very powerful and persuasive selling presentation. The concept was actually a poor one; but the video was superb!

In a similar vein, the use of emotionally loaded words in your concept presentation may actually backfire—it may act as a lightening rod, eliciting negative reaction and biasing the results downward:

- A new financial service may not be "sophisticated" and "elegant." The language is too powerful or simply inappropriate, causing customers to focus on this issue and fail to perceive other benefits.
- A supermarket ice cream brand could be "luscious," "rich," and "thick," but "gourmet" in a supermarket line may simply not be believable.

3. *Be clear.* Customers must fully understand the concept, if the responses and feedback they give are to be meaningful. Too often a product description is given that is vague, confusing, or superficial, and then the customer is queried about whether he or she would buy the product or not. The results are pure guesses on the part of the customer.

   A food manufacturer undertook a concept test with a frozen yogurt bar, whose major benefits were its delicious taste and the fact that it contained no artificial preservatives. Unfortunately the body copy talked about a "nutritious quiescently frozen confection on a stick." What exactly is a "frozen confection"? Is it like an ice cream? Or is it better than or different from ice cream? And what does "quiescently frozen" mean—I had to look the word up in the dictionary.

   Keep it simple, clear, and understandable, and use whatever communication tools—including visuals and models—that might help explain the concept most clearly to the prospective customer.

4. *Contact the right potential customers or users.* Make sure that the customers you involve in the concept test are indeed representative of your target market. If your target user is upscale, up-market, higher income professionals, there is no sense taking a sample of average consumers. Similarly, in an

industrial setting, if your target market is an entire industry, then undertaking a concept test solely on leading edge or innovative users is foolish—they're likely to give a much more positive response than the typical customer. Further, make sure that you seek opinion and feedback from a variety of people within the buying firm: there are often many purchase influencers in the decision to buy a new product.

With all its weaknesses, the concept test is still the best way of gauging likely product acceptance before you have actually developed a product. For familiar products in familiar categories (which are the bulk of product development efforts), it has proven quite predictive. The top box score (the percentage of people who replied "definitely would buy") is your best early indicator of how your product will fare, short of a test market or full launch.

Sadly there are no simple formulas for translating this top box score into a predicted market share. Some market research firms have developed elaborate models for estimating initial trial rates for certain types of consumer goods; and this initial trial rate combined with repurchase intent yields expected market share. But such formulas and norms tend to be very specific to certain industries and even product categories or classes within industries.

For frequently repurchased consumer goods, for example, a top box score of 40 percent or higher is considered a strong score. In hundreds of studies of concept test results versus test market results, such "strong" concepts result in an initial trial rate in excess of 30 percent, and there is a high likelihood of positive test market results. By contrast, "average" concepts that receive a top box score of 30 to 39 percent, achieve an initial trial rate of somewhat less than 30 percent, and result in positive test market results about one-third of the time. Any consumer brand scoring less than 30 percent "definitely would purchase" on the concept test gets a poor initial trial rate of well less than 20 percent and about one chance in ten that test market results will be positive. Figure 6.6 shows some of these relationships for frequently repurchased consumer goods.

Perhaps as important is the information obtained from the open-ended questions in a concept test, questions such as, "What did you like most about the product" and "Why did you rate brand X as better." If the concept is failing the test, then answers to these questions provide critical insights into what needs to be done to improve the product. Even for a successful test, these answers provide clues about how to fine tune the product design to make it even more attractive to the customer. Finally, the comments that potential customers make in response to the product provide hints into how the product might be positioned and communicated to users—what customer "hot buttons" have been hit.

Suggestion: Are you using concept tests effectively in your new product process? Do you take the time to verify that the proposed new product really is the right one before you charge off into development? Or do you assume that you have it right, and that you'll take your chances?

Build a concept test into your next important new product development *before development begins.* You don't need a prototype or sample product—just a firm idea of what the product will be. Present the product proposition as clearly

Figure 6.6:   Concept Test Relationships: Test Market Results versus Purchase Intent

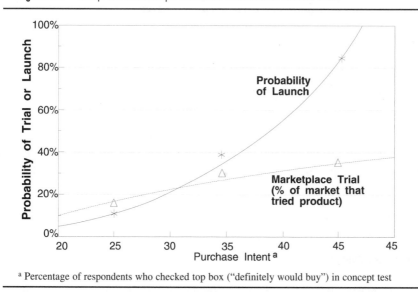

^a Percentage of respondents who checked top box ("definitely would buy") in concept test

as possible to selected customers, and remember: be realistic; don't oversell; be clear; and make sure you're speaking to the right people. Measure the customer's interest, likes, preference, and purchase intent—use scaled questions, and get quantitative answers (even in office interviews!). You'll be surprised at the insights you'll gain about your proposed product's commercial prospects. But exercise care in the use of these concept test results: intent-to-purchase figures don't translate directly into market share!

Financial Analysis

The various market studies—user needs-and-wants, the competitive analysis, and the concept test—help to map out the product definition. The target market is now sharply defined; the product concept and positioning strategy is confirmed; the benefits to be delivered are defined and validated, as are the physical attributes of the product—features, specs, and performance requirements. What remains is a business or financial justification of the project before one moves fully into the development phase.

Reasonable estimates can now be made for many of the inputs for a financial analysis. Market size and share estimates together with pricing analysis should yield expected revenues. The product's design characteristics are now known, so the detailed technical assessment should yield cost estimates and reasonable projections of profit margins. Marketing requirements and the expected launch costs have been investigated, and capital equipment needs have been forecast. These estimates are the inputs to a financial analysis.

Two types of financial analysis have merit as we move into Gate 3: the payback period and a discounted cash flow analysis, which can be used in conjunction with sensitivity analysis. More about these financial techniques in the next chapter, where we explore project evaluation methods.

Plans of Action

The final component of the business case is the action plan. Usually the rule is that a detailed plan of action should be put together for the next stage, and tentative plans for subsequent stages all the way through to launch. Following this rule, the business case plans consist of:

- a recommendation on the future of the project: Go versus Kill versus Hold.
- the detailed development plan. Its components are described in Chapter 8.
- tentative plans for Stage 4, Testing and Validation. Actions frequently undertaken in this stage are also portrayed in Chapter 8.
- a tentative manufacturing, operations, or supply plan.
- a tentative marketing plan. The marketing planning process is outlined in Chapter 9.

On to Development

The market has been researched. The product has been defined. The technical route has been mapped out. The financial and business justification has been prepared. And the action plan or path forward for the next stage (and subsequent stages) has been developed. The business case is now ready. These are the deliverables to the pivotal Gate 3 or business case decision. This critical gate opens the door to a significant commitment of resources and to a full-fledged development program. But because the homework has been proficiently undertaken in Stages 1 and 2 described in this chapter, development should proceed more smoothly: we now have clear and defined targets to speed towards.

Picking the Winners

If a man look sharply and attentively, he shall see Fortune; for though she is blind, she is not invisible.

Francis Bacon, *Of Fortune*, 1623.

Focusing Resources on the Right Projects

New product resources are too valuable and scarce to waste. The trouble is that most new product projects are losers. Either they fail commercially in the marketplace, or they are cancelled prior to product launch. Project selection—the ability to pick the right project for investment—therefore becomes a critically important task.[1] There are two reasons for this.

First, the great majority of projects are probably unsuitable for commercialization. While some failures no doubt are the result of poor project management, others are simply bad projects to begin with—they should have been killed much earlier. The ability to *spot these losers early in the process* (and before too many resources have been spent on them) is one key to improved new product profitability.

Second, there are far more new product opportunities than there exist resources to commercialize them. So tough choices must be made! One trap that too many firms fall prey to is trying to do *too many projects.*

> One of the first tasks of a newly appointed business unit manager at Du Pont was to assess his portfolio of new product projects. He asked each senior scientist to submit a list of the new product projects each was working on, indicating how much time was allocated to each project, and how long each had been on the books.
>
> To his chagrin, not one person submitted a list shorter than two pages long. The typical reply was: "I'm working on 12 projects; they're all critical; I spend a few days per quarter on each; and they've been on the books for eight years!"
>
> Undaunted, the business unit manager went to round two: "Please submit a list of the *three projects* that you're working on." The request had barely been circulated when he began to receive angry phone calls and visits from the scientists: "How dare you cut me down to three projects! All 12 of my projects are of critical importance to the company!"

What the business unit manager discovered the hard way was that people *could not, would not,* and *did not know* how to make tough choices. They lacked the will; they lacked the criteria; and they lacked the methods. And so priorities had never been set, and no focus ever achieved in the business unit.

Project selection is about tough choices: its purpose it to concentrate the scarce resources on the truly meritorious projects. The result is better focus, improved prioritization of projects, and ultimately faster development for the chosen projects.

In an ideal new product process, management would be able to identify the probable winners early in the game, and focus resources on those projects. Failure rates would be kept low, misallocated resources kept to a minimum, and the return maximized. This chapter is about gates: it tackles the difficult question of how to select winning new product projects. In it, we look at various approaches to project evaluation, with a particular emphasis on the earlier gates in the new product process.

Project evaluation is not as easy as it seems. Many firms have a mediocre track record in picking winners. For example, for every four projects selected for development, only one becomes a commercial success.[2] Management appears to be in error about 75 percent of the time: we'd be better off tossing a coin! In too many firms project evaluations are weak, deficient, or even nonexistent. In one of our studies, initial screening was found to be one of the most poorly handled activities of the entire new product process—screening was rated as "adequate" in only 12 percent of the cases![3] Further, 37 percent of projects did not undergo a business or financial analysis prior to the development phase, and 65 percent of projects did not include a precommercialization business analysis.

Tough Decisions

Designing an effective evaluation scheme is difficult. And if it wasn't difficult enough, there are a variety of complexities that make the task more arduous.

No Single Common Evaluation Technique. Project evaluation—making a Go/ Kill decision on a project—ideally should reoccur at a number of points in the new product process—our five gates in the game plan. But the amount of information increases substantially as we move from stage to stage, gate to gate. So do the amounts at stake. And thus the sophistication of successive evaluations, and even the methods of evaluation, should change from one gate to the next. For example, while financial analysis based on capital budgeting techniques may be appropriate as we near commercialization—at Gates 4 and 5—such analysis is likely to be highly unreliable at early gates and may do more harm than good. The result is that we end up with a new product process that *lacks a common and consistently applied evaluation technique*—a common thread that runs from Gate 1 to Gate 5.

Too Many Evaluation Methods.   A second difficulty is the confusion in choosing the appropriate evaluation method. Indeed there are a myriad of articles and books on the subject, each purporting to describe the method for selecting the right project; I've counted over one hundred different project evaluation techniques, from financial and risk models through to group sorting techniques and even portfolio optimization models. But a closer look at the various approaches reveals that each requires varying amounts of information, that each is best suited to a particular phase in the project, and that each has its particular strengths and weaknesses. In short, there is no one best way!

A Multiproject Decision.   The third difficulty with project selection is the impact of one project on another. What we face is not a single project decision; rather we must manage a portfolio of projects. So a Go/Kill decision on Project A should be made in the light of the costs, resource requirements, and pay-offs of Project B, Project C, and so on. In practice, this is often hard to do.

Imagine that you are a sailing instructor at a children's summer camp. Today is parents' visiting day. You've arranged a demonstration sailboat race. But unlike the usual boat race, the objective here is to have as many boats cross the finish line as possible (see Figure 7.1). You're in a canoe, supervising the junior sailors, and there's only so much help you can give. Just about every crew gets into trouble.

The management problem you face is this: how do you allocate your limited resources among the various sailing crews? To add to the complexity of the problem, each boat is at a different stage of completion of the race, and each boat needs different amounts and types of help. Should you help Boat C, which is so close to finishing, but clearly is in trouble? Or should you help Boat D, which is in great shape, but is just starting out, and will need resources to keep

Figure 7.1:   Allocating Resources among Projects

Different projects, each with unique resource requirements; how do you allocate scarce resources?

on course? In this boat race, as in new products, a decision on one contender cannot be made without taking into consideration the needs of the others.

To the management scientist, this portfolio management problem is one of constrained optimization under conditions of uncertainty: a multiproject, multistage decision model solved by mathematical programming. But these fancy optimization techniques have not proven to work well in practice in new product selection. Recent years have witnessed some simpler techniques aimed at tackling this portfolio management problem—techniques we'll look at later in the chapter. Regardless of the technique used, however, always recognize that the true problem is one of *resource allocation among a number of projects.*

More than just a Go/Kill decision. A further difficulty in project evaluation is what the decision means. At minimum, project evaluation should yield a Go/Kill/Hold/Recycle decision. The Go decision means "Go to the next stage of the process, after which the project will be reevaluated in the light of new and more concrete information." The Kill decision is self-evident: drop the project and cut your losses. The Hold decision means shelve the project—put it on the back burner: the project is a positive one, but there aren't sufficient resources to undertake it right now. And the Recycle decision means to rework the project: Go back to the previous stage for rework.

If the sole purpose of your project evaluations is simply to make Go/Kill decisions, however, your exercise is a pretty sterile one, and you're missing the real value of solid project evaluation. There are at least four purposes of an effective project evaluation.

The Project Evaluation Procedure

Purposes

Before designing a project evaluation procedure, consider the four main purposes of a gate:

1. *To make Go/Kill decisions:* This is the obvious purpose, the decision we just discussed above. The point here is that poor projects must be flagged and stopped; but in too many firms, projects seem to acquire a life of their own. They proceed like an express train, careening down the track, slowing down at the stations (review points), but never intending to stop until they reach their ultimate destination, market launch.|

2. *To make prioritization decisions:* Prioritization decisions are as important as Go/Kill decisions. Not all projects deserve equal treatment: it's important to make tough choices about which projects to really focus the resources on, and to accelerate through the process. Without prioritization, there is no concentration of resources, and little progress is made.

3. *To serve as a quality control check in the process:* We saw in Lesson 12 in Chapter 4 that completeness, consistency, and quality of execution are vital

to success. The gates or evaluation points become the quality control check points in the process. Here the purpose is to ensure that the project is being executed in a top quality fashion: that is, on schedule, on target, and with quality.

4. *To chart the path forward:* An effective evaluation decision should do more than make Go/Kill and prioritization decisions. If the decision is Go, the evaluation should provide an answer to the question, "Go where and do what?" In short, what is the path forward?

Fundamental to charting the path forward is *project analysis and diagnosis.* This includes understanding the project's strong points, its weaknesses, and its potential "killer variables." It means appreciating the project's key uncertainties and the critical areas of ignorance (the things we don't know).

Too often, management and project teams proceed with a project, yet fail to understand, appreciate, or acknowledge serious flaws in the project: There is no action plan to deal with these weaknesses; and the end result is disaster. We saw in earlier chapters that many of the reasons for project failure are preventable. Conversely, project proponents are guilty of inventing imaginary project strengths—seeing strengths where none exist—and proceed on false hopes. Finally, most projects are characterized by major areas of uncertainty and ignorance—we don't have the facts. Sadly, in some firms, no one faces up to this lack of facts, and no attempt is made to acquire the needed information. So an important facet of each gate evaluation is to understand the project's strengths and weaknesses, to pinpoint the critical areas of ignorance and uncertainty, and to identify potential killer variables so that the path forward or action plan for the next stage can be mapped out.

Requirements

Many approaches to project evaluation and idea selection have been developed. When designing an approach to project evaluation and selection, you must bear in mind a number of points.

Each decision point is only a tentative commitment in a sequential and conditional process. Each Go/Kill decision is only one in a sequence of such decisions.[4] A Go decision is not an irreversible one, nor is it a decision to commit all the resources for the entire project. Rather project evaluation can be viewed as a series of decisions, beginning with a flickering green light at the idea screen, with progressively stronger commitments made to the project at each successive decision point. For example, at Gate 1, the idea screen, a commitment is made to spend a limited amount of time and money on the project—perhaps $10,000 and two months on Stage 1—after which the project will undergo a more extensive evaluation at Gate 2. This Gate 2 decision is based on the new information gleaned during Stage 1. To use our earlier gambling analogy, this Gate 1 idea screen amounts to "buying an inexpensive look at the project," after which we'll decide if we're still in the game. And so it continues from gate to gate. In effect, we buy discrete pieces of the project at each evaluation point or gate: the entire new product project is incrementalized in order to manage risk.

The evaluation process procedure must maintain a reasonable balance between the errors of acceptance and errors of rejection.   Too weak an evaluation procedure fails to weed out the obvious losers and misfits, and results in misallocation of scarce resources and the start of a creeping commitment to the wrong projects. And once past Gate 3 and into development, projects tend to build up a head of steam: they get a life of their own and it becomes extremely difficult to stop them, even when all signals point to an impending disaster. We saw previously that about 50 percent of the resources that management spends on new products are spent on projects that fail; and that only one project in four that is given the green light to development actually succeeds commercially! Remember: the easiest points at which to kill bad projects are at the first few gates—Gates 1, 2, and 3. After that point, resources are committed, people become intensely involved, and in some cases "super-advocates" appear, and so killing a poor project becomes more and more difficult.

On the other hand, a too rigid evaluation procedure results in many worthwhile projects being stopped or rejected. This is especially true at the very early gates, where the project is little more than an idea: it is extremely fragile and vulnerable. The cost of rejecting good projects is perhaps even higher than the cost of proceeding with bad ones: the cost of lost opportunities. An overly rigorous and conservative screening process that weeds out everything but the "sure bets" invariably leads to elimination of all but the least innovative product types: minor modifications, product tweaks, and extensions. This can result in a "win the battle, lose the war" outcome for the new product program.

Project evaluation is characterized by uncertainty of information and the absence of solid financial data.   The initial decisions to move ahead with a project amount to decisions to invest that must be made in the absence of reliable financial data.[5] The most accurate data in the project are not available until the end of the development stage or even after testing and validation and as the product nears commercialization—information on manufacturing costs, capital requirements, and expected revenue.[6] Many of the activities, such as pilot production runs, customer field trials, and test markets, are aimed at obtaining reliable information on costs and revenues. But these activities tend to occur later in the new product process. Thus, as the project advances and as the fund of knowledge is augmented, project evaluations become more reliable and should be more demanding. But at the early gates, data on projected sales, costs, and capital requirements are little more than educated guesses (if they exist at all). This lack of reliable financial data throughout much of the new product process emphasizes the substantial differences in the methods needed for new product screening and predevelopment gate evaluations versus those required for conventional commercial investment decisions.[7]

Project evaluation involves multiple objectives and therefore multiple decision criteria. The criteria used in project Go/Kill decisions should reflect the corporation's overall objectives, and in particular its goals for the new product program. Obvious new product objectives are to contribute to corporate profitability and growth. But there could be other specific ones, including opening up new windows of opportunity, operating within acceptable risk boundaries, focusing on certain arenas of strategic thrust, or simply complementing existing products. Moreover, as was seen in Chapter 3, many qualitative characteristics of a new product project are correlated with success and financial performance, and hence should be built in as goals or "desired characteristics" as part of the evaluation criteria.

Not all of these goals and selection criteria are easily quantifiable. For example, the desire to move into a new technology or to develop synergistic products is not as easily quantified as a "20 percent discount cash flow (DCF) return." Nor are the criteria necessarily consistent with one another. There might arise conflicts among the "new technologies" criterion and the "synergistic" and "20 percent return" goals. Finally, the evaluation criteria do not necessarily remain the same as the project progresses from gate to gate. As better data become available towards the commercialization stage, the decision criteria become better defined, and may even change over time.[8]

The evaluation method must be realistic and easy to use. Project evaluation tools must be user-friendly. In short, they must be sufficiently simple and time efficient that they can be used by a group of managers in a meeting setting. Sophisticated computer-aided decision tools often fail this test, as do elaborate questionnaires and complicated checklists. The method must be easy to use in its data requirements, operational and computational procedures, and interpretation of results.

At the same time, the method must be realistic: for example, it cannot entail so many simplifying assumptions that the result is no longer valid. Many operations research evaluation tools fail on this point, largely because their simplifying assumptions render the method unrealistic: resources are often assumed to be easily transferable between one project and the next or between projects at different stages in the process, which is simply not valid; estimates of probabilities of success or expected revenues are called for early in the project, estimates which are pure guesses; and so on.

No one evaluation method meets all the requirements outlined above. In the section that follows, we review a variety of project screening, selection, and evaluation methods in the hope of finding some that come close to the ideal.

Four Approaches to Project Evaluation

The four main approaches to project evaluation include:

- benefit measurement models;
- economic models;

- portfolio selection models; and
- market research models.[9]

Benefit Measurement Models

Benefit measurement models require a well-informed respondent or group to provide subjective information regarding characteristics of the project under consideration.[10] Such methods typically avoid conventional economic data, such as projected sales, profit margins, and costs, but rely more on subjective assessments of strategic variables, such as fit with corporate objectives, competitive advantage, and market attractiveness. Included in this category are *checklists* and their extension, *scoring models*. In the latter, ratings of project attributes are weighted and combined to yield a project score. We take a much closer look at these popular methods later in the chapter.

Benefit measurement techniques recognize the lack of concrete financial data at earlier stages of the project and the fact that financial analysis is likely to yield unreliable results. So they rely on subjective inputs of characteristics that are likely to be known. As such, these techniques are most useful at Gates 1 and 2, and possibly Gate 3. But benefit measurement methods suffer from the fact that they treat each project in isolation, and do not take into consideration the impact of the project on the overall resource allocation question.

Economic Models

Economic models treat project evaluation much like a conventional investment decision. Computation approaches, such as payback period, break-even analysis, return on investment, and discounted cash flow (DCF or capital budgeting) methods, are used. To accommodate the uncertainty of data, probability-based techniques, such as decision tree analysis and Monte Carlo risk assessment, are proposed. (These financial or economic techniques are well-known methods; much has been written about them in other books; and they are generally available as software, for example, on spreadsheets. So we spend only a little time on them in this chapter.)

Although I recommend the use of certain of these financial methods—namely payback, DCF, and sensitivity analysis—at some gates, recognize their weaknesses too! Their main deficiency is simply the lack of solid, reliable financial data. The toughest project selection decisions lie in the first few gates of the process, when relatively little is known about the project. And it is here that traditional economic approaches suffer the most, because they require considerable financial data that are quite accurate. So, economic models are usually considered most relevant for "known" projects (such as line extensions or product modifications—projects that are close to home, and for which relatively good financial data is available), or at later stages of the new product process (for example, for Gate 3 and later).

Another weakness is that, like benefit measurement models, economic models treat each project in isolation—for example, a return or payback is calculated for this one project, which is then compared to some magical hurdle rate. The approach does not deal with the overall resource allocation problem.

Portfolio Selection Models

The original portfolio selection models were highly mathematical, and employed techniques such as linear, dynamic, and integer programming. The objective is to develop a portfolio of new and existing projects to maximize some objective function (for example, the expected profits), subject to a set of resource constraints. Anyone familiar with these programming techniques will immediately recognize the field day that the mathematician and management scientist would have solving this portfolio problem. But alas, in spite of the plethora of articles written, such techniques have not met with success in new products: they simply require far too much data, including financial data on all projects (both potential projects as well as those in the pipeline), timing information, resource needs and availabilities, and probabilities of success. A good summary article on such methods is "Decision Methods for Selecting a Portfolio of R&D Projects."[11]

The portfolio issue remains an important one, however, and has lead one expert to predict that "R&D portfolio analysis and planning will grow in the 1990s to become the powerful tool that business portfolio planning became in the 1970s and 1980s."[12] The last few years have witnessed simplifications in the portfolio approaches described above that have made them more understandable and useful. The typical simplification treats the new product portfolio problem much like the original Boston Consulting Group portfolio map for existing businesses (remember the portfolio maps featuring stars, cash cows, dogs, and wildcats?). This portfolio mapping method for new products is promoted by several noted consulting firms, and has seen limited success. More about these new approaches later in the chapter.

Market Research Approaches

Market research screens are usually used for relatively simple consumer products. Market research techniques, when used as a decision tool, assume that the sole criterion for moving ahead with a new product project is expected market acceptance. The assumption here is that strategic, technological, and production issues are not relevant (or can be easily dismissed). Given a strictly market-based screening decision, it makes sense to use a variety of market research–based techniques ranging from consumer panels and focus groups to perceptual and preference mapping.

> Atlantic Promotions is a proficiently managed, medium-sized firm in the business of marketing lower-priced consumer goods via heavy promotion on TV, and broad distribution via discount and junior department stores. Products include mostly household, automotive, and kitchen widgets. Technology and production is not an issue.
>
> New product selection is critical for the company, as the marketing launch costs are exceptionally high. Thus Atlantic adheres to a new product process, in

which Gate 2 is simply a set of consumer focus groups: that is, the focus consumers are exposed to various product concepts or facsimiles, and vote for the proposed products. These results of the votes become the Go/Kill decisions!

The danger, of course, is that this approach will produce a one-sided evaluation and that issues other than market acceptance will be neglected.

Which Methods Are Used in Practice?

Portfolio models: great in theory, but . . . Although conceptually appealing, and perhaps the most rigorous, mathematically based portfolio models see more visibility in text books and journal articles than in corporate offices. Studies done in North America and Europe show that managers have a great aversion to these mathematical techniques, and for good reason.[13] The major obstacle is the amount of data required—information on the financial results, resource needs, timing, and probabilities of completion and success for all projects. Much of this information is simply not available, and when it is, its reliability is suspect. Portfolio approaches also provide an inadequate treatment of risk and uncertainty; they are unable to handle multiple and interrelated criteria; and they fail to recognize interrelationships with respect to payoffs of combined utilization of resources. Finally, managers perceive such techniques to be too difficult to understand and use.

The appeal of a portfolio approach lingers on, however, in the form of simplified versions that have been more recently packaged and promoted to industry. Certain variants of the technique still suffer from many of the same problems that traditional portfolio methods do—namely the considerable data requirements, both financial and probability data. But the simplified portfolio methods are much easier to understand and use; don't require computer-based programming methods; and most important, present results in the form of visually appealing portfolio maps.

Note that portfolio methods are not project evaluation tools per se (that is, they're not Go/Kill decision models). Rather, they are prioritization and resource allocation methods, and hence can be used *in conjunction with some of the other methods* here, such as benefit measurement or economic models.

Economic analysis—good points, but use with care. Economic models are often used as project selection tools.[14] They are familiar to managers, and they are accepted for other types of investment analysis in the firm. But they do have limited applications. Economic models require financial data as input. Someone must make estimates of expected sales in year 1, year 2, and so on; and estimates are required for selling prices, production costs, marketing expenses, and investment outlays. Often these variables are difficult to estimate, especially in the early stages of a project. And even when estimates are made, they tend to be inaccurate. More's study on firms' abilities to estimate expected new product sales confirms that estimates were in error not by 10 percent or 20 percent, but by orders of magnitude![15]

Applying a financial screen to a high-risk or step-out project will tend to kill it. The problem is not the project, which may well be a viable one; the problem is the application of the wrong evaluation technique. A financial analysis that is done prematurely on a project will reject all but the sure bets—the uncertainties and risks come out too high—and will drive the firm into a conservative new product program.

Remember that financial analysis involving economic models (payback, ROI, DCF, etc.) is a powerful and useful tool in project evaluation, provided it is used at the right time and for the appropriate project type. If used too soon, or used for the wrong projects, it can do much damage. Qualitative and nonfinancial considerations must also enter the decision to move ahead. Therefore, limit reliance on financial evaluation to "known" projects—line extensions, product modifications, and the like—at the early stages. For more venturesome new products, avoid the use of financial techniques until a later gate in the game plan.

Market-based screening methods—a little one-sided. Market research techniques also see some degree of use in screening new product projects. For relatively simple new products, this may make sense. But often there are considerations other than simply market acceptance that must be evaluated prior to proceeding with a project. Before you move ahead with a market-research screen, the project should, at minimum, meet a set of "must" and "should" screening criteria.

The benefits of benefit measurement. Benefit measurement methods are generally recommended for many of the gates in the game plan. At the earliest gates, for example—because only a tentative commitment is required (early stages are relatively inexpensive ones) and because available information tends to be limited—benefit methods are the most logical evaluation tool. And even at later gates—for example, Gate 3—benefit measurement methods have much to offer.

Of all the benefit methods, the checklist and scoring model (based on a weighted checklist) appear most popular. The Conference Board reports that about 53 percent of the firms studied use written guidelines or rules for project selection, usually in the form of checklists or scoring models.[16]

An investigation of 26 project selection techniques, including scoring, financial, and portfolio methods, was undertaken by Souder.[17] The managers who took part in the study rated the mathematical portfolio models the highest in terms of realism, flexibility, and capability. (Note, however, that they are also the most difficult to use and require data inputs beyond the capability of most managers.) Scoring models were rated the highest in terms of cost and ease of use. Souder concludes that scoring models are "highly suitable for preliminary screening decisions where only gross distinctions are required among projects."

Suggestion: Take a look at how the various gates or decision points are handled in your firm's new product scheme. For example:

1. How are new product ideas screened in your firm? Is screening recognized as a distinct decision point or gate in the process, at which a conscious and deliberate Go/Kill decision is made? Or do ideas sort of meander into the process, almost by osmosis?

2. Look at your other predevelopment decision points (the equivalent of our Gates 2 and 3). What method is used to make these early Go/Kill decisions? If you're not using any method at all, or if you're relying strictly on a financial analysis, chances are your new product screening can be improved. Read on to see how you can use benefit measurement methods to implement screening and evaluation methods that work.

A Closer Look at Benefit Measurement Models

Benefit measurement models are popular and are recommended by a number of experts. Let's take a closer look at various types of approaches useful in screening new product projects. Approaches intended to integrate subjective inputs include comparative approaches, profile charts, benefit contribution techniques (financial indices), simple checklists, and scoring models (weighted checklists).

Comparative Approaches

Comparative approaches include such methods as Q-sort, project ranking, and paired comparisons. Each requires evaluators to compare one proposal to another proposal or to some set of alternative proposals. The evaluator must specify which of the proposed new product projects is preferred, and, in some methods, the strength of preferences. In some of these methods, a set of project benefit measurements is then computed by performing mathematical operations on the stated preferences.

The Q-sort method suggested by Souder is one of the simplest and most effective methods for rank-ordering a set of new product proposals.[18] Q-sort combines the use of psychometric methods with controlled group interaction. Each member of the group is given a deck of cards, with each card bearing the name or description of one of the projects. Each member then sorts and resorts the deck into five categories, from a "high" group to a "low" group (or into simple "Yes" or "No" categories), evaluating each project according to a prespecified criterion. (The criterion could be, for example, expected profitability.) The evaluators' results are anonymously tallied on a chart and displayed to the entire group. The group is then given a period of time to debate the results informally. The procedure is repeated, again on an anonymous and individual basis, followed by another discussion period. By the third or fourth round, the evaluator group usually moves to consensus on the ranking of the projects in each criterion. The method is simple, easy to understand, and straightforward to implement; it provides for group discussion and debate, and moves the group towards agreement in a structured way.

Comparative methods such as Q-sort do have their limitations. Perhaps their weakest aspect is that evaluators must give an overall or global opinion on a project. Individual facets of each project—for example, size of market, fit with distribution channels, likelihood of technical success—are never directly compared and measured across projects. It is left to each evaluator to consider these individual elements consciously or unconsciously and to arrive somehow at a global assessment. This may be asking too much of some evaluators. Moreover, the group discussion may focus on a few facets of the project and overlook other key elements.   A second problem is that no cut-off criterion is provided; projects are merely rank-ordered. It is conceivable that even those projects ranked highest will be mediocre choices in a field of poor ideas.

Profile Models

Profile models display a set of information-accumulation patterns over the entire new product process.[19] At each gate, a standard profile of the necessary information that must have been gathered by that point is specified—for example, what information on market size, on the competitive situation, or on development costs should be available by Gate 2 or by Gate 3? Then, for each project, the evaluators simply indicate their confidences in the information on each factor available at that gate. The information profile of the project in question is then compared to the desired information profile.

To develop these profile charts, a time scale is shown (see Figure 7.2), beginning with initial screening and ending with Gate 5, the precommercialization

Figure 7.2:   Profile Chart of a New Product Project

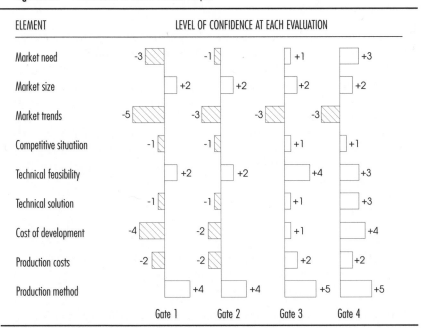

ELEMENT	LEVEL OF CONFIDENCE AT EACH EVALUATION			
Market need	-3	-1	+1	+3
Market size	+2	+2	+2	+2
Market trends	-5	-3	-3	-3
Competitive situatiion	-1	-1	+1	+1
Technical feasibility	+2	+2	+4	+3
Technical solution	-1	-1	+1	+3
Cost of development	-4	-2	+1	+4
Production costs	-2	-2	+2	+2
Production method	+4	+4	+5	+5
	Gate 1	Gate 2	Gate 3	Gate 4

gate. The elements of information shown down the left and ratings from −5 to +5 indicate the level of confidence in information on each element as a function of the elapsed time of the project. That is, how good is the information on each element at each gate? Figure 7.2 shows a project at Gate 4, with increasingly improving information on several key elements from Gates 1 to 4. Only a handful of elements are shown; in practice there is a longer list.

This chart is then compared to a standard profile previously developed and agreed to by management. If information is substandard on any element, more and better data must be acquired before the project is allowed to proceed. Negative information, of course, may signal a Kill decision.

The profile chart method is more a *quality control tool* than a Go/Kill decision tool. It is a technique that is useful at all gates from screening to precommercialization; it is also a convenient project tracking device. But the profile chart's main use as a control device is its ability to *prevent a project from advancing to the next stage where key information is missing.* It also helps determine what action is needed to move the project towards successful completion.

One major weakness of the profile method is that the preparation of profiles, whether standard or for one project, is no easy task. First, the choice of the elements for consideration and the choice of what constitutes a desirable profile are arbitrary. Second, the evaluators must ask themselves how they "feel" about the "goodness of information" for a given project. Finally, the method does not signal a Go or Kill decision, but merely Go or Recycle. As a project selection device the profile chart has limited application, but as a information quality control tool, it has merit.

Benefit Contribution Models

Benefit contribution models require the evaluator to gauge the project's attractiveness in terms of its specific contribution to new product or corporate objectives. Since new product objectives are usually financial, the benefit contribution method typically amounts to *simple measures of monetary return.* Various economic indices—quick-and-dirty financial calculations—are employed.

At the early gates in the new product process, simple cost-and-benefit comparisons are employed. Such index methods require only the most rudimentary of financial data, and hence are particularly suitable for early gate decisions. The attractiveness of a new product proposal can be measured via the following equation:

$$\text{attractiveness index} = \frac{\text{expected benefit to company}}{\text{cost}}$$

where:

$$\text{expected benefit} = \text{benefit to the firm} \times \text{probability of success}$$
$$\text{benefit} = \text{some simple measure of profits}$$
$$\text{cost} = \text{cost to execute the project.}$$

Various financial indices have been proposed and some are listed in Appendix B.

As an illustration, one major and highly successful producer of industrial products deliberately avoids the use of complex financial calculations in the early phases of a project. Instead it uses the following financial index:

$$\text{attractiveness index} = \frac{\text{sales} \times \sqrt{\text{life}}}{\text{cost}}$$

where "sales" is the likely sales for a typical year once the product is on the market; "life" is the expected market life in years of the product (the square root of life is merely the firm's way of discounting the future and particularly long life products); and "cost" is the cost of getting into the market (development, launch costs, and capital expenditures). This company uses two arbitrary hurdle points, X and Y. If the index exceeds X, the project passes; and if the index is between X and Y, more investigation is required. Below Y, it is killed. Company people view this financial index as a sanity check—as one person put it, "more a check to make sure we're not spending $10 million to enter a one-million-dollar business." In conjunction with this financial index, this company also uses a scoring model approach to assess the qualitative merits of the project.

A financial index approach is clearly a gross simplification of a rigorous financial analysis. But at the early stages, only gross distinctions between good projects and sure losers are required. The method has the advantage of not requiring detailed financial data and thus suits the initial screening and early gate decisions well.

Checklist Methods

One of the simplest approaches to evaluating new product proposals is the checklist method. This approach can be likened to questionnaires that follow magazine articles on some new dreaded disease. At the end of the article is a list of 20 questions. If you answer more than 12 "yeses" out of 20, then you should see your doctor—there's a good chance you have the disease. These types of diagnostic checklist questionnaires are found in many fields from medicine to psychology to personal planning. They are the original expert system, and have proven to be reasonably accurate in terms of predicting or diagnosing some ailment or condition.

How are checklists developed? A group of experts constructs a list of questions that they believe are useful discriminators in predicting or diagnosing a situation. The system is validated using past cases—does the list of 20 questions really discriminate between the yea and the nay cases? A cut-off score is established—how many "yes" or "no" answers it takes to indicate the existence of a problem.

Checklists work well in new product evaluation, particularly at the early gates. Many companies use nothing more than a checklist of ten or so questions as the idea screen or Gate 1.

At all gates, the *"must meet" criteria* are best handled by a checklist—these are criteria where the answer must be a *yes* (or rather cannot be a *no*) in order that the project passes. In some checklist schemes, there is also a set of *"should meet" questions*—questions where a *yes* answer is not mandatory, but where a certain minimum number of *yeses* must be attained. These *should meet questions* measure whether or not the project possesses certain desirable, but not essential, characteristics.

In the design of a checklist scheme, the *must meet criteria* typically capture strategic issues, feasibility questions, and resource availabilities:

- Does the new product project fit the strategic direction or mandate of the firm?
- Is it technically feasible?
- Do we have the resources required to undertake the venture?

By contrast the *should meet items* describe the relative attractiveness of the project:

- Is the market large?
- Is it growing?
- Can the product be manufactured in an existing company plant?
- Does the product have sustainable competitive advantage?

A *no* answer to any one of these *should meet questions* certainly won't kill the project. But enough *nos* and the project may simply not be attractive enough to pursue.

In using the checklist, the project is presented to a group of evaluators or gatekeepers. Following a project briefing, the evaluators answer the set of questions on the checklist, providing "yes/no" or "favorable/unfavorable" answers. The answers are tallied and a profile or score for the project is determined. A suitable pattern of responses (for example, a prespecified number of "yes" replies) signals a Go decision.

Checklist methods offer an attractive approach to new product evaluation. Implementation is straightforward; a number of criteria are considered, not just a single one; the list ensures that vital considerations are not overlooked; the evaluation is a consistent one, as all projects are subjected to the same set of criteria; and finally, the method does not require detailed financial inputs nor rely on a single financial criterion.

There are problems with checklists, however. The choice of items for the list is arbitrary—they represent the compiler's best guess as to what factors are important to consider in evaluating a project. Some elements are likely to be more important than others—for example, having a sustainable competitive advantage versus having synergy with the plant—and the checklist does not build in a weighting scheme. The issue of what constitutes "an acceptable pattern of responses" remains a difficult one. Finally the inputs or answers to the questions are subjective, may be largely conjecture and opinion, and may not even reflect careful thought.

Scoring Models

An extension of the checklist is the scoring model. Here projects are rated on a number of criteria, but this time on rating scales (for example, 0–10 or 1–5 scales). These ratings are then added together in a weighted fashion to yield an overall project score. The scoring model thus overcomes many of the criticisms of the checklist. Specifically:

- the scoring model allows for degrees in each characteristic—it's not just "yes" or "no";
- it recognizes that some questions are more important than others, and incorporates a weighting scheme; and
- it provides a combining formula that yields a single score, so that projects can be rank-ordered against each other, or be compared against some cut-off or minimum score.

In using a scoring model, the project is often first subjected to a set of *must meet* criteria using the checklist approach. These are the mandatory questions—a single *no* spells a kill. These questions are relatively easy to answer, and weed out obviously unsuitable projects. Those projects that pass these *must meet items* are then subjected to a set of *should meet items* using a scoring model. Independently of one another, the evaluators rate the project on each of a number of characteristics using a numeric scale. The scores are tallied across evaluators, and a mean score for each question is computed. The mean score for each question is then multiplied by the weighting factor for that question, and summed across questions to yield a project score.

Let's look at a very simplified version of a scoring model. Assume that there are three *should meet criteria* (in practice, 20 to 30 criteria are typical). These three criteria are:

- the synergy level—how closely the resource needs of the project fit the resources and skills of the firm;
- market attractiveness—market size, growth, competitive situation, etc.;
- product advantage—product superiority relative to competitive products.

Assume that management believes that the last item, product advantage, is the most important and is weighted at 10. Market attractiveness is next at 7. Synergy is less important and is given a weight of 3. After the development of the scoring model, three projects are reviewed. One is rejected on the *must meet criteria* during the gate meeting. The remaining two projects are then scored on the *should meet items*.

Project A is a "close to home" project and fits the company well: it can be made in your plant, sold by your existing sales force, and developed using in-house development skills and people. Score it 10 out of 10 on the synergy criterion. But its market is only so-so: score it 6 on market attractiveness. The product itself is fairly similar to competing products, and rates only 2 out of 10 on product advantage.

Figure 7.3:   Sample Results of Scoring Model Evaluations

Element	Importance weighting	Scores		Scores × importance	
		Project A	Project B	Project A	Project B
Synergy or fit	3	10	3	30	9
Market attractiveness	7	6	7	42	49
Product advantage	10	2	10	20	100
Totals	20			92	158

Project B, in contrast, has significant product advantage, and the evaluators give it 10 out of 10 on that element. The market is slightly more attractive than A's, and rates a 7. But the fit with the company's strengths is low, and B scores only 3 out of 10 on this synergy dimension.

Figure 7.3 shows how these two projects look using a scoring model. The first column shows the importance weights, which are decided when the model is developed and remain fixed from project to project. Note that the sum of these importance weights is 20, so that the maximum possible project score is 200 (that is, if a project was rated 10 out of 10 on all three questions). The next two columns show the ratings for the two projects. The last two columns show the weightings times the ratings.

What have we learned from this exercise? First, Project B looks better than Project A. Project B's total score is 158 versus only 92 for A. If you were considering several dozen projects, you would be able to rank order these from best to worst using the project scores. Second, Project A's score is 92 out of a possible 200 points, or a score of 46 percent. Project B scored 158 out of 200, or 79 percent. Many firms use a score of 50 or 60 percent as a cut-off, according to which Project A would fail and Project B would pass. In effect, the scoring model has enabled the Go/Kill decision for these two projects.

Third, the scoring model provides insights into the projects. Why did A do so badly? Can anything be done about it? Why did B do so well? Are you sure that its positive features have been assessed accurately? Figure 7.3 reveals that the factor that killed project A was a lack of product advantage—it was rated only 2 out of 10. Perhaps there's an opportunity to rectify this lack of product superiority by building some new features or benefits into the product. If not, the project remains dead.

Now consider Project B. Its main driving factor was product advantage: of its 158-point score, 100 points or two-thirds of the total came from this one element. But if product advantage was more fiction than real, then the project is in serious difficulty. The next logical step in Project B is to verify its competitive advantage in the marketplace via a market study of potential customers' reactions to the product concept.

One challenge in developing either a checklist or a scoring model is arriving at a list of acceptable criteria. One useful list for new product project selection has been published by the Industrial Research Institute's Research-on-Research Subcommittee.[20] The 13 key criteria are

1. cost to do,
2. likelihood of technical success,
3. profitability,
4. size of potential market
5. development time,
6. fit with overall corporate objectives and strategy,
7. the firm's capability to market the product,
8. market trends and growth,
9. the firm's capability to manufacture the product,
10. market share expected,
11. patent status,
12. potential product liability,
13. capital investment required.

This list is useful. But don't forget those factors that we found *directly related to new product success* and profitability in Chapters 3 and 4! They too should be built into your scoring model or checklist.

Of the various project evaluation techniques, scoring models appear to fare the best in practice, particularly for the early gates. They reduce the complex problem of making a Go/Kill decision on a project to a manageable number of specific questions. As with checklists, each project is subjected to assessment on a complete set of criteria, ensuring that critical issues are not overlooked, as so often happens in unstructured discussion meetings. The method forces managers to consider the project in greater depth, and provides a forum for discussion. Unlike the checklist approach, scoring models recognize that some questions are more important than others, and individual ratings can be combined into a single project score.

In spite of their popularity, there are problems with scoring models. They rely on the subjective opinion of managers, and the input data may not be completely reliable. But at the predevelopment gates, often the only "data" available are management opinions. Most firms use multiple evaluators, together with confidence scores, to heighten the reliability of inputs. The premise is that the "average" decision maker is optimal. The dilemma is that the likelihood of any one evaluator being "average" is just about zero—hence the desire for multiple inputs.

Another criticism of scoring models concerns the arbitrariness of questions and the weights assigned to those questions. The question of the cut-off point— why not use a cut-off score of 50 instead of 60?—also is a contentious issue, as is the real meaning of the "project score." These criticisms, as we shall see later, have been largely overcome in recent years.

The NewProd Model

Scoring models have been improved and refined: more user-friendly, more predictive, and more useful output is generated in the form of diagnostics. For example, NewProd is an empirically derived, computer-based new product scoring model, which was derived from the experiences and outcomes of hundreds of past new product launches.[21] It is premised on the fact that the profile of a new product project, in terms of a number of qualitative characteristics, is a reasonable predictor of success: *new product success is predictable* (see Lesson 11, Chapter 4). These qualitative characteristics include measures of synergy, differential advantage, market attractiveness, project familiarity, and so on (see Appendix C for a list of the 30 NewProd questions).

In use, up to 12 evaluators assess the project on each of 30 key questions using 0–10 scales. These questions are proven discriminators between winners and losers. Two answers per question are solicited: an assessment of the project on that characteristic (a rating), and then the evaluator's indication of how confident he or she was in his or her answer (a confidence score). The profile of the project, based on these ratings and confidences, is analyzed by computer and, in effect, compared with the profiles of hundreds of projects in the database that have known commercial outcomes. In this way, a likelihood of success and the project's strengths and weaknesses are determined.

NewProd attempts to predict whether a new product will be a success or not, and thus is an important input into the Go/Kill and prioritization decisions. The NewProd model is also a facilitating tool used to analyze or diagnose a project and hence to better understand that project. NewProd thus helps the project's evaluators or the project team itself uncover the project's strengths, weaknesses, and uncertainties; it leads to a common understanding of the project; and it helps them develop an action plan for the project.

This commercially available NewProd model has been adopted as a selection and diagnostic tool in about 100 companies in Europe and North America. It has been successfully validated in Holland, Scandinavia, and North America and yields predictive abilities in the 73- to 84- percent range—not perfect, but considerably better than the typical manager's ability to pick winners!

A Closer Look at Economic Models

The two most popular and perhaps best financial methods for new products are *payback period* and capital budgeting (DCF). Both are cash flow techniques as opposed to traditional accounting accrual methods, hence they avoid disputes such as what can be capitalized and written off versus what must be expensed in year 1; or what depreciation rate to use. Moreover, cash flow methods result in the "correct return" or yield from the project.

In the *payback period method,* a year-by-year cash flow projection is prepared for the project—cash in versus cash out. Initial expenditures in R&D, capital equipment, and launch in year 0 place the project in a highly negative cash position, but begin to be recovered as revenues commence in year 1. The payback period answers the question: "when do I get all my money back?" The payback method has three main advantages.

- It is simple and easily understood.
- It uses a cash flow approach, hence avoids accounting method disputes.
- Projections only as far into the future as the payback period are required—we don't need ten-year projections.

The most rigorous method of financial analysis for new products is capital budgeting—that is, *present value or DCF methods.*[22] DCF analysis requires a similar year-by-year cash flow projection as in payback, but here the net cash flows for each year are discounted to the present using a discount rate—usually the minimal acceptable return or hurdle rate for the company. This stream of future cash earnings, appropriately discounted to the present, are then added; and initial outlays are subtracted to yield the Net Present Value (NPV). If the NPV is positive, the project has cleared the hurdle or discount rate. Most computer spreadsheet programs come with a DCF capability, which also permits the calculation of the Internal Rate of Return (IRR)*—the true yield on the project (as a percentage).

DCF analysis also has certain advantages.

- It recognizes that time is money—that money has a time value. And it tends to penalize those projects with more distant launch dates.
- It too is a cash flow method, and avoids the usual problems of accounting and accrual techniques.
- It yields the "true" return as a percentage.
- It tends to place much less emphasis on cash flow projections that are many years into the future (that is, the result is not particularly sensitive to revenue and cost estimates made for many years out, particularly if the discount rate or IRR is high).

To help identify project risks, *sensitivity analysis* is recommended. Sensitivity analysis is quite easy to do, especially if the data are already in a spreadsheet format. In sensitivity analysis, key assumptions are tested: for example, what if the revenue drops to only 75 percent of projected; what if the manufacturing cost is 25 percent higher than expected; or what if the launch date is a year later than projected? Spreadsheet values are changed, one at a time, and the financial calculations are repeated.

If the returns are still positive under these different "what if" scenarios, the conclusion is that the project justification is not sensitive to the assumptions made. However if certain "what if" scenarios yield negative returns, then these assumptions become critical: key project risks have been identified.

Several improvements to these well-seasoned DCF methods are suggested by Graves and Ringuest, which take into account the decisions-maker's preferences for differing time flows of money and differing risk levels of projects.[23] Non-

---

* In the IRR calculation, the discount rate is determined such that the NPV equals zero.

constant discount rates (or discount rates that change over the life of the project) for projects for which the risk is due to some discrete identifiable event is one solution proposed.

The Allocation Decision: Portfolio Methods

Portfolio methods are used to prioritize projects and allocate resources among competing projects, and are useful when combined with another approach such as a scoring model, checklist, or DCF method above. Two portfolio approaches are proposed by two different consulting firms to provide insights into the portfolio decision.

Strategic Decision Group

The Strategic Decision Group method (SDG) is financially based and looks at the expected commercial value of the project to the company and also its probability of technical success.[24]

The first factor, *Expected Commercial Value,* is based on net present value techniques. It represents the future stream of earnings from the product, discounted to the present, and assumes success. That is, if the project were a success, what would its net present value (commercial value) to the company be? The second factor, *Probability of Success,* is simply the likelihood of technical success.*

These two factors—Expected Commercial Value and Probability of Success—are then plotted as a bubble diagram on a two-dimensional grid: Figure 7.4 shows a typical example taken from a true company situation. The size (area) of the circles or bubbles denotes the resources devoted to each project (annual budget), and hence display the "size" of each project. The quadrants are labeled:

- *Oysters:* the lower left quadrant, represents potential pearls—lower probability of technical success, but with high commercial value to the company. These must be cultivated to yield "pearls" to assure the future of the organization.
- *Pearls:* the upper left quadrant, which are the highly desirable projects, having both high commercial value and a high likelihood of technical success.
- *Bread and Butter:* the typical project—low risk, but with ordinary to low commercial value to the firm (often includes extensions, modifications, and minor projects). These projects are often necessary in that they fuel the organization. (You may also see the term "rice bowl" used in lieu of "bread and butter"; for example, in the Japanese version of the SDG model, the analogy is made with "bowls of rice fueling the person.")

* Potential problems with the method are that the commercial or marketplace success seems to be ignored (only likelihood of technical success is explicitly considered); also expenditures on capital, launch, and R&D are not factored into the commercial value calculation. We attempt to rectify these weaknesses with an adaptation of the SDG approach.

Figure 7.4:   Portfolio Map for Prioritizing New Product Projects

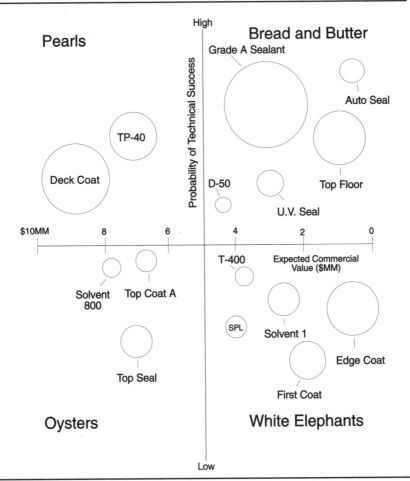

Example based on a sealants and coating firm (disguised).

- *White Elephants:* bad projects—a low commercial payoff and low likelihood of success. They require much care and expense and yield little profit. As SDG notes: "The king of Siam supposedly would give disagreeable courtiers white elephants, the upkeep of which caused financial ruin."

The portfolio grid is used at gate meetings, as well as during the annual planning or budgeting exercise, to ensure a reasonable balance of projects. Decision rules might be: seek as many pearls as possible; invest in some oysters; try to cut back on the bread and butter ones (there are usually too many of these); and delete the white elephants.

To make the model more complete, expenditures on R&D, capital items, and launch should be subtracted from the economic value of the project. Also, the probability of commercial success may be more critical than the probability of

Figure 7.5: Determination of Expected Commercial Value of Project

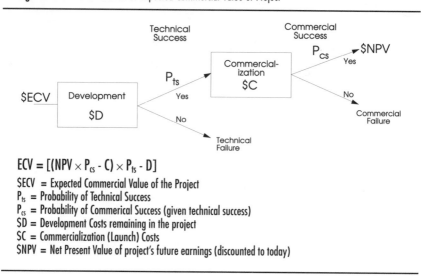

$$ECV = [(NPV \times P_{cs} - C) \times P_{ts} - D]$$

ECV = Expected Commercial Value of the Project
P_{ts} = Probability of Technical Success
P_{cs} = Probability of Commerical Success (given technical success)
D = Development Costs remaining in the project
C = Commercialization (Launch) Costs
NPV = Net Present Value of project's future earnings (discounted to today)

technical success, so cannot be ignored. Figure 7.5 shows our adaptation of the SDG model, which incorporates these missing elements.

Arthur D. Little

The Arthur D. Little (ADL) approach argues that financial or NPV methods used to generate portfolio maps may not only be meaningless but could also be harmful.[25] ADL considers a number of qualitative characteristics of each project that render a project attractive. Many of these same characteristics are found in checklist or scoring model systems described above under benefit measurement models. In ADL's scheme, specific project attractiveness characteristics include:

- fit with business or corporate strategy (a judgment rating from excellent to poor).
- inventive merit and strategic importance to the business (a judgment from high to low).
- durability of the competitive advantage (measured in years: projects that yield a long term competitive advantage are more attractive).
- reward: based on financial expectations (but can also be "necessity work"). Reward is usually expressed as a qualitative proxy for financial payoffs—from modest to excellent.
- competitive impact of technologies (base, key, pacing, and embryonic technologies).
- probabilities of success (technical success and commercial success; overall

Figure 7.6: An Alternative Version of a Portfolio Map

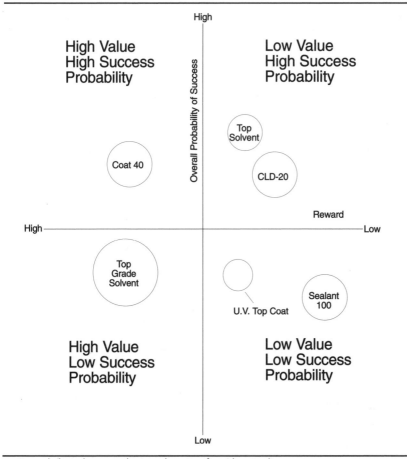

Example based on a sealants and coating firm (disguised).

success is the product of the technical and commercial success probabilities).
- R&D costs to completion (dollars).
- time to completion (months).
- capital and marketing investment required to exploit the technical success (dollars).

This ADL portfolio method requires the plotting of a number of these characteristics against each other on two-dimensional grids. The number of plots seems endless however; this does get a bit tedious, leads to information overload, and detracts from the method. Perhaps the single most useful plot shows the reward (a scaled measure from modest to outstanding) plotted against the probability of overall ouccess (Figure 7.6). Note that this useful grid closely resembles the SDG model, except that SDG's commercial value (an NPV calculation) is replaced by ADL's reward measure (a qualitative, scaled assessment).

Both methods essentially boil down to plotting a likelihood of success versus some measure of the economic value of the project. Perhaps the greatest benefit is simply having a display of all projects underway on a single map, so that management can see a bird's eye view of the projects in the pipeline.

Which Project Evaluation Method Is Best?

None is best! Despite its shortcomings, however, a *scoring model* used in conjunction with a *checklist of must meet criteria* is an effective way to handle the first three gates in the new product game plan. These methods render a highly judgmental decision somewhat less arbitrary and subjective; they systematize the review of projects; they focus attention on the most relevant issues; they force management to state goals and objectives clearly; they are easy to understand and use; and they are generally applicable to a broad range of situations and project types. Portfolio maps (such as ADL's or SDG's described above) might be used along with checklists and scoring models to help prioritize those projects that passed to help allocate resources.

Financial or economic methods also have a role to play at gates, and should see increasing use as the project moves from development towards commercialization—that is, from Gate 3 onward. The point is: by all means, undertake a thorough financial analysis at Gate 3; but don't base the project selection decision solely on it! At later gates in the process—Gates 4 and 5 for example—the nature of the evaluation does change: here it usually boils down to financial and risk considerations (handled by standard economic models) and a checklist consisting of a handful of *must meet* questions.

The Design of a Gate

We've had a look in this chapter at various approaches to evaluating and ranking new product projects. Now the task is to develop an appropriate evaluation or project selection approach for your firm—one that can be applied at the various gates. The problem is particularly difficult at the first few gates—Gates 1 to 3—where information is so lacking, notably financial information. Gates 4 and 5, while not easy ones, tend to benefit from better information, and can be largely reduced to a handful of questions, with a particular emphasis on profitable, risk, and financial outcomes. These financial methods are well known, so the remainder of the chapter focuses on nonfinancial approaches and on designing the first three gates in the process.

Before embarking on this task of designing the gates, let's reflect for a moment on how these gates work and on their role in the new product game plan. Remember: The entire new product process is built around a set of gates or decision points. These gates precede each stage, and open or close the door for the project to continue. In effect, they serve as the critical "quality control check points" in the new product process. Gates are much like quality checks on a production line, identifying substandard projects, and making sure that they are either stopped or fixed before significant spending continues on them. Gates deal with three critical quality issues:

1. *Is this the right project on which to spend your valuable resources?* In short, is this a quality project with value to the company that justifies further expenditures? Is it a good business proposition?
2. *Is the execution of the project being handled in a quality fashion?* That is, are the project leader and team members doing their job in a quality fashion? And are the deliverables to the gate in good shape?
3. *Is the "path forward" a quality one?* That is, is the proposed action plan reasonable, and are the resources proposed—people, money, and time—appropriate and realistic?

Gate Format

Gates have a common format (see Figure 7.7), with three important elements:

- *Deliverables:* These are what the project leader and team must deliver to the gate and are the results of actions in the preceding stage. Deliverables become the objectives of the project leader and team. Standard lists of deliverables are defined for each gate. As well, at the preceding gate, both the path forward and the deliverables for the next gate are decided.
- *Criteria:* These are what the project is judged against in order to make the Go/Kill and prioritization decisions. These criteria are usually a standard list for each gate, but usually change from gate to gate. They include both financial and qualitative criteria, and are broken down into required characteristics versus desired characteristics.

Figure 7.7:   The Structure of a Gate

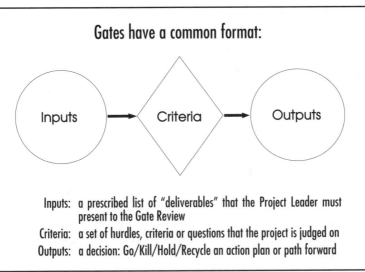

Gates have a common format:

Inputs → Criteria → Outputs

Inputs: a prescribed list of "deliverables" that the Project Leader must present to the Gate Review

Criteria: a set of hurdles, criteria or questions that the project is judged on

Outputs: a decision: Go/Kill/Hold/Recycle an action plan or path forward

Figure 7.8: The Two-Part Decision Process

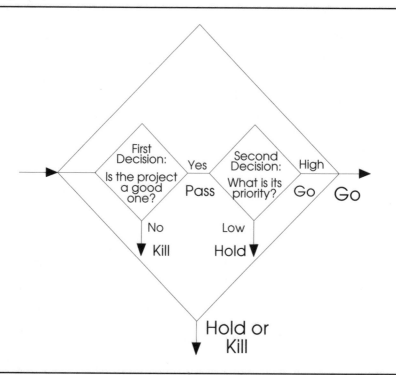

- *Outputs:* These are the results of a gate, and include a decision (Go/Kill/ Hold/Recycle) and a path forward (an approved action or project plan and the list of deliverables for the next gate).

A Two-Part Decision

The real problem in project evaluation at the earlier gates is allocating scarce resources across different projects, each at different stages of completion. Remember our sailboat analogy and the various portfolio models? In practice, the gate decision breaks down into a two-part decision—see Figure 7.8.

The first decision is: is the project a good one? If this were the only project available, would we proceed with it? Here the project is evaluated on its own merits against a set of standards. Think of this decision as a Pass-versus-Kill decision.

The second decision is a prioritization one: Given that the project is a good one, and considering the other projects already underway and the resources available, what is the priority of this project? Is it high priority—a strong green light and an emphatic Go? Or is it a Hold—one we put on the shelf until resources become available at a later date?

The first decision—the Pass versus Kill—is conceptually a much simpler one. And here there are excellent tools to assist you in making better decisions. A suggested approach is described below. The second decision, the prioritization one, however, is more problematic—conceptually complex and lacks widely accepted tools—so it tends to be more judgmental in nature (although some of the portfolio tools we outlined earlier may have applicability here). Nonetheless, the fact that the quality of the first decision can be greatly improved means that the prioritization decision is also likely to be a better one.

Culling Questions

As we design a typical early gate, remember that project selection is a culling process. The scheme is to subject projects initially to simple, easy-to-ask questions; in this way, you pare down the list of projects to a more manageable subset, which you then subject to more thorough evaluation.

The first part of each gate—the initial culling questions—is a simple quality check that the deliverables are in place, and that the activities that underlie these deliverables were executed in a quality fashion. This simple quality check involves a set of *must meet questions.*

The next set of questions ask whether or not the project is a good business proposition—they confirm that the project has positive economic value for the company. The justification of any project can be reduced to *three critical questions:*

- Is it real?
- Is it worth it?
- Can we win?*

Is It Real?

Is it real? poses fundamental questions about whether the project merits any consideration at all. For example, is the project in bounds or out of bounds? Is it feasible? Is it consistent with company policies? These "first pass" questions are usually *must meet criteria,* and, like the deliverables check, are best handled by a checklist. *Is it real?* questions deal with the following issues:

- *Strategic alignment:* Is the project within the new product mandate of the firm? Does it fall within an area of strategic focus—an area defined as "fair game"? This question presupposes that you have defined a new product strategy and areas of strategic focus that are in bounds versus out of bounds for your firm or division. More about strategy in Chapter 11. A lot of projects are eliminated at this stage simply because they are out of bounds.

---

* This is a variation of the Schrello "Real, Win, Worth" model, an excellent tool marketed by the Forum Corporation of North America.

- *Feasibility:* Is the project feasible . . . that is, can it be done? And most important, can *we* do it? Do we have the resources and skills to undertake the project (or could these be readily obtained?) If it's not feasible—because the product's not technically feasible, or because it's too big a project or outside your technical, marketing, and production capabilities, or simply too farfetched an idea—kill it here and now. And when you consider obtaining resources via a third party—for example, via a strategic alliance, partnership, or joint venture—be very careful in your assumptions about what resources and skills your partner brings to the table.
- *Company policies:* Does the project comply with company policies with respect to health, safety, and the environment? Does it meet company legal and ethical standards? These and other policies are obviously crucial ones to consider early in the life of a project and are potential knock-outs.
- *Killer variables:* Are there any other potential killer variables, such as impending changes in legislation and regulations, a new, emerging technology or competitive moves—that would simply destroy your project? If there are, then you can't wish these killer variables away—now is the time to recognize them.

Is It Worth it?

Is it worth it? is the second critical question. Although a relatively simple question, it is often difficult to answer, especially in the early phases of a project. Here we query whether the project is likely to have commercial value to the company, enough to justify the expected expenditures. In asking the *worth* question, we assume that the project will be a success: that is, given that the new product is successful, will its revenues and profits justify the investment? These financial issues are often uncertain at the first few gates, but nonetheless, first-cut estimates must be made if for no other reason than as a sanity check. At later gates, the *is it worth it?* question becomes paramount, as detailed financial analyses become a critical component of each gate. *Worth* criteria considered here, depending on the gate, may include:

- *minimum market size:* that the existing or potential market exceeds a certain size.
- *minimum margins in this market:* that margins earned by the players in this market at least exceed a certain percentage.
- *financial index:* whether or not the project's financial prospects exceed some financial index value or quick ratio. Some examples of these quickie financial ratios or indices are given in Appendix B.
- *payback period:* a determination of how long it will take to recoup the outlays in development costs, capital expenditures, and launch costs of the project. This is a cash flow method and can often be done simply and quickly.
- *net present value and internal rate of return (IRR):* here DCF analysis yields the "true" return of the project in the form of IRR, and the NPV gives the commercial value of the project to the company, taking into consideration

the cost of capital and the time value of money. These methods are usually reserved for later gates (Gate 3 and later).

Often other and strategic criteria take precedence over financial measures of worth—for example, the fact the new product is a strategic initiative and will open up new technology or market windows of opportunity; or that the new product is essential strategically as a defensive move against a threatening competitor.

Will We Win?

Will we win? is the third and perhaps the *most difficult question,* and the one we get wrong the most often. Figuring out the economic worth of a project is relatively simple, if the assumption is that we win. When was the last time you ever saw a project justification presentation made, financial calculations and all, on the assumption that the project would lose? The assumption always seems to be that we'll win! But here management is very often wrong: remember, for every four projects that are released for development, only one becomes a commercial winner.

Fortunately *we know what the ingredients of a winner are*—the profile of a winning new product has been uncovered in countless studies of new product success and failure. So *let's use some of these characteristics that are so strongly correlated with winning as selection criteria.* Note that no project will meet all of them, so here we look for a reasonable profile or point count across the set of criteria. In short, these *winning profile* characteristics are highly desirable, but not essential characteristics: a low score on any one is not grounds for killing the project. Unlike the *must meet criteria* above, these desirable characteristics are a matter of degree and become *should meet criteria.*

Table 7.1 lists these *should meet criteria,* ready to be translated into a scoring model format similar to the one you should be using in your gate meetings. (See also Appendix C for format.) The criteria in this table are typical of those at Gate 2 or Gate 3.

The criteria outlined above—real, worth, and win—are only sample criteria. The ones you should use in your company may differ. But the lists of questions provided above and those in Table 7.1 provide a great starting list. In the next section, you'll learn how to develop your list of criteria and a scoring model for your firm. Appendix C shows the set of evaluation questions from the NewProd model, which might also be included in your scoring scheme. And finally the results of the success/failure studies—what separates winners from losers—provide a comprehensive set of key discriminators useful in evaluation tools (see Chapter 3).

Prioritizing Projects

If the project passes the *must meet questions* and clears the minimum hurdle or score on the *should meets*, the project is a good one—it is a "pass." Now the

Table 7.1: Sample Gate 2 or 3 "Should Meet" Questions*

Product Advantage
The degree to which the proposed new product . . .

— offers unique benefits to customers or end users.

— offers the customer good value-for-money.

— solves a problem the customer has had with previously used products.

— has highly visible benefits.

— is higher quality than competitivie products.

Market Attractiveness
The degree to which the market . . .

— is a large one.

— is fast growing—well over GNP growth.

— has a significant long-term potential.

— earns exceptionally high margins for others.

— has no intensive nor aggressive competition.

— has no dominant competitor.

— is served poorly by competitors.

Synergy or Fit with the Firm
The degree to which synergies exist in the following areas:

— sales force distribution

— customer base

— R & D

— production facitlities and personnel

Other Should Meet Items
Does this project have . . .
— a champion to drive the project forward?

— a sponsor to shepherd this project?

— a positive impact on other products? (Will the product aid and abet the sales of other products in the firm? Or does it threaten other products?)

— other benefits?

*All items can be scored on scales of 1–5 or 0–10.

---

thorny question of prioritization arises: should we devote resources immediately or put it on hold. And what intensity of resources? As indicated above, this prioritization issue is largely handled judgmentally. Nonetheless, how the project fares on the should and must questions—how *strong* a pass—obviously is a useful input to the prioritization decision. Another useful input or tool is the portfolio map outlined earlier in this chapter, where the expected commercial value (or reward) of the project is plotted against probability of success. Using the portfolio map, the project in question can be considered against all other projects currently under way, and decisions made about reallocating scarce resources.

A word of caution: *project prioritization cannot be conveniently ignored*—you can't keep adding Go projects to the active list. Project prioritization, including removing projects from the active list, is an essential facet of each gate!

Developing the Must and Should Criteria

How does one go about developing a checklist and a scoring model to handle the Gates 1 to 3 in the new product process? Here are two approaches and both have their merits.

Management Consensus

One approach to developing a scoring model is the management consensus method.[26] This method can best be illustrated by an example. An all-day meeting is convened for the purpose of developing a screening tool. Present are managers who are involved in the gate decisions and who have had past new product experience. The session begins with an open discussion; the facilitator asks that all the *must meet* or knock-out criteria be identified. A freewheeling debate and discussion ensues, and a list of "absolutely essential" project characteristics is derived and agreed to. This list captures the "real" and "worth" questions. The lists provided above and in Table 7.1 might be a good place to begin.

Next the discussion moves to the *should meet* or desirable characteristics. These are essentially proxies for "will we win?" The facilitator asks participants to identify those characteristics that are thought to be ingredients in a winning project and also are likely to be known at this specific point in the project. Again a freewheeling discussion ensues, and the group should have no difficulty in producing a list of 30 or so desirable characteristics. Again Table 7.1 and Appendix C might be a good beginning point.

What about the weights for the *should meet questions?* To keep things simple, some companies elect to go with an *unweighted list of evaluative criteria*—one in which all items have the same importance and the ratings are simply added to yield a project score. But let's assume that management decides to place weights on the criteria, in order to acknowledge that some things—such as elements of product advantage—are perhaps more important than others—for example, synergy.

After the list of items is rewritten, clarified, and cleaned up (for example, removing duplicate items or items that measure essentially the same thing), the group is asked to consider the *importance* of each item. One approach is to collectively choose the item that is the most important. This item is assigned an importance weight of 10. Then, privately and independently, each manager assigns weights to each of the other items, all in relation to the most important (on a 0–10 scale, where zero means "not too important"). These weights are then tallied and anonymously displayed. Discussions take place on each question, focusing on those where there are large deviations among group members. Often consensus can be reached here. If not, the facilitator asks the group to repeat the exercise—to assign weights once again. By the second or third round, invariably agreement is reached on all items.

Using this approach, the management team identifies the *must meet criteria,* develops a comprehensive list of *should meet items,* and agrees on the importance weights for the should criteria. Note that the evaluation scheme—items and weights—has been developed and agreed to by the very people who must use it, thus ensuring commitment. An appropriate cutoff criterion can be established, and the model can be validated by running previous company projects, both successes and failures, through the model.

Review of Past Projects

The second approach to developing an evaluation tool is more analytical, more expensive, and more powerful. It requires a fairly large sample of past new product projects for raw material, and its use is thus restricted to larger firms.

As in our previous example, managers meet to identify a list of *must meet criteria* and a possible set of *should meet items.* But management opinion ends there. Next a sample of past commercial successes and failures is identified. People who are familiar with the projects are then asked to rate them, retrospectively, on the *should meet criteria* (0–10 ratings). Up to ten evaluators (usually about four or five) conduct this retrospective analysis of each project. The relative commercial success or failure of each project is also assessed—the degree to which the product exceeded or fell short of the minimal acceptable profitability criteria for this type of investment. With a large sample of projects and by use of appropriate statistical methods (such as factor analysis and multiple regression analysis), a success equation can be generated that relates the degree of success to each of the various *should criteria.* The coefficients of this equation then become the weights on the criteria.

In short, this analytical approach simply relies on empirical evidence—on past experiences—to derive a predictive equation or model that can be used to assess future projects. The NewProd model in Appendix C was derived in this manner.

Conducting a Gate Review

A number of companies use formal gate reviews, complete with written criteria, to heighten the sharpness of their project selection decisions. In practice, the project team and leader submit their deliverables or inputs to the gate, usually several days before the actual meeting. Remember: these deliverables were decided upon and agreed to at the previous gate. Deliverables should be short and to the point: some companies even place a stringent page limit on deliverables at each gate to eliminate unnecessary and unwanted paperwork. Gatekeepers receive copies of the deliverables in advance and have a chance to prepare for the meeting.

The Briefing

Depending on the gate, the project leader and team usually make a brief presentation of the project to the gatekeepers. This briefing session is designed to bring the group of evaluators up to speed on the project. In practice, the gatekeepers do not change much from gate to gate (although more senior people may be added as the spending requirements increase), hence the project team is not faced with totally reeducating the gate reviewers at each gate. Following this briefing, a question-and-answer period ensues, whereby project team members and gatekeepers share information and opinion.

The Gate Criteria

Once all the facts are on the table and the briefing session is complete, the formal evaluation begins, using the gate criteria. This is best handled by issuing each gatekeeper a blank scoring sheet, with the questions and scales based on those listed earlier in this chapter and in Table 7.1 (the format shown in Appendix C may be used). These scoring sheets are also displayed on an overhead projector.

The gate chairperson first walks the gatekeepers through the *must meet criteria*—one criterion at a time. Remember: a single *no* signals a Kill decision and brings the meeting (and the project) to a quick end. Thus, each *must meet criterion* is discussed openly, and a consensus view sought on each that it is positive.

Next, the chairperson leads the gatekeepers through each *should meet criterion,* again one item at a time. Each is discussed, but this time no consensus or votes are publicly called for. Each evaluator simply notes a score on his or her scorecard for each question: the "voting" or evaluation is done anonymously in order to avoid peer pressure or "group think."

After all *should meet questions* are discussed, the scorecards and answers are then tallied onto a single scorecard (usually the overhead transparency).

The Debriefing

A debriefing session ensues. This session is likely the most valuable facet of the evaluation process. Here the gatekeepers see each other's evaluations and scores (displayed via an overhead projector). Here are some of the topics in this debriefing.

Areas of disagreement are readily identified. For example, in the evaluation of a new high-strength–carbon reinforcing fiber, some of the evaluators assumed that the new product was indeed a leapfrog effort, far surpassing competitive products in terms of performance. The rest of the evaluators were much more skeptical, noting that the product was quite close to competitive products, particularly on the critical performance characteristics that mattered to customers. The different opinions of these two different sets of evaluators were not apparent during the open discussion, but became very clear after the ratings and scores were displayed on the overhead. In the discussion that followed in the debriefing session, the reasons for these differences became evident, and a discussion of performance characteristics (and relative importance to the customer) quickly ensued.

Areas of ignorance and uncertainty also become clear. For example, in the review of a new ion–exchange resin based on a totally new technology, there was considerable discomfort surrounding some of the questions that captured market need, size, and growth. It was clear that the project team had done a superb job dealing with the technology issues, but a much weaker job defining and qualifying the target market. The path forward for the project team was evident: get the missing market information!

Strengths and weaknesses of the project are discussed. The next step is to clearly understand weaknesses, so that needed actions can be taken either to eliminate the weakness, or at least to defend against the weakness. Similarly, strengths are identified, and the discussion often focuses on whether these strengths are real or are fiction. For example, in the evaluation of a new building material, the project fared relatively well on most points—a good fit with the company, a solid and growing market, and relatively weak competition. The product's advantages were rated quite negatively, however: the product didn't offer the customer any more benefits than the one they were already using. This one negative factor proved to be particularly damaging to the project's overall assessment. Discussions followed, and the project leader (a technical person) confessed that in pursuing the project, his goal was simply to develop a product that was equal to the competition—a "me too" product. The outcome of this facet of the debriefing meeting was a recognition that some element of product advantage was essential to the new product's success.

A Go/Kill decision is reached. For the first three gates, this decision is based on answers to the *real, worth, win* questions: how the project fares on the *must meet checklist items* (a single *no* signifies a kill); how the project scores on the scoring model—the *should meet questions* (the project score must clear a minimum hurdle); and in the case of Gate 3, how the project fares on the NPV and IRR financial criteria.

The project's prioritization is set. This is decided by looking at the strength of the project against the criteria (for example, the financial expectations and the project score on the *should meet items*). The current portfolio of projects (the portfolio map) is reviewed, and the impact of adding this new project (or expanding the resource commitment to this project as it moves from one stage to the next) is assessed.

A Course of Action

The *path forward* is next decided. Usually the project team has submitted a proposed plan of action to the gate, but the gatekeepers must review and possibly change the proposed actions in light of the revelations at the gate meeting. The debriefing session is particularly useful in this respect: when areas of disagreement and uncertainty and potential killer variables are highlighted, the action requirements become obvious. Typical questions addressed include: Why was the project rated so positively (or negatively)? What are its good points? Are we sure about them? What are its bad points? Can these be fixed? And so on.

Areas of disagreement that remain even at the end of the gate meeting must be resolved early in the next stage and certainly before the next gate. These often require specific studies. For example, in the case of the carbon-reinforcing fiber above, one action item added to the plan for the next stage included a customer study to determine the order-winning criteria and the relative importance of various product performance characteristics. A second action item was a closer look at competitive products—a competitive product analysis.

Similarly, *critical areas of ignorance* and uncertainty must be eliminated (or reduced). For example, in the ion-exchange resin project, the team was charged with getting the missing market information before any more technical dollars were spent: a market study was outlined at the gate meeting, involving visits to key and leading potential customers to ascertain interest level, economic value of the product to the customer, and purchase intent.

Negative facets of a project must at least be recognized and acknowledged, and, where possible, fixed. For example, the gate review of the "me too" building material resulted in two tasks as part of the action plan for the next stage: an end-user study to identify weaknesses in competitors' products, as perceived by the potential customer; and in-house creativity sessions (brainstorming) that focused on ways that the proposed new product could be significantly improved so as to outshine the competition.

Remember, the output of a well-conducted project review is not only a Go/ Kill and prioritization decision, but a *solid plan of action* for the next steps in the project.

The gate meeting concludes. The action plan is agreed to. The gatekeepers commit to the project, and assign resources to it. The list of deliverables for the next gate is spelled out. And the team is off and running for the next stage of the project with benefit of a strong management commitment, a clearly defined path forward, and a concrete set of objectives.

Speeding the Approval Process

One of the most positive facets of a formal new product process complete with defined gates is the speed of the approval process. In too many large firms, a significant percentage of the project leader's time is spent seeking approvals or sanctions from more senior people: the simple act of getting signatures on a piece of paper. Incredible as it sounds, I've seen this process hold up projects for weeks, and sometimes months! Reducing the approval process to a few days is one of the most dramatic things you can do to reduce cycle time.

The gates provide the mechanism. Here, all the key decision makers gather in one room. They hear the case for the project, evaluate it against a preset list of criteria, make a decision, and then commit resources to an action plan. It happens in one room and in one day!

Remember: as go the gates, so goes the process!

The Gatekeepers

Who are these people that man these critical gates—the gatekeepers* who make the Go/Kill and resource allocation decisions and that are essential to making the new product game plan work? Obviously the choice of the gatekeepers is specific to each company and its organizational structure. But here are some rules of thumb:

1. The gatekeepers at any gate must have the *authority to approve the resources* required for the next stage.
2. To the extent that resources will be required from different functions, then the gatekeepers must *represent different functional areas*—R&D, marketing, engineering, manufacturing, and perhaps sales, purchasing, and quality assurance.
3. The gatekeepers usually *change somewhat from gate to gate*. Typically Gate 1, the initial screen, is manned by a small group—perhaps two or three people—who need not be the most senior in the organization. Here the spending level is quite low. By Gate 3, however, where financial and resource commitments are substantial, the gatekeepers typically include more senior managers, for example, the directors of R&D, marketing, and manufacturing, and perhaps the divisional or business unit manager.
4. There should also be some *continuity of gatekeepers* from gate to gate. In short, the composition of the evaluation group should not change totally, requiring a total start-from-the-beginning justification of the project at each gate.

In many companies, which have implemented stage-gate systems, the greatest behavioral change occurs at the gatekeeper level—the decision process. Gatekeepers must abide by several essential rules—rules that represent a *major departure* from the old way of doing things—in order that the game plan be effective.

The first rule is: *a decision must be made.* If the deliverables are "on the table" and in good shape, a Go/Kill decision and decision on the action plan must be made that same day. The decision cannot be to defer making the decision.

---

* Here we use the term "gatekeeper" to mean a person who sits on a gate decision point, and makes Go/Kill and allocation decisions. In new product management, gatekeeper can also mean a person on the project team who is well networked with others inside and outside the company, and functions as an information gatekeeper.

Table 7.2: Summary of Gates and Methods

GATE	OBJECTIVE	METHOD	GATEKEEPERS
1: Initial Screen	To spend a little money to see if the idea merits spending more.	Checklist of (6–12) *must meet criteria;* scoring model for *should meet items* (optional).	Two or three middle-level technical and marketing people.
2: Second Screen	More rigorous test that opens the door to an expensive investigation stage.	Repeat checklist of Gate 1 *must meet* items; scoring model for *should meet items;* payback period as a sanity check.	Senior marketing, business, and technical people.
3: Decision on Business Case	To make the critical commitment to full product development.	A repeat of Gate 2 *must meet* (checklist) and *should meet* (scoring model) criteria; financial review based on Net Present Value and Internal Rate of Return together with sensitivity analysis; a portfolio impact assessment via portfolio maps.	Key decision-makers in the business unit or division: senior technical, marketing, sales, manufacturing, and management people.*
4: Postdevelopment Review	To make sure development met goals and product meets requirements; opens door to stages moving towards commercialization.	Checklist of *must meet* items (e.g., deliverables in place, plans OK); complete financial review, as at Gate 3.	Same as Gate 3.
5: Precommercialization Business Analysis	Final decision point prior to launch.	Same as Gate 4.	Same as Gate 4.
6: Postimplementation Review	Terminates new product project.	Review of project performance and key lessons.	Same as Gate 5.

* May also include senior finance, purchasing, and quality assurance managers.

The gatekeepers *also must be disciplined:* They must *use the stated criteria,* and not rely on "hidden" criteria, "gut feelings," or "from the hip" criteria in making the Go/Kill decisions. Management's track record is quite poor when it is swayed by these subjective factors.

In addition, gatekeepers must ensure that *all projects are treated consistently and fairly*—for example, not bypassing the gate for pet or personal projects. The gatekeepers must *be at the gate meeting.* (In one telephone company in the US, if the gatekeeper misses the meeting, then his or her vote is an automatic "yes"!) Finally, they must be prepared for the meeting—having read and thought through the advance briefing material.

Table 7.2 summarizes the methods and possible gatekeepers for Gates 1 through 5.

A Post-Game Gate: The Postimplementation Review

Gate 5 may be the final decision-point in the project, but it isn't the final review. In this game, not only must the team score a touchdown, but the players must sit on the football in the end zone to ensure that a goal really has been scored. The project team remains accountable and totally involved in the project through the launch and postlaunch activities.

Eventually, following this launch period (often 6–18 months), it is time to end the project. Here the project team is relieved of its accountability; the members are recognized and rewarded; and the product becomes a "regular product" in the firm's product line.

To mark the end of the project, a final review takes place: the postimplementation review. Here the main objective is to learn from the project so that the next project will be done even better. This is part of the quality process—the process of continual improvement. A second objective is to identify additional work that needs to be done on the new product for the years ahead—refinements, adjustments, line extensions, or perhaps the next generation or design.

Critical questions that are pondered by the gatekeepers and team at this final gate include:

1. What are the results of the project: sales, shares, margins, contributions, and profits (actual results and latest expected results)?
2. How do can these results compare to those projected at Gates 3, 4, and 5? If there are variances, what accounts for the discrepancies—why the gaps? And how we can become more accurate in the future—for example, what might we have done to more accurately forecast the product's performance?
3. What was done particularly well in the project? And what was handled weakly? What would we do differently the next time around?
4. Based on the answers to questions 1–3 above, what lessons have we learned? How should we modify our new product process to incorporate these new lessons?
5. What additional work needs to be done on this product? What new opportunities has the project or product identified? And what is the proposed plan of action?

Project Evaluation: A Final Thought

It is impossible to remove all the guesswork and risk from new products. We must always deal with the future, and hence with uncertain events. Sharper project evaluation is possible, however, and new product selection has been identified as one area needing much improvement. It is also an area where some firms have been doing a much better job in recent years.

Suggestion: Take a hard look at how new product projects are screened, selected, and prioritized, particularly at the earlier stages of a project. If your firm is typical, chances are that this process can be made more effective. If you've identified the Go/Kill decision points as less than excellent, why not move towards the development of a systematic evaluation, selection, and prioritization method, following the steps outlined here? In short, design your new product process around a set of effective gates.

Get a management group together, preferably the very people who will make the gate decisions. Develop a set of *must meet criteria* that deal with the *is it real?* and *is it worth it?* questions. Move on to the *should meet criteria*—criteria that are essential proxies for the critical question, *will we win?* Use a management consensus approach to develop the criteria and weights, or better yet, conduct a review of past projects—known successes and failures—to define the criteria, weights, and cutoff scores. Do this for each of the gates, especially the earlier ones—Gates 1, 2 and 3. Then design and implement a gate procedure, much like the one we've described in this chapter: deliverables in advance, a briefing session with questions and answers, the application of criteria, and finally the essential debriefing session that results in an agreed-to plan of action for the project.

Those firms that have made the effort—and there are a number that have carefully designed and implemented gates or key decision points using the approaches outlined above—are now reaping the benefits. They're seeing better, more thoughtful project selection and prioritization decisions; they're gaining improved focus (scarce resources going to the right projects); and they're using gate meetings to gain insights into the project to uncover what must be done to turn the project into a winner.

Development, Testing, and Validation

Everything that can be invented has been invented.
Charles H. Duell, Commissioner of the U.S. Patent Office (urging President McKinley to abolish the Patent Office)

The whole history of invention has been a struggle against time.
Charles Babbage, Grandfather of the computer (1791–1871)

On to Stage 3: Development

The project is Go for development. The up-front homework has been done and the product has been clearly defined: target market, product concept and positioning, benefits, and product requirements.

Stage 3, development, begins. Here we translate our business case plans into concrete deliverables. Remember: the deliverable at the end of Stage 4 is a prototype product that has been at least partially validated with customers and also via lab tests. As experienced project managers will attest, however, even in the most astutely defined product and project, much can go wrong from this point on. Two major problems often beset projects during this development stage.

1. *The product definition isn't quite right.* Problem number one is that the final product may not receive the same enthusiastic reception from potential customers that the product concept did in tests undertaken in Stage 2. This apparent inconsistency may be because the project team incorrectly translated the concept into a product—for example, ignored or down-played certain customer requests. Alternately, technical problems may have been encountered during development that forced a relaxing of certain performance requirements or an omission of features desired by customers. Worse, in the concept test, the customer may have been responding to an upbeat, perhaps even unrealistic, concept presentation; but the final product or prototype fell far short of the promised product as portrayed in the concept test.

2. *Things change.* The second problem occurs because the world does not stand still. Note that the entire project has been defined and justified on the basis of how things were just prior to the development stage. But development takes months, often years, and much that is unexpected can occur during this time frame. The market may change partway through development, making the original estimates of market size and product acceptance invalid. Customer requirements may shift, rendering the original set of product specs obsolete. Competitors may introduce a similar product in the meantime, creating a less receptive market environment. These and other external changes mean that the original product definition and justification are no longer valid.

These two pervasive problems present major challenges to the project manager as we enter the development stage. Challenge number one is to ensure that the product prototype or final design does indeed meet customer requirements. This means *seeking customer input and feedback at every step of the way throughout the entire development phase* as the product takes shape. One can never be sure about the success of a new product until it goes on sale in the marketplace. Thus it becomes imperative to build into the game plan a number of checks and tests to ensure that the project is still on target as we move through development and towards market launch. This is one of the key messages of this chapter: how to build in these checks and evaluations during and following product development. The name of this game is "no surprises."

Challenge number two is to move through development and into launch as quickly as possible. Rapid development is essential in order to enjoy the product's revenues sooner and to gain competitive advantage; but most important, *rapid development minimizes the impact of a changing environment:* if the product's development time can be reduced from 36 months to 15, the odds of things changing are similarly greatly reduced. For example, one of the problems with General Motors in the 1980s was the six-year cycle time from concept to launch; by the time the car was ready for market, consumers' tastes had changed, as had the competitive situation—so GM cars always looked a step or two behind the times. That's a second important message of this chapter—how to reduce cycle time during the development phase.

Ongoing Customer Input

Seeking customer input and feedback is a vital and ongoing activity throughout development, both to *ensure that the product is right and also to speed development towards a correctly defined target.* Don't be afraid to reach out to large numbers of customers to answer key design questions that arise during the development stage. The original market research that was done prior to product development may not be enough to resolve all your design dilemmas. Technical problems may arise during the development phase that necessitate a significant product design change. (Note that with better up-front homework, many of these technical roadblocks would have already been anticipated and appropriate measures built into the development plan to deal with them, hence minimizing the number of "on the fly" and unexpected changes needed during the development phase.) Nonetheless, unforeseen technical glitches invariably occur.

Avoiding the Edsel

If the impact of the product design change is likely to be visible to the customer, then check it out—don't assume! If market conditions are changing as a result of shifts in customers' tastes and preferences or because a new competitive product hits the market, don't be an ostrich. There's no disgrace in admitting that the up-front market investigations didn't answer every possible question. It's a fact of life that markets change and unforeseen technical problems occur.

In its day, the Edsel was one of the most carefully market-researched automobiles ever. Unfortunately, in the years between initial design work and product launch, customers' tastes changed, and so did the economy. Moreover, key design decisions were rarely checked out with customers—the styling of the car (which many people found repulsive), the electric push-button transmission located in the steering wheel hub, even the name of the car. What would have been the outcome if Ford had reached out to its customers at every step of the design and development process? The answer is obvious, as we witness the stunning success of the Sable and Taurus in the 1980s—a superb product development effort, one in which the customer was an integral part of the development process, every step of the way!

Astute product developers also recognize that additional market surveys may be required, even during the development stage. For example, in the development of a novel milk packaging system using polyethylene plastic bags, Du Pont of Canada's project team ran into a technical snag. The original concept was for milk to be packaged in one-quart plastic bags, and that these bags would have a tear-off tab for easy opening and resealing. The predevelopment market research tested and confirmed this product concept.

During development, however, technical difficulties arose that made the tear-off tab almost impossible. Rather than merely assuming that a change in product design would be acceptable to the consumer, the project team undertook a market survey of users to determine the importance of the tear-off tab. A hastily commissioned market survey revealed that the tear-off tab was desirable but not essential, and that product acceptance by the consumer would not be significantly affected by its absence. The tab was removed from the design and the product went on to be a great commercial success in Canada.

Designing Customer Tests

An often forgotten facet of customer testing is the *seeking of continual customer feedback during development*—that is, constant and iterative tests of the product as it takes shape during the lengthy development stage. In-house product testing (or lab tests) is normally an integral facet of product development.

But an in-house test only confirms that the product works properly under controlled or laboratory conditions. It says little about whether the product works under actual use conditions, and whether the customer finds the product acceptable. Customers seem to have an innate ability to think of novel ways of finding product weaknesses, ways the engineering-testing group could never have imagined. The "acid test" of the product design is with the customer.

There are many relatively simple customer tests that you can build into your game plan during Stage 3.

> Assume that you are partway through the development of a fairly complex product—for example, a new lawn-and-garden tractor aimed at homeowners. Key components—the new automatic transmission and dashboard instrument panel—have already been designed, developed, and tested in house. Both of these components are highly visible in the final product: they determine how the transmission shifts and how the dash looks and functions. Here's what you can do to assess the degree of customer acceptance:

1. Bring potential users (and your dealers) to the development site (or to a convenient location, such as a suburban hotel) to view and try out key components. You might mount the transmission on an existing tractor and display a mock-up of the dash available. Let the customer look, touch, and try. Record their reactions and comments (on tape, if you can). Obtain basic background information (demographics and other segmentation data), and then measure interest, liking, preference, and purchase intent much like in a concept test (and using the question format shown in Chapter 6 in Figure 6.5). Include probing questions, noting areas of particular likes and dislikes. If the customer has problems and voices complaints when he or she sees or tries the product or component, notes these as well.

2. The same procedure can be used with focus groups of customers. Start with an introductory group session. Then move to the display area so customers can touch and try. Finally, reconvene the group for a discussion of the merits and shortcomings of the tested components. The group session is more efficient than individual interviews (more inputs in a shorter period of time) and often leads to a more interesting and insightful discussion (the group members stimulate one another), but be careful of group dynamics: a single powerful member can sway the entire group to a positive or negative reaction to the prototype.

3. When the number of customers is small, try setting up a "user's panel"—an ongoing group of potential customers that acts as a sounding board or team of advisors during the development process. Whenever designs, design decisions, or components need to be checked, convene the customer panel to get its reaction.

4. Customer partnerships are perhaps the most certain way of seeking continual and honest customer input during the development phase. Customer partnerships work particularly well where both the customer and the developer each have something to gain from a cooperative development effort.

Seeking customer input in such an arrangement is rendered quite straight-forward: the customer's people become an integral part of your design team.

As you become more comfortable involving the customer in your Stage 3 development work, you can begin to accelerate the process. For example, in the case of computer software development, you might develop a small facet of the product in a few days—rapid prototypes of several screen displays. But don't keep these as a secret: show them to the customer, and seek fast feedback as you proceed to the next step in development. The *ideal action is fast, highly iterative, and parallel:* a rapid or partial prototype is quickly fashioned, fol-lowed by immediate customer feedback, followed by development of another part of the product or a more complete prototype, and so on—a back-and-forth pattern, as illustrated in Figure 8.1.

Suggestion: While this rapid, iterative prototype-and-test process is practiced by a minority of industries, such as software producers, the methodology has applicability to a much broader range of industries and settings. The point is: break the development of the product into pieces or parts; rapidly develop par-tial prototypes, working models, or parts of the product; then test these quickly with the customer. This iterative series of rapid-prototype-and-test steps will quickly move you down the field in Stage 3 to your goal of the right product, and in a much-collapsed time frame.

Figure 8.1:   The Iterative Nature of the Rapid-Prototype-and-Test Pattern

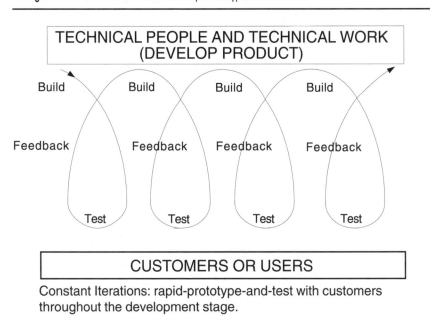

Constant Iterations: rapid-prototype-and-test with customers throughout the development stage.

Shortening Development Times

The second challenge introduced at the beginning of this chapter is to shorten development times so as to minimize the chances that the development target changes. Thus a sense of urgency is essential throughout Stage 3. This is one of the longest and potentially most troublesome phases of the project, but with the homework done up-front and with a solid product and project definition in place, many of the pitfalls and time-wasters typical of the development phase have been eliminated. We saw in Chapter 4, for example, five sensible ways to reduce cycle time. Build these into your new product process—this is the first way to reduce cycle time:

1. *Do it right the first time:* Build in quality of execution at every stage of the project. The best way to save time is by avoiding having to recycle back and do it a second time.
2. *Homework and definition:* Doing the up-front homework and getting clear project definition saves time downstream: it means clear product design targets and less recycling.
3. *Organize around a multifunctional team with empowerment:* The multifunctional team is essential for timely development: it cuts down on "siloing" up and down the vertical organization, and promotes parallel processing (rather than sequential problem solving).
4. *Parallel processing:* The relay race, sequential, or series approach to product development is dead: a more appropriate scheme is a *rugby game or parallel processing.* More gets done in an elapsed period of time; and the process becomes multifunctional.
5. *Prioritize and focus:* The best way to slow projects down is to dissipate your limited resources and people across too many projects. By concentrating resources on the truly meritorious projects, not only will the work be done better, it will be done faster.

In spite of these measures to reduce cycle time, there still is the commonly voiced complaint that the development phase takes far longer than expected; R&D or the design group is invariably accused of lacking a sense of time urgency. I hear this criticism often leveled at R&D or other technical groups by marketing and management people. Part of the problem may be indeed that technical people have a longer-term orientation and don't exhibit quite the same degree of "hustle" and responsiveness that marketers and business people do. But the problem may also be a management and planning one as well. For at the heart of every good development project is a *sound development plan.*

Timelines

The actual development of the product is driven by this development plan. This is the project plan approved at Gate 3, which includes:

- a chronological listing of activities, actions, and tasks.
- a timeline or time schedule, showing beginning and end points of these actions. Gantt charts, which provide a timeline and show activities along this line as bars (defining a start time and an end time), are appropriate for relatively simple projects, whereas critical path plans are needed for more complex ones.
- resources required for each action or task, notably personnel, person-days and dollars.
- milestones to be achieved are defined throughout the development phase (and are built into the timeline). These milestones are measurable and definable points in the project where a review of the project can be conducted to determine if it is on track, on schedule, and on budget.

The timeline or time schedule is a critical element in the plan. It must be aggressive, causing team members to stretch a bit. But it must also be realistic. Too often, a very compressed R&D plan is put together in response to marketing's demands. Unrealistic completion times are assigned to tasks. But within months or weeks of implementation, the truth is known: the plan of action is pure fiction, and its entire credibility is lost. So be aggressive, but be realistic too, in designing the timeline.

Deadlines must be regarded as sacred if speed is the objective.[1] Time-based innovation is impossible without a disciplined adherence to deadlines. Sadly, most companies only pay lip service to this principle. By sacred deadlines, we mean that a predetermined date is adhered to as a guideline for planning, with no excuses. The plan is developed, complete with the tasks to be done and their deadline dates. Delays are dealt with via extra input of effort and resources, *not postponement.*

Milestones

Milestones are important metrics in the timeline. Milestones are those checkpoints along the way where we check to make sure that we're on schedule and on budget. One rule of thumb that some firms employ is that if several milestones in a row are missed, the project should be flagged: the project is clearly in some sort of trouble, and the project leader must call for a full review of the project (in our model, the project cycles back Gate 3, so that gatekeepers can reconsider the wisdom of continuing with this project, now in trouble). In this way, milestone points can be used to blow the whistle on projects that are heading off course, before the problem becomes too serious.

To be effective, a milestone must be measurable and have a time frame attached. For example, in the development of a new software product, the proposal "to have most of the program written and partially debugged" is a very poor milestone. Words such as "most of" and "partially" are not measurable, and further, there is no time frame. Rather, the milestone should be quantifiable: "To have 30,000 lines of software written and fully debugged by day 95 of the project" is more appropriate.

Milestone checkpoints are not to be confused with the periodic review meetings that technical managers often hold. These review meetings typically are scheduled on a calendar basis (rather than in "real time" and after certain tasks have been completed): typical is the "quarterly review of all projects." These meetings are more for information purposes (rather than for control); but they do serve a useful role: here senior technical people are able to review progress to date during this development stage, and to provide insights, advice, and mentoring to the technical players on the team.

Discipline

Project plans—timelines and milestone checkpoints—are meant to be followed. When a project falls way behind schedule, too often it is because the project team just went through the motions of developing a plan of action complete with a time schedule, simply to meet management's requirements that such a plan be prepared. Then it was business as usual, and the plan and timeline were conveniently forgotten. Wrong! There must be constant self-discipline and accountability for these time schedules. Timelines are there for a purpose. One of the common traits I've observed among successful project leaders is a dedication to the plan and to the schedule. Some examples:

> A textbook case of a successful new product undertaken in Du Pont's automotive paint refinish business was driven by a (then) relatively inexperienced project leader. One of her keys to success, she told me, was her dedication to her schedule throughout the development phase of the project. She and her team used project management software (Harvard Project Manager) to lay out the plan for the two-year development phase. Every Monday morning at 7:30 A.M., the entire team would meet to review progress: what did we accomplish last week; where are we on the timeline; and what needs to be achieved by this time next week? Each Monday the critical path plan was updated, and a new time schedule generated. "It was this discipline—this religious adherence to the timeline—that drove the project so quickly and successfully," she exclaimed. The project was one of the most successful and time efficient that the division had ever experienced.

> The R&D manager at Adhesives Systems (a small, high-tech subsidiary of B.F. Goodrich) is in effect the technical leader on each project. The division has an enviable record of fast-paced, successful developments. His secret to success: good planning and tight control of projects. Every project must have a detailed plan of action before it begins. Once a project is underway, he has a weekly meeting with the technical players on the project; and every two weeks there is a full team meeting—marketing, R&D, and manufacturing players. But the weekly follow-ups are critical, he claims: "When the project is falling short, I know about it, and they (the players) know that I know about it! We have a (time) plan and I push hard to stick to it."

Many project teams and leaders have resorted to user-friendly software to help map out their projects. *MacProject, Harvard Super Project Manager,* and *On Target* are typical programs that help to lay out tasks, resources, and timelines. Besides being excellent tools to help structure and plan the project, these software packages also have the advantage of permitting weekly updates to the project's schedule and plan.

In Chapter 10, where we look at the implementation of the game plan, we consider a number of tactical tips and hints for reducing cycle time, not only for Stage 3, but from beginning to end of the project.

Other Actions during Stage 3

Remember that while the physical development of the product proceeds in Stage 3, many other activities (described in Chapter 4) are concurrently undertaken by other members of the project team. In parallel to product development, market analysis and competitive analysis both continue, in part based on the continuing feedback from customers. Detailed test plans are developed for the next stage, while marketing, production (or supply), and quality assurance plans are developed for the stages downstream. Regulatory and legal work continues, seeking to remove potential barriers to the project's progress. Financial and risk analyses are also updated: as the final product takes shape, estimates of manufacturing costs and capital equipment needs become much more certain.

On to Stage 4: Testing and Validation

A prototype or sample product has been developed. Thanks to the ongoing lab and customer testing that took place throughout Stage 3, the product has at least been partially proven even before it enters this testing and validation stage. The purpose of Stage 4 is to provide final and total validation of the entire project: the commercial product, its production, and its marketing. Typical activities in this stage include extended in-house product tests, customer field trials or usage tests, test markets, and trial or pilot production.

Testing with Customers

Not only must the product work right in the lab, it must also work right when the customer uses and abuses it. The product must also be acceptable to the customer (simply "working right" doesn't guarantee customer acceptance). Finally, the product must excite and indeed delight the customer: he or she must find it not only acceptable, but actually *like it better* than what he or she is buying now. In short, customer reaction must be sufficiently positive so as to establish purchase intent.

For some products the first time the customer can see and try the product is after the prototype or sample is completed. But this is risky! Don't wait until the product is fully developed before showing it to the customer. This grand unveiling could lead to some very unpleasant surprises rather late in the game. Nonetheless, there are some situations where customers cannot be a part of the development phase, and hence Stage 4 is the first chance you have to seek customer reaction. This might be true in the case of highly confidential developments, or perhaps some consumer goods (where the final sample or prototype is required before customer reactions are meaningful). It may also be true for more complex products, where the product is such that individual components (or working models) cannot be tested with customers. An example of the latter is an office telecommunications/information system, for which separate components including software, desktop hardware, large switching devices, and communications networks mean very little to an office customer until they are working together as a system.

Remember: by delaying customer tests until the end of development—until Stage 4—the risks increase. Try building in customer tests during development. For example, customer testing of this office telecommunications system during Stage 3, development, might allow customers to try a *working model* of the desktop unit complete with *simulated screens on the CRT,* and a *mock-up of the output,* and so on.

One of the pitfalls here is the reluctance of the project team to unveil their "baby" too soon to customers, just in case the reaction is negative:

> A well-known firm was developing a new camera-microscope system for use in a lab. In the homework phase, team members had interviewed lab users to solicit their inputs, and also brought in expert microscopists to seek performance requirements. So far so good. But no concept test presenting specs and performance characteristics of the proposed product was ever done. Here the team leader argued that the customer would actually have to "experience the product" in order to respond intelligently.
>
> So he sought to develop a "working model"—this was supposed to be a very crude but working version of the product—so that the customer could have hands-on experience. The problem was that the so called "working model" ended up being almost the final prototype, and by this point the project was into the millions of dollars. The project leader's reluctance to show early versions of the product or even product concepts to customers is understandable. But his arguments were faulty: admittedly, a working model will yield better feedback, but concept tests and bringing customers in to see bits and pieces of the product, as it takes shape, also yield useful insights and solid feedback regarding product design; further, by deferring customer feedback and reaction to so late a point in the process, he placed the project and company in a needlessly high-risk situation.

Preference Tests

A preference test—in which customers, either individually or as a group, are exposed to the finished product and their interest, liking, preference, and purchase intent measured—does several things. First, it provides a more accurate reading of likely market acceptance than the predevelopment concept test or any of the customer tests done during development. We now have the "commercial" or finished product to show the user. By contrast, in the concept test, the customers saw only a description or a model of the proposed product—something fairly intangible. And even during the development stage, we only had pieces of the product, or a working model—but never the final product. During the Stage 4 preference tests, however, customers are exposed to the real product—one they can touch, taste, or try. Much more information is presented to them, and because they are better informed, their answers and reactions are likely to be better predictors of eventual market acceptance.

A preference test also provides clues to minor design improvements that can make the product even better. If the suggested design improvements turn out to be major, it's back to the drawing board for a total redesign and more customer tests.

The final purpose of preference tests is to determine how and why the customer responds to the product. For this purpose, tape recordings of customer responses are invaluable. The words and phrases the customers use in their comments provide valuable hints about how the product should be communicated to the customer. The attributes or features that strike the customer first can be used in designing ads, brochures, or sales presentations.

Once the preference testing is complete, what does one do with the data? Can market acceptance or market share be estimated from the data? Many of the same guidelines outlined in conducting a concept test also apply to the preference test in order to maximize the value of preference testing.

- *Be careful not to "oversell" the product to the customer.* If you make too forceful or biased a presentation, what you're probably measuring is how good a salesperson you are, not whether the customer really likes the product.

  In the case of a new telecommunications product, for example, the project manager (who also was the product champion) conducted user tests and follow-up interviews himself. He was delighted with the consistently positive customer reaction. A second wave of tests and interviews, done by a third party, revealed much more negative results. It was found that the enthusiastic product champion had so oversold his product's benefits that he virtually coerced the respondents into positive responses.

- *Be sure that the customer is sufficiently well-informed* about the product to be able to judge it. This is a particular problem with innovative products. If the potential customer doesn't understand the product, its use, and its benefits, his or her responses won't mean very much. An "information session" held prior to the product test should give the customer relevant facts concerning the characteristics, use, and purpose of the product if these are not immediately apparent.

- *Be cautious in measuring price sensitivity* in customer preference tests. A common ploy is to ask an "intent to purchase question" about a product priced at say, 99 cents. Then the question is repeated, and a price 5 cents higher is named. Not surprisingly, the proportion of "definitely would buy" responses goes down as the price goes up. This type of questioning is invalid, however. By quoting the first price as 99 cents, the interviewer has established a reference price that is likely to bias all subsequent price questions. Had half the respondents been presented one price, and the other half the higher price, the positive responses would have been much closer. The same problem arises when a list of possible prices is presented and the respondent is asked, "What's the most you'd pay for the product?" The reference range of prices influences the answer.

If price sensitivity is an issue—that is, if you want to measure intent to purchase as a function of price—one price should be presented to one group of respondents, a second price to another group, and so on. Even with these controls, however, measuring price sensitivity is tenuous at best.

- Don't take "preference" and "intent-to-purchase" data literally. A 52-percent preference level does not translate into 52 percent of market share. The concerns relating to concept test results also apply here—these were outlined in Chapter 6. The results usually must be discounted to adjust for "yea saying," the lack of dollar commitment on the part of the buyer, and split purchases.

  Some firms use the following rule of thumb: a minimum of 50 percent of the target market must prefer the product, either "somewhat" or "very much," over the brand or make they currently buy or use. If the figure is below 50 percent, the new product is in trouble. History is perhaps the best guide for translating preference and intent data into market-share estimates. This points to the need to conduct user tests for every new product and to build up a history of data.

- *Interpret results of preference tests of difficult-to-distinguish products carefully.* For example, one cigarette manufacturer consistently obtained preference results on new products in the 45-to 55-percent range—a respectable result, so management thought. Eventual market shares were disappointing, however. An investigation of the testing procedure was undertaken. It was found that when a preference test was conducted on cigarette A versus cigarette B, 40 percent of the people preferred A, 40 percent preferred B, and 20 percent liked both equally. The catch was that A and B actually were the same cigarette! The point is that people will often indicate a preference where no difference exists, particularly in product categories that offer few product cues to help users distinguish between products. Thus, the preference results of 45 percent obtained in the cigarette example aren't very meaningful: 40 percent was by chance, and only 5 percent was true preference. In product categories where cues do exist, however, preference results are more meaningful.

Extended or Field Trials

Extended user trials (or field trials) enable the customer to use a product over a longer time period, usually at his or her own premises. The customer's reactions and intents are thus likely to be based on better information. Extended tests are particularly appropriate for complex products, for products that require a learning period, and when it takes time for the customer to discover the product's strengths and weaknesses. An extended trial may also uncover product deficiencies not apparent in a short customer test or a lab test.

To undertake an extended trial, a sample of potential customers is identified and qualified (that is, they agree to participate). The product is then given or loaned to the customer. He or she proceeds to use it at home, at work, or in the factory. A debriefing session is held with the user (either in a personal interview or by phone). The usual questions—interest, liking, preference, and intent—are posed. Probing questions can be asked about the product's strengths and weaknesses, its ease of use, its frequency of use, and suggestions for improvement. Often the results are unexpected—witness the case of the wall telephone (described in Chapter 5) that fell off the hook when a nearby door was slammed. There are other examples.

> A manufacturer of heavy equipment developed a prototype tree-harvesting machine. The unit was designed to fell trees with a knifelike action, strip the branches, cut the tree into sections, and load the sections onto a carrying device. The unit was thoroughly tested by company engineers in nearby forests and pronounced satisfactory. The unit was then loaned for customer tests to a forest products firm. All went well at the first site. When the unit was operating at a second site during rainy weather, serious product deficiencies became apparent. The combination of a certain soft soil (common in many forests) and wet weather caused the unit to become hopelessly mired in the mud. The test revealed that major changes were required in the traction design of the product—expensive changes, perhaps, but far less costly than the prospect of having dozens of the units stuck in the mud of forests around the world.

When undertaking field trials or extended trials in the case of complex, technical, or industrial products, a little care taken at the beginning in the design of these trials can make the results so much more valid. Here are some tips:

1. *Pick the test sites carefully.* Certainly, convenience is a factor, but strive for representativeness too. If you only pick "friendly customers," then you're likely to get positively biased responses and may be in for a shock after market launch.
2. *Get a written agreement with the customer in advance.* This agreement should specify, first of all, that this is a product test (many new products are placed with potential customers by aggressive salespeople, but the customer is not fully appraised that this is only a test!). Next it should indicate something about the timing, test duration, test conditions, what will be measured, by whom and how. How many times have we witnessed disputes over test results because a different testing procedure or metric was used; it could have all been avoided if these were spelled out in advance.
3. *Be there!* Even if the tests are being done at two in the morning, be on site. Strange and unforeseen events have a habit of befalling otherwise straightforward product tests when the project leader isn't there to check up on things. Get your presence written into the agreement beforehand (item 2 above).

4. *Get the customer to sign off on the test results,* and most important, on the interpretation of these results—for example, that they were a success or a failure. Two people can witness the same event or test, and draw quite different conclusions from it. Get agreement, and get it in writing!

Customer Tests: Not the Place to Cut Corners

User tests and contacts, both during development and after the prototype or sample is ready, often prove critical to the success of the product. So don't cut corners here! Studies show that this customer test phase—whether or not done, and how well executed—is significantly correlated with new product success. Moreover, analyses of new product failures reveal that in *half the failures the customer test was poorly undertaken or skipped altogether.*[2] The objectives of these customer tests usually include some or all of the following:

• to determine whether the product works well in actual use conditions (if not, what improvements are required?);
• to gauge whether the product is acceptable to the customer (and why, or why not?);
• to measure the customer's level of interest, liking, preference, and intent to purchase (and the reasons for these);
• to gauge price sensitivity—how preference and intent are affected by price; and
• to determine those benefits, attributes, and features of the product to which the customer responds most strongly (information useful in the design of the communications strategy for the product).

Suggestion: The customer test phase is not a difficult step, nor is it unduly expensive. Given its pivotal role in identifying product deficiencies while there is still time to correct them, and in assessing likely market acceptance, I recommend that customer tests be built into your game plan, at minimum, following the development stage, and if possible, during and throughout the development process. Remember: check with the customer, and check again—no surprises!

The Final Trials

By now, the product has been tested with the customer, and has been pronounced satisfactory. Minor design improvements have been incorporated. At the same time, the marketing plan for the product is coming together. (Chapter 9 is devoted to the development of a marketing plan; note that this marketing planning exercise gets underway in parallel with product development.)

Finally, the time is ripe to test the product, its production, and the launch plan under commercial conditions. For the first time you pull together all the elements of the marketing mix—product, price, advertising, promotion, sales force, etc.—and test their combined effect. At the same time, you produce a limited quantity of the product in a trial or pilot production run. The aim, of course, is to determine whether the strategy and programs as envisaged will generate the sales and profits you expect. If the answer is no, then you can choose between modifying the strategy and killing the project. It's still not too late to turn back.

There are two possible ways to test the launch strategy. Both are essentially experimental. Both cost less and are less risky than a full-blown launch. Both serve to provide a fairly valid test of the launch strategy, while leaving time for course corrections to be made before the launch. And both are reasonably good predictors of eventual sales or market share.

The first method is a pre–test market or *simulated test market*—a simulated shopping experiment that has gained popularity among consumer-goods producers. The second is a test market or trial sell, which although more expensive, has wider applicability for different types of products. Let's look at each in more detail.

The Pre–Test Market

A pre–test market (or simulated test market) is a relatively inexpensive yet surprisingly useful method for predicting market share and sales from a *new consumer product*. There are a number of commercial versions of pre–test market studies offered by various consulting or market research firms. Examples include BASES, ASSESSOR, and TEMP.

Potential customers in a pre–test market study are brought to a testing facility, where they are exposed to advertising for the new product or to a concept statement. In some approaches, the advertising is built right into a television show, and consumers think they are there to view a pilot. Following the exposure, consumers are given the opportunity to go on a simulated shopping trip through a dummy store. They are given coupons or credits and asked to select some merchandise. Of course, the new brand is displayed in the store, along with a variety of other typical store products. If a consumer chooses the brand under test, he or she is interviewed a few weeks later, after using the product.

A pre–test market study yields important information. First, the simulated shopping trip provides a measure of the effectiveness of the advertising and the package in generating sales. Second, information on product use, liking, and repurchase intent is obtained. The initial trial rate combined with the repurchase intent permits estimates of sales or market share. Finally, these techniques produce valuable segmentation data: demographics and other pertinent information about study participants are obtained, and a more exact definition of the target market is developed. Each of the commercially available pre–test market techniques varies somewhat in terms of method, computation, and purpose. BASES is used primarily to predict Year 1 and ongoing volume, whereas ASSESSOR and TEMP predict ongoing market share.

Why have such techniques become so popular, particularly among consumer-goods producers? Cost is the big factor. A pre–test market costs about $100,000; a test market can cost ten times that amount. Moreover, pre–test markets are surprisingly predictive. Although the experiment is somewhat artificial—a simulated shopping trip, phony money, a dummy store, etc.—experience has shown that the results are very close to the market share finally achieved after launch.

One major consumer goods firm estimates that pre–test markets demonstrate an "accuracy rate" of plus or minus 2 percentage points. That is, if the predicted share was 10 percent, the actual share will be between 8 percent and 12 percent. Of 17 such pre–test market results, in only one case were the results so far wrong as to misguide the project. The pre–test market had predicted a substantially higher market share than was eventually realized; the product was launched, and failed.

Other reasons for using a pre–test market include speed (it doesn't take as long to set up and conduct as a test market); the depth of data provided (segmentation data on triers and repurchasers); exposure (in a pre–test market, there is far less chance that the competition will learn about your new brand, and even less likelihood that competitors will get their hands on a sample); and control. The last point merits mention. In a full-fledged test market, there are many variables beyond the control of those conducting the test. One of these is competitive activity. Stories are told of deliberate competitor interference: competitors cut their prices, increase promotional activity, and even sabotage the test displays, all in an effort to thwart the test market or invalidate its results. A pre–test market, in contrast, is much more controlled: the store, the competitive brands on the shelf, and the displays are all within the control of the company conducting the test.

The one serious problem with a pre–test market is its limited applicability. Pre–tests are typically limited to relatively inexpensive consumer goods—the kinds of products found on supermarket shelves. The dummy store, the simulated shopping trip, and the fake money are clearly inappropriate techniques to use with big-ticket consumer items or industrial products. For those products, a trial sell, or test market, is the best means of testing the proposed launch plan and product.

Test Markets

Test markets (or trial sells) are the ultimate form of testing a new product and its marketing plan prior to committing to the full launch. Of the testing techniques, a test market comes closest to testing the full launch strategy before it actually takes place.

A test market is essentially an experiment. As in any experiment, there are subjects, treatments, and a control group. A small representative sample of customers is chosen—they are the *subjects.* They are exposed to your new product and to the complete launch plan, which includes all the elements of the marketing mix. This is the *treatment.* (Several different treatments can be used on different groups to see which works best.) The *control group* is all people not exposed to the test market.

There are usually two reasons for conducting a test-market study. The most common objective is to determine (or verify) the expected sales of the new product. A reliable forecast of future sales is critical to the final Go/Kill decision at Gate 5. If the test market shows poor sales performance, the project can be killed, or perhaps recycled to an earlier stage for necessary revision of the product or its launch plan.

A second objective is to evaluate two (or more) alternative launch plans by testing two different treatments to see which gives better results. This type of test marketing is less common. For one thing, it's clearly more expensive. Besides, the hope is that by the time you're ready to test market, strategy questions will have been resolved. Nonetheless, in some cases the test market is used to decide which market strategy works best. The choice of an appropriate positioning strategy is one of those cases.

Some years ago, a food company planned to introduce a new instant breakfast drink. The product had some taste advantages over competitors; it also was more convenient to prepare and store in the home. One possible strategy was to position the product as a "great-tasting breakfast drink"; the other was to position it as "a convenient, easy-to-prepare breakfast drink." Four test market cities were chosen. Two were subjected to the "great taste" positioning strategy; the other two featured the "convenience" strategy, and the test market results contributed to the decision to use the "great taste" strategy for the national launch.

Test markets can also be used for industrial products, in which case they're usually referred to as trial sells. A trial sell goes hand-in-hand with a pilot production run of the product. If a limited quantity of the product can be produced, samples can be made available to a handful of company salespeople in one or two sales territories for trial sell. The elements of the trial sell are as close to those of the actual launch as possible: the price, the advertising literature, the direct mail, and sales presentation are identical. The only difference is that national advertising and promotion cannot be used for a single sales territory. As with a consumer test market, negative sales performance in a trial sell will signal either a KILL decision or significant changes in the launch plan before the product is sold nationally.

Designing a Test Market

When the decision is GO for a test market, a number of decisions will have to be made to ensure accuracy and reliability of results.

Locations. The test-market locations must be chosen. In the case of consumer goods, cities usually are selected; for industrial products, sales territories can be used. Locations should be chosen to be representative of the entire market. For consumer goods, this means representative in terms of demographics and other segmentation variables. Cities must be selected with the availability of appropriate local media in mind. For industrial goods, a "representative" sales territory means representative in terms of industry breakdown, size of buying firms, etc.

Two or more sites usually are selected for the test. If two alternative strategies are being tested, if the risks are high in the project, if uncontrollable variables are likely to be a factor, or if representativeness is a problem, then more than two sites probably will be required.

Execution. The test market itself amounts to an execution of the marketing plan, but only for the selected locations—a "mini-launch." All of the elements of the marketing mix should be as close to those of the final launch as possible, including pricing, advertising, channels, and sales presentations. The duration of the test market must be established; tests can range from several months to several years, although shorter tests usually are preferred. Products with longer repurchase cycles necessarily mean a longer test market period.

Measuring Results

Decisions must also be made on what data to gather. For consumer goods, warehouse shipments are a rough indicator of performance, but that figure also includes product already in the "pipeline." Sales to end users—retail sales via store audits—are the preferred measure. With industrial goods, sales to end-users can be more directly measured, since the distribution channels tend to be shorter.

Some firms include end-user surveys in their test markets. Now that the product is actually in the hands of a customer, the time is ripe to obtain critical information. The task is to conduct follow-up interviews with users to find answers to some or all of the following questions:

- Who bought the product (demographics and other segmentation data)? Such information helps to confirm or refute the original definition of the target market.
- Why did he or she buy it? A knowledge of the "whys" leads to insights into the effectiveness of the communications and positioning strategies, and into buyer motivations and preferences.
- Did the customer like the product after he or she tried it? Why or why not? Such information is critical to a confirmation of the soundness of the product's design, features, attributes, and benefits.
- Would the customer repurchase the product? Answers to this question enable a determination of the long-run market share to be made.

Incorporating an end-user survey into a test market provides far more information than the test market alone, which only measures sales results. The results of a survey can prove invaluable if the market-launch strategy needs modification or adjustment.

Identifying the User

Identification of the end-users can be a problem for manufacturers of some types of goods. If follow-up interviews are to be conducted, provision must be made in the design of the test market to determine who should be interviewed. For industrial goods, the "who" information can be recorded as part of the sale, either through your own sales force or with the help of distributors. (The "who" information might include not just the purchasing agent, but also the individual or departmental user.) For big-ticket consumer goods, a mail-back in the guise of a warranty card provides this data. For smaller items, in-store intercepts can be used, or some form of redeemable mail-back can be included in the package.

To Test or Not to Test?

Having examined the elements of a successful test market, we now move to the most important decision: whether to undertake a test market at all. One common school of thought argues that test markets aren't worth the time, trouble, and cost. Test markets are expensive, particularly in terms of competitive lead time. Moreover, a test market exposes your product to competitors, thus giving them time to respond. So if speed and the competitive situation are crucial factors, then consider omitting the test market—this may prove to be "intelligent corner cutting." But be aware of the risks, and try to *build other steps into your game plan* that address the customer acceptance issue much earlier in the process—for example, better up-front market research, constant customer feedback during development, and well-executed customer or field trials.

Cost in money is another big factor. Test markets cost hundreds of thousands, and sometimes even millions, of dollars. The value of the information generated by a test market must be weighed against the cost of conducting the test market.

Another argument against test markets is that they exemplify the "horse and the barn door" situation. By the time the test market results are in, the door is being locked just after the horse has fled. Basically, the development budget has been spent; the product is fully developed, the creative work has been done, the packaging costs incurred, and the plant tooled up, at least for limited production. What's left? It's almost too late in the game to make changes now—the time to have killed or modified the project was much earlier in the process. This argument is persuasive in cases when expenditures up to the point of commercialization (for example, development) are particularly high in relation to launch costs.

A final argument against undertaking a test market is the questionable validity of results. As noted above, much can go wrong with a test market. Many variables in the experiment are beyond the control of those conducting the test. Often those variables cannot be known until the test market is well under way, and by that time it's too late to do anything.

Test markets or trial sells are not necessarily needless or wasteful. Give serious thought, however, to the pros and cons of undertaking such a test: test markets should not be an automatic or routine part of every new product's game plan.

A test market is useful when the uncertainties and the amounts at stake are high. A test market is warranted in the following types of circumstance:

1. *When there is still a high degree of uncertainty* about the eventual sales of the new product as the launch phase approaches. When you've conducted all the appropriate tests but are still undecided about the product's market acceptance, a test market may be called for. On the other hand, if you built market studies into earlier stages of your game plan—a concept test in Stage 2, rapid-prototype-and-tests during development, and user and preference tests during Stage 4 (and these have been well executed)—then you should be fairly sure about market acceptance and hence may not need a test market.

2. *When the horse is still not completely out of the barn*—when there are many expenses yet to be incurred in the project before and during the full launch. If many expenditures remain to be committed in the project—for example, if a plant needs to be built or a production line retooled or set up; if an expensive national advertising campaign needs to be mounted; if a sales force needs to be hired and trained—then a test market can be used to provide valuable inputs to these final GO decisions. On the other hand, if the production facilities are in place, and the if launch is relatively inexpensive (that is, if future expenditures are low), the cost and time involved in a test market may not be justifiable.

Certain technical considerations must be borne in mind when deciding to go with a test market. Limited or trial production may not be practical for some products. As one manufacturer of telecommunications equipment put it: "For telephone handsets, there's no problem doing a test market. We can run a couple of thousand of these units down a quickly set-up production line quite easily. For major capital equipment, however, such as a new digital switch, the day we make our first production unit, that's the day we're in full-scale production. There's no halfway."

Limited marketing in one or two cities, regions, or sales territories must also be possible. For goods that rely on electronic media, local print media, direct mail, local distribution channels, and personal selling, the marketing effort can be made to focus on one region. If national advertising and promotion vehicles are key to the product's launch, then a test market may be ruled out.

Suggestion: If the risk remains high as the project approaches launch, consider building into your game plan a final trial: a pre–test market or a test market, accompanied by pilot or limited production. A pre–test market is recommended for consumer goods as a cost-effective predictor of market acceptance. For other types of goods, however, a full test market or trial sell is really the only method of accurately predicting the final sales results.

Test Markets: A Final Thought

Go into a test market with your eyes open. In too many cases test markets have been undertaken when they weren't really needed. Concept tests, preference tests, user trials, or pre–test markets had been undertaken with positive results, yet the firms proceeded with the test markets anyway. When they were asked why, their answer was, "It's company policy." Given the predictive abilities of pre–test markets and the problems and costs of test markets, clearly there are times when a test market can be safely omitted.

If you've done a thorough job on the up-front or predevelopment activities and carried out usage tests, preference tests, and pre–test markets, a test market may be unnecessary. The time to spot a bad product or a bad strategy is early in the game plan, not after the horse has bolted. In too many cases, unfortunately, a test market is a belated attempt to close the barn door. It's better to spend your time and money on up-front, "homework" activities.

If the decision is GO for a test market, remember that selection of locations, design of the test, and specification of what information will be gathered (and how it will be gathered) are critical issues, and require much thought. For example, think seriously about adding a buyer survey to the test market; for a small cost it provides the needed diagnostic insights that a simple test market doesn't yield. Too many test markets are badly designed, and others yield only limited information—yet they cost a fortune. Don't make that mistake in your test market.

Table 8.1   Summary of Stage 4 Actions: Testing and Validation

Conduct Extended Lab Tests	Final and validation lab tests are conducted to prove product performance and compliance with specs; final regulatory lab tests are conducted.
Conduct Customer Tests	Customer tests are designed to prove the product under real-life conditions and to establish purchase intent; may be of short duration (preference tests) or extended (field trials). Based on detailed test plans.
Undertake Trial, Pilot or Limited Production	Pilot, limited or trial production is undertaken to provide product for customer tests or test market, and also to prove the production system, production costs, throughputs, etc. The QA Plan (or standards) is tested.
Finalize Regulatory and Legal Issues	The legal/patent/copyright issues are finalized. All lab tests needed for regulatory approval are undertaken; approval is sought and obtained.
Revise and Finalize Marketing and Production Plans	Based on the results of the customer tests, test market and trial production runs, the Marketing Plan and Production Plan (as developed in Stage 3) are revised and finalized.
Revise and Finalize Financial Projections	The financial risk analyses are revised and finalized (as per Stage 3), but this time based on hard and reliable inputs: the results of the customer tests and test markets, combined with trial production results.

Go for Launch

The final evaluation decision—GO to full production and full market launch—is largely a financial one. Armed with the results of preference or end-user tests, test markets or trial sells, and pilot production runs, you can now make estimates of production and marketing costs, sales volumes, final prices, and profit margins with a high degree of confidence. Before the product moves to full-scale commercialization, a thorough financial analysis is essential.

By now, the market and production tests have yielded positive results. Armed with those results, the final DCF and sensitivity analyses are carried out. The expected return clearly exceeds the minimum acceptable level, even with pessimistic estimates of key variables. So the decision is GO for commercialization. It's time for the final play of the game—into the market!

The Final Play—Into the Market

Plans are nothing. Planning is everything.
Dwight D. Eisenhower.

The Marketing Plan

The marketplace is the battleground on which the new product's fortunes will be decided. Thus, the plan that guides the product's entry to the market is a pivotal facet of the new product strategy. In this chapter, we'll look at the factors involved in developing a marketing plan for your new product.

First, what is a marketing plan? It's simply a plan of action for new product introduction or launch. It specifies three things:

- the marketing objectives
- the marketing strategies
- the marketing programs

The marketing plan itself is a document that outlines or summarizes your objectives, strategies, and programs. The marketing-planning process is a series of activities undertaken to arrive at the marketing plan. Much of this chapter will deal with the process of developing a marketing plan—setting objectives, developing marketing strategies, and formulating marketing programs.

Timing Is Everything

When does the marketing-planning activity begin? This chapter occurs rather late in the book because the market launch is one of the final stages in the new product game plan. Be warned, however: this is not to imply that marketing-planning should be the final step prior to launch. If you leave it to the bitter end, you're likely to find you've done too little, too late.

During one of my investigations into how companies develop new products, I made an appointment to interview a senior executive in charge of new products.

The company was a large manufacturer of heavy equipment. I arrived at head-quarters for the interview, and was quickly directed to the engineering building several blocks away. "Mr. X, who's in charge of new products, is located in our engineering department," I was told. That should have been my first clue. During the interview, Mr. X spent several hours reviewing the development process. He focused almost entirely on the engineering, prototype-development, and product-testing phases. Finally I asked, "When do the other departments—manufacturing and marketing—get involved?" He replied, "manufacturing" They enter the scene after the product is tested and we've developed a set of manufacturing drawings. And marketing? Those sales fellows get involved as the product's getting ready for production—almost as the first unit comes down the production line." In subsequent conversations, it came as no surprise to learn that the firm's new product performance was indeed dismal, and that many problems could be traced to a lack of an effective and carefully conceived launch plan.

Start Early

Marketing planning is an outgoing activity that occurs formally and informally throughout much of the new product process. Informally, it begins during the first few stages of the game plan, right after the idea stage. By the time the project enters Stage 2, formal marketing planning is already underway as part of the development of the business case. Figure 9.1 shows that the development of a full marketing plan occurs simultaneously with product development to emphasize that a formal marketing plan should be in place long before the product is ready for market introduction or even for a trial sell.

Suggestion: Where in the new product process does marketing planning occur in your firm? Does it begin, as it does in many firms, at the very end of the game plan? Or do you start marketing planning in parallel with the development of the product? If it's a matter of "too little, too late," why not incorporate the marketing-planning activities alongside the development stage of your game plan?

An Iterative Process

The marketing planning process for a new product is an iterative one. The plan is not carved in marble at the early stages of the new product process. Even the formal marketing plan that should be in place prior to product test and trials is likely to be tentative. The first version of the plan probably will see many changes before it is finally implemented in the launch stage. In short, there will be many times when you will rethink and recast your marketing objectives, strategies, and programs before implementation.

Figure 9.1:   Marketing Planning in the Game Plan

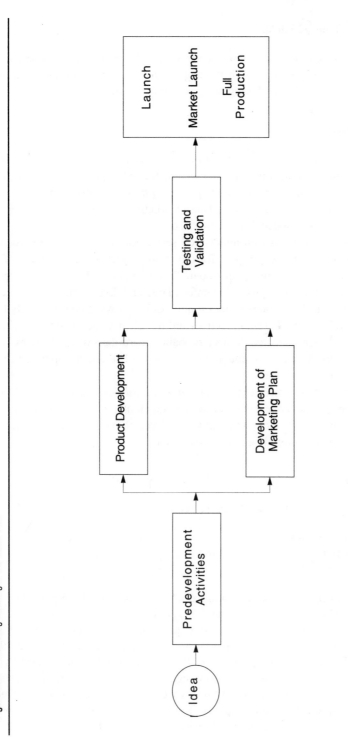

Setting Marketing Objectives

The marketing objectives that you specify for a new product must mean something. Why bother going through the aggravation of setting objectives at all? Objectives are part of a marketing plan for good reason.

The Role of Objectives

First, an *objective is a decision criterion.* When a manager is faced with two alternative courses of action, he or she weighs the consequences of each action against his or her objectives. The manager then picks the alternative that comes closest to meeting those objectives. Thus, marketing objectives help managers make decisions about specific marketing actions.

Second, a common and well-understood set of objectives for a new product *creates a sense of purpose*—a goal for the team players to strive toward. The written objectives communicate this goal. This common understanding is critical, particularly if the new product team is a large and diverse one. In too many new product projects the players are on quite different wavelengths simply because the product's marketing objectives are not clearly specified, not written down, and not communicated. You've probably heard the saying, "Having lost sight of our objectives, we redoubled our efforts." The remark applies in too many new product situations.

Finally, marketing objectives become *a standard for measurement.* Milestones or benchmarks are critical during the launch phase, when course corrections may be necessary. How will you know if you're on course if you haven't specified where you should be at any given time?

Good Objectives

What makes a "good objective"? Marketing objectives must

- set criteria for making decisions;
- be quantifiable and measurable; and
- specify a time frame.

A typical objective might be expressed as: "To gain a leadership position in the market." This sounds laudable, but it's a poor objective. First, it is not useful as a decision criterion. Second, it isn't quantified. What does "leadership" mean? Does it mean "50-percent market share or better," or does it mean "the highest market share among competitors"? And what does "market" mean? The whole market? Or a specific and narrow segment of the market? Third, because the objective isn't quantified, it can't be measured. For example, one year from now, after the product is on the market, how will the product manager know if the product is meeting its objective? Finally, no time limit has been specified. Is the objective to be reached in Year 1 or in Year 10?

There is a much better way to express the same marketing objective: "To obtain a 20-percent unit market share in the owner-operator segment of the class 8 diesel truck market during Year 2 in the market." Phrased in this way, the objective is a guide to action. Alternative plans can be assessed on their likelihood of achieving a 20-percent share; the objective is measurable and quantified; a time limit is specified; and market share can be measured during Year 2 to determine whether the product is on course.

Typical marketing objectives for a new product should include some or all of the following:

- unit or dollar sales of the product by year
- market share by year (be sure to specify the whole market or a segment, and whether the share is measured in terms of units or dollars)
- product profitability—percentage margins, annual profits by year (dollars or percentage), and payback period

Suggestion: Review several of your firm's past marketing plans for new product launches. Take a hard look at the "marketing objectives" section of the plan. Did the stated objectives establish good criteria for making decisions? Were they quantifiable and measurable? Did they specify a time limit? If not, strive for sharper objectives in future marketing plans using the list of typical objectives above as a guide.

Refining the Objectives

The process of setting objectives will involve iteration, or recycling. The setting of objectives is shown as the first step in the marketing-planning process in Figure 9.2. In practice, however, you must revisit this objective-setting stage a number of times as you move towards your final marketing plan.

At the early stages of the project, some rough numbers may be available that permit ballpark estimates of objectives. These early estimates may be little more than educated guesses, but at least you will have made your first attempt at setting some objectives for the product. As more and better information about the market, the product's expected advantages, and projected costs becomes available, the objectives will become better defined and more valid. Market studies, financial analyses, cost analyses, and other activities that are part of the new product game plan are inputs to the constant refinement of marketing objectives. By the time the product is ready for launch, the marketing objectives will have undergone extensive changes from the first rough estimates made at the beginning of the project.

Realistically, marketing objectives for a new product represent a *merging of what is desired and ideal* and *what is possible.* In the final marketing plan, the objectives for the product—sales, market share, margins—and the forecasts for the product become one and the same.

Figure 9.2:   Developing the Marketing Plan

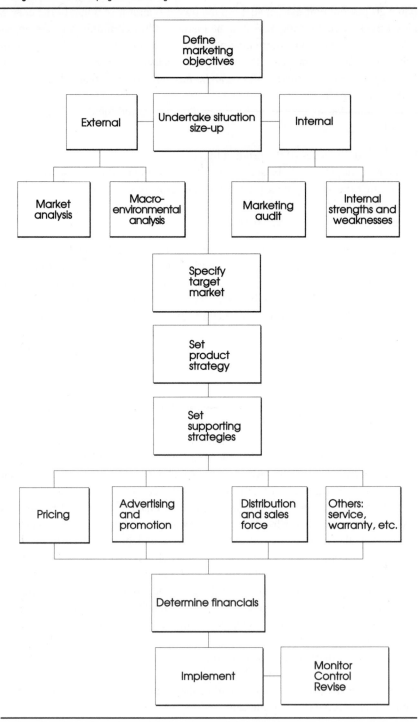

The Situation Size-Up

The situation size-up is a key facet of the marketing-planning process. Typically, it is shown as the step that precedes the development of strategies. In practice, however, size-ups are done often and at virtually every phase of marketing planning. A size-up is a situation analysis—it pulls together the relevant information and asks, "So what? What does all this information mean to the development of my plan of action? What are the action implications?" Many situation size-ups are long, boring, and overly descriptive, and fail to answer the question, "So what?" They begin with the heading: "Background," then move to "Description of the Market," and so on. They're full of information and long on description, but *short on action implications.* Make sure that your situation size-up includes the pertinent information, but always tell the reader, "Here's what this means in terms of an action plan for our new product." The major areas—both internal and external—that should be covered in a situation size-up in a new product marketing plan are shown in Figure 9.2.

The Market Analysis

The market analysis lowers the microscope on the market for the new product. A good market analysis addresses the following questions and issues.

- *Market overview:* What are the quantitative and qualitative aspects of market size, growth, and trends?
- *Market segments:* What market segments exist in this new product's marketplace? How is each segment unique? What are the quantitative and qualitative aspects of their size, growth, and trends?
- *Buyer behavior:* (in the segments in question) The who, what, when, where, why, and how of the purchase process are set out. Who buys? Who are the purchase influencers? What do the buyers buy, and when, and where? Why do they buy what they buy? What are their choice criteria (the order-winning criteria) and what are their preferences, wants, and needs?
- *Competition:* Who are the competitors? In which segments? What are their strengths and weaknesses? How good are their products? How does the customer rate their products? What are the competitors' strategies in pricing, advertising, and distribution? How well are they doing in market share and profitability? Why?

There are two points to remember: First, much of this market information will not be readily known at the outset of the new product project. By the time the project is ready to enter the development stage, however, market studies should have been undertaken in Stage 2, and a thorough market analysis, with action implications, should have been completed.

The second point is that *a good market analysis goes a long way towards charting a winning market strategy.* If the market analysis lacks insight and information, the marketing plan probably will be vague and not very hard-hitting.

A sound market analysis is the foundation upon which a winning launch plan is built. Don't skimp at this step.

Macroenvironmental Analysis

A macroenvironmental analysis looks beyond the immediate marketplace or the new product. Trends and factors outside the firm and the product's market that may have an impact on the market and product are analyzed. These include:

- the economic situation;
- the political, legislative, and legal situation;
- demographic trends;
- social trends; and
- technological developments.

For example, when assessing at the economic situation in the case of a new home gardening product—say, a rototiller—one would look at, among other things,

- the Gross National Product (as an overall indicator of wealth) and the disposable income (current and projected) of targeted families;
- costs and prices of garden produce and inflation rates; and
- fuel-cost projections.

Under the "demographics" heading, one would look at the age breakdown of the population, population locations, and so on.

Several general questions should be asked for each trend category in the macroenvironmental analysis:

- What is the situation or trend?
- What is the timing of the situation or trend, and how certain is it to occur? Is it here now or is it a "maybe and far in the future?"
- What are the implications of the situation or trend? Is it a threat or an opportunity? For example, what impact does the aging of the population have on the purchase of labor-saving home gardening products? For the design, positioning, and pricing of such products?
- What action is called for in light of the situation or trend?

The macroenvironmental analysis tends to be less concrete and less focused than the market analysis, and some of the conclusions or action implications will be fuzzy and contradictory. Nonetheless, the analysis is a useful one to build into your marketing planning effort. It doesn't take much time and effort, and on occasion some critical factors with a major bearing on the project are identified.

Internal Assessment

An internal assessment focuses on the company's internal strengths and weaknesses, particularly as they pertain to the project in question. A marketing audit typically is part of this assessment—it pinpoints your marketing "assets" and "liabilities."

- Look at your sales force. Is it good, bad, or indifferent? What are its strengths and weaknesses? Will it be able to do a good job with the new product? If not, what should be done?
- What shape is your customer service in? Are significant changes and improvements required to support the new product?
- Assess the status of your distribution or channel system, pricing policies, advertising approaches, etc. What needs to be done to bring them "on line" for the new product project?

The idea behind the marketing audit is to identify marketing strengths and resources that you can build on and use to advantage in the new product. Remember: The shrewd strategist always attacks from a position of strength. An essential step in the strategy-development process, therefore, is to understand what your strengths really are, and to identify and correct any weaknesses in the firm's marketing resources that could have a negative impact on the new product.

Another facet of the marketing audit is to look at your marketing performance over time—at current products and, perhaps, at other recent launches. Consider market shares, margins, and marketing costs against the strategies employed. The point here is to learn from your history, and to build these insights into a winning marketing strategy for your new product.

The internal assessment must also consider other facets of the company that will have a bearing on the launch plan for the new product. For example, you should be aware of the strengths and weaknesses of the manufacturing department—quality-control problems, availability of raw materials, people shortages, etc. Similarly, the strengths and weaknesses of other groups in the company, such as engineering, R&D, and finance, are equally critical. The object is to avoid being handicapped in your market launch by problems in other company departments.

Suggestion: Using past new product marketing plans in your company as test cases, assess the "goodness" of the situation size-ups that were undertaken. Was the market analysis a good one? Did it touch on the points outlined above? Was the environment reviewed and assessed? Was a "strengths-and-weaknesses" audit undertaken? Most important, did the situation size-up point to action implications? If your situation size-ups have typically been weak, why not begin with an outline or map of what you want to see in such an analysis? Remember that a solid situation size-up makes the job of strategy formulation much easier.

Defining the Target Market

The importance of target-market definition is a key element of the protocol statement or product definition (see Chapters 4 and 6). Clearly, one must have a precise definition of the target market before designing the product and before developing the launch plan. *From market segmentation, all else flows:* segmentation is fundamental to effective marketing planning. Yet many people get it wrong! Before embarking on a plan of action, it is essential that you know "the object of your affection."

How is a target market selected or defined? The first step is *segmenting the market*—that is, identifying the segments. The second step is *selecting the appropriate segment* to become the target market.

Segmenting the Market

Market segmentation is a popular topic among marketing strategists, and too complex to be fully discussed in this short chapter. Let's look at the highlights.

In the old days, economists spoke about "markets" as though they were relatively monolithic and homogeneous: "The market for X will behave this way or that way." Markets aren't homogeneous entities, however. They are people or groups of people buying things. No two people or groups of people are exactly alike, especially when it comes to their purchasing patterns. As consumers, we're all individuals: we have unique motivations, tastes, preferences, and desires. To treat all these different people or buying units as though they were painted with the same brush is naive. Moreover, to try to appeal to those different customers with the same strategy—one product, one price, one communications approach—is counterproductive.

Market segmentation is the delineation of groups or clusters of people within a market such that there is relative homogeneity within each group and heterogeneity between groups. That is, the people within one cluster or segment exhibit more or less the same buying characteristics, but are quite different from the people in other clusters or segments. The company that develops a strategy tailored to a specific buyer or type of buyer is likely to be more successful than the firm that has only a single strategy in the marketplace. Henry Ford's remark, "You can have any color as long as it's black," may have worked for the Model T and the early days of the automobile industry, but it fell flat once General Motors implemented a strategy of market segmentation in the 1920s: "A car for every purse and person." The idea behind segmentation is shown pictorially in Figure 9.3.

This quick look at segmentation theory reveals that segmenting a market is a lot more difficult than picking a few convenient variables—age, sex, income (or, for industrial products, company size or Standard Industrial Classification (SIC) code)—and splitting the market into groups or categories. That is one method of segmentation, but the results usually aren't very helpful.

Figure 9.3: Different Ways of Viewing a Market

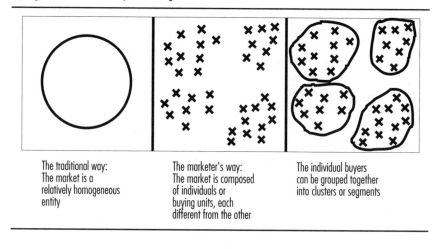

| The traditional way: The market is a relatively homogeneous entity | The marketer's way: The market is composed of individuals or buying units, each different from the other | The individual buyers can be grouped together into clusters or segments |

Bases for Segmenting Markets

Four broad categories of variables are useful in segmenting a market:

1. State of Being

Included in this category are familiar sociological variables such as age, sex, income, occupation, and the stage of the family cycle. The analogous variables for industrial goods are company size, industry classification (SIC code), and type of buying unit. Geography is another convenient variable: urban, suburban, exurban, and rural; regions of the country; and even regions of the world.

These "state of being" variables are the easiest to use: they're familiar and easily measurable, and published statistics relating to the variables are usually available. Frequently, however, they don't yield useful segments. The statement, "We're introducing a new brand of after-dinner liqueur aimed at women" is nonsense. The target market "women" assumes that all women's tastes are the same when it comes to after-dinner liqueurs, and that's simply not true. Remember, seek clusters of people that are relatively homogeneous—when it comes to buying your type of product, the buyers within a segment should behave much like one another.

2. State of Mind

The variables in this category describe potential customers' attitudes, values, and lifestyles. This type of segmentation is called "psychographics." Consider the over-the-counter drug market. Psychographically, some people are hypochondriacs, some are skeptics, some are authority seekers. Each type is a different segment, to which a different product or different marketing strategy can be targeted.

3. Product Usage

Product usage segmentation looks at how the product is bought or used. The three major bases for usage segmentation are as follows:

- *Volume segmentation:* the popular 80:20 rule applies for many markets—20 percent of the customers buy 80 percent of the product. Buyers can be divided into categories of heavy user, light user, and non-user.
- *Loyalty:* some customers are loyal to your firm, some are loyal to a competitor, and some move back and forth. The three different segments may deserve three different strategies.
- *Market factor:* different people respond to different elements of the marketing mix. In many markets, there are price-sensitive buyers, quality-conscious buyers, convenience buyers, service-seeking buyers, and so on. These types of buyers are different segments and should be treated accordingly.

4. Benefit Segmentation

Perhaps the most useful method of segmentation for use with a new product is benefit segmentation. Benefit segmentation recognizes that *people have different reasons and motivations for buying* a product, and therefore they seek different packages of benefits. When purchasing a new car, some people are looking for basic transportation—a reliable, practical, low-cost, safe car. Others seek a prestigious high-performance car loaded with creature comforts.

Benefit segmentation is particularly useful for new product strategy. Using this approach, the target market defines the benefits that must be built into the new product. Usually, these benefits can be translated into specific product features, which aids the product design process. The positioning and communications strategics also are largely defined by the benefit segment selected. Consider, for example, two target market definitions for a new alcoholic beverage:

- Target market A: "The product will be aimed at white, middle-income, American women in the 20 to 30 age group."
- Target market B: "The product will be aimed at women seeking a mild, nonfattening, sweet-tasting, smooth beverage to be used in a relatively upscale social setting."

The definition of target market A is an example of demographic segmentation. The definition is too vague to be useful in designing the product or creating an ad campaign. The definition of target market B is an example of benefit segmentation. The product can almost be designed and advertised simply by reading the statement. Benefit segmentation has its drawbacks, however. It invariably requires extensive market research. That research is difficult—many intangible variables must be measured. It's much easier to measure people's ages or occupations than it is to measure the benefits they seek.

Suggestion: No doubt there is a great deal of discussion in your firm about market segmentation and about selecting the right target market when developing a marketing plan for a new product. But have you ever tried to segment the market based on the different packages of benefits customers want from a given product? Try benefit segmentation. You'll find its a very powerful tool in designing a new product strategy. Some market research will be required to determine what benefits are sought, and which people seek what benefits.

Selecting the Right Target Market

A segmentation analysis should yield a number of potential market segments. At the same time, different versions of the product may be conceived to suit two or more segments. As Figure 9.2 illustrates, when one thinks of market segments one also thinks immediately of how to target the segments—for example, what product benefits and features can be built into the product to suit it to a particular segment or segments. The next task is to select the appropriate target market from among these options.

> Fibernyle, a division of the Lawson Mardon Group, a major international packaging firm, developed a packaging breakthrough—a plastic aerosol container designed to replace metal aerosol cans. The new product offered numerous benefits: better aesthetics, nonrusting, better feel, internal cleanliness, etc. Many possible market segments (and positioning strategies) were identified for the aerosol cans, from large-volume, low-price commodity segments such as toiletries (for example, shaving cream and hair spray) to speciality, low-volume (but potentially high–value-added) niche segments such as medical products (for example, contact lens sprays).
>
> The choice of segment (and positioning of the product) proved crucial to the entire project. Segment choice determines the nature of product specs that must be met and the product testing required, the benefits that will be emphasized, the pricing strategy, and even production equipment acquisition (high-volume versus low-volume).

Criteria for Market Selection

What are the criteria for selecting the target market (and product concept) from among a list of options? What criteria should Fibernyle management use for their plastic aerosol? Several straightforward criteria apply:

- *Segment attractiveness:* Which segment is the most attractive in terms of its market size, growth, and future potential?
- *Competitive situation:* In which segment is the competition the least, the weakest, or the most vulnerable?
- *Fit:* Where is the best fit between the needs, wants, and preferences of each segment and the benefits, features, and technological possibilities of your product?

- *Ease of access:* Which of the segments is the easiest for your company to reach in its selling effort, distribution channels, etc.?
- *Relative advantage:* In which segment do you have the greatest advantage over competitors in terms of product features and benefits, as well as other facets of your entry strategy? Note that "fit" and "ease of access" are not enough; they suggest mere adequacy. You must also look for areas in which you have a strong likelihood of outdoing your competitors.
- *Profitability:* It all boils down to profits! In which segment are you most likely to meet your sales and profits objectives?

Product Strategy

The definition of the product strategy—exactly what the product will be—goes hand-in-hand with the selection of the target market. Remember our discussion of the protocol or product definition: the protocol defines the target market and the product strategy. Target market definition and product strategy, together, are the leading edge of strategy development, and are front and center in the development of the marketing plan (see Figure 9.2).

What is meant by "product strategy"? For a new product there can be three or four components to the term.

The Product's Position

Product positioning is a combination of market segmentation and product differentiation. "Position" in the marketplace means "how the product will be perceived by potential customers." It's the continuation of the sentence: "Our product is the one that . . .". The position is usually defined in terms of key underlying dimensions by which customers perceive and differentiate among competitive makes. For example, a Volvo 764 is an automobile that is . . .what? It's safe, reliable, and lasts a long time (and is perhaps somewhat boxy and boring). By contrast, a BMW 500 series is . . .? It certainly isn't boxy and boring. No, it's been carefully positioned by BMW as the ultimate driving machine. Very different positioning, yet technically the two cars are fairly similar.

Step 1 in defining the product strategy is the specification of the product's position—usually a sentence or two defining how the product will be positioned in the market and in customer's minds, relative to competitive products and in terms of benefits offered. If you can't write down a clear, concise, and meaningful positioning statement, chances are you're headed for trouble. A fuzzy positioning statement is usually an indication of fuzzy thinking—no product strategy or, at best, only a vague notion of strategy.

Product Benefits

The benefits that the product will deliver to the customer should be delineated. Remember: a benefit is not a feature, although the two can be closely connected. A feature is part of the product's design—a physical thing. A benefit is in the eye of the beholder—some characteristic that is of value to the customer. For example, in the design of a new garden tractor, a benefit might be ease of use by elderly people. Corresponding features that translate into this benefit might be a clutchless transmission, a hydraulic lift mechanism for the mower deck, and power-assisted steering.

Features and Attributes

Step 3 is to translate the desired benefits into features, attributes, and product requirements. This step is likely to result in a much longer list of items, and one that gets very close to defining the product specifications. Here is where QFD may help (see Chapter 6). For example, in the case of a highway truck, if one benefit of the proposed vehicle was that it is "quick and easy to repair and maintain," then the corresponding list of features or product requirements might be

- a quick-disconnect radiator; 2–4 butterfly bolts, several hose connections, and the rad is out;
- facility to drop the engine between the frame rails—the engine is out in half an hour;
- color-coded hoses and wiring with quick connecters—snap in, snap out for easy replacement.
- modularized electrics in the dashboard so that faulty modules can be pulled and replaced in minutes;
- 90-degree tilt engine bonnet for easy engine access.

This three-step procedure—defining the position, listing the benefits, and itemizing the product features, attributes, and requirements—is a logical lead-in to the development of detailed product specifications. This fourth and final facet of the product strategy is an exact definition of what the product will be, and something tangible the development group can work towards. In some projects, detailed product specs may not be possible at this point, and creative solutions by the development team may be required.

Marketing Planning and the Game Plan

You will have noticed that the marketing-planning process, outlined in Figure 9.2, closely parallels the new product game plan. Indeed, if Figure 9.2 is superimposed on the game plan shown in Figure 9.4, key marketing-planning steps correspond to the various stages of the game plan. For example, the first few steps of developing the marketing plan—setting objectives and undertaking a situation size-up—correspond to the two up-front stages of the game plan. Target market definition and defining product strategy are critical facets of Stage 2, the detailed investigation and building the business case—the key stage just preceding product development. Thus, the marketing-planning process gets underway much earlier in the game than many people might imagine.

Figure 9.4: Development of a Marketing Plan (Integrated with the New Product Process)

Stages in the Game Plan

Corresponding Marketing-Planning Activities

| **Idea** |
| Idea generation |
| Initial screening (Gate 1) |

| **1. Preliminary Investigation** |
| Preliminary market, technical & financial assessments |

First Cut AT:
- Marketing objectives
- Size-up of market
- Defining target market
- Defining product concept & strategy
- Assessing market & sales potential

| **2. Detailed Investigation** |
| Build business case |
| User needs-and-wants studies |
| Competitive & market analyses |
| Concept tests |
| Detailed technical assessment |

Define Precisely:
- Target market & positioning
- Product benefits
- Product requirements & features
- Expected sales

First Cut AT:
- Preliminary Marketing Plan

| **3. Development** |
| Product Development |
| Iterations with customers |
| Develop test, marketing & production Plans |

Initial Customer Feedback:
- rapid-protypte-and-test with customers

Develop Supporting Elements of Plan:
- Pricing
- Advertising & promotion
- Customer service
- Sales force & distribution

| **4. Testing & Validation** |
| Full customer tests |
| Test market |
| Trial production |

Test the Marketing Plan:
- Product tests with customers (to validate product & confirm purchase intent)
- Test market or trial sell
- Revise & modify product & supporting elements of marketing plan
- Finalize product and marketing plan

| **5. Full Production & Market Launch** |
| Implement production and marketing plans |

Implement Marketing Plan
Measure, Control, and Adjust Plan

The Supporting Elements

By now the leading edge of the marketing plan has been developed—the target market and product strategy. The top of the pyramid in Figure 9.2 is in place. Now come the supporting strategies, the remaining blocks in the structure.

These are the elements of the marketing mix that will support the product launch. Let's have a quick look at the more critical ones.

Pricing Strategy

How does one go about pricing a new product? It is difficult to generalize, but there are some basic guidelines.

1.   What is the product's target market and positioning strategy?

Before you reach your pricing decision, both the target market and the product's positioning strategy must be specified. For example, if the product is aimed at a "niche" market, one with specialized needs, and if the positioning is a highly differentiated one, in essence you have a mini-monopoly situation: for that target market, you become the one and only product. A premium price strategy is likely the route to follow. Conversely, if the product is not well differentiated from competitive products, and if the target market is served by others, a competitive pricing policy is appropriate.

Just in case you're tempted to enter the market on a "low-ball" price basis (that is, using a low price as a means of gaining market share), remember that price is the easiest strategy for a competitor to counter, while a product advantage may take years to catch up with. Similarly, an advantage gained through a clever promotional program, a unique distribution effort, or a massive selling campaign may force the competitor to play catch-up ball for months or even years. In contrast, a price advantage is usually temporary: it can be countered tomorrow morning with a simple telex to all salespeople, dealers, and distributors announcing a similar price cut.

Our NewProd studies also confirm the fact that a low price entry strategy for a new product doesn't work all that well. For example, in NewProd III, low price was not found to have any impact on new product success at all.[1] Similarly, a NewProd study of the chemical industry found that of all the elements of product advantage found in new chemical products, low price was one of the few not correlated with success.[2] The message here is not that price is unimportant. Of course it is! Offering good value for money and being price-competitive are essential to success. But *low price as the leading edge of strategy* for new products may not be a winning strategy. There is a big difference between being price-competitive (offering good value for money) versus electing a low-price strategy!

It does make sense, however, to use price as a leading weapon when you have a sustainable and real cost advantage: when your costs are truly lower than competitors' by virtue of product design, low-cost access to raw material, cheaper labor, or higher production volumes. Unfortunately, most firms are not in the position of being *best cost producers,* especially in the case of a product new to the company. A low price decision means sacrificing immediate profits in order to "buy" market share for the future, or to open a window for future new products. (These topics are discussed in more detail below.)

2. What are the other strategic issues?

There are a number of strategic issues that may affect your pricing decisions.

Skimming versus penetration. One school of thought argues that a pricing policy that yields low selling prices, high volumes, and low production costs is desirable. The profit per unit is low, but bigger profits come from volume. Usually, a larger investment in production facilities is required. The idea is to dominate the market through penetration pricing, and reap the long-term rewards of a leading market share. An assessment of your own strengths and weaknesses, your financial capacity and risk averseness, the slope of the learning, or experience curve (costs versus cumulative production volume), the price sensitivity of the marketplace, and possible competitive reactions will dictate whether such a policy is a viable option.

The high-volume, low-price policy has many adherents. The PIMS studies (Profit Impact of Market Strategy) point to market dominance and high market shares as the key to profitability.[3] Similarly, the BCG model (the Boston Consulting Group's approach to strategic planning) relies heavily on experience curves and on gaining market share as the key to having a portfolio of "star products."[4]

The alternative to high volumes and low prices is a skimming policy. The new product is aimed at the market segment for which the product has the most value, and which will pay a premium for it. Profit per unit is high, but volumes are lower. Investment in production facilities is also lower, so the risk is often lower. While the product may never dominate the entire market, it may dominate the one segment and prove very profitable.

A combination of the two strategies is also possible. A skimming strategy is implemented to start with, attacking the high-value market segments. The initial risk is low. Should the product gain acceptance, and when the investment is partly paid back, then a penetration policy is adopted: increase production, drop prices, and go for dominance across the entire market. Timing is critical. The shift must take place before competitors invest in the development and production of similar products.

Corporate strategy. The new product's pricing must be established in the light of the corporate strategy. The new product is not a "stand-alone" item; it is part of a grander plan. For example, senior management may have decided that a specific market or product category is top-priority, and will commit significant resources, at a loss if necessary, to gain a foothold in the market. The new product may be the advance landing party that will sustain heavy losses while paving the way for more profitable future entries. Normal pricing practices may give way to larger issues.

> For example, in the 1980s, Daimler-Benz made a decision to enter the North American heavy truck market. Its two-pronged strategy was based on price. First, it purchased an independent but significant US truck manufacturer, Freightliner, and proceeded to wage a price war in the United States and Canada. (Some industry experts speculate that the firm was prepared to commit—to lose—up to $1 billion to gain a foothold in the mar-

ket.) Second, it imported a truck manufactured in South America into the United States, again on a price basis. Relative to Daimler-Benz's European trucks, the design was obsolete, but the price was attractive. These low-priced products were the advance landing party designed to establish a beachhead; high profits were temporarily sacrificed in exchange for effective market penetration.

3. What is the product's value?

All new product pricing boils down to an assessment of the product's value or worth to the customer. Value, like beauty, is in the eye of the beholder—the customer, in this case. Value is subjective; perceptions vary with the buyer. The price is objective, set by the seller. Ideally, the price accurately reflects the product's value.[5]

Because two people can look at the same product, however, and judge it to have a different value, the first question to ask is: value to whom? If you've done an effective job in defining the target market, that question will have been answered. The next question is: what is the product's value or worth? In assessing value to the customer, one usually looks at what the customer's options are. If similar products are available to the customer, then your product's value is simply the price of the alternative to the customer, plus or minus a bit, depending on the advantages of your product, service delivery, reputation, etc., relative to the competitors'. In pricing in highly competitive markets characterized by relatively homogeneous products, start with competitive prices and work upward or downward from there.

If your product is significantly different from what is now on the market, it is often possible to impute a value by comparing the product's worth relative to the product the customer is now using to solve his or her problem.

> For example, some years ago, a firm introduced a new building material aimed at builders of prefab homes. The product was a 4-by-8 foot panel of very thin bricks attached to a backer sheet and was designed to replace conventional brickwork on the exterior of a prefab home. The product's main advantage was that it could be factory-installed, thus eliminating on-site labor. The product was an innovation, so there were no directly competitive products upon which to base a pricing policy. The customer's alternative was conventional bricklaying at the job site; the value of the new product to the customer was calculated based on those material and labor costs.

When the new product has economic benefits to the customer—for example, measurable cost savings, as in the brick panel example above—a value-in-use can be calculated and used as a standard for the product's value to the customer. The product's value sets the upper limit on price.

4. If in doubt, research the customer

Often, the only way to assess accurately the product's value to the customer is through market research. This research can be combined with the concept test or the product tests. There are several ways to gauge product worth and price sensitivity:

- Ask the potential buyer, "What is the maximum price at which you would buy this product?" Naturally, you'll get different answers from different people, but plotting "percentage of respondents (cumulative)" versus "maximum price" gives an indication of price sensitivity (or price elasticity).
- In measuring the intent to purchase, expose different groups of people to different prices. For example, divide your research sample into three groups. Present the product concept to group A at price 1; to group B at price 2; and to group C at price 3. Measure the intent to purchase, and plot "the percentage who said definitely yes" versus "price level." Again, this curve gives an indication of price sensitivity.
- Use trade-off analysis in your concept tests. Different versions of the same product are presented to the respondent. The product can be varied along a number of possible dimensions, of which price is one. Sophisticated data analysis is used to determine the utility (or worth) of different features or attributes to the user.

A test market or trial sell also can be used as an experiment to test different price strategies.

5. What is the contribution profit?

The place to start a pricing analysis is at the top line, not the bottom line, of a profit analysis. The first question to ask is: at what price might the product sell? Based on the assessment of the product's value to the customer, there will probably be a range of possible prices—several possible prices to consider.

Next, consider the contribution profit per unit. Contribution profit is the selling price less variable costs per unit (direct labor, materials, sales commissions, etc.). Thus subtract the variable costs per unit from each proposed selling price. Variable costs are those that vary directly with output or production volume. They include items such as material, labor, the variable part of overhead costs, and some marketing expenses, such as sales commissions. Don't include fixed costs—those that are incurred regardless of the production or sales volume of the product. Fixed costs typically include items such as depreciation on production equipment, management costs, light, heat, and rent.

This contribution profit at each proposed selling price is crucial. It tells us the relative volumes we must sell at each price in order to make the same annual profit. The contribution profit analysis thus gives significant clues as to the direction in which our pricing policy should move.

Now it's time to start thinking about possible sales volumes at the different prices. Often the sales volumes need only be educated guesses. If adequate research has been done to gauge the product's worth to the target customer and to obtain an idea of price sensitivity, then this calculation becomes more valid.

The total contribution profit is found by multiplying relative volumes at the different prices by the contribution per unit—this figure signals the best price (or at least the price that yields the maximum expected contribution profit).

Usually, estimates of expected volumes at different prices are highly uncertain, even after conducting extensive market research. So use sensitivity analysis. That is, chose pessimistic, likely, and optimistic estimates of volumes at each price, and produce three sets of contribution profit calculations. Chances are that you'll see that the "best price" doesn't change all that much as we move from pessimistic to optimistic scenarios.

Where do fixed costs fit into this contribution profit analysis? In a nutshell, they don't! Fixed costs are relevant in the decision to enter a business. Once you are in, however, variable costs are relevant for pricing decisions.

The one place where fixed costs might enter the figuring is in the determination of break-even volumes. It's wise to determine your break-even volumes at different prices—how many units do we have to sell at different prices to cover our fixed costs?—and then to compare these break-even volumes to what you expect to sell. Too often the break-even volume is too close to expected sales!

6. Promotional pricing

There can be a big difference between the ongoing or "normal" price and the introductory price of a new product. The pricing calculations, market research, and positioning strategy may all point to a premium price. But management may lose heart and feel that the price is too high to induce initial sales. A lower, less than optimal, price may be chosen. If obtaining initial trials is a major problem, don't sacrifice a well-conceived pricing strategy to do so. An introductory "promotional" price can be used to induce those first sales.

Promotional pricing can take many forms. For consumer goods, it can be coupons, a cents-off deal, or a company rebate. For industrial goods, a simple explanation that an introductory price is being offered to the first customers to buy the product will suffice.

There are several advantages to using an initial promotional pricing strategy. First, the normal price is retained for the long term. The customer is aware that the usual price is higher, but since the product is new it can be had for a limited time for the introductory price—a real deal. Second, the positioning strategy remains intact. If the product really is a differentiated and superior one, then it *should be priced higher.* The customer sees the normal price, which reflects the product's worth or positioning. Remember: from the customer's perspective, price is an indicator of quality!

Finally, it's difficult to justify a price hike to the customer after the product is first priced low. With an introductory offer, however, making the transition from the introductory price to the normal and higher price is easy, and is actually anticipated by the customer.

Suggestion: Although pricing is one of the most critical decisions of the new product's marketing strategy, all too often the pricing decision is handled in a sloppy fashion. Moreover, too often managers get locked into a "cost plus" mentality—prices are based on costs rather than on what the product is worth to the customer. In this section, six key points to remember have been highlighted. Use this list the next time you face a new product pricing decision.

The result will be a much more thoughtful approach to pricing, and usually a better decision.

Advertising: Getting the Message Across

A company can have the best product in the world and sell it at a fair price. If no one knows about it, however, the battle is lost. The product's virtues must be communicated to its target market. Advertising is an effective communication tool.

Normally, the advertising plan is developed by an advertising agency or an in-house advertising or graphics department. The new product project leader is often tempted to wash his or her hands of the advertising function—to subcontract this facet of the marketing plan, and assume that "those advertising folks will handle it."

This attitude is wrong. An effective advertising campaign begins with the project leader. While the details of the media plan and development of the "creative" (the artwork and copy) may be the task of others, the communications strategy itself is the project leader's responsibility. Here are some simple "before" and "after" steps that can be taken to ensure a more effective advertising effort for the new product.

Before meeting with the advertising agency (the term "agency" is used to denote either an outside or in-house group), here's what to do:

1. Specify the advertising objectives

Advertising can do many things. It creates awareness, knowledge, and understanding. It can shape attitudes and create a desire or a preference for a product. In the case of direct marketing, it can even create a sale. Advertising can do all these wonderful things—for a cost! Before talking to the agency, pin down *what you want your advertising to do for you*. The product's advertising objectives should be specific and quantifiable. Some examples:

- to create an awareness, within three months of launch, among 50 percent of the defined target market, that Product X is now available.
- in six months, to have 30 percent of municipal water engineers, buyers, and consultants aware that a new water pipe is corrosion resistant and has doubled the life of a traditional ductile iron pipe.

The role of advertising in the total selling effort must be decided before specifying detailed advertising objectives: how much of the communications job will advertising do, and how much will be done by the sales force or other mechanisms?

2. Specify the target market and positioning strategy

Good advertising people will insist on knowing these in detail. Without a clear definition of the target market, how can they design a media plan? And without a positioning strategy, how will they know what the message is to be?

3. Describe the target market

The project leader must provide as much detail as possible on the target market and how it behaves: demographics, locations, occupations, etc. Other types of segmentation may have been used, such as benefit or volume segmentation. That's fine for most of the elements of the marketing strategy, such as product design, pricing, and so on. But remember, the advertising industry, and certainly the media plan facet, still relies heavily on traditional segmentation variables in the choice of appropriate media. For consumer products, readership and viewership are still reported in terms of age, sex, income, etc., and for industrial goods by industry and by the reader's occupation or position.

4. Communicate the product to the agency

The agency should study the product thoroughly before embarking on campaign development. You can help by providing as much detail as possible on how the product works, how it is used, and what its benefits, features, and attributes are.

David Ogilvy, one of the gurus of the advertising industry, preaches to members of his industry about the importance of a painstaking study of the product prior to creative development. He cites the example of his Rolls-Royce advertising: how was the true "meaning" of a Rolls-Royce automobile to be translated into a print ad? After three weeks of reading about the car and visiting Rolls's facilities, Ogilvy hit upon the statement, "At 60 miles an hour the loudest noise comes from the electric clock." That became the headline message of this now-famous campaign.[6]

With these four key steps in place, it's time to turn the advertising development over to the agency. The agency will devise a media plan—which media will be used, the frequency and timing of appearance, and the budget allocation—and the advertisement itself. When the agency presents the results of its efforts, the project leader must once again become a key player in development of the advertising plan.

The review and approval of the proposed advertising plan is next. The steps are as follows:

1. Review the media plan

The essential question is whether the proposed media plan will reach the target audience with the desired frequency. The plan should specify the *expected reach* and *frequency* of the campaign: how many potential customers the campaign will reach, who these people are, and how often they will receive a message.

First, look at each medium recommended by the agency, and in particular at the readership or viewership of that medium. Then compare that with the defined target audience and the advertising objectives. Second, determine how often the target customer will be hit with a message. The choice of frequency is largely based on experience. A good rule of thumb is that it takes at least three impressions for a person to get a message. A mere awareness of your product is likely to require a minimum frequency of three; more ambitious objectives—knowledge of product benefits or features, liking, or preference—will require a higher frequency.

2. Review the creative

Does the message back the product's position? Does it get across the product's benefits to the reader or viewer? An ad may be extremely creative and artistic, and may even win awards. The real purpose of an ad, however, is effective communication of the product. Don't feel shy about asking probing questions and critiquing the ad's potential effectiveness as a communication piece.

3. Run tests on the creative

If the advertising budget for the product is large enough, you may want to test the ad. For example, the pre–test market procedure described in Chapter 8 can be used to perform a test of an ad's effectiveness. Another method is to measure customers' preferences for products on a list before and after viewing the ad. The advertising agency will be able to design appropriate testing procedures.

For low-budget campaigns, the testing should be done on a smaller scale and at a lower cost. There's no sense spending $50,000 to test the effectiveness of a $100,000 ad budget! Advertising for industrial products, for example, is often low-budget, and may take the form of a brochure, a direct mailing, or trade journal advertising. You should still test, however: Obtain feedback on your proposed ad by exposing it to a handful of customers, either individually or as part of a focus group, to measure its suitability and effectiveness.

4. Assess the worth of the objectives

Now comes the tough question. The proposed plan from the agency will include a budget. Review the advertising budget with the original objectives in mind. You can then decide whether to accept the costs as reasonable in light of the objectives, or to back off on some of the objectives—perhaps they were too ambitious to start with.

5. Build in measurement

The only way to know whether the advertising plan is achieving its objectives is to build in some techniques of measurement. Decide, with the agency, how advertising effectiveness will be measured. This will usually involve a market research study. For example, if one of the advertising objectives was that "in six months, 30 percent of municipal engineers will know that our pipe has double the life of the competitor," then plan to take a representative sample of municipal engineers in six months. Ask them what they know about the new kind of pipe. If significantly less than 30 percent of the sample don't know that is has double the life of the competitor, then the ad didn't achieve its objective.

Commercial services are an alternative to market research: such services regularly measure viewership or readership of ads in various media.

Suggestion: You've probably heard someone remark that 50 percent of advertising dollars are wasted. The problem is that no one knows which 50 percent! It's true that advertising is very much an art. Well-informed advertising decisions can be made however. Use the "before" and "after" steps and rules outlined in this section; be tough on the advertising people, and see if you can't improve this important element of the launch effort.

Sales Force Decisions

For the majority of new products, sales force decisions will be straightforward: the product will be sold by the company's existing sales force and/or through its existing distribution system. In the gating or project selection process, several important questions will have been asked:

- Will the product be sold to a market we now serve?
- Will the product be sold to our existing customers?
- Will the product be sold by our sales force and/or via our present distribution system?

If the answers to those questions were "yes"—and they are for most new product projects that pass the early gates—then the sales force plan boils down to tactical issues:

- training the sales force in the selling of the new product;
- providing the sales force with the appropriate selling aids;
- devoting effort to the new product (for example, developing a call plan with the sales force to introduce the product); and
- motivating and "incenting" the sales force (doing "internal marketing" to ensure that the sales force enthusiastically supports the new product).

Don't underestimate this last item. In some companies, this internal marketing effort—getting the sales force on your side—is as critical (and almost as time-consuming) as the external marketing program!

For some new products, however, the use of the existing company sales force and/or distribution system may be inappropriate. If changes or additions to your sales force are to be made, two important questions must be answered:

- What is the nature of the selling job for the new product?
- Is the nature of the selling job compatible with the talents, training, and the way the current sales force (or distributor) operates?

An example: A manufacturer of scientific lasers and instruments marketed a product line of nitrogen lasers and other light sources in a low price range, typically $1,000 to $5,000 per unit. Its "sales force" consisted of a network of manufacturers' reps throughout North America, Europe, and Japan who called on scientific accounts. As scientific products went, the sale was a relatively simple one. The product was easily understood by buyers; it was easy to explain and demonstrate on site by salespeople; it was a low-risk purchase item; and the client's purchase decision was typically quick and uncomplicated.

A new product introduced by the firm represented a significant departure. Unlike the simple lasers, this new optical instrument was a system—a sophisticated unit, priced at about $100,000. It could not be demonstrated on site; many people were involved in a lengthy purchasing process; considerable explanation of the system's features was required; and it was a high-risk purchase decision for the customer. Naively, the company moved the new product through its usual sales force system. The product manager was available to the reps for back up. Not surprisingly, the reps failed to perform. The selling task was so different from that for the usual products the reps handled that they were simply unable to cope with the new product.

In making sales force decisions for your new product—whether to use your existing sales force, hire a new sales force, or use a third party (a middleman)—the decision rests on a few critical factors:

- the fit between the nature of the selling job for the new product and the talents, training, and operating methods of the sales force—how they sell now;
- the degree of control over the selling effort that you need to exercise; and
- the relative costs of each option, and whether those costs are fixed or variable.

Other Supporting Strategies

The main elements of the launch are now in place: the product and target market definition, the pricing strategy, the advertising program, and the sales force effort. The remaining elements, not discussed in detail here, are physical distribution, promotion, customer service, and warranties. Each of these remaining elements is critical to the success of the new product, of course, and each must be built into the launch plan. Fortunately, most of the remaining elements are in place as ongoing programs in your company, and it's simply a matter of making use of what's already there for your new product.

The Final Step: The "Financials"

The financial statements are an integral part of any launch plan. They cover two topics:

- what the plan will cost to implement (the budget); and
- what the plan will achieve (sales and profits projections).

The "financials" are detailed proforma profit-and-loss statements for the new product for Year 1, Year 2, Year 3, etc.—in essence, a financial plan for the project.

Most new product project leaders and teams are somewhat suspicious of financial people. They tend to view them as too narrow (strictly financially driven); too short term; and too prone to kill a project prematurely. And so the project team tries to avoid financial people, financial scrutiny, and financial analysis. Although the new products game is very much future-oriented, and as noted in Chapter 7, financial analysis must be used with caution, this is one time when a solid financial analysis and a financial plan are essential.

The financial plan is important for several reasons. First, it serves as a budget for the new product—an itemized accounting of how much will be spent, and where. Second, the financial plan is the critical input for the final Go/Kill decisions as the project moves closer and closer to full launch and commercial production. The expected return from the product can be computed from the financial plan. Finally, the financial plan provides benchmarks. These benchmarks are critical to the control phase of the launch plan—making sure that the new product is on course. A launch plan should also include contingency plans for actions to be taken if the results deviate from the expected course.

In developing a launch plan, and particularly for the first attempt or first iteration for a specific new product, the financial plan is often the acid test. Any major discrepancies in strategic thinking are discovered and dealt with at this point; for example, there may be major differences between the objectives and the financials. The original sales and profit objectives set out at the beginning of the planning exercise may be miles apart from the sales and profits spelled out in the financial projections. Or, there may be inconsistencies between costs of achievement and expected results. The financials often reveal that the costs of implementing the plan are simply not warranted by the results the plan will achieve.

The existence of such discrepancies is no surprise. The marketing-planning exercise is very much an iterative one. This was the first attempt—a roughed-out, tentative plan. Now, go back to the beginning of the planning exercise, and start and start again—the refining process. Rethink the objectives; redo the size-up; reformulate the action plans; recalculate the financials. These iterations or recycles take time and effort, so it's important that you begin this marketing-planning exercise early in the new product process—ideally before Gate 3.

As the product moves closer and closer to the launch, and with each successive iteration and refinement to the plan, the launch plan starts to crystallize. And if the homework, tests, and trials have been properly executed, it should be a matter of clear sailing into a successful launch . . . with another winner on your hands!

Implementing the Game Plan: The Industry Experience

... there is nothing more difficult to carry out, nor more doubtful of success, nor more dangerous to handle than to initiate a new order of things. For the reformer has enemies from all those who profit by the old order, and only lukewarm defenders in all those who would profit by the new order, this lukewarmness arising partly from their fear of their adversaries, who have the laws in their favor, and partly from the incredulity of mankind, who do not truly believe in anything new until they have had actual experience of it.

Machiavelli, *The Prince,* 1532.

Let's Implement the Game Plan

So when do we start? Let's do it!

You've just about finished reading this book; you've talked to a few of your colleagues; you've also read a few of the articles referenced here, and a few more. Your company has already endorsed the Total Quality Management concept, and this *stage-gate approach* seems to tie in nicely. So you're convinced: the prospect of adopting a formal new product process or *stage-gate system* in your company is increasingly appealing.

Next you contact a few acquaintances at other firms that have implemented such new product game plans—companies such as 3M, Polaroid, H-P, Exxon Chemicals, Northern Telecom, Corning, Black & Decker, Procter & Gamble, various divisions in Du Pont, and others. You learn from these firms that stage-gate systems do indeed work: they reduce the errors and omissions, they reduce the rework and failure rates, and they even decrease the cycle time. But you also learn from these other companies that *it's not quite as easy and straightforward as it seems.*

For the first part of this chapter, let's consider the results of implementing a formal new product process. Later in the chapter, we'll look at some of the key implementation issues.

Some Evidence: Performance Results

Do formal new product processes really work? The overwhelming evidence suggests they do.[1] Stage-gate systems are a great success, according to the man-

Figure 10.1: Overall Contribution of Formal New Product Processes

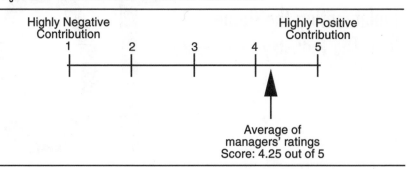

agers who took part in our in-depth study of their firms' new product process-es.* Managers were first asked to assess the *overall contribution* of their formal new product process to their company's development program. A five-point scale ranging from 1 (highly negative impact) to 5 (highly positive impact) was used. The results are clear: managers wholeheartedly endorsed the new product process, the mean score being 4.25 out of 5 (see Figure 10.1). Comments tend-ed to be enthusiastic:

> "It's critical for success!"
> "It keeps us on track and streamlines the process (of product development)."
> "The process requires marketing people to do analysis up front—what the market needs is very clearly defined now."

No system designed to improve product innovation is without its weaknesses. And there were some cautious assessments too:

> "A positive contribution . . . a little bureaucratic, but otherwise good."
> "It has created some time consuming steps, but the overall effect is good."

The *specific performance results* achieved by implementing stage-gate sys-tems are also impressive. Managers were asked to describe the actual results of implementing a new product process in their own firm—an open-ended, "top-of-mind" discussion. The discussion comments were coded and categorized to identify and rank areas of major impact.

Improved product success rates, higher customer satisfaction, and meeting time, quality, and cost objectives were the most frequently cited areas of positive impact (see Figure 10.2). More than one-third of managers, without any prompt-ing, indicated that the process' strongest impact was on the *success rate* of new products and on the *customer satisfaction* achieved. Managers revealed that a much stronger market orientation had been built into their new product game plan, and that key activities such as market studies and concept tests were now an integral facet of their product development efforts. The results were positive:

> "Product success is more likely now."
> "We've managed to greatly improve customer satisfaction."

* Twenty-nine managers in nine divisions in five leading U.S. firms that had implemented formal new product processes took part in the study.

Figure 10.2:   Impact of Formal New Product Process

Comment	Managers citing (%)[a]
Improved product success rate and higher customer satisfaction	34%
Product developed on target (meets time, quality, and cost objectives)	34%
Faster-to-market	31%
Improved profit performance (sales and margins)	28%
A learning tool: educate our people	24%
Improved cooperation and coordination among people involved in the projects, e.g., different departments or functions	21%
Fewer errors; less recycling; less redesign	17%
Improved communication	17%
Better project control	10%

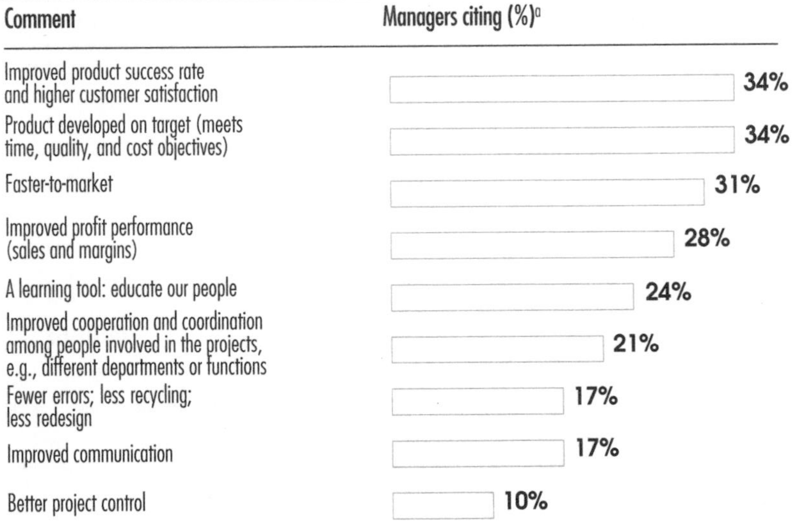

[a]Adds to more than 100% due to multiple responses

R. G. Cooper and E. J. Kleinschmidt, *Formal Processes for Managing New Products: The Industry Experience*, McMaster University, 1991.

"Our products really meet market needs, and they succeed more often—fewer failures."

Being on *time and on budget*—that is, meeting project and product objectives—was seen as another payoff from formal processes, also cited by 34 percent of managers. New product processes brought discipline into product development, where previously there had been chaos; and more attention was focused on time schedules, deadlines, and project costs and objectives:

"The projects are on target (now): on time, and on quality and cost targets."

Being *faster-to-market* and obtaining *better profit performance* from new products were other comments volunteered by the study's participants (see Figure 10.2). There were virtually no negative comments in this open-ended discussion of the impact of the formal new product process.

These top-of-mind comments provide some assurance that stage-gate approaches do work. The *degree of improvement* in six key areas was rated on five-point scales (1 = no improvement, 5 = great improvement) to provide quantitative measures of performance impact. The results, given in Figure 10.3, are provocative and provide strong support for implementing a stage-gate model. On all six dimensions of performance, there was significant improvement. Although answers varied, there were very few instances where "no improvement" was cited. The major benefits of implementing a new product process, in rank order, are:

Figure 10.3:   Improvements Achieved by Implementing a Formal New Product Process

Performance dimension	Mean improvement[a]	Range of answers[a]
Improved teamwork/better communication	4.11	2–5
Less recycling/less rework on project	3.85	2–5
Improved new product success rate	3.80	2–5
Better launch	3.41	1–5
Earlier detection of failures	3.35	1–5
Improved time efficiency/shorter elapsed time to launch	3.32	1–5

[a]Responses of 29 managers on 1–5 scale where 5 = great improvement and 1 = no improvement

R. G. Cooper and E. J. Kleinschmidt, *Formal Processes for Managing New Products: The Industry Experience,* McMaster University, 1991.

1. *Improved teamwork:* Managers saw significant improvement in interfunctional teamwork. The fact that new product processes stress multifunctional activities, and use multifunctional criteria at each gate, promotes and demands this teamwork:

   "There is a much smoother transition from lab to manufacturing. Manufacturing is involved (in the project) almost from the beginning."
   "Common priorities are now supported by all functions."
   "There are more multifunctional discussions and information exchange, and earlier commitment by marketing and manufacturing."

2. *Less recycling and rework:* The amount of recycle and rework—going back and doing it again—was greatly reduced. New product processes generally have a number of quality checks built into the process to ensure that critical activities are carried out, and in a quality fashion, thereby reducing the incidence of recycle:

   "There are fewer design changes late in the project—we get the specs definition right."
   "The number of engineering change notices after release to manufacturing has dropped. We keep a detailed record of these."

3. *Improved success rates:* Managers noted that the proportion of new products that succeeded was higher, and the profitability from new products was also better. The fact that stage-gate systems build in better project evaluations at the gates (hence cull out potential failures earlier) and focus more attention on key success activities, such as market studies, sharper and earlier product definition, and customer tests, accounts for this improvement:

"The number of projects that exceed (sales and profit) targets has risen considerably."

"There are fewer customer complaints now. Our products are 'right' when production starts."

"We measure our new product performance based on profit contribution . . . we know the success rate is up."

4. *Earlier detection of failures:* Potential failures were spotted earlier, and either killed outright or steps taken to avert disaster. The use of gates with clear Go/Kill criteria, typical of most firms' processes, helped to sharpen the project evaluations:

"Checkpoints throughout the process are key to spotting failures."

"We actually kill projects now. In the past, we'd just let them continue."

"Our major review points usually detect weaknesses in projects."

5. *Better launch:* Marketing planning and other market-oriented activities are integral to most firms' new product processes, resulting in more involvement in the project by marketing, and a better launch:

"There is better internal coordination between marketing and manufacturing."

"We meet launch dates now, and on budget."

"Customer acceptance levels are higher (at launch)."

6. *Shorter elapsed time:* This result was surprising: The common view is that a more thoroughly executed new product project takes a longer time. Not so, according to the managers interviewed. Better homework, more multifunctional inputs, better market and product definition, and less recycle work all serve to shorten the idea-to-launch time:

"Compared to similar projects prior to having our new process, our times to launch are down."

"The number of iterations in development has been reduced."

"We stay on schedule more often now."

This conclusion on cycle time reduction, although somewhat of a surprise, has also been backed up by yet another study—this one an extensive internal study within one firm.[2] Here the time-to-market for a large number of new product projects was considered, both before and after the implementation of a formal new product process. Cycle times, of course, depend on project complexity, and so a measure of complexity was developed, and cycle times plotted against this measure (see Figure 10.4). Two plots are shown—"before" and "after" the introduction of a formal new product game plan. The results:

- The formal process reduced the cycle time: it reduced the slope of the relationship between time and complexity by about one-third; and it reduced the intercept by one-third (see Figure 10.4). The end result is that the introduction of a formal stage-gate type system cuts cycle time by about one-

Figure 10.4:   Cycle Time Reduction with New Product Process

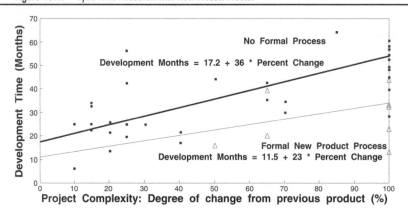

Reprinted with permission of the publisher from "Metrics for Measuring Product Development Cycle Time" by A. Griffin. Thomas P. Hustad, Editor. *The Journal of Product Innovation Management* 10(2): 112-25.

third for simple projects and by *considerably more than one-third for more complex ones!*

- The formal new product process also made the complexity-time relationship much more predictable. The lower of the two lines in Figure 10.4—results seen *after* a new product process was introduced—provides a much better fit for all the data points than the upper "before" line. The unexplained variance, "noise," or unpredictability in time-to-market was reduced from 65 percent to 35 percent.

These time-to-market metrics in Figure 10.4 admittedly are limited to the experiences of a single company. But such measures are hard to come by. This metric study, together with our study's more qualitative assessments across a number of firms and divisions, provides concrete evidence that stage-gate systems really do work and also lead to time compression!

The Nature and Use of the New Product Process

The performance results of implementing a new product process are impressive. But what are the characteristics of the process used? Chapter 5 portrayed the typical stage-gate process. But this was a generic process; clearly, each company modifies and adapts the process to its own needs.

Time in Use

New product processes are relatively recent developments in most companies studied. The mean time in operation was 5.6 years, and only one firm had used the system for more than 10 years.

Figure 10.5:   Characteristics of New Product Process

Nature of process	Managers citing (%)
Universal Process	
Totally universal: used for all projects within Division	34%
Universal, but not used for small projects or minor improvements	14%
Total: Universal system	48%
Selective Process	
Inconsistent use: for some projects, not for others	31%
Inconsisent use: depends on the department handling the project	14%
Inoconsistent use: decision by management	7%
Total: Selective process	52%

R. G. Cooper and E. J. Kleinschmidt, *Formal Processes for Managing New Products: The Industry Experience,* McMaster University, 1991.

Universal versus Specific Use

About half the processes studied were universally used throughout the division or company (see Figure 10.5). That is, all new product projects, with the exception of very small projects and minor modifications, required the use of the pro-cess. For half the firms, however, the new product process was used less consistently. For example, some firms used the process for certain classes of products, but not for others; there were differences from department to department in the use of the process; and certain types of projects, such as pure research projects, were exempt from the process.

Formality

The formality and rigidity of processes varied from firm to firm. On average, managers thought that their process was quite formal, but not overly rigid (see Figure 10.6). In discussing formality, managers cited the following characteristics of their processes:

- The process includes formal gate meetings, complete with Exit or Go/Kill criteria, and with sign-offs required (52%).*
- The process provides detailed descriptions of the tasks and activities to be completed at each stage or phase (34%).

* The percentage of managers noting. The total is more than 100 percent since comments are not mutually exclusive.

Figure 10.6:   Rigidity, Formality and Expected Changes in the New Product Processess

Characteristic	Rating scale (1–5)
Degree of formality (5 = extremely formal)	3.82
Degree of rigidity (5 = extremely rigid)	2.59
Expected changes in the process in the future (5 = expect major changes)	2.43

R. G. Cooper and E. J. Kleinschmidt, *Formal Processes for Managing New Products: The Industry Experience,* McMaster University, 1991.

- The process requires careful documentation and reports. These requirements are spelled out in the process (14%).
- The process specifies a set of "deliverables" or inputs for each gate. These deliverables become the objectives of the project team (10%).

Many managers commented that although the process was formally laid out, paperwork was kept to a minimum.

Lack of flexibility in the process was not a major concern. Figure 10.7 provides a summary of the nature of flexibility or latitude allowed. Only 11 percent of managers

Figure 10.7:   Flexibility of the New Product Process

Nature of flexibility	Managers citing (%)
The process is flexible: it is situationally dependent	39%
The process is flexible and deviations are permittted, providing management approves	29%
The number of stages or phases used depends on the project	11%
The activities and tasks are flexible provided major requirments are met	7%
The Gates are fixed, but their application is flexible	4%
The process is rigid—all stages are set and fixed	11%

R. G. Cooper and E. J. Kleinschmidt, *Formal Processes for Managing New Products: The Industry Experience,* McMaster University, 1991.

saw their processes as totally rigid: that is, all stages and all gates must be adhered to, regardless of the project and situation. Typical comments were:

"Each project has its own requirements and hence differing degrees of adherence to the total system."
"The decision to bypass certain activities or review points can be made with the approval of management."

Expectation of Change

Major changes or overhauls were not generally expected in these new product processes in the near future, indicating a fairly high degree of user satisfaction. Almost two thirds (62 percent) of managers saw minor modifications and adjustments only; and another 13 percent saw no changes at all (see also Figure 10.6 above). Of those expecting major changes, the nature of the changes included:

- increased marketing involvement (10%); and
- a more simplified process (7%).

Rationale for a New Product Process

What were the motivations that underlay the implementation of a stage-gate system? The majority of reasons lie within six main categories; three motivations dominate (see Figure 10.8).

Figure 10.8:   Motivations for Implementing a New Product Process

Reason	Managers citing (%)[a]
Better cooperation, coordination and communication among those involved in the project	69%
Better and faster quality of execution of key tasks in the project: effectiveness and timeliness	59%
More control, discipline and information: a management information and control system	55%
More structure: a road map or layout of the key tasks, so that none are overlooked or left until too late	24%
Better resource allocation decisions	10%
Lower level decision-making; team empowerment	10%

[a]Adds to more than 100% due to multiple response.

R. G. Cooper and E. J. Kleinschmidt, *Formal Processes for Managing New Products: The Industry Experience*, McMaster University, 1991.

The most often cited motivation was the desire for *better cooperation, communication, and coordination* among people directly and indirectly involved in a new product project. Most often, these people reported to different functional areas, and the need for teamwork was frequently mentioned:

> "We needed a common understanding among the different departments involved in the project."
> "We wanted marketing and manufacturing to be more involved and much earlier."
> "We needed to 'blur the lines' between different departments so that we could work as a team."
> "We desired a system to coordinate activities and improve communication, because many people are involved in a project, and over a long period of time."

A second major motivation was the desire to improve the *quality and timing of the activities* that comprise the project. A total of 59 percent of managers cited a need for more effective and efficient execution of project tasks:

> "We wanted to improve our efficiency, product quality, and timing."
> "(The need was) to accelerate the new product process for faster market entry."
> "(The process would) provide for better homework at the front end, yielding sharper product definition prior to development."
> "We had too much recycling . . . going back and doing it again. We wanted better quality of execution the first time."

The desire for more *control and information* was the third major reason for implementing a stage-gate system: a system that would yield discipline, control activities, and provide information for top management (55 percent of managers citing). Typical comments included:

> "(The process) was needed to ensure that projects met company goals."
> "We needed better check points throughout the process."
> "Top management wanted to be kept informed and involved in the development process."
> "We desired a tracking of the status of all projects."

The need for *structure*—a road map to guide the project—was mentioned by a minority of respondents (24 percent). Here the major concern was that key activities or tasks were not left until too late, or forgotten altogether. A new product project is complex, often entailing hundreds of tasks at different stages. A standardized lists of tasks, broken down by stage, helps to ensure no critical errors of omission.

Other reasons cited for implementing a new product process included the desire to improve *resource allocation* or budgeting decisions (10 percent citing); and the need to *move decisions lower* in the organizational structure to the project team level (10 percent citing).

The Previous Process

What system had the new stage-gate system replaced? Managers were queried about the process that had been in place prior to the current formal one. Almost one-third indicated that they had no process, or at best, a very informal, ad hoc process. Another 24 percent said that a particular process was used, but that key phases of the project, important activities, and needed functional groups were not a part of the process:

"We focused on getting the design to production, but not the product to market. Marketing was not a part of our process."

Some managers (21 percent) indicated that they had always used the current process, and that the "old process" was too long ago to remember. Yet another 10 percent complained that their old process had been highly structured, rigid, and restrictive:

"We had very rigid procedures coupled with ad hoc interventions by senior managers."
"(It was) a very structured process, with laborious check-off procedures."

When asked about what was wrong with the previous product innovation method, the majority of managers pointed to a lack of coordination between functional areas, and too long a process (see Figure 10.9). Comments such as "there was enmity amongst different groups" and "there were heated disagreements among functions" were common. Too long a process was also a complaint:

"The (old) process was simply too burdensome and bureaucratic to meet the time pressures—it took forever to get products to market."

Other complaints were that the previous process was inefficient and costly (16 percent citing); that key steps and activities were often missed (16 percent); that there was lack of top management involvement and control (11 percent); and that there was insufficient flexibility (11 percent).

Figure 10.9:   Problems with Previous Methods for Developing New Products

Reason	Managers citing (%)[a]		
Lack of cooperation/disagreements between functional groups and departments			37%
Process too slow		26%	
Inefficient and costly	16%		
Missing steps; key activities not done	16%		
Too flexible	11%		
Lack of top management involvement and control	11%		

[a]Of those previously employing an alternate method. Total is more than 100% due to several multiple responses.

R. G. Cooper and E J. Kleinschmidt, *Formal Processes for Managing New Products: The Industry Experience,* McMaster University, 1991.

Implementation Problems

A vital question concerns how such stage-gate systems were implemented: for example, was it a management edict, or was there bottom up development and support? The most common mechanism was via a new products committee, which made the decision to implement, and then designed a process (26 percent of firms). Other approaches included a top down directive (15 percent); and a gradual development—the process simply appeared and grew over time (15 percent).

Initial response to the new system was *by no means universally positive* within firms. On a five-point scale, the initial response averaged a mid-range 3.5, where 1 meant "poorly received" and 5 meant "very well received." Comments broke down as follows:

- Well or fairly well received (58%)
- Perceived as bureaucratic by many people (14%)
- The process needed revision initially (10%)
- Mixed reception: well by some, poorly by others (7%)
- Poorly received (3%)

The range of responses suggests that even the best designed new product process can be expected to meet with mixed reviews on introduction. The subsequent positive results achieved, however, changed the views of the skeptics.

The majority of firms *did not provide formal training* for their people when they first introduced their stage-gate system. The breakdown was:

- Learned the process on the job (55%)
- Some formal training provided, but mostly learned on the job (24%)
- Only meetings and discussions held when introduced (11%)
- Formal training provided (10%)

This *lack of training and education explains some of the initial skepticism* and the lack of universal acceptance when the system was first introduced.

Most managers (90 percent) indicated that there had been start-up problems when their new product process was first implemented. In 80 percent of these cases, the problems were not deemed to be serious. When queried further, the majority of managers (55 percent) indicated that the problems were applications problems rather than with the process itself. That is, they or their staff had difficulty undertaking some of the tasks that the game plan required; and the process itself was not problematic. Again, this points to the lack of education, training, and facilitation as a possible cause. But 45 percent of managers saw the process itself, not its application, as the root of the problem.

A number of steps were undertaken to overcome these problems and weaknesses in initial implementation. Seventy-eight percent of firms worked on team building and teamwork solutions; 17 percent witnessed organizational redesign; 17 percent obtained greater involvement of more senior managers; and 10 percent simplified the design of the process.

The goal of higher new product success rates, shorter development times, and more profitable new products will continue to be an elusive one. The design and implementation of stage-gate new product processes has produced enviable results for the few firms that we studied. The evidence is clear: formal new product processes really do work!

Designing and Implementing a Stage-Gate Process

You've seen the positive results in other firms. Now it's time to charge ahead in your company. But recognize at the outset that the design and implementation of a stage-gate new product process is *certainly no easy task.* In many ways, it resembles the implementation of a TQM process, but with a much narrower focus—on new products only, and not the entire company. But the steps, intensity of effort, and frustrations are much the same as trying to introduce TQM to a firm. And if you've already been through the TQM process, you understand what I mean when I say: don't underestimate the amount of work involved in the design and implementation of a stage-gate new product process—on the surface it looks easy, but, to use the metaphor of a gracefully swimming duck, underneath there's a lot of paddling going on!

The design and implementation of a new product process—let's abbreviate this to NPP—usually proceeds in three steps or phases:

- Phase 1: Conceptual design.
- Phase 2: Detailed design, including development of detailed documentation.
- Phase 3: Implementation.

Usually these three steps are undertaken by the same group or task force, although clearly additional resources are required during the implementation phase.

Phase 1: Conceptual Design

The conceptual design phase is the design of a skeleton or outline of the proposed NPP—for example, a flow model much like the one presented in Chapter 5. This task sounds relatively straightforward; in fact, some people are even tempted to "lift" the model right out of this book, and proclaim, "voila, we have our system!" But hold on. Unless you want to face diaster a few months down the road, there are quite a few other facets to this conceptual design phase.

Let's back up a bit. The notion of having an NPP has been floating around the company for some months. You have exposed top management to the concept and they have bought in; finally, the needed management authority and commitment to proceed is obtained. A *task force is struck* to handle the design and implementation of the process. Common questions before you even get going are:

1. Who should be on this task force?

Clearly the task force must be carefully selected to include knowledgeable, bright, thoughtful, experienced, and influential people from the different functions involved in product development (and the different geographic areas involved too). Additional members might include an executive sponsor (who represents senior management and lends credibility and authority to the task force) and an outside expert, consultant, or facilitator (someone who has been through the exercise before).

2. How large should this task force be?

This group should not be a committee with a cast of thousands—rather this is a lean, action-oriented task force. But there must be enough people to obtain diversity of opinion, function, and geography. The best task forces I've seen operate with about five to nine people. Three or four is too few—not a broad enough perspective; ten or more is too many—the group becomes cumbersome, and it's almost impossible to schedule meetings.

One of the best NPP task forces that I have served on was Biocides business unit at Rohm and Haas. Team members were carefully selected: the sales and marketing managers from Europe, the sales and marketing managers from North America, and two R&D section mangers. The executive sponsor was the Director of R&D, and I was the outside facilitator. One weakness was that certain functions (notably manufacturing) and certain regions (specifically the Pacific and South/Central America) were not represented, but total representation would have required a task force twice the size. Special efforts were made to keep these other people involved in the task force's work.

3. What about time commitments by the task force?

Anticipate a fairly intense effort, especially towards the beginning. Task force member's calendars need to be freed up for key dates well in advance. I usually undertake phases 1 and 2—the conceptual and detailed designs—in "rounds."

Here's what a "round" looks like: the task force meets intensively for two days at an offsite location; within one week, the material or output from this meeting is written up (for example, a draft version of the stage-gate model) and circulated to task force members; each of them holds "show and tell" sessions and seeks feedback from their constituencies (their "clients"); the feedback is circulated to the task force; and the agenda and objectives for the next two-day meeting are set.

Each "round" takes about one month, but this requires a tough task force master or chairperson: One of the most demanding tasks is the quick write-up of material, and getting it out to people within one week. Estimate about one or two rounds for phase 1, the conceptual design, and another two to three rounds for phase 2, the detailed design. Implementation, or phase 3 varies considerably by company.

There are other preliminaries as well. For example, the task force should *not proceed in an information vacuum.* Before the task force gets underway, here are some actions you might consider:

- *Current practices and problem detection:* Consider conducting an audit or study within the firm to determine the major problems, barriers, pitfalls, and deficiencies that plague the way we currently do new product projects. This list of problems provides an excellent incentive to get started on the design and implementation of a new product process; it also provides some guide-lines and objectives for the task force (see Appendix A for a sample set of audit questions). Two examples:

Procter & Gamble's current new product process traces its roots to retrospective studies of new product successes and failures undertaken in the mid 1980s. Here, 60 past new product projects were studied in depth (350 P&G people took part in the study) to find out what was going well and what was lacking in their current methods. This extensive study laid the foundation for the company's new product process.

Research management at Tremco, a B.F. Goodrich subsidiary, held a series of "town hall meetings" with technical, marketing, and manufacturing people to identify what was wrong, and what was right about their new product practices. These meetings were open and public forums where anyone could voice an opinion. When the NPP task force got down to work, it was presented with the list of problems and deficiencies identified at these town hall meetings—and one goal of the task force became the solution of these deficiencies.

- *Information session kickoff:* One serious trap that a well-intentioned NPP task force can become entangled in is the failure to keep the rest of the organization informed. In short, the task force becomes so focused on their objective that they fail to communicate with others outside the task force. And those in the company with a real interest in new products, but who aren't on the task force, quickly view the task force as "ivory tower" and distant. So six months later, when the new game plan is about to be launched, there already exists a significant constituency of nay-sayers.

    The key rule here is: keep your clients informed and involved! Don't forget: the rest of the folks in the organization are your customers or clients—the people that will ultimately use this stage-gate process. So before the task force even starts out on its journey, it's best to have an information session—a new products day or kick-off, which often covers the following topics:

    — your firm's new product objectives versus your new product performance (this often identifies a gap);
    — your current new product practices (perhaps based on some internal study or audit, as outlined above);
    — the need for a new way of handling new products;
    — the concept of the stage-gate process and its positive impact at other firms (use the results presented earlier in this chapter);
    — introduction of the task force: its mandate and composition; and
    — the role of other players present.

    One item I've often successfully built into this kickoff event is work-shops in which teams break out, identify a list of key problems, and, most important, recommend potential solutions. They then reconvene and present their results to the other teams. One result, invariably, is the recognition of the need for a new product process. Organizational buy-in has already begun!

Following these preliminaries—getting top management buy-in, selecting the task force, undertaking a current practices audit, and the kickoff—the task force is ready to move. This conceptual design phase, as noted above, usually proceeds in one or two rounds, with feedback from others in the company sought after each meeting. The end result is a draft of a conceptual model that has received general approval from both the task force members and those outside the task force: management and the likely team players.

This conceptual model is little more than a few pages: a flow diagram not unlike the one shown in Chapter 5. It identifies and names the stages and gates; provides the spirit or flavor (the purpose) of each stage and gate; and lists the likely activities in each stage. But details, such as in-depth descriptions of activities, deliverables, and gate criteria, as well as organization and procedures, are not yet spelled out.

Phase 2: Detailed Design

The conceptual design or skeleton of the model has been accepted by the organization and by senior management. Now it's time to put some meat on this skeleton. Two to three more rounds are usually required. Here the following questions are addressed as the detailed model takes shape:

- *Stage descriptions:* Specifically, what actions or activities are required at each stage? Often an overview or brief description of each activity is developed to provide the project team with a flavor for what is expected.
- *Gate descriptions:* What deliverables are required for each gate (and in what level of detail)? What are the gate criteria—the *must meet* and *should meet items* outlined in Chapter 7? How will projects be prioritized? Once a project is given a Go decision at a gate, is this a firm and binding decision (or can the project be reprioritized in a month or two if a better project comes along)? And how do gates mesh with quarterly reviews of projects, project milestones, and annual budget setting?
- *Gate procedure:* Who are the gatekeepers for each gate? How is the meeting run—for example, is there a chairperson, a referee, or a facilitator present? What method should gatekeepers use to score the project against the criteria? How are decisions ruled? Should the project team be present for the entire meeting? And so on.
- *Organizational:* What should the composition of cross-functional teams be? Where in the process should the team be formed? Who does the work on the project prior to this point? Who should the team leaders be? Is it the same leader from beginning to end of the project? How much empowerment should the team be given? How should team members be relieved of their normal duties? Who does the annual performance evaluation of each team member? And how are team members recognized and rewarded?

Remember: throughout these rounds, as the game plan takes shape, there is *constant information flow between task force members and the various constituents* in the organization: senior management, potential gatekeepers, team leaders, and members. The idea here is to seek both feedback as well as buy-in.

Documentation and presentation are important, and so one result of this detailed design phase is normally the development of a fairly detailed "user's manual" as well as a quick guide. Towards the end of this phase, implementation issues begin to be aired, and often an implementation plan is developed as the final task in phase 2.

Phase 3: Implementation

Implementation is by far the longest, most difficult, and most expensive phase. It consists of a set of events and activities designed to inform people about the NPP and train them in its use; to seek buy-in and commitment from the organization; and to bring projects—both new and existing—into the new system. The implementation phase normally is initiated at some event or company conference whereby senior management indicate their commitment, and an overview of the process is presented. But each company's implementation plan must be designed to suit its own culture and needs. The mechanics—the design of a process—are relatively easy; but the behavioral side—getting commitment and change in behavior—isn't!

Bringing Projects into the NPP

Decisions must be made about how to bring current projects into the system. The use of piloting as one technique to gain organizational commitment is outlined below. This is a gradual approach to bringing projects on board, in which only a few test cases are initially introduced to the NPP.

Other companies simply announce a starting date: all new projects are "in the system" after that date; and leaders of all existing projects must declare where they are in the process—what stage or gate—by that date. An additional requirement is that all existing projects must clear one gate within, say, six months of the starting date. This gate may be the next gate, or if the project is not far enough into the stage, then the preceding gate.

Getting Commitment

The entire team must be committed: senior managers, coaches, and players! No new order of things will be successfully internalized in an organization unless there is commitment and buy-in from those at the top, from those at the middle level and from those lower down who actually must use the new system.

If those at the top—senior management—don't commit to this new product process, then very quickly the word will spread through the organization that the model isn't for real: that the most senior people don't support it! Moreover, top management has the authority to commit the vital resources, without which the new process will barely limp along.

My personal observation is that there has never been a successful implementation of a formal NPP (or stage-gate system) without the commitment and dedication of top management. As one champion of a stage-gate system confessed:

> "The breakthrough came when senior management actually started to use the language of the process . . . when they started asking questions such as 'is the project in Stage 2 or 3?' ; 'when's the next gate?' or 'are the deliverables in place?'. It was then that we all got the message that the senior people were serious about us using our new process."

Top management commitment alone isn't enough, however. Sure, the CEO can place his or her blessing on the new system, and say the right words at senior management meetings. He or she can even dictate the implementation of the new process and allocate people to do so. All these items are a step in the right direction. But alone they won't yield a successful new product process.

Managers at the next levels down in the organization must also be on board. These are the decision-makers for the majority of new product projects—the business unit manager, the marketing and sales managers, the R&D or engineering manager, the manufacturing and QA managers, and so on. These are the people that *man most of the gates or key decision points* in the process, not the CEO or executive vice presidents!

If these key middle-level people have not committed to the concept and procedures of the NPP, then all is lost. For if they run gate meetings badly—they are poorly prepared, fail to use the stated gate criteria, shoot from the hip, let half-baked projects slip through gates with half the deliverables missing (or worse yet, let projects simply slide around gates), ask inane questions, seek irrelevant information, or kill projects for the wrong reasons—then even the best-designed NPP will quickly break down and fall into disuse. Unfortunately I have seen all of these abuses within supposedly well managed firms.

Fact: The *greatest change in behavior* is required, not at the project leader and team level, but at *the decision-making level.* Managers who man the gates face the greatest learning challenge. Thus the buy-in of these middle-level managers is critical to the success of the stage-gate implementation. For as go the gates, so goes the process!

Management commitment alone is not enough. The senior executives can say all the right things and even commit people and money. But that is no guarantee of success. The middle-level managers—the people that man the gates—can run sharp, disciplined gate meetings. But there's more to success than this. Never forget: Implementation really happens in the trenches. Implementation means ordinary team members and project leaders buying into the process: R&D people, engineers, marketing people, and manufacturing folks—the real "doers" on the organization—will ultimately make it happen. If they are not committed to making this new product process work—if they see it as useless, bureaucratic, or another "flavor of the month" from management upstairs—then the process is doomed to failure. They'll simply pretend to be using the process: they'll go through the motions and say the right words, but in reality, it's business as usual.

Here are some of the ways that other firms have used to get people "on board" and committed to their new product process.

1. Position the NPP as one facet of your TQM program.

Total Quality Management programs are increasingly popular these days, especially amongst senior management. The two new insights that TQM programs bring are:

- a recognition that *all work is a process,* and that any process can be managed to be more effective and efficient.
- the understanding that it takes a lot of time and work to successfully implement a new process—it's not a quick fix. But the *results are worth the effort.*

These "truths" that the TQM proponents have brought into organizations also apply to the NPP. In "selling" your new product process, position it as part of the firm's overall program on TQM. Argue that the NPP is simply the application of TQM approaches to new products. Show that new product development is merely a process, and that this process too can be managed more effectively. Talk about gates, not as harsh hurdles, but as quality-control checkpoints in the process—to ensure that the project is a quality one. And finally, make the point that, like TQM methods, implementation of the NPP will be difficult, long and require resources, but that the results are worth the effort.

2. Sell everyone on the need for more new products!

Surprising as this seems, not everyone in the organization is as convinced as you are of the need for new products. The "champions of the process" by definition are the most supportive of a strong new product effort; the rest of the organization is often not quite as eager or convinced that new products are top priority. The implication here is that not only must you sell the concept of a stage-gate system, you must first promote the notion that "new products are vital for the health, prosperity, and even survival of the organization." There is much evidence available to support this view. Use it.

Suggestion: Use industry data to make your case for the need for new products; for example, some of the data from Chapter 1: in US industry in 1981, new products represented 33 percent of corporate sales. By 1986, this had risen to 40 percent. In 1992, it was 46 percent!

Look at your own track record. What percentage of sales come from new products? What is your objective? What has been your growth driver? Compare your performance—profits, growth, etc.—to competitors or other business units in your corporation.

Once convinced that new products are essential, the next question is: how do we get more winners? And that's where the NPP is proposed as the solution.

3. Use facts to underpin the potential benefits of the NPP.

There are many skeptics in any organization. As the quotation from *The Prince* that opens this chapter suggests, this skepticism arises from the "incredulity of mankind, who do not truly believe in anything new until they have had actual experience of it." If your colleagues don't have direct experience, then bring experiences in from other organizations where stage-gate systems have been used with success. That is, don't promise imaginary benefits based on speculation and hearsay; deal with facts and solid evidence.

To substantiate the need for formal new product processes, for example, take apart any unsuccessful project. At the root of its problems, you'll probably find serious process deficiencies: poor quality of execution; certain key activities not done at all or done too late; poor or nonexistent gates or decision points; and so on. If you can't provide the evidence from your own company, then at least rely on research studies done in others. Use our NewProd studies outlined in Chapter 3, where the overriding conclusion was that most firms' product development processes are in serious trouble; and that success and failure depends to a large extent on process.

There is not much published evidence of the performance results of *implementing new product processes,* but those studies that have investigated the impact of stage-gate systems provide universally positive results. The data on how formal NPPs affect results (provided earlier in this chapter) give you the ammunition to prove your point.

4. Deal with the barriers and preconceptions.

The initial reaction to an NPP by many in the organization is less than positive, as the study above showed. Common views are, first, that an NPP is unnecessarily bureaucratic; and second, that it will now take longer to develop and launch new products. Both assumptions are wrong! Nonetheless, these are the nightmares of people charged with running NPPs in other firms. There is a real danger that the process does indeed become bureaucratic, and that it does extend the time-to-market. *So every effort must be taken to minimize bureaucracy, and to speed products to market.* More about speed later. Further, be sure to come armed with the evidence and make the point strongly: in well-run NPPs at other companies, the evidence is clear: the "system" has evolved to a slick, streamlined process, which accelerates products to market.

5. Buy-in starts top down.

Encourage and train senior people to start "talking the talk and walking the walk" of the NPP. They must "model the way" and set the example for others. If they use the language of the NPP, ask the "process questions" (for example, ask about stages and gates), and refer to gate criteria (even in casual conversation or ordinary meetings), then the rest of the organization gets the message.

6. **Get the commitment to the NPP written into the business unit's mission and strategic plan.**

This is not a major item, but one move that several companies have found as yet another way of focusing the spotlight on the NPP.

7. **Use pilots.**

Identify a handful of projects, and use these as test or demonstration cases of "how to do it." Make sure that these projects are really well run: select good potential projects—ones destined for success; choose an able leader and a proficient team; provide good mentoring and facilitation; and commit the right resources. Throughout their development, hold these projects up as shining examples to the rest of the organization: they are both illustrations of the use of the NPP, as well as proof that the new process works!

Getting organization buy-in and commitment is the first prerequisite for successful implementation of a new process. This involves changing attitudes, values, and actions. It relies on effective communications, presentations, and internal marketing. These requirements lead us into the next two critical items: communications and training.

Communication

Effective communications and presentation of the NPP are cornerstones of its success. I've witnessed several instances when initial attempts to implement a well-designed NPP were dealt *fatal blows by poor communications pieces:* the written documentation (for the introduction of the system) was too lengthy; it was complex, hard to follow, and not user-friendly; and it simply turned the reader or audience off before he or she had completed page 1.

Remember: first impressions are lasting ones, and the initial documentation or presentation sets the stage for all that is to follow.

1. **Design a quick guide for introduction.**

Virtually every company with a successful new product process has not forgotten the "internal marketing" facet. They have designed simple, appealing introductory pieces for their NPPs. Most have been professionally designed and have production quality equal to a company sales brochure. The argument here is that in any organization, internal marketing is every bit as important as external marketing, *so do it professionally.* This quick guide is not the full manual, but simply an introduction—to create a positive first impression. Some examples:

*   Procter & Gamble's initial written presentation (four years ago) was a detailed "user's manual" in a loose-leaf binder. Although well-written and an

invaluable guide to the would-be product developer, it saw most of its service on office bookshelves rather than in project team meetings. It was politely ignored; most recipients, it was suspected, hadn't read past the table of contents.

Internal marketing research was then conducted on managers to find out what was appealing—what they would read. Various concepts and mock-ups were presented to managers.

The "rebirth" of P&G's NPP introduced a simple, colorful, and effective four-page brochure, which lays out the entire process. It's very much a selling document, emphasizing the benefits of the process, with just enough meat to give the reader a taste for the system. This brochure is one of the best I've seen as a quick guide in any company.

- Wavin, a Shell-Europe subsidiary in the PVC business, developed a novel booklet, which features a cartoon character who leads you through their NPP. Although the version I saw was not written in English, so clear were the visuals that I was easily able to follow their seven-stage process.

  Wavin has also developed appealing posters that are displayed on company bulletin boards. The same cartoon character leads you through the process on these full-sized posters.

- Exxon Chemicals developed a more sedate, but nonetheless effective, four-page brochure, which highlights the company's NPP and its rationale. Exxon uses this not only for internal marketing, but also with customers (for example, in the event of a joint development project with a customer).

The quick guide is the introduction—the teaser. It is a simple road map—intended more as a selling piece—and is not a substitute for the detailed instruction manual.

2. Design a user-friendly instructional manual.

Do you remember when you acquired a new piece of software for your PC? It most likely came with a user's manual—a gray 3-ring binder measuring about six inches square (and about three inches thick!). Did you find this inviting . . . did you have trouble restraining yourself from reading it cover to cover?

The software people have smartened up a lot in the last few years: they've designed manuals that are easy to read, well illustrated, and actually useful! Maybe we can learn from their experiences.

The description of the NPP delivered by the typical task force tends to be simply that: a detailed description of the NPP. But it's usually not a very good *user's manual*—it never was intended to be; rather it is a working document.

Companies with successful stage-gate systems invariably put considerable thought and effort into appropriate documentation. Some examples:

- Exxon Chemicals has developed an NPP user's manual that is a slick as any professional software manual today. It is professionally typeset; there are illustrations, diagrams, boxed insets, and other devices to make its reading appealing, easy, and understandable. The booklet is about 50 pages in length, and inviting to read.

- Procter & Gamble uses an electronic user's manual. The entire manual has been developed as a windows-style computer software presentation. Using a mouse to access pop-up windows, the user can get information on any facet of the NPP, and at various levels of detail.
- NCR is developing a self-help package of computer software to facilitate the front end of their NPP. The software asks pertinent questions about the proposed project and helps the champion structure his or her idea and project.

Some examples of how not to do it:

- IBM's "red-book" process is described in painful detail in 11 volumes of loose-leaf binders. It is agonizing to read—it appears as though it was put together by a joint committee composed of former software manual writers and members from the company's legal department. It describes in minute detail how every step in the process should be carried out. Not fun stuff! To no great surprise, no one I have ever met at IBM has totally read it.
- AT&T put together their *Product Management Process*, a lengthy, detailed document that resembles a textbook on product development. Its length, small typeface, and lack of illustrations and color, made it simply a boring document to plow through. Most AT&T people agreed; they didn't read it!

The point here is, don't assume the working document that your task force develops is the user's manual. It probably isn't! And if you try to make it the user's manual, experience suggests that you'll fail! So engage someone to translate your document into one that will serve users well. Take a look at software user's manuals, pick the ones you like, and use them as a model for your NPP documentation.

3. Develop a professional live presentation package.

During the first year of implementation, you'll be presenting and "selling" your NPP, possibly to numerous audiences within the corporation. The problem is that most managers are not very good at making such formal, large- audience presentations. And why should they be—they're not professional actors and not seasoned performers. Get some professional help and develop tools that will heighten the professionalism and effectiveness of your presentation.

Recently, I witnessed two different NPP task forces making oral presentations to various groups in their companies. In both cases, the presentations did not go as well as was hoped. One was simply boring: the presenters didn't excite the audience. In the other, I witnessed the task force leader "die on stage" in front of an audience of over 50 people. He was simply poorly prepared: terrible, almost unreadable visuals; an unrehearsed talk; and serious content problems in the presentation (for example, the audience consisted of a number of senior salespeople, yet the NPP failed to include sales in product development!). By the end of the presentation, there was actually hostility in the room!

In designing the NPP presentation, develop an outline of a script—the key points in this selling presentation; then reduce these to professional visuals—color overheads or 35-mm slides. Develop an outline of a script so that anyone can give the presentation. And test the presentation on a live audience. You can also use my video, *Winning at New Products*[3]—it may not describe your NPP exactly, but it sets the stage for you by demonstrating positive use of NPPs in other companies, such as Du Pont, Polaroid, and B.F. Goodrich (Tremco Division).

Remember the purpose of these presentations: the *official purpose* is instructional and informational—to teach people about this new process. But let's not kid ourselves: the *real purpose* is selling—to get organizational buy-in! If you don't secure buy-in, then the instructional facet of these presentations is wasted. So treat this effort very much as a sales pitch.

4.   Come up with a good name for the process.

Would a rose by any other name still be a rose? Maybe and then maybe not! Many of those involved in NPP implementations concur that even seemingly trivial issues—the name you put on your process—are important. You're selling a "product" here, so *worry about its brand name!* Some names used by the different companies include:

> Ameritech: Product Development Process
> Black & Decker: Global Product Development Management System
> Corning: New Product Innovation Process
> Exxon Chemicals: Product Innovation Process
> ICI (U.K.): New Product Commercialisation Scheme
> Northern Telecom: New Product Gating System
> Procter & Gamble: Product Launch Model
> Polaroid: Product Delivery Process
> Tremco (B.F. Goodrich): Tremco New Product Process

Some companies have gone as far as researching different names internally. Even the names of some of the components of the system have come under scrutiny. For example, Corning found the term "gate" had a negative connotation, and hence uses the term "diamond decision point"; both Skil Tools and Black & Decker use the term "tollgate" instead of gate. (B&D researched different words, and found that potential users saw a tollgate as a positive thing: "once you paid your money, you had a clear and open highway till the next tollgate!")

Training

The need for training and facilitation in the use of the NPP cannot be understated. Yet in our study above, many companies confessed to weaknesses in their initial attempts: they simply underestimated the training needs of users. The majority did not provide training as part of implementation, and this was cited as one of the reasons their NPPs were not favorably received. Training is important for two reasons:

1. *We dislike the unknown.* Things we don't know or don't understand we tend to have a negative predisposition towards. So if your audience—the intended users—doesn't understand the system (or worse yet, has incorrect views or misperceptions about it), then watch out: you're in for an uphill battle trying to get implementation. Training, if nothing else, creates familiarity and sense of comfort about new and foreign things.
2. *People don't know how to use the process.* Your NPP requires many people—team leaders, team members, and gatekeepers—to do new and different things, or to do old things in a new way. Without instruction, guidance, and facilitation, there is a high likelihood that people will simply get it wrong: they'll do a poor job on these new tasks. Learning by doing is great in theory, but the problem here is that you may not have this luxury. *The NPP must work reasonably well the first time;* if it doesn't, users will become frustrated; the process will be blamed; and good luck trying to implement it then! Training provides people with the necessary skills and knowledge to carry out these new tasks that the NPP demands of them.

Everyone who has been through the implementation of an NPP agrees that training is important. But there is anything but unanimity on the nature and format of that training. I have witnessed discussion on a variety of issues.

What topics should be covered in the training program? Three general areas emerge:

- *Soft skills:* The NPP demands certain "people skills" or "soft skills" that may be new to some players. These include: team leadership; interpersonal skills; time management; meeting management; conflict resolution; etc.
- *Hard skills:* The NPP requires certain people to undertake (or at least oversee) tasks they haven't done before (particularly in the case of technical people). Hard skills topics include: financial and business analysis; market research and market information gathering; market segmentation and target market selection; competitive analysis; project management (including the use of new software for project management); designing and conducting field tests; and designing a marketing plan.
- *The use of the NPP:* Users must be trained in the use of the new process. Specific topics here might include: the process—how it works; expectations at each gate (deliverables); gate criteria; the details of each stage; how a gate meeting works; etc. Here, users include both team members as well as gatekeepers.

Polaroid spent considerable time and money training team members—scientists, engineers, marketers, etc.—in the use of their new Product Delivery Process. Sadly they neglected the gatekeepers. "These were senior people, and didn't need training," it was argued. Wrong! Within several divisions, gatekeepers simply failed in their task: they did not know how to run a gate meeting: they came in unprepared, asked the wrong questions, and didn't understand or didn't use the criteria. Polaroid has now embarked on a "train the gatekeepers" initiative.

There are mixed views on how much soft-skill and hard-skill training should be included during the implementational phases of the NPP. Some companies argue that these skills are acquired and available on a routine basis as part of their company's normal training program. But there is *unequivocal support* for the notion of a *training program in how to use the NPP system:*

- Exxon Chemicals has put together a two-day training program on the use of their NPP. Within three years, over 1,000 people have been put through this program.
- Corning has charged its human resources department with the implementation of its NPP. Not only do they provided hands-on facilitation, but they also have designed and put in place a three-day training program on the NPP, with an almost-full-time instructor.

A variety of different training methods and formats are recommended for the implementation of your NPP. Some firms use a program of formal seminars, which NPP users take in advance of their projects. This seminar format is relied on mostly for the initial training on introduction of the NPP (for example, the two-day Exxon NPP course and three-day Corning NPP course). These introductory seminars consist of a combination of lectures and discussions; company cases, team exercises, and role playing (e.g., running a gate meeting). Additionally, some firms such as Hewlett-Packard, offer a full complement of hard-skills courses (and some soft-skills seminars) appropriate for product development teams.

Other companies provide JIT, or "just-in-time" training to each project team when and how they need it. What this entails is a combination of custom-tailored seminars together with standard training packages.

Some firms rely heavily on the use of facilitators to help the project teams and gatekeepers:

- Corning provides facilitators to work closely with the project team. The facilitator acts as a consultant, a mentor, and a trainer.
- Polaroid has a New Product Process Office, which provides help and facilitation both to project teams (for example, a facilitator works with the team in helping them prepare their business case) and to gatekeepers (the facilitator can attend gate meetings to ensure they run properly).

Having good materials and documentation can go a long way as a substitute for formal or JIT training. For example, Procter & Gamble's PC-based documentation is almost a "self-help, do-it-yourself" training program for team members. NCR's IDEA software guides the product champion through the front-end of the NPP. Other companies develop extensive illustration materials taken from real company cases, with examples of a business case, project plan, competitive analysis, and so on. These models show clearly and visibly what is expected of teams. In short, "don't tell me, show me an example!"

Reducing Cycle Time

Cycle time reduction is both a topical and critical issue, and moves front-and-center especially during NPP implementation. Some people in your company fear that the NPP will increase cycle time. Not so! You have the evidence above—use it! But *you must deal with these fears!*

The facts are clear: *a formal new product process does reduce cycle time when it is properly implemented.* The new product process builds in many approaches designed not only to lead to success, but a *faster success!* Remember Lesson 14 in Chapter 4:

"Speed is everything! But not at the expense of quality of execution."

Here we introduced *five sensible ways to reduce cycle time*—ways that are totally consistent with sound management practice, and which have been built into the stage-gate process. Let's have a quick review:

- *Do it right the first time:* The best way to save time is by avoiding having to recycle back and do it a second time.
- *Homework and definition:* Doing the up-front homework and getting clear project definition saves time: it means less recycling back to get the facts and a sharper product target to work towards.
- *Organize around a multifunctional team with empowerment:* Multifunctional teams are essential for good communication, rapid decision-making, and parallel problem-solving—all key ingredients in saving time. The whole team—marketing, R&D, manufacturing, engineering—is on the field together and actively participates in each play.
- *Parallel processing:* Run your new product projects, not like a relay race, but like a *rugby game*—use *parallel processing,* where three or four activities are done simultaneously and by different people from various functions. More gets done in an elapsed period of time and there is less chance of an activity being arbitrarily omitted due to lack of time.
- *Prioritize and focus:* Speed up your process by concentrating resources on the truly meritorious projects: not only will the work be done better, it will be done faster. But this means tough Go/Kill decisions and prioritizations at the gates.

In addition to these, here are some "nuts-and-bolts" ways to reduce cycle time. Consider making them part of your implementation efforts.

- *Use flow-charting:* that is, map out each and every activity in a project (or in your NPP), and remove the time wasters. Any NPP can be accelerated by shortening each stage.[4] Shortcuts, or omitting the unrequired, are obvious time savers. Ask how every activity can be reduced in time. Be ruthless. This is not rocket science, just simple flow-charting. Adhesives Systems, a B.F. Goodrich division, is doing this currently with every project.
- *Use planning tools:* utilize critical path-planning and project management software. Look for opportunities for undertaking tasks concurrently, or for beginning one task before another ends.

- *Add flexibility* to the process to ensure greater speed (and be sure to *emphasize this in your presentations*). Overlap stages; bring activities forward into an earlier stage, especially long–lead time activities; have multiple gate approvals—for example, a combined Gate 2 and 3 meeting—at one time; use intelligent corner cutting—it's OK to relax the rules of a well-defined process once you have the NPP up and running.
- *Deadlines must be regarded as sacred* if speed is the objective. Time-based innovation is impossible without a disciplined adherence to deadlines. Delays are dealt with via extra input of effort and resources, *not postponement.*
- *Have flexible funding:* that is, set aside envelopes of money (or resources) so that one does not have to wait for a new budget year for money to start a promising project.
- *Move ahead anyway:* If gatekeepers cannot make timely decisions (for example, cannot arrange a time for a meeting, or don't show up to the meeting), the decision is an automatic Go. Make this a company rule.
- *Keep it simple:* Find opportunities for unbundling products and projects. For example, instead of a project that requires three inventions, break it into three separate new product projects: introduce three successively better generations of products. The rule here is: project complexity doubles and triples the cycle time; so work to reduce the complexity of projects!

Suggestion: When implementing the NPP, *make every effort to reduce cycle times* of projects. The mere fact that you're now using an NPP that builds in quality of execution, homework and early definition, multifunctional teams, parallel processing, and focus means automatic cycle time reduction. But do more than this. Use the approaches outlined above during your implementation—flow-charting, planning tools, process flexibility, sacred deadlines, flexible funding, fast gate decisions, and complexity reduction. But be sensible too: Often the "quick fix" methods designed to speed things up—for example, cutting corners or omitting steps—yield precisely the opposite effect, and in many cases are very costly.

NPP Metrics

Is it too early to start thinking about NPP metrics? Certainly not! I strongly subscribe to the view that "you cannot manage what you cannot measure" and "what gets measured gets done." Some firms have made the mistake of not implementing measurement of their NPP until too late in the game.

In designing metrics, the general principle is: understand who needs the information, and what purpose it will be used for. Then start thinking about what to measure. The kinds of metrics various firms use fall into one of four broad categories (see Figure 10.10 for details):

Figure 10.10:   New Product Process (NPP) Metrics.

---

1   What are the "vital signs" of new product projects in the pipeline?

- What are the profiles of projects that are at various stages of the new product process? Here we consider the key success factors identified in Chapter 3, and translate these into surrogates for ultimate success. These metrics contain many of the gauges found in screening criteria (Chapter 7), but go beyond these.

- Key metrics include:
  - various measures of expected product advantage: product benefits, relative product quality, value-for-money, etc.
  - synergy measures—marketing, technology, and production.
  - gauges of market attractiveness (size, growth, margins, competition, etc.).
  - quality of execution of stages and tasks completed to date.
  - organizational measures: is there a team? is it truly multifunctional? is it working well? is there a leader? accountability? empowerment? etc.

- These measures are developed and projects are monitored on them as they progress.

2. Are people using the NPP?

- What percent of projects are truly in the process? To what degree? (by stage; by activity; and by team member and function).

- What percent of the development budget is going to projects actually "in" the NPP?

- Do people understand the NPP? When gatekeepers or team members indicate that they're using the system. then ask them some simple questions about the NPP: "list the criteria at any Gate? what's involved in a business case? what are the deliverables for any gate?" etc. If they can't answer, chances are they're not using the NPP.

3. Are people using the NPP well?

Questions or metrics for teams:

- Are you really using the NPP to move your project along, or are you just filling out the forms?

- Do you challenge other team members?

- Are the teams empowered (or are the gatekeepers "micro-managing")?

- Do you have the skills, tools, and training needed to do the job as a project team member?

- Do you agree with the results of the NPP (for example, gate decisions, project prioritization, resource allocations, etc.)? Do you understand how and why decisions have been made?

- Are you meeting gate review dates and milestones in your project?

- Do you feel that you have gatekeeper and/or management support for your project? Are the gatekeepers (or management) serious about your new product and do they value your efforts?

- Are the gatekeepers doing a good job? For example: Are they prepared? Do they use the gate criteria? Do they ask relevant questions? Are they disciplined? Are all projects treated fairly and consistently? Do all projects go through the gates? Are gate decisions based on the criteria? Are decisions timely?

Questions or metrics for gatekeepers:

- Are project teams meeting your expectations?

- Are projects meeting gate deadlines and milestones?

- Are the deliverables to gates in good shape? Are they quality deliverables (the result of good work)?

- Do you have the skills, tools, and training needed to do the job as a gatekeeper?

- Do the gatekeepers assure funding? Help the team get what it needs? Generate organizational confidence? Provide guidance, acting as a sounding board for the leader and team? Facilitate and buffer the team?

- Do gatekeepers balance "mentoring" versus "meddling?"

4. Is the output or result of the NPP successful?

Assess the results in terms of:

- Profit: the hit rate (i.e., the percentage of new products that are financially successful).

- Resource allocation and gate decisions:
    — What proportion of resources spent at each stage go to successful, unsuccessful, or killed projects?
    — Are the right projects being stopped?
    — What is kill rate at each gate?

- Impact:
    — new products (introduced in last 3 or 5 years) as a percentage of current sales.
    — strategic impact: the number of new categories, new platforms or new technologies entered and (percentage of business in each).

- Cycle time: Does it meet goals? How does it compare to cycle times pre-NPP?

---

1. What are the "vital signs" of projects in the pipeline.

These metrics are based on the key success factors (identified in Chapter 3) and provide a profile of the projects as they progress from stage to stage. These measures capture the "health" of projects currently underway, and provide an early warning of impending trouble (see Figure 10.10).

2. Are people using the NPP?

The naive observer can be fooled by the answers to this question. Ask any project team, "Are you using the NPP?" and they'll answer "Yes." Lower the microscope and you'll find the truth: some team members, some activities, and some stages are following the NPP; but many aren't. In short, this needs to be a probing set of metrics, that asks for evidence and specifics. The emphasis is on "show me."

These short-term metrics (items 1 and 2) are crucial ones to have in place during the early years of the NPP. They are the first indicators of trouble and they pinpoint the need for course corrections (see Figure 10.10).

3. Are people using the NPP well?

People may be familiar with the NPP, and are even trying to use it. But they may not be doing a very good job at it. Here are metrics aimed at both gatekeepers and teams that address proficiency issues. In both cases, some form of audit tool or questionnaire is used to solicit answers; some of the answers in Figure 10.10 will obviously be opinion.

4. Is the output or result of the NPP successful?

This captures the longer term performance of the company's NPP: profits, hit rates, and percentage sales by new products. Sadly, it may take five years or more to obtain definitive measures on these metrics. But the time to start is now.

Note that although cycle time is a popular concept, its measurement is fraught with problems. First, when does the clock start ticking—at the idea stage? at Gate 1? or when serious development begins at Gate 3? Second, what do we measure cycle time against? We must have a yardstick.

Measuring profit is somewhat easier: it is reported relative to a minimum hurdle rate; or relative to last year's return; or relative to the cost of capital. There exist yardsticks for comparison. But cycle time presents problems. If we measure it relative to previous year's projects, this assumes the nature of the projects (for example, complexity) hasn't changed (and also that we kept records from previous years). If we measure it against time goals, who says the goals were realistic—maybe they were wishful thinking? If we measure cycle time versus *how long the project should have taken,* then how do we know how long it should have taken! The point is: cycle metrics are very problematic.

A Process Manager

Many companies with a successful NPP have a full-time process manager. In the case of some firms, the NPP had been designed and had been in the implementation phase for several years, but was limping along and led by a committee (often the task force that had designed it). But it was only when a dedicated champion was appointed to devote his or her energies to the NPP that it really was implemented:

- Polaroid's old process was housed in quality assurance as a part-time activity for several years. It took a full-time manager of their new Product Delivery Process (PDP) to truly implement this NPP, however. This person largely acts as an ambassador, consultant, and trainer, but is ultimately responsible for seeing that the PDP process is implemented across the company.
- The champion for the NPP at Corning was found in human resources (an expert on organizational change). He worked full time on the implementation and management of their NPP, and with continuing support from the executive sponsor (Corning's president). Successful implementation took two years.

Give serious consideration to having a full-time manager of the NPP, certainly during its initial years. Committees and task forces tend to do a rotten job of implementation!

A Final Thought on Implementation

Many investigations, including my own NewProd studies, have provided clues and insights into how to mount a successful product innovation program. Now you move ahead and translate these and other insights and lessons into a carefully crafted new product process—a game plan that provides a road map and discipline, focuses on quality of execution, builds in the up-front homework, is strongly market-oriented, and is backed by appropriate resources.

The implementation of a stage-gate game plan is far more complex than its mere design, however. Implementation means effecting organizational change, which is perhaps the most difficult of all challenges in today's corporation. Being a change agent requires much planning and work, as this chapter has made clear. If the experiences of other firms are any guide, however, then the results of a successfully implemented new product process are well worth the effort. But don't underestimate the effort required!

The Long Term: What Markets, Products, and Technologies?

I find the great thing in this world is not so much where we stand, as in which direction we are moving: To reach the port of heaven, we must sail sometimes with the winds and sometimes against it—but we must sail, and not drift, and not lie at anchor.
Oliver Wendell Holmes, *The Autocrat of the Breakfast Table,* 1858.

Win the Battle, Lose the War?

What if . . .

- What if a manager implemented the game plan—the new product process from idea to launch as outlined in the last ten chapters?
- And what if she religiously followed the game plan?
- And what if the steps were executed well?
- And even assuming luck was on her side . . .

would the result be a steady stream of successful new products with a high profit impact on the firm? Not necessarily. One ingredient is missing, and that ingredient makes the difference between winning individual battles and winning the entire war.

The key ingredient is the new product strategy or *the product innovation charter* (PIC).[1] The new product strategy charts the strategy for the firm's entire new product initiative. It is the master plan: it provides the direction for your company's new product efforts, and it is the essential link between your product development effort and your firm's corporate strategy.[2]

How does the firm's new product strategy fit into the game plan? Some strategic models show it as preceding the idea-generation stage, as though strategy development were simply one stage of many in the game plan. But the product innovation strategy is more than that; it *overarches the game plan and influences every stage of the new product process.* The role of new product strategy is shown in Figure 11.1.

Figure 11.1: The Product Innovation Strategy and the New Product Process

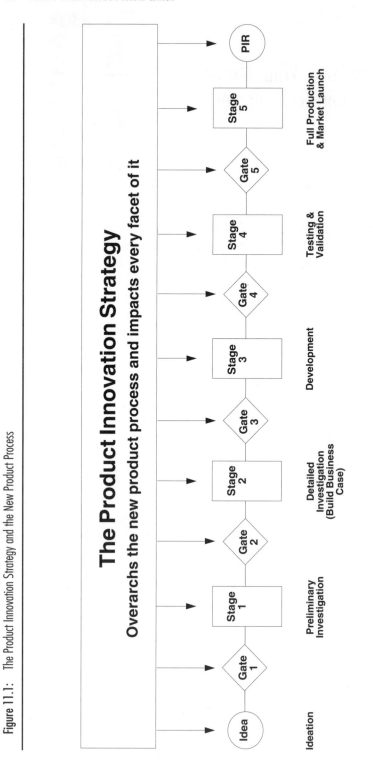

The Product Innovation Strategy
Overarchs the new product process and impacts every facet of it

| Ideation | Preliminary Investigation | Detailed Investigation (Build Business Case) | Development | Testing & Validation | Full Production & Market Launch |

Reprinted from *Business Horizons*, May–June 1990. Copyright 1990 by the Foundation for the School of Business at Indiana University. Used with permission.

This chapter begins with a look at the need for a product innovation strategy, and reveals a shortage of useful frameworks for developing such a strategy. The components of an innovation strategy are then defined, followed by a glimpse into some of the broad strategic options or scenarios that your firm might elect in product innovation. We then look at the hard evidence to see what types of innovation strategies appear to deliver the best results, and to understand what success factors the winners shared. Next, approaches to developing an innovation strategy are outlined—approaches where we define and elect arenas of strategic thrust for your new product efforts. We also look at entry strategies: that is, having defined our strategic direction, how does one go about entering that arena? The chapter ends on a controversial note, namely the thorny issue of planning theory versus planning practice. So let's move forward, elevating ourselves above the individual new product project, and look at strategy and direction for the firm's entire new product effort.

The Importance of a New Product Strategy

New product development and technology bear an integral relationship to a company's thinking by helping to define the range of that company's choices.[3] For many companies, new products have become the leading edge of corporate strategy, opening up new markets and new business opportunities.[4]

The companies that are most likely to succeed in the development and launch of new products are those firms that implement a company-specific approach, driven by corporate objectives and strategies, with a *well-defined new product strategy* at its core. This was one of the findings of an extensive study of new product practices: the new product strategy was viewed as instrumental to the effective identification of market and product opportunities.[5]

A number of firms do develop such innovation strategies. For example, PICs were described by Crawford in his study of 125 firms.[6] He notes that firms are now beginning to pull all the multifunctional elements together in one document, which specifies the types of markets, products, technologies, and orientation the company will pursue with its new product strategy.

What Is a Product Innovation Strategy?

A product innovation strategy is a strategic master plan that guides the new product game. But how does one define or describe a new product strategy? The term "strategy" is widely used in business circles today. The word is derived from the ancient Greek word meaning "the art of the general." Until comparatively recently, its use was confined to the military. In a business context, strategy has been defined as "the schemes whereby a firm's resources and advantages are managed (deployed) in order to surprise and surpass competitors or to exploit opportunities."[7] More specifically, strategic change is defined as "a realignment of firm's product/market environment."[8] Strategy is closely tied to a product and market specification; Corey identifies market selection and product delineation as the two key dimensions of corporate strategy.[9]

Product innovation strategy, while closely related to corporate strategy, tends to more specific. Typically, it contains two or three key elements.

- *Objectives and role:* The product innovation strategy specifies the objectives of the new product effort, and it indicates the role that product innovation will play in helping the firm achieve its corporate objectives. It answers the question: how do new products and product innovation fit into the company's overall plan? Statements such as "By the year 2000, 30 percent of our corporate sales will come from new products that we will develop and launch in the next five years" are typically found in the innovation strategy. Performance objectives can also be included in this strategy, such as the desired number of new product introductions, expected success rates and acceptable financial returns from new products.
- *Arenas and strategic thrust:* The second component of an innovation strategy is the specification of the arenas in which the game will be played. That is, it defines the types of markets, applications, technologies, and products on which the firm's new product efforts will focus. The specification of these arenas—what's "in bounds" and what's "out of bounds" is fundamental to spelling out the direction or *strategic thrust* of the firm's innovation effort, and is the result of identifying and assessing new product opportunities at the strategic level.
- *Plan of attack or entry strategy:* A third component that is often found in a product innovation strategy concerns the "how"—that is, how the company intends to exploit opportunities in the defined arenas to achieve its innovation objectives. This action plan tends to be firm-specific, but can capture a number of elements of the plan. For example, entry strategies might be outlined and can include internal product development, licensing, joint venturing, and even acquisitions of other firms.

Why Have a New Product Strategy?

Developing a new product strategy or PIC is hard work. It involves many people, and especially top management. Why, then, go to all the effort? Most of us can probably name countless firms that do not appear to have a master plan for their new product efforts. How do they get by?

Doing Business without a Strategy

Running an innovation program without a PIC or strategy is like running a war without a military strategy. There's no rudder, there's no direction, and the results are often highly unsatisfactory. We simply drift. On occasion, such unplanned efforts do succeed, largely owing to good luck or perhaps brilliant tactics.

A new product initiative without a strategy will inevitably lead to a number of ad hoc decisions made independently of one another. New product and R&D projects will be initiated solely on their own merits and with little regard to their fit into the grander scheme. The result is that the firm finds itself in unrelated or unwanted markets, products, and technologies: there is no focus.

Objectives: The Necessary Link to Corporate Strategy

What types of direction does a PIC give a firm's new product efforts? First, the objectives of a strategy tie the product development effort tightly to the firm's corporate strategy. New product development, so often taken as a given, becomes a central part of the corporate strategy, a key plank in the company's overall strategic platform.

The question of spending commitments on new product is dealt with by defining the role and objectives of the new product initiative. Too often the R&D or new product budget is easy prey in hard economic times. Research and development tends to be viewed as "soft money"—a luxury. But with product innovation as a central facet of the firm's corporate strategy, and with the role and objectives of product innovation firmly established, cutting this budget becomes less arbitrary. There is a continuity of resource commitment to new products.

The Arenas: Guiding the Game Plan

The second facet of the PIC, the definition of arenas, is critical to guiding and focusing the new product efforts (see Figure 11.2). The first step in the game plan is idea generation. In Chapter 6, a proactive idea generating system was

Figure 11.2:   The Choice of Arenas Guides the New Product Process

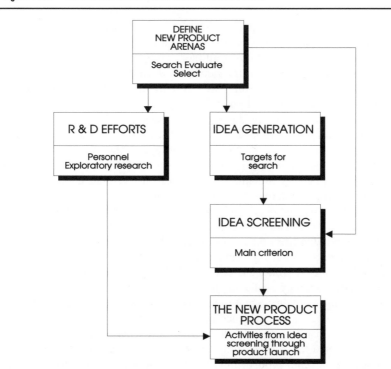

Reprinted by permission of *Business Quarterly,* published by the Western Business School, the University of Western Ontario, London, Ontario, Canada, from R. G. Cooper, "Strategic Planning for Successful Technological Innovation," Spring 1978.

proposed as both practical and desirable. But where does one search for new product ideas? Unless the arenas are defined, the result is a scatter-gun search effort, undirected, unfocused, and ineffective.

The first gate in the game plan is idea screening. The key criterion for this early Go/Kill decision is whether the proposed new product falls within the company's mandate for its new product initiatives. That is, does the proposed project have strategic alignment? Is it aligned with the firm's strategy? This usually translates into "Is this the kind of market, product, and technology that we as a company have decided is game for us?" Without a definition of your game—arenas of strategic thrust—good luck in trying to make an effective screening decision!

The definition of arenas also guides resource and personnel planning. If certain markets are designated top priority arenas, then the firm can acquire resources, people, skills, and knowledge to enable it to attack those markets. Similarly, if certain technologies are singled out as arenas, the company can hire and acquire resources to bolster its abilities in those fields. Resources building doesn't happen overnight. One can't buy a sales force on a moment's notice, and one can't acquire a critical mass of key researchers or engineers in a certain technology at the local supermarket. Putting the right people, resources, and skills in place takes both lead time and direction.

Where's the Evidence?

The argument in favor of a deliberate assessment of opportunities and the development of an innovation strategy, although logical, may be somewhat theoretical. One can't help but think of all those companies that have made it without a grand strategy. Further, the notion of deciding what's in versus out of bounds is foreign to many firms: after completing his large sample study on innovation charters, Crawford notes that "the idea of putting definitive restrictions on new product activity is not novel, but the use of it, especially sophisticated use, is still not widespread."[10] Quinn's work on how managers *really* develop corporate strategy concludes that "the approaches they [managers] use frequently bear little resemblance to the rational-analytical systems so often described in the planning literature."[11] He goes on: "Overall corporate strategy tended to evolve as internal decisions and external events flowed together to create a new consensus for action." He argues that strategies evolve and crystallize over time, often in a piecemeal fashion and based on interim decisions. His argument is not that firms have no strategies, but the way the strategy is developed often does not hinge on formal planning methods.

Regardless of how strategy is developed, the question remains: does a product innovation strategy really matter? Perhaps current practice observed by Quinn is wrong, and firms ought to approach strategy development a little more formally! So where's the evidence in support of having a product innovation strategy? There isn't much, unfortunately. One reason is that very few studies have investigated the role and impact of an innovation strategy. Most of the business research into product innovation has focused on the individual new product as the unit of analysis—for example, on why a new product succeeds or fails—but not on a company's entire new product efforts and which innovation strategies succeed or fail.

The studies that have looked at firms' new product strategies have a clear and consistent message: new product strategies at the firm level are critical to success, and some strategies clearly work better than others.

- Booz, Allen & Hamilton's study of new product practices in corporations found that "successful companies are more committed to growth through new products developed internally" and that "they are more likely to have a strategic plan that includes a certain portion of growth from new products."[12] The authors of this study go on to explain why having a new product strategy is tied to success:

  "A new product strategy links the new product process to company objectives, and provides focus for idea/concept generation and for establishing appropriate screening criteria. The outcome of this strategy analysis is a set of strategic roles, used not to generate specific new product ideas, but to help identify markets for which new products will be developed. These market opportunities provide the set of product and market requirements from which new product ideas are generated. In addition, strategic roles provide guidelines for new product performance measurement criteria. Performance thresholds tied to strategic roles provide a more precise means of screening new product ideas."

- The PIMS studies (Profit Impact of Market Strategy) considered new product strategies, but in only a peripheral way.[13] The studies looked at why certain business units were more profitable than others, and attempted to link profitability to the market strategy elected. Research and development spending and product quality level were two of many strategy variables considered in the studies, and both were found to be connected to profitability.

- Nystrom and Edvardsson studied a number of industrial product firms, and identified how various new product strategies were tied to performance.[14] Strategies emphasizing the synergistic use of technology, a responsive R&D organization, and an externally oriented R&D effort were generally more successful. While the study was limited to a handful of strategy dimensions, the message is clear that strategy and performance are closely linked.

- In one of my own studies, I looked at the *performance impact of product innovation strategies* in 120 firms.[15] This study is one of the few investigations undertaken on a large number of firms that considers many strategy dimensions, and how the strategy of the firm's entire new product effort is tied to performance results. The overriding conclusion was that product innovation strategy and performance are strongly linked. The types of markets, products, and technologies that firms elected and the orientation and direction of their product innovation efforts had a pronounced impact on success and profitability. Strategy really does count.

How Product Innovation Strategies Affect Performance

What are the secrets of a successful innovation strategy? To answer this question, I observed the product innovation strategies of 120 firms, measured on 66 strategy variables. These strategy variables described the types of markets, products, and technologies that the firms elected for their new product efforts, and their direction, orientation, and commitment to this initiative. The performance of the firms' new product efforts was measured on 10 different scales. The conclusions, set out below, are based on concrete data and the results of a scientific investigation, not on wishful thinking, conjecture, or speculation. They will prove useful in the formulation of a new product strategy.

Conclusion 1. There is a strong connection between the new product strategy a firm elects and the performance results it achieves. New product strategy and performance are closely connected. The underlying hypothesis of the study— that strategy leads to performance—was strongly supported. Five different strategy types or scenarios were uncovered, and each was associated with a different performance level and type. One strategy, called "Strategy Type B" (a balanced strategy), yielded excellent results overall, and in a convincing manner.

New product success is not solely a matter of good fortune, or even of being in the right industry. Admittedly, firms in certain types of industries—growth industries, technologically developing industries, and high-technology industries—on average achieved better new product performance. This comes as no surprise. The point must be made, however, that the new product strategy elected had a pronounced and independent effect on performance. That is, the types of arenas selected, and the firm's direction and commitment to the new product effort, all helped to determine performance.

The implications of this strategy-performance link are critical to the management of a firm's new product efforts. The existence of this link points to the need to define clearly the firm's new product strategy as a central and integral part of the corporate plan. The development of a new product strategy becomes a pivotal management task.

During discussions with managers, I found that the great majority either lacked a written product innovation strategy, or admitted to having only a superficial plan. Many firms did not even have quantifiable objectives for their new product initiatives. For example, managers often did not know key performance results of their new product efforts, and had to do considerable digging to answer questions on straightforward objectives-and-control gauges, such as percentage sales by new products, or success, fail, and kill rates.

Suggestion: New product strategy pays off. If your firm does not have an explicit written PIC or strategy, complete with measurable objectives and specification of arenas as a guide to your firm's new product efforts, now is the time to begin developing one.

Conclusion 2. On average, new product development initiatives performed well. Product development has a much better performance record, on average, than previously assumed. Over the years, some startling "statistics" surfaced, such as the often quoted "90 percent of all new products fail" and others. Crawford's study helped to dispel many of these myths by showing that most of the reported figures were based on speculation, on personal claims, or on studies of questionable merit.[16]

Consider our findings on new product performance. Overall, the average success rate for developed products was 67 percent. Only 17 percent of launched products failed in the marketplace, and another 16 percent were killed prior to launch. Admittedly, these figures do not include the many projects that were killed partway through development, after substantial amounts of money and time were spent on them.

New product performance was also positively rated on other performance criteria. New products introduced in the five years prior to our study represented, on average, 36.5 percent of the current sales of the firms. On a number of scaled questions that gauged performance—contribution to corporate sales and profit objectives, overall profitability, success versus competitors, and overall success—companies scored on the positive side of the ratings.

The disconcerting evidence, however, was the wide variation in those performance measures:

- Success rates for developed products ranged from 0 percent to 100 percent. More than 25 percent of the firms had a 50 percent success rate (or worse) on launches.
- Percentage sales by new products (the percentage of current corporate sales that came from products introduced in the last five years) also ranged from 0 to 100 percent. Almost 40 percent of the firms reported that 20 percent or less of their sales were from new products.
- On the scaled ratings of performance (0–10 scales), the average rating was 6 to 7; answers showed high variations among firms, however, from lows of 0 to highs of 10.

The point must be made again: Most new products do succeed, and most firms' new product efforts contribute in a major way to the sales and profits of the firm. These results do much to dispel the negative myths that product development is a luxury only a few firms can afford, that R&D spending is a questionable expenditure yielding low returns, and that only a fortunate few succeed in the new product game.

Suggestion: Does your firm suffer because too many people believe the myths—that the new product game is too high-risk, that the payoffs are low, and that one is better off avoiding the game? If so, use the concrete evidence in the studies to help dispel the myths and to put new product development in a more positive light in your firm.

Conclusion 3. All firms do not follow the same new product strategy; five separate strategy types exist.

The details of each strategy type are shown in Figure 11.3.

Type A: *the technologically driven strategy,* the most popular (followed by 26.2 percent of firms), featured a technologically driven sophisticated approach to product innovation. The new product effort lacked a strong market orientation, however, and there was little fit, synergy, or focus in the types of products and markets exploited. The markets targeted tended to be unattractive ones.

Figure 11.3: The Five Strategy Scenarios

A TECHNOLOGICALLY DRIVEN	B BALANCED STRATEGY	C TECHNOLOGICALLY DEFICIENT	D LOW-BUDGET, CONSERVATIVE	E HIGH-BUDGET DIVERSE
Poor product fit and focus	Strong product fit and focus	Product differential advantage: quality and superiority	Production and technological synergy	Poor program focus
Targets low potential, low growth markets	Avoids competitive markets	Defensive orientation	Low R & D spending	High R & D spending relative to sales
Technologically sophisticated, oriented, and innovative	Seeks high potential growth markets	Serves needs new to firm	Low product differen-tial advantage: impact and features	Targets competitive markets
Low marketing synergy	Avoids serving needs new to firm	Strong program focus	Serves needs new to firm	Targets markets new to firm
Weak market orientation	Strongly market oriented	Low technological sophistication, orientation, and innovativeness	High product fit and focus	Premium priced products
Avoids competitive markets	Technologically sophisticated, oriented, and innovative	Market oriented	Low product differen-tial advantage: quality and superiority	Poor production and technological synergy
Low product differential advan-tage: quality and superiority	Strong program focus	Poor production and technological synergy	Avoids dominant competitor markets	Low technological sophistication, orientation, and innovativeness
Strong program focus	Premium priced products	Avoids markets new to firm	High marketing synergy	Seeks high-potential, growth markets
Avoids serving needs new to firm	Avoids custom products	Targets dominant competitor markets	Low technological sophistication, orientation, and innovativeness	Weak market orientation
	Product differential advantage: quality and superiority	High R & D spending relative to sales	Targets highly competitiive markets	Poor product fit and focus
	Product differential advantage: impact and features	Avoids premium-priced products	Avoids premium-priced products	Avoids serving needs new to firm
	Avoids markets new to firm	High marketing synergy		Product differential advantage: impact and features
High impact; low succcess rate; poor profitability	Top performers; best on every performance gauge	Very poor results	Good success rate; low-impact program	Very poor results

Adapted with permission from R. G. Cooper "The Performance Impact of Product Innovation Strategies," *European Journal of Marketing* 18 (1984): 1–54.

This technology-driven strategy generally led to mediocre performance re-sults—it failed to meet the firm's new product objectives, it yielded a high pro-portion of cancellations and failures, and it was unprofitable. The strategy did have a high impact on corporate sales, however. In sum, the technologically driven strategy produces a technologically aggressive, moderately high-impact initiative, but is costly, inefficient, and plagued by failures because of a lack of focus and a lack of marketing orientation and input.

Type B: the *balanced strategy* (15.6 percent of the companies studied) fea-tures a technologically sophisticated and aggressive effort, a high degree of product fit and focus, and a strong market orientation. New products were aimed at attractive high-growth, high-potential markets where competition was weak. New products were premium-priced and featured a strong differential advantage: high-quality products that performed a unique task and met customer needs better; and products with a strong customer impact that offered unique features and benefits to the customer.

Not surprisingly, this strategy led to the best results: the highest percentage of sales by new products (47 percent versus 35 percent for the other firms); the highest success rates of developed products; a higher profitability level; and greater impact on corporate sales and profits.

Type C: the *technologically deficient strategy* (15.6 percent of companies) lacked technological sophistication. Firms using this strategy pursued products that were low-technology, "me too," low-risk and relied on simple, mature technologies. These developments proved to be a poor fit with the existing technology and production base of the company. These companies lacked an offensive stance, and attempted to serve market needs that they hadn't served before.

Predictably, Strategy Type C results were dismal. New products represented a low proportion of their annual sales (31 percent), the lowest of any group, and a high proportion of their new products failed commercially. Finally, their new product initiatives were rated the lowest in terms of meeting corporate objectives and in their impact on company sales and profits.

Type D: the *low-budget conservative strategy* (23.8 percent of firms) featured low R&D spending and new products with minimal differential advantages ("me too" products). These new product efforts were focused and highly synergistic, tending toward a "stay close to home" approach. New products matched the firm's production and technological skills and resources; fit into the firm's existing product lines; and were aimed at familiar and existing markets.

In spite of their lack of spending, firms using this strategy achieved moderately positive results: a high proportion of successes and low failure and kill rates. The new product effort was profitable, but yielded a low proportion of sales by new products and had a low impact on corporate sales and profits. This conservative strategy resulted in an efficient, safe, and profitable new product initiative, but one without a dramatic impact on the corporation.

Type E: the *high-budget diverse strategy* (18.9 percent of companies) was essentially a non-strategy. It featured heavy spending on R&D, but in a scattergun fashion; there was no direction, no synergy, no focus, no fit. The firms attacked new markets and new technologies, and used unfamiliar production technologies—a clear case of not sticking to their knitting. These firms were tied with the Type C firms as the worst performers.

Suggestion: Take a step back for a moment, and consider your firm's or division's new product efforts. Is there a strategy at all, either implicit or explicit? If so, which of the five strategy scenarios comes closest to describing your firm's approach? How do your performance results compare?

Conclusion 4. One strategy—Type B, a balanced strategy—yielded exceptional performance results. The strategy that outperformed the others called for a *balance between technological sophistication and aggressiveness* and *a strong market orientation.* The performance results of the firms that elected the balanced strategy were dramatically better than those of the rest of the firms. The Type B firms were significantly higher than the other four strategy groups in terms of:

- new product success vis-à-vis competitors' efforts;
- importance in generating corporate sales and performance;
- meeting new product strategy objectives; and
- the overall success of the effort.

The Type B firms tended to excel in sales by new products (47 percent versus 35 percent for the other firms); success, failure, and kill (72 percent success rates versus 66 percent for the other firms); and product development profitability.

Several characteristics distinguished the high performers from the rest. First, they had a strongly market-oriented and marketing-dominated new product effort; they were technologically sophisticated, oriented, and aggressive; and they were highly focused. Second, they selected familiar markets that were noncompetitive, high-potential, and high-growth, with needs that the firm had served previously. Third, they developed new products that fit into their current product lines and that were closely related to each other. The products had two types of differential advantages: product quality and superiority, and unique features and benefits with a high customer impact. The products tended to be premium priced, but were not limited-scope, custom products.

The orientation of these firms' strategies serves as a guide to other companies. Type B companies were the only firms to achieve both a *strong market orientation* and a high level of *technological sophistication and aggressiveness.* These firms possessed technological prowess comparable to that of many other firms, yet they had based their new product efforts on the needs and wants of the marketplace. Their new product ideas were derived from the marketplace; a proactive search effort was made for market need identification; a dominant marketing group was involved in the new product process; and the entire process had a strong market orientation.

The types of products and markets that these top performers selected (outlined above) were unique, and can serve as a guide to you in the selection of arenas as part your company's new product strategy.

Finally, the balanced strategy yielded positive results independent of the characteristics of the firm's industry or the firm itself. Industry growth rate, technology level, and technological maturity of the industry all affected performance, but the most important factor was the choice of the right strategy. Moreover, the balanced strategy gave consistently positive results regardless of firm or industry. This winning strategy is also a universally applicable strategy.

Suggestion: Compare your firm's explicit or implicit innovation strategy to the one elected by the Type B strategists. Do you share the same orientations? Do you select the same types of markets? Do you develop similar types of products? Go through the list of distinguishing characteristics of these firms, and see how you rate on each item. This exercise should shed light on your strategic strengths and weaknesses.

Conclusion 5. Adopting some, but not all, of the elements of the winning strategy is not sufficient. Certain elements of the balance strategy can be found in other strategy types. None of those types performed nearly as well as Type B, however. For example:

- Strategy D, the low-budget conservative approach, shared certain elements with B, namely a good product fit and focus. The Type D firms also possessed a high degree of technological and marketing synergy between their new product projects and the firm's resource base. The result was second best, however, and far short of the winning strategy. In particular, while the success, failure, and kill rates of new products were positive, the low-budget, technologically unaggressive strategy simply lacked the R&D commitment and technological prowess of Strategy B. The result was a low-impact new product initiative—a case of winning the battle, but losing the war.
- Strategy A firms adopted a technologically aggressive stance, like the winning Type B firms. But they lacked a market orientation, developed products that were a poor fit with their marketing resources, and tended to target low-growth, low-need markets. The result was a moderately high-impact new product effort, but one with a poor success, failure, and kill rate.

The conclusion is that a technologically driven and dominated strategy, on its own, is wrong. Equally wrong for most firms is a conservative, stay-close-to-home approach to new products. The most successful strategy is one that marries technological prowess, a strong market orientation, and a high degree of fit and focus: Strategy B.

Conclusion 6. A low-budget conservative strategy yields fairly positive results, especially for some types of firms and industries. Strategy D—the low-budget conservative approach—was one of the most popular strategies. It worked well only for some types of firms, however. Companies adopting the conservative strategy featured new product efforts that:

- had a high degree of technological and production synergy;
- had a low level of R&D spending; and
- created products with the fewest differential advantages—"me too" products in their customer impact and features.

To a lesser extent, the same companies' new product initiatives

- had a low level of technological sophistication and orientation;
- created products with little differential advantage in product quality and superiority;
- had a high degree of product fit and focus;
- featured products priced lower than competitors';
- were targeted at markets synergistic with the firm, but involving needs new to the firm; and

- were targeted at highly competitive markets, but markets with no dominant competitor.

On average, firms adopting the low-budget conservative strategy achieved positive results in profitability (returns versus expenses) and new product success rates. The end result was a low-impact new product effort, however, with a lower-than-average percentage of sales from new products (31 percent versus 38 percent for all the other firms). For certain types of firms the low-budget conservative strategy worked particular well. Companies with strengths in marketing (strong sales force, channel system, advertising, and market research skills) and firms in technologically mature, slower-growth industries performed extremely well by adopting this strategy. Sound performance was restricted to their profitability and success rates, however; the total new product effort was still low impact.

One conclusion is that firms that possess certain distinctive competencies—marketing power, for example—might rely on those strengths as the key to moving relatively ho-hum new products to the market. But the results for Type D firms were still inferior to the balanced-strategy firms that faced similar markets and had similar strengths. Moreover, for firms lacking key strengths or facing developing and higher growth industries, the conservative strategy typically yielded results far inferior to the balanced-strategy approach. Further, while a conservative strategy may work well for some firms and over the medium term, if the firm's markets or technologies change dramatically, the firms are caught in a vulnerable position—victims of the "product life-cycle trap."[17]

Suggestion: Is your company a Type D firm—facing mature markets, but with key marketing strengths in your company? Have you elected the low-budget conservative approach to new products? If so, and if you're typical, the results of your new product efforts are probably adequate. But they could be even better if you adopt the balanced-strategy approach.

Selecting the Right Strategic Arenas

The performance impact study, which identified Strategy Types A to E above, yields insights into the ingredients of a successful product innovation strategy for your company. Take a hard look at Strategy B, for example.

Two Types of Success Factors

The investigation also identified criteria that are useful in the evaluation and selection of arenas—the kinds of markets, technologies, and products that successful companies focused their innovation efforts on. A number of strategy factors were found to *affect* the new product performance of firms. These success factors fit into one of two categories: *they describe the types of new product arenas* the firm had chosen; or they capture the *basis of how the firm elected to compete.*

Factors that capture *descriptors of the chosen arenas* can be further categorized into:

- the attractiveness of the arena (for example, whether arena markets are growing or not, and the magnitude of market opportunities in the arena); and
- the strength or ability of the firm to exploit the arena (for example, whether or not the firm brings the right resources and skills to the table).

These arena descriptors are spelled out in detail later in this chapter, where they are used to develop a checklist of criteria to help you evaluate potential new product arenas and choose directions of strategic thrust for your company's new product strategy.

The second category of success ingredients, factors that capture the *basis of competition,* portray the orientation and commitment to the company's new product efforts. They include factors such as technological aggressiveness and sophistication, market orientation, focus and level of R&D spending—useful guides to how a new product strategy should be oriented. Specifically:

- *Technologically sophisticated strategies do better.* Firms that are "high" on this dimension employ sophisticated development technologies, and develop high-technology, technically complex new products. These firms are strongly R&D–oriented, proactive in acquiring new development technologies, and proactive in generating new product ideas. They develop innovative, higher-risk, venturesome products that offer unique features and benefits to customers. They employ state-of-the-art development and production technologies, and the company's product innovation effort is viewed by management as offensive (as opposed to defensive) and as a leading edge of corporate strategy.
- *Market-oriented and marketing-driven strategies do better.* Firms that are "high" on this marketing dimension feature a new product process that is strongly market-oriented and one dominated by the marketing people in the company. These companies are proactive in market-need identification and new product ideas are primarily market-derived. The picture emerges here of a firm whose new product effort is highly responsive and sensitive to market needs and wants, and where products are developed that are closely in tune with market wants.
- *A focused new product effort is more successful.* Strongly focused firms develop new products that are closely related to each other—the opposite of a highly diverse or shotgun approach. The products that these firms develop employ related development technologies and production methods. They are aimed at closely related markets, and the new products themselves are closely tied to each other.
- *An offensive orientation out-performs a defensive stance.* Firms with an offensive orientation view their new product initiatives as aggressive ones— aimed at growth and gaining market share (rather than merely protecting a position). Their new product efforts feature an active search effort for new product ideas, and are proactive in terms of market-need identification.

The Big Message

Our extensive study of firms' innovation strategies shows clearly that successful product innovation begins with the determination of a new product strategy. The strategy-performance link uncovered in the study is solid evidence of the need for strategy definition. The study provides many insights into the ingredients of a successful innovation strategy—the types of objectives that are both reasonable and measurable, and the criteria that are useful in the selection of arenas (the kinds of products, markets, and technologies that successful firms elect). Finally, the practices of the top performers—an aggressive and focused initiative with a strong market orientation married to technological sophistication—provide strong hints about how the new product game should be played.

A Lack of Good Frameworks

In spite of the apparent importance of having a product innovation strategy, you may be stopped dead in your tracks. Frankly, there isn't much in the traditional literature about how to develop a solid new product strategy for your company. For example, few guidelines have been developed to assist you in the choice of arenas and the direction for your new product efforts.[18] That is, there exist few conceptual frameworks or proven methodologies for formulating a new product strategy. Moreover, as noted above, little empirical research has been undertaken to determine the components and results of firms' new product strategies: that is, how companies directly or indirectly choose new markets and areas of technology, and organize and focus their R&D efforts in different directions.[19]

Although many corporate strategy models and frameworks have been developed, virtually all are for *existing businesses*—they deal with resource allocation, prioritization, and strategy development for businesses and products that you're already in! For example, product portfolio techniques have gained widespread acceptance for managing a portfolio of business units or products—stars, cash cows, dogs, and so on.[20] But as Day points out, "a product portfolio analysis identifies the need for new products . . . but does not indicate where to look."[21] Similarly the PIMS model is a useful diagnostic and forecasting tool, but strictly for existing businesses and products. In short, today's strategy models deal with *what is* rather than *what might be!* What is lacking in these approaches, argues Day, is "a systematic procedure for generating and choosing new strategic options," including new product arenas.

Let's not give up, however. Simply because the tools are neither well developed, nor see widespread use is no reason to quit. Remember the positive impact of having a strategy, and the dangers of sailing without a rudder or a map. So let's start out on the first steps of our strategy voyage.

Developing a Product Innovation Strategy: Setting Objectives

A few years ago, I boarded an early morning flight on a major airline. The captain began his announcement: "Welcome aboard flight 123 en route to. . . ah . . .".

There was a long pause. The pause was punctuated by laughter and wisecracks from the passengers; the captain didn't know where the flight was going! Fortunately, within 30 seconds, he remembered our destination. If he hadn't, the plane probably would have emptied. Who would stay on a plane where the captain didn't know his destination? Many of us, however, seem content to stay on board new product efforts that have no destination.

Defining objectives for your product-development strategy is essential; most of us accept that premise. Yet my strategy study revealed that many firms actually lacked written and measurable objectives for their firms' innovation initiatives.

What types of objectives should be included in an innovation strategy? First, the objectives should be measurable so that they can be used as benchmarks against which to measure performance. For example, Booz, Allen & Hamilton notes that firms are now measuring the results of their innovation efforts.[22] Second, the objectives should tie the firm's new product initiatives tightly to the corporate strategy. Finally, they must give the new product team a sense of direction and purpose, and be criteria for decision making.

Role Objectives

One type of new product objective focuses on the role that the new product effort will play in achieving corporate objectives. Some examples:

- The percentage of company sales in Year 5 that will be derived from new products introduced in that five-year period. (Five years is a generally accepted time span in which to define a product as "new," although given today's pace, three years may be more appropriate). Alternately, one can speak of absolute sales—dollars in Year 5 from new products—rather than relative sales or percentages.
- The percentage of corporate profits (gross, contribution, or net) in Year 5 that will be derived from new products introduced in that five-year span. Again, absolute dollars can be used instead of relative profits.
- Sales and profits objectives expressed as a percentage of corporate growth. For example: 70 percent of growth in company sales over the next five years will come from new products introduced in this period.
- The strategic role, such as defending market share, exploiting a new technology, establishing a foothold in a new market, capitalizing on a strength or resource, or diversifying into higher-growth areas.[23]
- The number of new products to be introduced. There are problems with this type of objective, however: the products could be large-volume or small-volume ones, and the number of products does not translate directly into sales and profits.

Note that the objectives listed above can be broken down by business unit or company division, or even by new product type; for example, 50 percent of new product sales from extensions and modifications, 30 percent from new items in existing lines, 20 percent from new lines and/or new-to-the-world products.

The specification of role objectives gives a strong indication of just how important new products are to the total corporate strategy. The question of resource allocation and spending on new product efforts can then be more objectively decided.

Performance Objectives

A second type of objective deals with the expected performance of the new product effort. Such objectives are useful guides to managers within the new product group. Examples include

- success, failure, and kill rates of new products developed;
- number of new product ideas to be considered annually;
- number of projects entering development (or in development) annually; and
- minimum acceptable financial returns for new product projects.

Many of the performance objectives flow logically from the role objectives. For example, if the firm wants 70 percent of sales growth to come from new products, how does that figure translate into number of successful products; number of development projects; success, failure, and kill rates; and number of ideas to be considered annually?

Setting these objectives is no easy task. The first time through, the exercise is often a frustrating experience. Yet these objectives are fundamental to developing an innovation strategy, not to mention a logically determined R&D budget figure.

Suggestion: Step 1 in developing a product innovation strategy is defining objectives. Start with the role objectives listed above, then move to the performance objectives.

Defining Target Arenas

The specification of arenas provides an important guide to your product innovation efforts. As Day notes, "what is needed is a strategy statement that specifies those areas where development is to proceed and identifies (perhaps by exclusion) those areas that are off limits."[24] The arenas guide the search for new product ideas; they help in project selection (for example, as noted in Chapter 7, a typical and important *must criterion* in project selection is: does the project fit within the firm's new product mandate? The "mandate" is defined by the arenas). Finally, delineation of where the firm wishes to focus its new product efforts is critical to long-term planning, particularly for resource and skills acquisition.

Defining the target arenas answers the question: on what business, product, market, or technology areas should the firm focus its new product efforts? Conceptually, the task is one of *opportunity identification* followed by *opportunity assessment*.

Two issues immediately arise. First, one may question the need for focus at all. Note, however, that new product focus has been found to be an important ingredient of successful innovation strategies.[25] Focus provides direction for idea generation, criteria for project screening, and targets for resource acquisition.[26] A second criticism is that focus will inhibit creativity; some of the best ideas, which may lie outside the target arenas, will be rejected. The counterargument is that focus improves creativity by targeting energies on those areas where the payoff is likely to be the greatest.[27] Further, significant new product breakthroughs outside the bounds of the product-development strategy statement can usually be readily accommodated in an ongoing project screening process, or via free-time or scouting projects. Finally, inevitably there will be products that "got away" in any new product effort, just as there will be the proverbial "fish that got away"; but there will continue to exist ample opportunities within the defined arenas for the firm to exploit, provided management has done a credible job in arena definition.

There are two steps to defining the target arenas. The first is developing a comprehensive list of possible arenas—opportunity identification. The second is paring the list down—assessing the opportunities—to yield the target arenas.

What Is a New Product Arena?

How does one define a new product opportunity or arena? Literature in the field of "business definition" provides some guidance. In his article "Marketing Myopia," Levitt urges managers to remove their myopic blinders and to define the business, not in terms of products, but in terms of the generic needs of customers the firm serves.[28] Thus railroads should not have defined their business as "railroading," but as "transportation of people, goods and other `things'" (including, for example, data transmission). In Levitt's mind, arenas are "market/need" areas, and the main criterion for search and selection of new arenas is "consistency with the market/need areas now served by the firm."

Levitt's argument has become embedded in marketing thought, and has become one the tenets of the *marketing concept.* In the business policy literature, however, Ansoff points out that in pursuing a market path in the identification and selection of new business opportunities, there is no guarantee of synergy.[29] Synergy, Ansoff argues, is the common thread—the essential relationship between the new business and the old—which is the key variable in the choice of new business areas. Through synergy, the whole is greater than the sum of its parts; the new business builds on the old, and utilizes resources from the old business at marginal cost; and together the combined return on the firm's resources is greater than if each business had been undertaken separately. If Levitt's thesis were pursued to its logical conclusion, U.S. railroads would have been in the taxi and car rental businesses, and perhaps even the manufacture of automobiles and trucks—all part of transportation. But in the latter cases, synergy would have been lacking.

Ansoff makes two main points. First, new business areas should be defined in terms of product/market opportunities (not just market need). And second, synergy with the base business should be the key criterion in the identification and selection of new product/market areas for exploitation. Corey uses a parallel approach, and proposes that we build two-dimensional matrices, with the dimensions labeled "products" and "markets" in order to identify new business arenas.[30] He notes that markets, together with the products that can be developed in response to needs in these markets, define the opportunities for exploitation: the arenas.

In *Defining the Business*, Abell takes this matrix approach one step further by proposing that a business be defined in terms of three dimensions:[31]

1. *Customer groups served.* For a computer manufacturer, customer groups might include banks, manufacturers, universities, hospitals, retailers, etc.
2. *Customer functions served.* These might include applications support, services, software, central processing, core memory storage, disk storage, etc.
3. *Technologies utilized.* For core memory storage, several existing and new technologies might have application to the random access memory function.

The result is a three-dimensional diagram, with new business arenas defined in this three-dimensional space.

Finally, Crawford's study of firms' innovation charters points to several ways in which business managers define new product arenas in practice.[32] Arenas are specified by:

- product type (for example, liquid pumps);
- by end-user activity (process industries);
- by type of technology employed (rotary hydraulics); or
- by end-user group (oil refineries).

On its own, each of these arena definition schemes has its problems. For example, a product type definition is limiting: product classes or types die. Similarly, an end-user group definition could lead the firm into a number of unrelated technologies, products, and production systems.

A review of these and other schemes for defining a business arena reveals that a single-dimension approach is likely too narrow. A three dimensional approach, similar to Abell's, probably will suit most business contexts.[33] Under this scheme, a new product arena can be defined in terms of:

- *Who:* the customer group to be served.
- *What:* the application (or customer need to be served).
- *How:* the technology required to design, develop, and produce products for the arena.

These three dimensions—who, what, and how—provide a useful starting point to describe new product arenas.

Figure 11.4: Defining New Product Arenas: The Three Dimensions

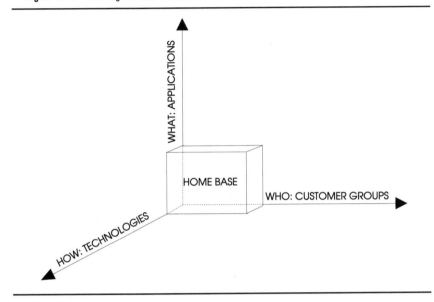

Identifying Possible Arenas

The next step is the search for new product arenas. A three-dimensional diagram is used to illustrate this search (Figure 11.4). The three dimensions of customer groups, applications, and technologies are shown as the X,Y, and Z axes of the diagram. Home base is located, and then other opportunities are identified by moving away from home base in terms of other (but related) customer groups, applications, and technologies.

An example: A company we'll call Chempro is a medium-sized manufacturer of blending and agitation process equipment for the pulp and paper industry. The company's major strength was its ability to design and manufacture rotary hydraulic equipment. The market served was the pulp and paper industry. The application was agitation and blending of liquids and slurries. The company's current or home base is shown as the cube in Figure 11.5.

What new product arenas exist for the company? Clearly, the home base is one of these, and indeed the firm was active in seeking new product ideas for agitation equipment in the pulp and paper field. Most of these opportunities, however, were limited to modifications and upgrades.

One direction the firm could take is to develop new products aimed at alternative customer groups. These customer groups might include the chemical, food-processing, petroleum-refining, and hydrometallurgical fields. The options are shown on the X or horizontal axis of Figure 11.5.

Similarly, new products in related applications can be sought. These related applications include the pumping of fluids, fluid aeration, and refining and grinding, as shown on the vertical or Y axis of the arena matrix.

Figure 11.5:   The Arena Dimensions for Chempro

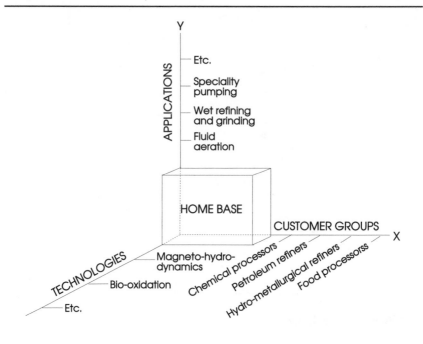

Considering these two dimensions—different applications and different customer groups—we can now proceed to define a number of new arenas. Working with a two-dimensional diagram (Figure 11.6), we see that besides the home-base arena, there are 12 other arenas that the firm could consider for its new product focus. For example, the firm could develop blending and agitation equipment (same application) aimed at the chemical or petroleum industries (new customer groups). Alternatively, Chempro could target aeration devices (new application) at its current customers, namely pulp and paper firms. Each of these possibilities represents a new arena for the firm.

The firm might also be able to change its third dimension by moving from its home base of rotary hydraulic technology to other technologies. If the alternatives are superimposed along the third dimension atop the matrix, the result is a much larger number of possible arenas. (This third dimension expansion is not shown in Figure 11.6—it's a little hard on the eyes! Possible alternative arenas include magneto-hydrodynamic pumps and agitators for a variety of end-user groups, bio-oxidation reactors for the food industry, and many others.)

Suggestion: Draw an arena diagram for your company or division. (You may need several diagrams.) Use the three dimensions of customer groups, applications, and technologies. Locate your home base, and then move out on each of the three axes, identifying other customer groups, applications, and technologies. This exercise should help you uncover a number of new but related product arenas.

Figure 11.6: Identification of Product Innovation Arenas for Chempro

	CURRENT CUSTOMER GROUP	NEW CUSTOMER GROUPS		
	Pulp and paper	Chemical process industry	Petroleum refining	Hydro-metallurigical
CURRENT APPLICATION Agitation and blending liquids	Agitators and blenders for pulp and paper industry	Chemical mixers	Petroleum storage blenders	Hydro-metallurgical agitators
NEW APPLICATIONS Aeration	Surface aerators for pulp and paper waste treatment lagoons	Aerators for chemical wastes	Aerators for petroleum waste treatment	Aerators for flotation cells (hydro-metallurgy)
Wet refining and grinding	Pulpers, repulpers and refiners			
Specialty pumping	High-density paper stock pumps	Specialty chemical pumps	Specialty petroleum pumps	Slurry pumps

Reprinted by permission of *Business Quarterly*, published by the Western Business School, the University of Western Ontario, London, Ontario, Canada, from R. G. Cooper, "Strategic Planning for Successful Technological Innovation," Spring 1978.

Selecting the Right Arenas

The task now is to narrow down the many possible arenas to a target set—the one that will become the focus of the firm's innovation strategy. To a certain extent, a prescreening of these arenas has already occurred: most of the arenas have been identified as being related to the base business on at least one of the three dimensions. Some synergy exists for each arena.

The choice of the right arenas is based on a single "must" criterion, and two "should" criteria. The must criterion is an obvious one: Does the arena fit within the corporate mission? The other two criteria were identified in studies of successful new product efforts. These criteria are *arena attractiveness* and *business strength* (see Table 11.1).

Arena attractiveness is a global dimension that captures how attractive the external opportunity is for that arena. In Table 11.1, arena attractiveness consists of

- *market attractiveness:* the size, growth, and potential of market opportunities within the arena; and
- *technological opportunities:* the degree to which technological and new product opportunities exist within the arena.

Table 11.1 Characteristics of Successful New Product Arenas

KEY CRITERION	WEIGHTS[a]
Arena Attractiveness:	
1. Market attractiveness	
• The size of the markets in the arena (dollar volume) are very large.	5
• There exist a large number of potential customers for the product in the arena.	9
• Markets in the arena have a large long-term potential.	11
• Markets in the arena are growing very quickly.	17
Subtotal: Market attractiveness	42
2. Technological opportunities	
• Products sold in this arena are very high-technology products.	12
• The arena is characterized by leading and state-of-the-art technologies.	19
• The arena features products based on very sophisticated technologies.	27
Subtotal: Technological opportunities	58
Total for Arena Attractiveness	100
Business Strength	
1. Technological synergy	
• Production processes used in this arena fit well the production processes, resources, and skills of the firm.	11
• The R&D skills/resources required in the arenas fit well the technical skills/resources of the firm.	14
• The engineering/design skills/resources required in the arena fit well the engineering/technical skills/resources of the firm.	4
Subtotal: Technological synergy	29
2. Marketing synergy (or fit with the firm)	
• The sales force and/or distribution channel system required for the arena fits those of the firm.	8
• The advertising and promotion approaches and skills required in the arena fit well those of the firm.	14
Subtotal: Marketing synergy	22
3. Potential for product advantage (or superiority)	
• Our new products in this arena will have a major impact on customer use and behavior.	18
• Our new products will be unique (differentiated from) competitive products.	20
• Our new products will meet customer needs better than competitive products.	11
Subtotal: Potential for product advantage	49
Total for Business Strength	100

[a] Weights are based on my study of 120 firm's new product strategies and their performance results. Factor analysis and multiple regression analysis were used to derive these empirically-based weights.

In practice, arena attractiveness is an index constructed from the answers to a number of individual questions. Table 11.1 shows a sample list of factors found in my study of product innovation strategies, although this list may not be an exhaustive one. Typically, an arena is assessed against each question and is given a rating; these ratings are then multiplied by the item weight shown in the table and summed to yield an index of arena attractiveness.

Arenas that feature large, growing, and high-potential markets and are characterized by products with sophisticated and leading-edge technologies score high on the arena attractiveness dimension.

Business strength is the other global criterion. Business strength focuses on the firm's ability to successfully exploit the arena. Synergy is a key concept here—the ability to leverage the firm's resources and skills to advantage in the new arena. Business strength is again a composite dimension, consisting of three factors:

- technological synergy
- marketing synergy
- potential for product advantage or superiority.

Arenas that build on the firm's distinctive competencies, that are highly synergistic with its marketing and technological strengths and resources, and that offer the firm an opportunity to gain a product advantage or product superiority are the ones that score high on the business strength dimension.

How the various arenas score on the two criteria can be shown pictorially in the arena assessment diagram of Figure 11.7. Arena attractiveness is shown as the vertical dimension, and business strength as the horizontal. The result is a four-quadrant diagram, not unlike traditional portfolio models, but with different dimensions and different components to each dimension.

Each quadrant represents a different type of opportunity. The arenas shown in the upper left quadrant, which feature high arena attractiveness and business strength, are clearly the most desirable. These are called the "good bets." Diagonally opposite, in the lower right quadrant, are the "low-low" arenas—those arenas that neither build on the firm's strengths nor offer attractive external opportunities. These are the "no bets." The "high-risk" bets are in the upper right quadrant: they represent high-opportunity arenas where the firm has no exploitable strengths. Finally, the lower left quadrant houses the "conservative bets"—arenas where the firm can utilize its strengths to advantage, but where the external opportunity is not so attractive; these are opportunities to be pursued at little risk, but offer limited returns. Using such a diagram, management can eliminate certain arenas outright (those in the "no bet" quadrant), and select a reasonable balance or set of arenas from the other three quadrants. The "good bets," in the upper left quadrant, are usually the top-priority ones.

Assessing the Arenas at Chempro

At Chempro, in our example above, the problem of arena assessment was simplified by recognizing the firm's technological and financial resource limitations. The company's main asset was its ability to design and engineer rotary hydraulic equipment. The prospect of embarking on new and expensive technologies, such as magneto-hydrodynamics or bio-oxidation, was out of the question. Moreover, having identified its current technology as a field of particular strength, and recognizing that there were many opportunities that could

Figure 11.7:   Arena Assessment: Arena Attractiveness versus Business Strength

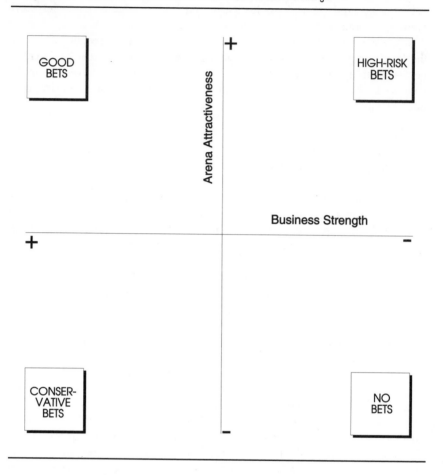

build on this strength, Chempro elected to stay with its current technology. Management chose to attack from a position of strength, and so the third dimension—alternative technologies—was erased. The result was the two-dimensional array you saw in Figure 11.6.

Next, the 12 new arenas plus the home base had to be rated on the two key dimensions of market attractiveness and business position. For this example, a list of questions was employed similar to Table 11.1; each arena was rated on each question. The questions were then weighted, and a business strength and arena attractiveness index were computed for each of the 13 possible arenas. The results for Chempro are shown in Figure 11.8.

Suggestion: Now that you've identified a list of possible arenas, try to rate each on the two key dimensions of market attractiveness and business positions. You might consider developing a list of questions for each dimension, and score each arena. Draw an arena assessment map (similar to that of Figure 11.8) to see where your arenas lie.

Figure 11.8: Arena Assessment for Chempro

Figure 11.8: Arena Assessment for Chempro

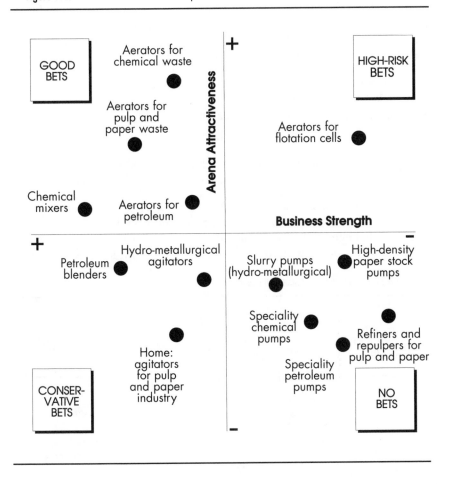

Selecting Chempro's Arenas

The choice of arenas depends on the risk/return values of management. Selecting only those arenas in the top half of the arena assessment diagram—the good bets and the high-risk bets—emphasizes the attractiveness of the external opportunity, and places no weight at all on the business-strength dimension: a high return, but a higher-risk choice. The other extreme—selecting only those arenas on the left of the vertical, the good bets and conservative bets—boils down to a low-risk, low-return strategy: selection of only those arenas in which the firm possesses strong synergy and a good business position. Ideally, one looks for a combination of the two: arenas in which the market attractiveness and the business strength both are rated high—the good bets in the upper left quadrant of Figure 11.8.

For Chempro, six arenas were rated positively on both dimensions. In order to quantify or rank order these opportunities, a cutoff or 45-degree line was drawn (see Figure 11.9). Arenas to the left of and above this line were considered positive; those to the right and below were negative. The perpendicular distance of each arena from that line was measured. The longer the distance, the more desirable the arena. Based on this exercise, three good bets and one conservative bet were defined as new arenas for Chempro:

- aerators for the chemical industry (waste treatment);
- blenders for the petroleum industry;
- agitators and mixers for the chemical industry;
- surface aerators for the pulp and paper industry.

The decision was made to continue seeking new products in the home-base arena as well. Several other arenas were put on hold for future action.

Suggestion: Use an arena assessment diagram similar to that shown in Figure 11.8 to identify your top priority arenas. Start with a 45-degree cutoff line, as illustrated in Figure 11.9, and measure the distance to each arena. Use a sharper angle for your cutoff line if you want to isolate less-risky, lower-return arenas.

Figure 11.9: Assigning Priorities to the Arena

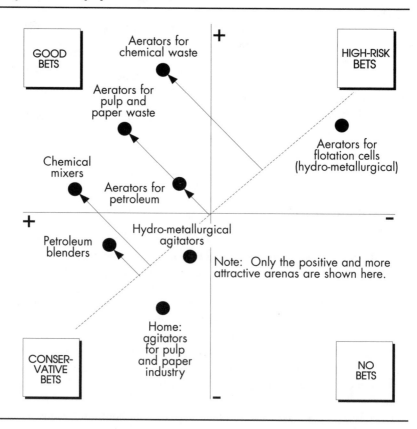

(Note that a 90-degree or vertical line yields only good bets and conservative bets.) A more nearly horizontal cutoff line results in a higher proportion of arenas in the high-risk quadrant.

An Alternate Approach to Selecting Arenas

The question of arena definition and selection is handled somewhat differently at Pugh Roberts & Associates.[34] Technology planning, in this firm's view, involves three basic decisions:

1. determining options for the investment of technology resources: the possible arenas
2. assessing and prioritizing these arenas in terms of potential market opportunities, competitive assessment, and technology impact
3. developing action plans and entry strategies for top priority arenas

An option for investment or an arena is defined to be the intersection of

- technology skills required to exploit the arena;
- products or systems that would be sold in the arena; and
- market areas.

Figure 11.10: The Technology Planning Framework

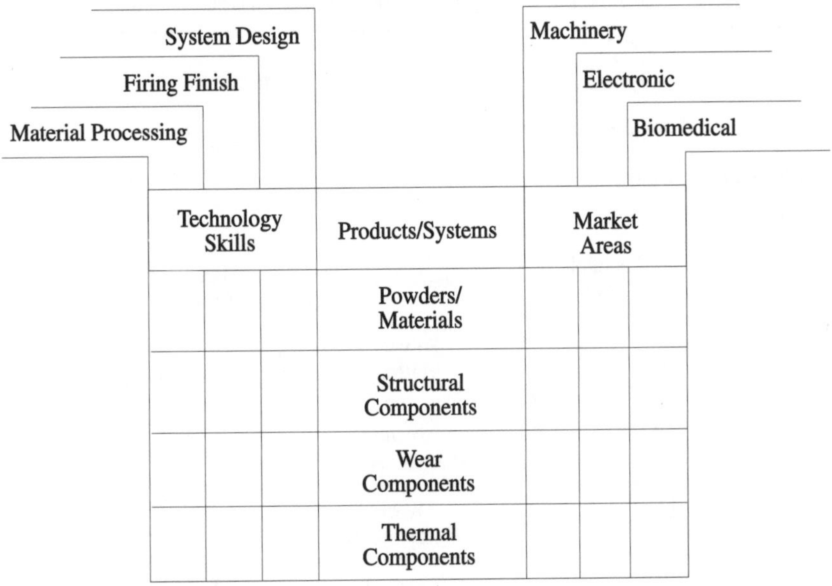

Reproduced with permission of Pugh Roberts & Associates, Boston, MA.

These three dimensions, and an example for a materials company, are plotted in Figure 11.10. (Note that these three dimensions parallel closely the arena definition of Figure 11.4.)

Figure 11.11 is used to identify possible arenas of interest. Next follows an assessment of each arena, relying on the following criteria:

1. *Potential marketing opportunities ($):* Here, product and market segments of interest are defined within each arena and are rated in terms of dollar volume, growth prospects, margins, profit potential, the firm's knowledge of the market, fit with the firm's technological capabilities, and the elasticity of the market to technological improvements.

2. *The firm's position (S):* The firm's strengths are assessed relative to each arena. Here a competitive analysis is undertaken, in which competitors in selected market segments are rated. The *commercial position* of each competitor involves a review of product line performance, market share, manufacturing and distribution costs, reliability, customer service, and reputation/ image. The *relative performances* of competitors' *products* are also assessed, but in terms of key technical performance criteria. Finally, the competitors' *technology positions* are assessed: technology capability; technology experience; production experience; proprietary position; and innovation track record.

3. *Technological impact (T):* The third criterion looks at whether new or improved technologies are likely to have a strong positive impact in each of the product market segments within an arena. Here the relevant existing and

Figure 11.11: The Use of the Technology Planning Framework for a Materials Company

System Design				Machinery		
Firing Finish				Electronic		
Material Processing				Biomedical		
Technology Skills			Products/Systems	Market Areas		
S, T			Powders/ Materials	$ S, T	$ S	$ T
S, T	S	T	Structural Components	$ S, T		$ T
S, T	S	T	Wear Components	$ S, T		$ T
S			Thermal Components		$	

$ = Potential market opportunities of large volume, high margin, future growth, high elasticity, etc.;
S = strong position relative to current and potential competition; T = new technology expected to have great impact.

potential technologies are first identified. Next, the life cycles and current position of each technology on its life cycle are determined. (The technology S-curve concept is used here.) Technology forecasts are developed, along with the timing and impact of probable technologies on key cost/performance characteristics of the product area. The idea here is to identify technologies with high "leverageability"; i.e., where technological returns or improvements will be high for the effort and investment expended (a steep S-curve slope).

Figure 11.11 shows the materials company example with each arena rated. Arenas that score strong on all three criteria—potential market ($), business position (S), and technological impact (T)—are singled out as arenas for exploitation.

Entry Strategies

This chapter so far has focused on the question: which new product arenas should a company enter? A second question is: how should the firm enter these arenas to avoid failure and maximize gain? Although these questions are fundamentally different, Roberts and Berry note that they should not be answered independently of one another.[35] Entering a new business arena may be achieved by a variety of mechanisms, such as internal development, joint ventures, and minority investments of venture capital. As Roberts indicates, each of these mechanisms makes different demands upon the corporation.[36]

Roberts and Berry propose an entry-strategy selection framework based on market and technological dimensions.[37]

1. *Newness of Technology:* the degree to which that technology has not formerly been embodied within the products of the company.
2. *Newness of a Market:* the degree to which the products of the company have not formerly been targeted at that particular market.
3. *Familiarity with a Technology:* the degree to which knowledge of the technology exists within the company, but is not necessarily embodied in its current products.
4. *Familiarity with a Market:* the degree to which a market is known by the company, but not necessarily as a result of selling into that market.

If a business in which the firm currently competes is defined as its *base business,* then market factors associated with the new business may be characterized as *base, new familiar,* or *new unfamiliar.* The same is true for technological factors.

The thesis underlying Roberts and Berry's framework is that the newer or more unrelated an arena is to the base business, the poorer the results to the firm. This leads to the logical conclusion that *entry strategies requiring high corporate involvement* should be reserved for *new arenas with familiar market and technological characteristics.* Similarly, entry mechanisms requiring low corporate input seem best for unfamiliar arenas.

Various entry strategies are shown in the matrix of Figure 11.12 for different degrees of market and technological newness and unfamiliarity. Roberts and

Berry support their matrix approach with 14 actual cases, showing the success/failure patterns across the matrix.[38] Various entry strategies and their appropriateness are discussed below, and the advantages of each are summarized in Table 11.2.

Internal development

Internal development exploits internal resources as a basis for establishing a new business or entering a new arena for the company. According to several studies, returns from such efforts are distant, with 8 years required to generate positive returns, and 10 to 12 years to achieve returns comparable to mature businesses.[39] Lack of familiarity with markets and technologies in the new business arena often leads to major errors, and is one reason for poor performance. Roberts and Berry recommended internal developments only for base business arenas and those involving new but familiar markets using base technologies, or new but familiar technologies targeted at base markets (see Figure 11.12).

Acquisitions

Acquisitions may be attractive not only because of speed of execution, but also because they offer a much lower cost of entry into a new arena. Acquisi-

Figure 11.12: Optimum Entry Strategies

Market factors	Base	New familiar	New unfamiliar
New unfamiliar	Joint ventures	Venture capital or Venture nurturung or Educational acquisitions	Venture capital or Venture nurturing or Educational acquisitions
New familiar	Internal market development or Acquisitions (or Joint ventures)	Internal ventures or Acquisitions or Licensing	Venture capital or Venture nurturing or Educational acquisitions
Base	Internal base developments (or Acquisitions)	Internal product developments or Acquisitions or Licensing	"New style" joint ventures

	Base	New familiar	New unfamiliar

Technologies or services embodied in the product

Adapted from: E. Roberts, and C. A. Berry, (1985) "Entering New Business" *Sloan Management Review*, pp.3-17.

tions are appropriate for new but familiar arenas, as shown in Figure 11.12 and Table 11.2.

Licensing

Acquiring technology through licensing represents an alternative to acquiring a complete company. Killing points out that licensing avoids the risk of product development by exploiting the experience of firms who have already developed and marketed the product.[40] Licensing is particularly appropriate when entering new but familiar technology arenas.

Internal Ventures

Roberts notes that many companies adopt new venture strategies in order to meet ambitious plans for diversification and growth.[41] In this strategy, a firm attempts to enter different markets or attempts to develop substantially different products from its base businesses by setting up a separate entity within the existing corporate body. The concept is to establish small businesses—entrepre-

Table 11.2   Entry Mechanisms: Advantages and Disadvantages

NEW BUSINESS DEVELOPMENT MECHANISM	MAJOR ADVANTAGES	MAJOR DISADVANTAGES
Internal development	Uses existing resources	Time lag to break even tends to be long (on average eight years) Unfamiliarity with new markets may lead to business errors
Acquisition	Rapid market entry	New business area may be unfamiliar to parent
Licensing	Rapid access to proven technology Reduces financial exposure	Not a substitute for internal technical competence Not proprietary technology Dependent upon licensor
Internal venture	Uses esxisting resources May enable a company to hold a talented entrepreneur	Mixed record of success Corporation's internal climate often unsuitable
Joint venture or alliance	Technological/marketing unions can exploit small/large company sunergies Distributes risk	Potential for conflict between partners
Venture capital and nurturing	Can provide window on new technology or market	Unlikely alone to be a major stimulus of corporate growth
Educational acquisitions	Provides window and intial staff	Higher initial financial commitment than venture capital Risk of departure of entrepreneurs

neurial, venture businesses—within the large corporation, taking advantage of the corporation's resources, but freeing the venture team from the usual corporate barriers to entrepreneurial behavior.

Joint Ventures or Alliances

When projects get larger, technology too expensive, and the cost of failure too large to be borne alone, joint venturing becomes increasingly viable.[42] According to Roberts and Berry, despite changes in U.S. law that permits or encourages research-based joint ventures involving many companies, traditional joint ventures, which result in the creation of third corporations, seem to have limited life and/or growth potential.

"New style" joint ventures are of particular interest, in which a large and a small company join forces to create a new entry in the marketplace. In these efforts of "mutual pursuit," usually without the formality of a joint venture company, the small firm provides the technology, the large enterprise provides the marketing capability, and the venture is synergistic for both parties. Large company/small company alliances, called "strategic partnering," often involve the creative use of corporate venture capital and are growing in importance as a joint venture mechanism.[43]

Venture Capital and Nurturing

The venture strategy that permits some degree of entry, but the lowest level of corporate commitment, is that associated with external venture capital investment. Major corporations invest venture capital in developing or start-up firms in order to become involved in the growth and development of such firms, and may eventually acquire them outright. The motivation is to secure a "window on technology" by making minority investments in young, growing, high-technology enterprises. When the investing company provides managerial assistance as well as venture capital to the small firm, the strategy is classed as "venture nurturing" rather then pure venture capital. This nurturing strategy appears a more sensible entry in achieving diversification objectives as opposed to simple provision of funds, but it also needs to be tied to other company diversification efforts.[44]

Educational Acquisitions

Although rarely discussed in the management literature, targeted small acquisitions can fulfill a role similar to that of a venture capital minority investment and, in some circumstances, offer significant advantages. In such an acquisition, the large firm acquires a small firm, usually with an "interesting" technology at the early stage of development. The acquisition is made, but not so much for financial return reasons, but to acquire know-how and familiarity at minimal cost. The acquiring firm immediately obtains people familiar with the new technology area, whereas in a minority investment, the parent company relies on its existing staff to build familiarity by interacting with the investee. Acquisitions made for educational purposes may therefore represent a faster route to familiarity than the venture capital "window" approach, and are recommended as one possible entry strategy for new, unfamiliar arenas (the top right cell in Figure 11.12).

Putting the Product Innovation Strategy to Work

The objectives and the top priority arenas for the firm's new product strategy have been defined. So have the entry mechanisms. Let's look at how this product innovation strategy guides the management of the company's development efforts.

Searching for Product Ideas

The definition of objectives and arenas provides guidance to the idea search effort. Armed with a knowledge of the new business areas the firm wishes to pursue, those in the company charged with seeking new product ideas will have a clear definition of where to search. Moreover, it now becomes feasible to implement formal search programs—suggestions schemes, contests, sales force programs, creativity methods, and all the other methods outlined in Chapter 6—to flush out new product ideas. The search for ideas will be more efficient, generating product ideas that are consistent with the firm's focus.

In Chempro's case, all personnel, from the president to sales trainees, gained a clear view of which new product arenas the company wished to concentrate on. These new insights make it possible for good new product ideas in the designated arenas to pour in.

More Effective Screening

One of the most critical screening questions highlighted in Chapter 7 was whether the new product idea fits within the firm's mandate for new products. Put another way, does the firm have any "right" to even consider the product idea? All too often the question is answered with blank stares and shrugs.

A clear delineation of the firm's new product arenas provides the criterion essential to answer the "mandate fit" question. Either the new product idea under consideration fits into one of the designated arenas, or it does not. If it does not, the proposed project is an automatic kill. The result is a more effective and efficient screening of ideas. Precious evaluation time and resources are not wasted on product ideas that may seem attractive on their own merits, but simply do not fit into the long-term innovation strategy of the firm.

Personnel and Resource Planning

Resources essential to new products—R&D, engineering, marketing, production—cannot be acquired overnight. Without a definition of which arenas the firm intends to target, planning for the acquisition of these resources is like asking a blindfolded person to throw darts.

For Chempro, aerators for the pulp and paper industry were defined as a top priority arena. R&D management hired researchers in the field of biochemistry and waste treatment; the engineering department acquired new people in the field of aeration design and aeration application engineering; and plans were made to add aeration experts to the sales force. Finally, several exploratory technical and market research programs were initiated in aeration and bio-oxidation.

Theory versus Reality

The premise of this chapter so far is that an innovation strategy is a useful concept to guide the innovation process: that is, specifying objectives, defining arenas, and deciding entry strategies will enhance the product innovation effort. A second facet of this chapter has been to outline various tools that help identify arenas (Figures 11.4 and 11.10), prioritize these arenas (Figures 11.9 and 11.11), and elect entry strategies (Figure 11.12 and Table 11.2).

Now to throw some cold water on all this theory! There is mounting evidence that *such formal approaches to planning see more light in text books,* academic publications, and classrooms than in corporate board rooms. In the context of developing corporate strategies, Quinn argues that firms typically evolve strategy and that managers move towards strategy consensus over time.[45] In short, the notion of a logical, sequential planning approach—Quinn calls this the rational-analytical system—is more fiction than fact. For example, "the precise directions that R&D may predict for a company can only be understood step by step as scientists uncover new phenomenon, make and amplify discoveries, build prototypes, reduce concepts to practice, and interact with users during product introductions."

Quinn's point is a valid one. How can a strategist identify an arena as a top priority until the firm has actually tried several new products in that arena? Only when individual new product projects get underway are new scientific discoveries made, and new market needs discovered or confirmed—opportunities that might never have been thought of at the initial planning and arena selection stages. And so the operational results at the project level yield further insights into the arena, and provide feedback to the planning process (Figure 11.13). For example, a common criticism of the arena selection methods and criteria outlined above is that, a priori, managers do not know the answers to the arena selection questions. The question, "Are there ample new product opportunities within this business arena for our technologies?" cannot be answered, in some cases, until the firm actually enters the arena. It's almost a case of "you don't know what you'll find until you get there!"

The top part of Figure 11.13 shows the formal planning process—identification and selection of arenas and formulation of entry strategies—as described previously in this chapter. The bottom half shows the innovation process at the operational level, yielding new discoveries, insights, and information, which

Figure 11.13: Interaction of the Formal Rational-Analytical Process (top) with the Operational Facet of Product Innovation (bottom)

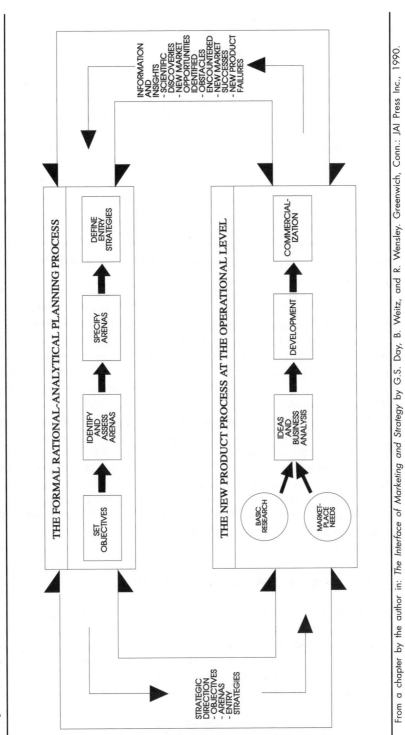

From a chapter by the author in: *The Interface of Marketing and Strategy* by G.S. Day, B. Weitz, and R. Wensley. Greenwich, Conn.: JAI Press Inc., 1990.

come only as a result of investing in an arena, and gaining firsthand experience within that arena.

The same is true in the case of acquisitions. The formal or rational-analytical model suggests a sequential set of activities: clarifying overall corporate objectives; setting forth goals for the acquisition program; defining specific criteria that acquisition/diversifications should meet; systematically searching out acquisition candidates; and so on. Fine in theory, but only as each acquisition candidate is sequentially identified, investigated, negotiated for, and integrated into the organization can one predict its ultimate strategic impact on the total enterprise, argues Quinn.[46]

The outcome is an incremental or evolutionary strategy development process, with the rational-analytical process and the implementational process feeding each other. Quinn concludes that "successful managers, who operate with logical incrementalism, build the seeds of understanding, and identify and commit into the very processes that create their strategies." By the time the strategy begins to crystallize and focus, some of the pieces have already been implemented and tested.[47]

The point of this discussion is not to refute the utility of undertaking formal planning and the development of an explicit product innovation strategy. First, simply because firms and managers behave a certain way does not necessarily mean that they are correct. History has shown many corporate practices and examples of so-called "sound management" to be wrong.* Second and most important, formal planning should play an integral role in enhancing the effectiveness of what Quinn describes as the incremental and evolutionary process of strategy development.

In short, both processes are important to defining strategy, and as shown in Figure 11.13, they complement each other. If only the operational/ implementational facet of the process (the bottom half of Figure 11.13) were in place, there would be chaos: a "ready, fire, aim" situation. We'd be testing a lot of opportunities with a very low hit rate. Conversely, a strictly normative approach—relying only on the rational-analytical planning framework and assuming that we can accurately foresee that nature of each opportunity—is not likely to be effective on its own either, the result being a lot of aiming, some firing, and quite a few surprises!

Some Final Thoughts on Product Innovation Strategy

New product strategy or innovation strategy is receiving increasing attention in the literature and corporate offices. As firms face mature and flat markets, increasing competition from home and abroad, and accelerating technological change, more companies are looking to product innovation as a strategic weapon. With the increasing importance of innovation also comes a desire to manage innovation, hence the wish to develop product innovation strategies.

---

* The book *In Search of Excellence* is a classic case, where many of the firms, cited as examples of sound management practice, fell on hard times within a few years of the book's publication. T. J. Peters and R. H. Waterman Jr., In Search of Excellence. New York: Harper & Rowe, 1982.

What we have seen in this chapter is a distinct lack of conceptual frameworks and empirical evidence to guide this strategy formulation process. Indeed, even the term "product innovation strategy" is not well understood or familiar to most managers. This chapter has attempted to highlight some of the approaches and tools proposed to deal with innovation strategy development. Clearly, there are evident gaps and weaknesses.

In spite of the challenge, a product innovation strategy is a must for all firms that are serious about building new products into their long range plans. Many firms operate without such a charter, and the managers in those firms know the problems only too well. There is no direction to the idea search, or there is no idea search at all. Much time is wasted in screening proposed projects and agonizing over the same question: Should we be in this business? Personnel and resource planning is hit-and-miss, and there are difficulties in securing a long-term, sustained budget commitment for new products from senior management.

Several methods of defining the new product strategic direction have been outlined in this chapter. They begin with a recognition of the need for and rewards of such a strategy. Objectives are defined that give the firm's new product effort a sense of purpose, and tie it firmly to the corporation's overall objectives. Arenas—the who, what, and how—are identified and pared down to a set of top priority fields for exploitation. These arenas give the new product initiative direction and focus, ingredients that are critics to a successful innovation strategy. And entry strategies for each arena—ranging from internal product development to acquisition—are developed. Recognize that operating in parallel to this rational-analytical planning process is a more serendipitous phenomenon—an evolutionary and incremental approach to strategy development. Both strategy processes have merit: implement the one and harness the other, and you reap the best from both.

The War Plan and the Battle Plan

Define the objectives of the new product effort. Choose the arenas upon which to focus. Decide the entry strategies. These are the ingredients of the war plan, or the product innovation strategy. Then move towards the battle plan, a step-by-step sequence of actions—a stage-gate system—to bring products from mere ideas to money-making successes in the marketplace. This is the new product process, the tactics or game plan.

There are no guarantees, of course. Even the best war plans and battle plans have been laid to waste by bad luck, unforeseen events, and poor execution. Product innovation is a future-oriented, hence uncertain and high risk, endeavor. Having no plan or no process at all, however, is simply begging disaster to strike. Product innovation is too important to be left totally to chance. The processes outlined in this book provide a discipline that builds the success ingredients into product innovation by design rather than by chance. By doing so, they increase your odds of *winning at new products*.

Audit Questionnaire for Diagnosing Strengths and Weaknesses in Your Firm's Product Development Efforts

[Note to reader: This questionnaire is designed to be self-administered to people closely involved in product development in your firm, division, or business unit. I have provided a much truncated version here, but the full questionnaire can be over ten pages in length. In designing your questionnaire, provide lots of space for answers, and promise anonymity.]

I. New Product Project Analysis

This first section is designed to probe what's going well and what's going badly as we move a new product project from idea to launch.

Please select a new product project in your Division that your are quite familiar with—perhaps one you worked on. Ideally, it should be a completed project, and can be either a commercial success or a failure.

My project for discussion is: _____

This project ...   ____ is rated as a commercial success
(check only one) ____ was killed; never went to market
                              ____ went to market, but failed commercially
                              ____ is not yet finished.

Listed below are a number of activities that might have been undertaken in your new product project. We want four answers for each activity:

a) *Proficiency:* Your assessment of how well this activity was handled or executed (quality of execution). Here: 10 = excellent; 0 = very poor; ND = not done, but should have been (an error of omission); NA = not applicable; (e.g., not done, but this was Ok—there was no need for this activity).

b) *Explanation of deficiency:* If the activity was deficient (i.e., low score or ND—not done, but should have been), why? What went wrong? Was there no time? No money? People availability? Lack of skills? A lack of appreciation of the activity's importance? No precedent? What were the reasons for a low score?

c) *Improvements needed:* What should have been done here, in hindsight? What improvements? Try to give a little detail.

d) *Importance of improvements:* Your assessment of how important it is to improve this activity . . . for this project, and for projects in general. Here: 10 = great need for improvement; 0 = no need for improvement.

Remember: Four questions per activity—two are scaled (0–10) and two require verbal answers. Note: if the project is not yet complete, then write across that activity "NOT YET DONE."

1. Idea generation—coming up with the original idea.
   a) Proficiency: (circle a number from 0–10 <u>or</u> check ND <u>or</u> check NA).
   very poor 0 1 2 3 4 5 6 7 8 9 10 excellent; or ___ ND; or ___ NA
   b) If deficient, why: _____
   c) What improvements needed?_____
   d) Need for improvements: (circle a number from 0–10 or check NA)
   no need 0 1 2 3 4 5 6 7 8 9 10 great need;   or ___ NA

[Note to reader: Repeat question 1 (a to d) for all activities from idea to launch. Include decision points as well (see Table 2.1 in Chapter 2 for a list and definition of possible activities. For example, repeat for the following activities (the wording will vary by firm):]

2. Initial screening—the first decision to go ahead with this project.
3. Preliminary market assessment—an initial, quick market appraisal.
4. Preliminary technical assessment—the first and quick technical look.
5. Detailed market study—market research, detailed customer interviews, etc.
6. Detailed technical assessment—a more in-depth technical look, prior to development.
7. Decision to develop—the decision to move into a full-fledged development project.
8. Development—the actual development of the physical product.
9. In-house product tests—internal, lab, or alpha tests of the product.
10. Customer tests—field trials.
11. Trial sell (or pre-test or test market)—to prove market acceptance.
12. Trial production—limited, trial, or batch production—to prove production.
13. Precommercialization business analysis—the final decision to commercialize.
14. Production start-up—the start of commercial production.
15. Market launch—full marketing of the product.
16. Post launch review—a full review of the project after launch is completed.

And now, some other questions about this project:

17. Organization: How was the project handled (check one):
    ___ As a multidisciplinary, multifunctional team, with identified members from various functions—R&D, marketing, manufacturing, purchasing, etc.—as active members of the team; or
    ___ As a functional effort: each function doing its part of the project, but not really as a team.
    Comments: _____

18. Was there a project leader, clearly identified, who lead and was accountable for the project from its early stages through to launch?

           ___Yes ___ No

Comments: _____
19. Did the project move as quickly as it might have?   ___Yes ___ No
If No, why not? What slowed it down? _____

II. The New Product Process: General Practices:

Moving away from this specific project, let's look at the Division's new product
practices in general.

For the questions below, to what extent are the following statements true about
product development in the Division. Please answer using this 0–10 scale,
where 10 = Definitely yes; all the time, and 0 = Definitely not; not at all.

A. Ideas
   1. Idea generation is in good shape—there are quality ideas and lots of them
      (circle a number).

          Definitely not 0 1 2 3 4 5 6 7 8 9 10 Definitely yes

Comments: _____

_____

[Note to reader: Use the same 0–10 format with room for comments for items
2–28 below.]
   2. We are getting more than enough new product ideas as inputs to the pro-
      cess.
   3. The ideas are *quality* ones.
B. Our new product process
   4. We use a *formal new product process*—a standardized process to guide
      product development from idea to launch.
   5. There are clearly defined stages that make up this process—these stages
      are highly visible and known by all.
   6. Activities are clearly defined for each stage of this process—what is re-
      quired or expected is very visible.
   7. Go/Kill decision points are clearly defined for each stage of the process.
   8. There are clear criteria for Go/Kill decisions—these are spelled out and
      known by all.
   9. These criteria are *really used* by decision makers in making these Go/Kill
      decisions (as opposed to "hidden criteria," or gut feel, etc.).
 10. Go/Kill decisions are made in a timely fashion—approvals are handled
      efficiently and quickly.
 11. The decision makers are clearly defined for the process—who will make
      the Go/Kill decisions.

C. Practices and orientation

12. We have a strong commitment to *quality of execution*—every activity from ideation through to launch must be carried out in a quality fashion.

13. We have a commitment to *completeness*—every key step must be carried out (no uncalled-for shortcuts).

14. The deliverables to each decision point (or project review) in the process are in good shape . . . *quality deliverables*.

15. There is a strong focus on *predevelopment or up-front homework* (e.g., market studies, technical appraisal, financial and business analysis, etc.) prior to opening the door to full-scale development.

16. There is a strong focus on *product and project definition* prior to the beginning of development—target market, product concept, benefits, features, and requirements are sharply defined and agreed to before development work can begin.

17. We are committed to a *market orientation*—an emphasis on the customer and marketplace via market studies, market research, customer trials, etc.

18. We *involve the customer* throughout development—our people, who work on the project, constantly interface with customers.

19. There are *tough and demanding decision points* (or Go/Kill points) where tough choices are made and projects really do get killed.

20. These Go/Kill project decision points are handled well—they are solid, rigorous reviews.

D. Organization

21. All projects have an identifiable and accountable leader—you can point to a person who's in charge and responsible for driving that project.

22. The leader is dedicated to the one project (that is, he or she doesn't have a dozen projects under way at any one time).

23. The leader is responsible for the project from idea right through to launch—that is, carries the project right through the process and not just for one or a few stages.

24. Every project has a clearly identified core team of players.

25. The project team is multidisciplinary (or multifunctional)—the players are from different functions in the company (R&D, marketing, manufacturing, etc.).

26. The members of this project team are given release time from their normal jobs to work on this project.

27. The project team members are physically close to each other—their offices, labs, or work areas are within 100 yards of each other.

28. The team aspect of new product development is working well—where we have people from different departments working on a project team.

III. Performance and Suggestions

In this final section, stand back and give us your thoughts on how effective the Division's new product efforts are, and what needs improving—the "big picture."

1. How would you rate the success of the Division's new product efforts in recent years?

   dismal failure -5 -4 -3 -2 -1 0 1 2 3 4 5 great success

2. Why did you rate it the way you did? _____

3. What are the major positive aspects of the Division's new product efforts? What's good about it? _____

4. What are the negative aspects? What's bad?_____

5. What are the major barriers to a highly successful new product effort in the Division?_____

6. Are projects moving along as quickly as they should—rate the timeliness of projects.

   poor 0 1 2 3 4 5 6 7 8 9 10 excellent

   Comment on timeliness: _____

7. Do we have the necessary resources in the Division to do projects properly (e.g., time, money, people availability)?

   not at all 0 1 2 3 4 5 6 7 8 9 10 very much so

   Explain: _____

8. Are we trying to do too many projects for the resources available?

   not at all 0 1 2 3 4 5 6 7 8 9 10 very much so

   Explain: _____

9. What aspects of product development need improving? What specific recommendations do you have for making the Division's new product process more effective?_____

10. Please use the last blank page to add any relevant comments that might help us improve the way we go about conceiving, developing, and launching new products in the Division.

11. Your name (your answers are confidential!): _____

Financial Indices

A number of financial indices have been proposed to provide a short-cut financial assessment of projects. These simpler ones are not intended to be total substitutes for more rigorous methods, such as Discounted Cash Flow (DCF). Rather, they are meant to be used at very early gates—for example, at Gates 1 and 2—when only the most rudimentary of financial data are known. More complex indices can be used in conjunction with DCF methods, and indeed often require DCF profits as inputs.

The simplest are straightforward ratios:

$$\text{Payback Index (years)} = \frac{C}{S \cdot M}$$

This gives a crude, first-cut, payback period. (All symbols are defined at the end of this appendix.) And the *reciprocal* of this index gives a very crude estimate of the return as a percentage.

A second ratio was outlined in the text in Chapter 7. It simply compares the payback period (above) to the expected life of the product (here product life is discounted by taking the square root).

$$\text{Life vs. Payback Index} = \frac{S \cdot M \cdot \sqrt{L}}{C}$$

The argument here is that one should opt for projects with a somewhat longer payback period, provided that the product will generate sales and profits for a longer time period.

Some indices consider probabilities of success, both technical and commercial success. Further, by including the annual profit, PR (rather than just annual sales and margins), the index below suggested by Pacifico requires a somewhat more sophisticated data:[1]

$$\text{Index} = \frac{P_t \cdot P_c \cdot L \cdot PR}{I + RD}$$

Several of the indices are quite complicated and are clearly more than simple "sanity checks." Rather these more complicated indices are intended to *help prioritize projects.* One of the most sophisticated formulas is a combination one suggested by Teal.[2] He looks at four subindices: an R&D index (the ratio of profits to R&D expenses of the project); an investment index (the ratio of profits to investment); the sales contribution index (the ratio of product sales to company sales); and the market share index (the ratio of sales to market size):

$$\text{Index} = \frac{(\Sigma PR)}{(25\,RD)} \cdot \frac{(\Sigma PR)}{.27\,(I+RD)} \cdot \frac{(25\,S)}{(T)} \cdot \frac{(2\,S)}{(MS)}$$

Another prioritization index, proposed by Disman, considers many of the same elements as found in the SDG portfolio model introduced in Chapter 7.[3] Here the term PR denotes product profits for any given year, and this is discounted over the life of the product at the discount rate R:

$$\text{Index} = \frac{P_t \cdot P_c \cdot 2\,\overline{(1+R)^n}}{RD}$$

The assumption here is that R&D resources are the scarce or limiting resource. Ranking projects according to this index will yield a portfolio of projects with the highest expected profits from a given (or limited) R&D dollar expenditure.

Nomenclature:

C = cost to develop and commercialize the product.

I = total investment in the product or project (excluding developing costs).

L = economic life of the product (years).

M = profit margin as a percent of sales (expressed as a decimal; e.g., 0.30).

MS = market size ($/year).

P_c = probability of commercial success, given technical success (percent).

P_t = probability of technical success (percent).

PR = annual profits from the product in a typical year.

R = discount rate (percent).

RD = the R&D or development costs of the product.

S = annual sales of the product ($/year) for a typical year.

T = total annual company sales.

The NewProd
Diagnostic and Screening
Model Questionnaire

C

Instructions

1. For each of the following 30 questions, indicate your level of agreement or disagreement by circling a number from 0 to 10. Read each question carefully! Anchor phrases are provided to help define what is meant by a 10 or a 0.

2. Answer every question. Give your best estimate, even though you may not be sure of an answer.

3. Indicate how sure or confident you are about each answer. Do so by writing a number from 0 to 10 on the blank line following the numeric scale. Here:

   > 10 = 100% confident; I am certain about this answer.
   >
   > 0 = no confidence; a pure guess.

4. Use a black pen. Circle and write clearly . . . press hard. Try not to cross out answers.

5. Most people take about 15 minutes to answer the questionnaire. New users are advised against agonizing over questions and their exact meaning. Answer quickly . . . with feedback you can revise your answers.

6. Remember: two answers are required for each question—a rating and a confidence, both 0–10.

* * * *

Company _____ Tel _____
Product name _____ Ref _____
Evaluator's name _____
Title _____
Department _____ Tel _____

* * *

I. Resources Required

The first 8 questions are designed to probe whether our company has the capabilities, talents, skills, resources, physical facilities, and experience necessary to undertake the project, assuming that we were to move ahead with the project. The fact that these resources might otherwise be occupied at present is not relevant.

If certain facets of the project are to be carried out by others (e.g., subcontracted production or product design; distribution via middlemen; etc.), these available outside resources should be considered as available to the project. Be careful to be realistic about the availability and quality of these outside resources.

Remember: for each question
  * circle a rating (0-10) of the resource adequacy; and
  * indicate your confidence (0-10) in your rating on the blank line.

	STRONGLY DISAGREE	STRONGLY AGREE	CONFIDENCE (0 TO 10)
1. Our company's financial resources are more than adequate for this project. (10 = far more than adequate; 0 = far less)	0 1 2 3 4 5 6 7 8 9 10		_____
2. Our company's R&D skills & people are more than adequate for this project. (10 = far more than adequate; 0 = far less)	0 1 2 3 4 5 6 7 8 9 10		_____
3. Our company's engineering skills and people are more than adequate for this project. (10 = far more than adequate; 0 = far less)	0 1 2 3 4 5 6 7 8 9 10		_____
4. Our company's marketing research skills and people are more than adequate for this project. (10 = far more than adequate; 0 = far less)	0 1 2 3 4 5 6 7 8 9 10		_____
5. Our company's management skills are more than adequate for this project. (10 = far more than adequate; 0 = far less)	0 1 2 3 4 5 6 7 8 9 10		_____
6. Our company's production resources or skills are more than adequate for this project. (10 = far more than adequate; 0 = far less)	0 1 2 3 4 5 6 7 8 9 10		_____
7. Our company's sales force and/or distribution resources and skills are more than adequate for this project. (10 = far more than adequate; 0 = far less)	0 1 2 3 4 5 6 7 8 9 10		_____
8. Our company's advertising and promotion resources and skills are more than adequate for this project. (10 = far more than adequate; 0 = far less)	0 1 2 3 4 5 6 7 8 9 10		_____

II. Nature of Project

These 3 questions provide some general descriptors of the product or project.

Here the terms "market," "customer," and "competitor" must be defined. The market is defined both geographically and in terms of applications: think in terms of which users our product is targeted at—the target users—in order to define the "market." Competitive products are those products that these customers now use that our product is intended to replace.

	STRONGLY DISAGREE	STRONGLY AGREE	CONFIDENCE (0 TO 10)
9. Our product is highly innovative— totally new to the market. (10 = totally new; 0 = a direct copy)		0 1 2 3 4 5 6 7 8 9 10	_____
10. The product specifications—exactly what the product will be—are very clear. (10 = very clearly defined; 0 = not defined at all)		0 1 2 3 4 5 6 7 8 9 10	_____
11. The technical aspects—exactly how the technical problems will be solved— are very clear. (10 = very clear; 0 = not clear; not known)		0 1 2 3 4 5 6 7 8 9 10	_____

III. Newness to the Company

Is this a familiar project to our company or a totally new one to us? These next 4 questions probe how new or "step out" the project and product are to our company. Again, be sure to define what you mean by "market," "customer" and "competition" (see note before question 9 above).

	STRONGLY DISAGREE	STRONGLY AGREE	CONFIDENCE (0 TO 10)
12. The potential customers for this product are totally new to our company. (10 = totally new; 0 = our existing customers)		0 1 2 3 4 5 6 7 8 9 10	_____
13. The product class or type of product itself is totally new to our company. (10 = totally new; 0 = existing product class for us)		0 1 2 3 4 5 6 7 8 9 10	_____
14. We have never made or sold products to satisfy this type of customer need or use before. (10 = never; 0 = have done so, or are doing so now)		0 1 2 3 4 5 6 7 8 9 10	_____
15. The competitors we face in the market are totally new to our company. (10 = totally new to us; 0 = competitors we have faced before)		0 1 2 3 4 5 6 7 8 9 10	_____

IV. The Final Product

The next 7 questions probe our product advantage. Be sure to think in terms of our product versus competitive products . . . the products or solutions that the customer is now using to solve his/her problem.

	STRONGLY DISAGREE	STRONGLY AGREE	CONFIDENCE (0 TO10)

16. Compared to competitive products
(or whatever the customer is now
using), our product will offer a number of unique features, attributes or
benefits to the customer.   0 1 2 3 4 5 6 7 8 9 10   _____
(10 = many positive, unique features and benefits; 5 = same; 0 = fewer)

17. Our product will be clearly superi-
or to competing products in terms
of meeting customer needs.   0 1 2 3 4 5 6 7 8 9 10   _____
(10 = clearly superior; 5 = equal to; 0 = inferior to competitors)

18. Our product will permit the customer
to reduce his/her costs, when com-
pared to what he/she is now using.   0 1 2 3 4 5 6 7 8 9 10   _____
(10 = major reduction; 5 = same; 0 = higher costs)

19. Our product will permit the customer
to do a job or do something that he or
she cannot do with what is now avail-
able on the market.   0 1 2 3 4 5 6 7 8 9 10   _____
(10 = clearly yes; 5 = same; 0 = less so)

20. Our product will be of higher quality
—however quality is defined in this
market—than competing products.   0 1 2 3 4 5 6 7 8 9 10   _____
(10 = much higher quality; 5 = same; 0 = inferior to competitors)

21. Our product will be priced consider-
ably higher than competing products. 0 1 2 3 4 5 6 7 8 9 10   _____
(10 = much higher; 5 = same; 0 = much lower)

22. We will be first into the market with
this type of product.   0 1 2 3 4 5 6 7 8 9 10   _____
(10 = first in; 0 = one after many)

V. Our Market for This Product

These last 8 questions look at the nature of the marketplace. Again, be sure to define what you mean by "market," "customer" and "competition" (see note before question 9 above).

23. Potential customers have a great need
for this class or type of product.   0 1 2 3 4 5 6 7 8 9 10   _____
(10 = great need; 0 = no need)

24. The dollar size of the market (either
existing or potential market) for this
product is large.   0 1 2 3 4 5 6 7 8 9 10   _____
(10 = very large; 0 = very small).

25. The market for this product is grow-
ing very quickly.   0 1 2 3 4 5 6 7 8 9 10   _____
(10 = fast growth; 0 = no growth or negative growth)

RESOURCES REQUIRED	STRONGLY DISAGREE	STRONGLY AGREE	CONFIDENCE (0 TO 10)

26. The market is characterized by intense price competition.   0 1 2 3 4 5 6 7 8 9 10   _____
    (10 = intense price competition; 0 = no price competition)

27. There are many competitors in this market.   0 1 2 3 4 5 6 7 8 9 10   _____
    (10 = many; 0 = none)

28. There is a strong dominant competitor—with a large market share—in this market.   0 1 2 3 4 5 6 7 8 9 10   _____
    (10 = dominant competitor; 0 = no dominant competitors)

29. Potential customers are very satisfied with the (competitors') products they are currently using.   0 1 2 3 4 5 6 7 8 9 10   _____
    (10 = very satisfied; 0 = very dissatisfied)

30. Users' needs change quickly in this market—a dynamic market situation.   0 1 2 3 4 5 6 7 8 9 10   _____
    (10 = change very quickly; 0 = stable needs, no change)

Return completed questionnaire to:

NewProd Evaluation Manager/Coordinator _____

Department _____ Tel _____ Date _____

Please complete and return before: _____

Endnotes

Chapter 1

1. Booz, Allen & Hamilton, *New Product Management for the 1980s* (New York: Booz, Allen & Hamilton Inc., 1982).
2. A. L. Page, "PDMA New Product Development Survey: Performance and Best Practices" (Paper presented at PDMA Conference, Chicago, Nov. 13, 1991).
3. Ibid.
4. Ibid. Average annual sales for companies in the survey were $529 million; R&D expenditures averaged 3.8% of sales.
5. "Year End R&D numbers," *Research & Technology Management.* vol. 34 no. 6 (Nov.–Dec. 1991): 6. Foreign data was converted to U.S. dollars using Purchasing Power Parities. Based on data from: OECD Scientific, Technological and Indicators Division, 1991.
6. R. G. Cooper, "Stage-Gate Systems: A New Tool for Managing New Products," *Business Horizons,* vol. 33, no. 3 (May–June, 1990).
7. "Most Admired Corporations," *Fortune,* Feb. 11, 1992, p. 52.
8. Booz, Allen & Hamilton, *New Product Management for the 1980s.*
9. Ibid.
10. R. G. Cooper, "New Product Success in Industrial Firms," *Industrial Marketing Management,* 11 (1982): 215–23. See also R. G. Cooper, "The Impact of New Product Strategies," *Industrial Marketing Management* 12 (1983): 243–56.
11. C. M. Crawford, "New Product Failure Rates—Facts and Fallacies," *Research Management* (Sept. 1979): 9–13.
12. Cooper, "New Product Success in Industrial Firms." See also: R. G. Cooper, "The Performance Impact of Product Innovation Strategies," *European Journal of Marketing* 18, 5 (1984): 5–54; and R. G. Cooper, "Overall Corporate Strategies for New Product Programs," *Industrial Marketing Management* 14 (1985) 179–83.
13. A. L. Page, "PDMA New Product Development Survey."

14. D. S. Hopkins, *New Product Winners and Losers*, Conference Board Report no. 773 (1980).
15. Booz, Allen & Hamilton, *New Product Management for the 1980s.*
16. Ibid.
17. A. L. Page, "PDMA New Product Development Survey."
18. Booz, Allen & Hamilton, *New Product Management for the 1980s.*
19. Ibid.
20. E. J. Kleinschmidt and R. G. Cooper, "The Impact of Product Innovativeness on Performance," *Journal of Product Innovation Management* 8 (1991): 240–51.
21. Ibid.

Chapter 2

1. Booz, Allen & Hamilton, *New Product Management for the 1980s* (New York: Booz, Allen & Hamilton Inc., 1982).
2. R. G. Cooper, "The Performance Impact of Product Innovation Strategies," *European Journal of Marketing* 18, no. 5 (1984): 5–54. See also C. M. Crawford, "New Product Failure Rates—Facts and Fallacies," *Research Management* (Sept. 1979): 9–13; D. S. Hopkins, *New Product Winners and Losers*, Conference Board Report no. 773 (1980); and A. L. Page, "PDMA New Product Development Survey: Performance and Best Practices" (Paper presented at PDMA Conference, Chicago, Nov. 13, 1991).
3. T. J. Peters and R. H. Waterman Jr., *In Search of Excellence* (New York: Harper & Rowe, 1982).
4. D. S. Hopkins, *New Product Winners and Losers.* See also D. S. Hopkins and E. L. Bailey, "New Product Pressures," *Conference Board Record* 8 (1971): 16–24; and National Industrial Conference Board. "Why New Products Fail," *The Conference Board Record* (New York: NICB, 1964).
5. Hopkins and Bailey, "New Product Pressures."
6. Much of this section is taken from an article by the author R. G. Cooper, "Why New Industrial Products Fail," *Industrial Marketing Management* 4 (1975): 315–26.
7. The remaining 6 percent of effort goes to other activities, including financial and evaluative activities. R. G. Cooper and E. J. Kleinschmidt, "Resource Allocation in the New Product Process," *Industrial Marketing Management* 17, no. 3 (1988): 249–262.
8. Cooper, "Why New Industrial Products Fail."
9. R. Calantone and R. G. Cooper, "A Discriminant Model for Identifying Scenarios of Industrial New Product Failure," *Journal of the Academy of Marketing Science* 7 (1979): 163–83.
10. Much of this section is taken from articles and research by the author and Professor Elko J. Kleinschmidt. See R. G. Cooper and E. J. Kleinschmidt, "An Investigation into the New Product Process: Steps, Deficiencies and Impact," *Journal of Product Innovation Management* 3, no. 2 (1986): 71–85.
11. Ibid.
12. E. Mansfield and J. Rapoport, "The Costs of Industrial Product Innovation," *Management Science* 21 (Aug. 1975): 1380–86.

13. Booz, Allen & Hamilton, *New Product Management for the 1980s.*
14. Cooper and Kleinschmidt, "Resource Allocation in the New Product Process."
15. Booz, Allen, and Hamilton, *New Product Management for the 1980s.*

Chapter 3
1. Some of this section is taken from an article by the author. See R. G. Cooper, "New Products: What Distinguishes the Winners," *Research and Technology Management* (Nov.–Dec. 1990): 27–31.
2. S. Myers and D. G. Marquis, "Successful Industrial Innovations," *National Science Foundation* NSF 69–17 (1969).
3. R. W. Roberts and J. E. Burke, "Six New Products—What Made Them Successful," *Research Management* 16 (May 1974): 21–24.
4. R. Rothwell, "Innovation in Textile Machinery: Some Significant Factors in Success and Failure," *SPRU Occasional Paper Series* no. 2 (Brighton, Sussex, U.K.: SPRU, Sussex University, 1976). See also R. Rothwell, "Factors for Success in Industrial Innovations" in *Project SAPPHO—A Comparative Study of Success and Failure in Industrial Innovation* (Brighton, Sussex, U.K.: SPRU, University of Sussex, 1972); and R. Rothwell et al., "SAPPHO Updated—Project SAPPHO Phase II," Research Policy 3 (1974): 258–91.
5. R. Rothwell, "The 'Hungarian SAPPHO': Some Comments and Comparison," *Research Policy* 3 (1976): 30–38.
6. H. Kulvik, *Factors Underlying the Success or Failure of New Products,* Report no. 29 (Helsinki, Finland: University of Technology, 1977).
7. J. M. Utterback et al. "The Process of Innovation in Five Industries in Europe and Japan," *IEEE Transactions on Engineering Management* (Feb. 1976): 3–9.
8. A. H. Rubenstein et al. "Factors Influencing Success at the Project Level," *Research Management* 16 (May 1976): 15–20.
9. R. G. Cooper, "Identifying Industrial New Product Success: Project NewProd," *Industrial Marketing Management* 8 (May 1979). See also R. G. Cooper, "The Dimensions of Industrial New Product Success and Failure," *Journal of Marketing* 43 (Summer 1979): 93–103; and R. G. Cooper, "Project NewProd: Factors in New Product Success," *European Journal of Marketing* 14 (1980): 277–92.
10. M. A. Maidique and B. J. Zirger, "A Study of Success and Failure in Product Innovation: The Case of the U.S. Electronics Industry," *IEEE Transactions on Engineering Management* EM–31 (Nov. 1984): 192–203. See also B. J. Zirger and M. A. Maidique, "A Model of New Product Development: An Empirical Test," *Management Science* 36 (July 1990): 867–883.
11. Ibid.
12. Booz, Allen & Hamilton, *New Product Management for the 1980s* (New York: Booz, Allen & Hamilton Inc., 1982).
13. Based on an internal study and described in Edith Wilson, *Product Development Process, Product Definition Guide, release 1.0,* internal Hewlett-Packard document, Jan. 1991.

14. E. W. Larson and David H. Gobeli, "Organizing for Product Development Projects," *Journal of Product Innovation Management* 5 (1988): 180–90.
15. Much of this section is taken from articles and based on research by the author and Professor Elko J. Kleinschmidt. See R. G. Cooper and E. J. Kleinschmidt, *New Products: The Key Factors in Success,* monograph (Chicago: American Marketing Association, 1990). See also Cooper, "New Products: What Distinguishes the Winners,": 27–31.
16. C. M Crawford, "Protocol: New Tool for Product Innovation," *Journal of Product Innovation Management* 2 (1984): 85–91.
17. R. G. Cooper and E. J. Kleinschmidt, "Resource Allocation in the New Product Process," *Industrial Marketing Management* 17, no. 3 (1988): 249–262.
18. This international facet is described in Cooper and Kleinschmidt, *New Products: The Key Factors in Success.* See also E. J. Kleinschmidt and R. G. Cooper, "The Performance Impact on an International Orientation of Product Innovation," *European Journal of Marketing* 22 (1988): 56–71.
19. R. G. Cooper and E. J. Kleinschmidt, "Major New Products: What Distinguishes the Winners in the Chemical Industry," *Journal of Product Innovation Management,* 10 no. 2 (March 1993), 90–111. See also R. G. Cooper and E. J. Kleinschmidt, "How the New Product Process Impacts on Success and Failure in the Chemical Industry," *Industrial Marketing Management* 22, no. 2 (1993): 85–99.

Chapter 4

1. Various firms' new product processes, including a 3M division's, are described in R. G. Cooper and E. J. Kleinschmidt, *Formal Process for Managing New Products: The Industry Experience* (Hamilton, Ont., Canada: McMaster University, Michael DeGroote School of Business, 1990).
2. Havelock and Elder as cited in Everett M. Rogers, "The R&D/Marketing Interface in the Technological Innovation Process," in Massoud M. Saghafi and Ashok K. Gupta, eds., *Managing the R&D/Marketing Interface for Process Success: The Telecommunications Focus, Vol. I, Advances in Telecommunications Management* (Greenwich, Conn., JAI Press Inc, 1990.)
3. Booz, Allen & Hamilton, *New Product Management for the 1980s* (New York: Booz, Allen & Hamilton Inc., 1982).
4. R. G. Cooper, "Stage-Gate Systems: A New Tool for Managing New Products," *Business Horizons* 33, no. 3 (May–June, 1990).
5. Ibid.
6. R. G. Cooper, "The New Product Process: A Decision Guide for Managers," *Journal of Marketing Management* 3, no. 3 (1988): 238–255.
7. R. G. Cooper, "New Products: What Distinguishes the Winners," *Research and Technology Management* (Nov.–Dec. 1990): 27–31; R. G. Cooper and E. J. Kleinschmidt, "An Investigation into the New Product Process: Steps, Deficiencies and Impact," *Journal of Product Innovation Manage-*

ment 3, no. 2 (1986): 71–85; R. G. Cooper and E. J. Kleinschmidt, "New Products: What Separates Winners from Losers," *Journal of Product Innovation Management* 4, no. 3 (1987): 169–84; and R. G. Cooper and E. J. Kleinschmidt, *New Products: The Key Factors in Success,* monograph (Chicago: American Marketing Association, 1990).

8. C. M. Crawford, "Protocol: New Tool for Product Innovation," *Journal of Product Innovation Management* 2 (1984): 85–91.

9. Edith Wilson, *Product Development Process, Product Definition Guide, release 1.0,* internal Hewlett-Packard document, Jan. 1991.

10. M. A. Maidique, and B. J. Zirger, "A Study of Success and Failure in Product Innovation: The Case of the U.S. Electronics Industry," *IEEE Transactions on Engineering Management* EM–31 (Nov. 1984): 192–203.

11. Tom Peters, *Thriving on Chaos* (New York: Harper & Row, 1988), 261.

12. E. W. Larson and David H. Gobeli, "Organizing for Product Development Projects," *Journal of Product Innovation Management* 5 (1988): 180–90.

13. Peters, *Thriving on Chaos.*

14. Cooper, "What Distinguishes the Winners"; Cooper and Kleinschmidt, "An Investigation into the New Product Process"; Cooper and Kleinschmidt, "New Products: What Separates Winners from Losers"; and Cooper and Kleinschmidt, New Products: The Key Factors in Success.

15. Booz, Allen & Hamilton, *New Product Management for the 1980s.*

16. Peters, *Thriving on Chaos,* 302.

17. Booz, Allen & Hamilton, *New Product Management for the 1980s.*

18. M. E. Porter, *Competitive Advantage: Creating and Sustaining Superior Performance* (New York: Free Press, 1985).

19. See, for example: D. F. Abell and J. S. Hammond, *Strategic Marketing Planning.* (Englewood Cliffs, N.J.: Prentice-Hall, 1979).

20. Maidique and Zirger, "A Study of Success and Failure in Product Innovation.

21. Cooper and Kleinschmidt, *New Products: The Key Factors in Success.*

22. Ibid. See also Maidique and Zirger, "A Study of Success and Failure in Product Innovation."

23. Cooper and Kleinschmidt, "An Investigation into the New Product Process," 71–85.

24. R. G. Cooper, "Selecting Winning New Products: Using the NewProd System," *Journal of Product Innovation Management* 2 (1987): 34–44; See also R. G. Cooper, "The NewProd System: The Industry Experience," *Journal of Product Innovation Management* 9 (1992): 113–127.

25. R. G. Cooper and E. J. Kleinschmidt, "Resource Allocation in the New Product Process," *Industrial Marketing Management* 17, no. 3 (1988): 249–62.

26. Peters, *Thriving on Chaos,* 257.

27. R. G. Cooper, "Stage-Gate Systems."

28. Ibid.

29. Booz, Allen & Hamilton, *New Product Management for the 1980s.*

Chapter 5

1. A quotation describing the quality process, which has equal applicability to the new product process. See Thomas H. Berry, *Managing the Total Quality Transformation* (New York: McGraw-Hill Inc., 1991).
2. This chapter is taken from four sources, all by the author: R. G. Cooper, "A Process Model for Industrial New Product Development," *IEEE Transactions in Engineering Management* EM–30 (Feb. 1983): 2–11; R. G. Cooper, *Winning at New Products* (Reading, Mass: Addison Wesley, 1986); R. G. Cooper, "The New Product Process: A Decision Guide for Managers," *Journal of Marketing Management* 3, no. 3 (1988): 238–55; and R. G. Cooper, "Stage-Gate Systems: A New Tool for Managing New Products."
3. These examples are taken from Cooper, "Stage-Gate Systems: A New Tool for Managing New Products."
4. Bro Uttal, "Speeding New Ideas to Market," *Fortune* (March 1987): 62–66.
5. E. W. Larson and David H. Gobeli, "Organizing for Product Development Projects," *Journal of Product Innovation Management* 5 (1988): 180–90.
6. R. G. Cooper, "The New Product Process: A Decision Guide for Managers"; and Cooper, "Stage-gate Systems: A New Tool for Managing New Products."
7. These 60 cases yielded tentative models of the new product process. See R. G. Cooper, "The New Product Process: An Empirically Derived Classification Scheme," *R&D Management* 13 (Jan. 1983): 2–11.
8. Cooper, *Winning at New Products.* See also Cooper, "The New Product Process: A Decision Guide for Managers"; Cooper, "Stage-Gate Systems: A New Tool for Managing New Products"; and R. G. Cooper and E. J. Kleinschmidt, *New Products: The Key Factors in Success* (monograph) (Chicago: American Marketing Association, 1990).

Chapter 6

1. E. A. Von Hippel, "Has Your Customer Already Developed Your Next Product," *Sloan Management Review* (Winter 1977): 63–74. See also E. A. Von Hippel, "Successful Industrial Products from Customer Ideas," *Journal of Marketing* (Jan. 1978): 39–49; E. A. Von Hippel, "Get New Products from Customers," *Harvard Business Review* (March–April 1982): 117–22; and E. A. Von Hippel, *The Sources of Innovation* (New York: Oxford University Press, 1988).
2. Ibid.
3. C. M. Crawford, "Unsolicited New Product Ideas: Handle with Care," *Research Management* (Jan. 1975): 22.
4. Much of this section is taken from an excellent summary of QFD: A. Griffin and J. R. Hauser, "The Marketing and R&D Interface," in *Handbook: MS/OR in Marketing*, G. L. Lillien and J. Eliasberg, eds. (Amsterdam: Elsevier Scientific Publishers, 1992).

5. John R. Hauser and Donald Clausing, "The House of Quality," *Harvard Business Review* (May–June 1988): 33–56.
6. Griffin and Hauser, "The Marketing and R&D Interface."
7. Ibid.
8. Ibid.

Chapter 7

1. R. G. Cooper, "The NewProd System: The Industry Experience," *Journal of Product Innovation Management* 9 (1992): 113–127.
2. Booz, Allen & Hamilton, *New Product Management for the 1980s* (New York: Booz, Allen & Hamilton Inc., 1982).
3. R. G. Cooper and E. J. Kleinschmidt, "An Investigation into the New Product Process: Steps, Deficiencies and Impact," *Journal of Product Innovation Management* 3, no. 2 (1986): 71–85.
4. A. Albala, "Stage Approach for the Evaluation and Selection of R&D Projects," *IEEE Transactions on Engineering Management* EM-22 (Nov. 1975): 153–62.
5. R. G. Cooper, "A Process Model for Industrial New Product Development," *IEEE Transactions on Engineering Management* EM-30 (Feb. 1983): 2–11.
6. Albala, "Stage Approach for the Evaluation and Selection of R&D Projects."
7. Ibid.
8. N. R. Baker and W. Pound, "R&D Project Selection: Where We Stand," *IEEE Transactions on Engineering Management* EM-11 (Dec. 1964): 124–34.
9. N. R. Baker, "R&D Project Selection Models: An Assessment," *IEEE Transactions on Engineering Management* EM-21 (Nov. 1974): 165–71. See also N. R. Baker and J. Freeland, "Recent Advances in R&D Benefit Measurement and Project Selection Methods," *Management Science* 21 (1975): 1164–75.
10. Baker, "R&D Project Selection Models."
11. Byron Jackson, "Decision Methods for Selecting a Portfolio of R&D Projects," *Research Management* (Sept.–Oct. 1983): 21–26.
12. Philip Roussel, Kamal N. Saad and Tamara J. Erickson, *Third Generation R&D, Managing the Link to Corporate Strategy* (Boston, Mass.: Harvard Business School Press and Arthur D. Little Inc., 1991).
13. Baker, "R&D Project Selection Models." See also Baker and Freeland, "Recent Advances in R&D Benefit Measurement."
14. E. P. McGuire, *Evaluating New Product Proposals,* Report no. 604 (New York: Conference Board 1973).
15. R. A. More and B. Little, "The Application of Discriminant Analysis to the Prediction of Sales Forecast Uncertainty in New Product Situations," *Journal of the Operations Research Society* 31 (1980): 71–77.
16. McGuire, *Evaluating New Product Proposals.*

17. W. E. Souder, "A Scoring Methodology for Assessing the Suitability of Management Science Models," *Management Science* 18 (June 1972): B526–43.
18. W. E. Souder, "A System for Using R&D Project Evaluation Methods," *Research Management* 21 (Sept. 1978): 29–37.
19. D. R. Augood, "Review of R&D Evaluation Methods," *IEEE Transactions on Engineering Management* EM–20 (Nov. 1973): 114–20.
20. Lowell W. Steele, "Selecting R&D Programs and Objectives," *Research & Technology Management* (March–April 1988): 17–36.
21. R. G. Cooper, "Selecting Winning New Products: Using the NewProd System," *Journal of Product Innovation Management* 2 (1987): 34–44. See also Cooper, "The NewProd System: The Industry Experience," *Journal of Product Innovation Management* 9 (1992): 113–27.
22. Samual B. Graves and Jeffery L. Ringuest, "Evaluating Competing R&D Investments," *Research & Technology Management,* (July–August 1991): 32–36.
23. Ibid.
24. Parts of this section are taken from J. E. Matheson, M. M. Menke and S. L. Derby, "Improving the Quality of R&D Decision: A Synopsis of the SDG Approach," *Journal of Science Policy and Research Management* (in Japanese) 4, no. 4 (June 1989).
25. Roussel, Saad & Erickson, *Third Generation R&D, Managing the Link to Corporate Strategy.*
26. W. E. Souder, "Achieving Organizational Consensus with Respect to R&D Project Selection Criteria," *Management Science* (Feb. 1975): 669–681.

Chapter 8
1. W. J. Vrakking, "The Innovative Organization," *Long Range Planning* 23, no. 2 (1990): 94–102.
2. R. G. Cooper, "Why New Industrial Products Fail," *Industrial Marketing Management* 4 (1975): 315–26. See also R. G. Cooper and E. J. Kleinschmidt, "An Investigation into the New Product Process: Steps, Deficiencies and Impact," *Journal of Product Innovation Management* 3, no. 2 (1986): 71–85.

Chapter 9
1. R. G. Cooper and E. J. Kleinschmidt, "What Makes a New Product a Winner: Success Factors at the Project Level," *R&D Management* 17, no. 3 (July 1987): 175–89.
2. R. G. Cooper and E. J. Kleinschmidt, "Major New Products: What Distinguishes the Winners in the Chemical Industry," *Journal of Product Innovation Management* 10, no. 2 (March 1993) 90–111.
3. R. D. Buzzell et al., "Market Share—A Key to Profitability," *Harvard Business Review* (Jan.–Feb. 1975): 97–107, See also S. Schoeffler, "Impact of Strategic Planning on Profit Performance," *Harvard Business Review* (March–April 1974): 137–45.

4. *The Product Portfolio,* pamphlet no. 66 (Boston: The Boston Consulting Group, 1970).
5. R. C. Bennett and R. G. Cooper, "The Misuse of Marketing: An American Tragedy," *Business Horizons* (Nov.–Dec. 1981): 51–61.
6. D. Ogilvy, *Ogilvy on Advertising* (London: Orbis Publishing and Pan Books, 1983).

Chapter 10
1. R. G. Cooper and E. J. Kleinschmidt, *Formal Processes for Managing New Products: The Industry Experience* (Hamilton, Ont., Canada: McMaster University, 1991). See also: R. G. Cooper and E. J. Kleinschmidt, "New Product Processes at Leading Industrial Firms," *Industrial Marketing Management* 10, no. 2 (May 1991): 137–47.
2. A. Griffin, "Metrics for Measuring Product Development Cycle Time," *Journal of Product Innovation Management* 10, no. 2 (March 1993): 112–125.
3. *Winning at New Products* (28 minute video) (Ancaster Ont., Canada: Management of Technology and Innovation Institute, 1991).
4. Milton D. Roseanau Jr., "Phased Approach Speeds up New Product Development," *Research and Development* 30, issue 11 (Nov. 1988): 52–55.

Chapter 11
1. The term "PIC" was coined and defined by Merle Crawford: See C. M. Crawford, "Defining the Charter for Product Innovation," *Sloan Management Review* (1980): 3–12.
2. Much of this chapter is taken from works by the author. See R. G. Cooper, "*Winning at New Products* (Reading, Mass: Addison-Wesley 1986). See also R. G. Cooper, "Defining the New Product Strategy," *IEEE Transactions on Engineering Management,* EM-34, no. 3 (1987): 184–93; also R. G. Cooper, "Identifying and Evaluating New Product Opportunities," in *The Interface of Marketing and Strategy* by G. S. Day, B. Weitz, and R. Wensley, vol. 4 of *Strategic Management Policy and Planning: A Multivolume Treatise* (Greenwich, Conn.: JAI Press Inc, 1990).
3. A. M. Kantrow, "The Strategy-Technology Connection," *Harvard Business Review* (July–Aug. 1980): 6–21.
4. R. G. Cooper, "The Performance Impact of Product Innovation Strategies," *European Journal of Marketing* 18, no. 5 (1984): 5–54.
5. Booz, Allen & Hamilton. *New Product Management for the 1980s* (New York: Booz, Allen & Hamilton Inc., 1982).
6. Crawford, "Defining the Charter for Product Innovation."
7. D. J. Luck and A. E. Prell, *Market Strategy* (Englewood Cliffs, NJ: Prentice Hall, 1968), 2.
8. I. H. Ansoff, *Corporate Strategy* (New York: McGraw-Hill, 1965).
9. R. E. Corey, "Key Options in Market Selection and Product Planning," *Harvard Business Review* (Sept.–Oct. 1978): 119–28.

10. C. M. Crawford, "Strategies for New Product Development: Guidelines for a Critical Company Problem," *Business Horizons* (Dec. 1972): 49–58.

11. J. B. Quinn, "Formulating Strategy One Step at a Time," *Journal of Business Strategy* 1 (1981): 42–63.

12. Booz, Allen & Hamilton, *New Product Management for the 1980s*.

13. R. D. Buzzell et al., "Market Share—A Key to Profitability," *Harvard Business Review* (Jan.–Feb. 1975): 97–107.

14. H. Nystrom, "Company Strategies for Research and Development," in *Industrial Innovation*, ed. N. Baker (New York: MacMillan, 1979). See also H. Nystrom, *Company Strategies for Research and Development* (Uppsala, Sweden: Institute for Economics and Statistics, Report S-750 07, 1977); also H. Nystrom and B. Edvardsson, *Research and Development Strategies for Swedish Companies in the Farm Machinery Industry* (Uppsala, Sweden: Institute for Economics and Statistics, 1978); also H. Nystrom and B. Edvardsson, *Research and Development Strategies for Four Swedish Farm Machine Companies* (Uppsala, Sweden: Institute for Economics and Statistics, 1980).

15. R. G. Cooper, "The Performance Impact of Product Innovation Strategies," 5–54. See also R. G. Cooper, "How New Product Strategies Impact on Performance," *Journal of Product Innovation Management* 1 (1984): 5–18; also R. G. Cooper, "The Strategy-Performance Link in Product Innovation," *R&D Management* 14 (Oct. 1984):151–64; also R. G. Cooper, "New Product Strategies: What Distinguishes the Top Performers," *Journal of Product Innovation Management* 2 (1984): 151–64; also R. G. Cooper, "Industrial Firms' New Product Strategies," *Journal of Business Research* 13 (April 1985): 107–21; also R. G. Cooper, "Overall Corporate Strategies for New Product Programs," *Industrial Marketing Management* 14 (1985): 179–83.

16. C. M. Crawford, "New Product Failure Rates—Facts and Fallacies," *Research Management* (Sept. 1979): 9–13.

17. R. C. Bennett and R. G. Cooper, "The Product Life Cycle Trap," *Business Horizons* (Sept.–Oct. 1984): 7–16.

18. G. S. Day, "A Strategic Perspective on Product Planning," *Journal of Contemporary Business* (Spring 1975): 1–34.

19. Nystrom, *Company Strategies for Research and Development*.

20. G. S. Day, "Diagnosing the Product Portfolio," *Journal of Marketing* (1977): 29–38.

21. G. S. Day, "A Strategic Perspective on Product Planning," *Journal of Contemporary Business* (Spring 1975): 1–34.

22. Booz, Allen & Hamilton, *New Product Management for the 1980s*.

23. Ibid.

24. Day, "A Strategic Perspective on Product Planning," 1–34.

25. Cooper, "The Performance Impact of Product Innovation Strategies," 5–54.

26. Booz, Allen & Hamilton, *New Product Management for the 1980s*.

27. Day, "A Strategic Perspective on Product Planning."

28. T. H. Levitt, "Marketing Myopia," *Harvard Business Review* (July–Aug. 1960): 45–86.
29. Ansoff, *Corporate Strategy.*
30. Corey, "Key Options in Market Selection and Product Planning."
31. D. F. Abell, *Defining the Business* (Englewood Cliffs, N.J.: Prentice Hall, 1980).
32. Crawford, "Defining the Charter for Product Innovation," 3–12.
33. The original concept for this method is found in R. G. Cooper, "Strategic Planning for Successful Technological Innovation," *Business Quarterly* 43 (Spring 1978): 46–54. See also Cooper, "Defining the New Product Strategy," 184–93; and Cooper, "Identifying and Evaluating New Product Opportunities."
34. Internal documents provided by Pugh Roberts & Associates, Boston, Mass.
35. E. B. Roberts and C. A. Berry, "Entering New Businesses: Selecting Strategies for Success," *Sloan Management Review* (Spring 1983): 3–17.
36. E. B. Roberts, "New Ventures for Corporate Growth," *Harvard Business Review* (1980): 3–17.
37. Roberts and Berry, "Entering New Businesses."
38. Ibid.
39. Ibid.
40. J. P. Killing, "Diversification through Licensing," *R&D Management* (1978): 159–163.
41. Roberts, "New Ventures for Corporate Growth."
42. Killing, "Diversification through Licensing."
43. Roberts, "New Ventures for Corporate Growth."
44. Ibid.
45. Quinn, "Formulating Strategy One Step at a Time."
46. Ibid.
47. Ibid.
48. T. J. Peters and R. H. Waterman Jr., *In Search of Excellence* (New York: Harper & Rowe, 1982).

Appendix B

1. D. R. Augood, "Review of R&D Evaluation Methods," *IEEE Transactions on Engineering Management* EM-20 (Nov. 1973): 114–120.
2. Ibid.
3. Ibid.

Index